INTRODUCTION

Susannah Clapp

Angela Carter was fifty-one when she died of lung cancer in 1992. She left behind her fifteen books, two partly assembled collections – and a louder chorus of praise than she ever heard in her life. Her reputation soared like her trapeze-artist heroine Fevvers, the 'Cockney Venus' of *Nights at the Circus*, 'shaking out about her those tremendous red and purple pinions, pinions large enough, powerful enough to bear up such a big girl as she. And she was a *big* girl . . . Now all London lies beneath her flying feet . . .' Three days after she died Virago had sold out of her books.

It is not, of course, that her novels and stories went unacknowledged in her lifetime. Angela Carter was no Barbara Pym. She was given solus reviews and publishers' parties; she went on telly; she was taught as a set book in schools, courted by universities and nobbled by fans. But she was never treated as the object of acclaim and deference that the welter of huge obituaries might suggest. She was a decade too old and, she believed, too female to be mentioned routinely alongside Amis–Barnes–Ishiguro as among the younger pillars of British fiction. She was two years too young to receive a full entry in Margaret Drabble's 1985 edition of *The Oxford Companion to English Literature*, which featured only writers born before 1939. She won the Somerset Maugham Award in 1968 (and described with some pleasure how she used the money to run away from her first husband: 'I'm sure Somerset Maugham would have been very pleased'), but she never won the Whitbread, was not once even shortlisted for the Booker Prize. Three months before her death she announced that she had a plan to put this last omission right: she had cracked what made a Booker Novel and she was going to write it – it would feature a philosophy don, his mistress, a bit of time-travelling, and many pages, and was to be called *The Owl of Minerva*. She knew it would win.

Her work is voluptuous, political, fantastic, snarling, erotic, learned. It is the work of a writer who was singular in seeing no paradox in being a dandy as well as a socialist. Her vocabulary was both far-flung and down-to-earth; her mode of address veered from the abstruse to the anecdotal. It was characteristic of her – Angela did not study fairy tales and medieval literature for nothing – that in order to talk about her last novel, *Wise Children*, she should use an emblem, disguised as a parenthesis: 'Can I digress,' she asked in an interview, with the elaborate politeness that brooked no opposition, 'about the Granada Theatre Tooting?' She did so, explaining that the Granada – a Thirties super-cinema with a hall of mirrors and a cyclorama of the night sky projected onto one ceiling – had been extremely important to her as a child. She had thought it terrifically beautiful; it had also given her an intimation of what it was to play with style: 'it's a very, very difficult mix of real craftspersonship, real marble and fake . . . you never quite know what's what until you touch it . . . the stairs are real fabulous marble but the pillars are painted plaster . . . it's a masterpiece of kitsch but in a hundred years' time no one's going to be able to tell that it's kitsch.'

Playing with style, making fairy tale and fantasy tell new truths, was part of the point of her work. 'Is she fact or is she fiction?' was Fevvers's slogan, and it could have been Angela's on the page, and in life. She was not at first easy to make out, and never easy to second-guess. Her face was strong-boned, but fluid, almost fuzzy; she was a great curser (a message left on my answering-machine at the outbreak of the Gulf War consisted entirely of oaths), but byzantinely courteous – an icily disarming 'forgive me' accompanied by a salaam and a chuckle was a favourite introit. She had exceptional verbal sharpness but surrounded her trenchancies with long pauses, huge wheezes of silent laughter, verbal flutters in which south London slang took over from her usual piping tones. She skidded into some of her best *mots* through a series of hesitancies which were a world away from diffidence: I remember her some years back stunning a television books panel who had been reverencing D. H. Lawrence, by announcing, after an extremely long goose-pimpling pause: 'I've always thought that Gudrun was, well, the vasectomy queen of the North.'

Her prose, like her own speaking voice, was allusive, parodic and playful. Performance and performers delighted her in life and were celebrated in her books. She wrote about cinema and circuses and the music-hall; she created the somersaulting Fevvers and, in her last novel, *Wise Children*, the stalwart hoofers Nora and Dora Chance, with their legend 'What a joy it is to dance and sing!' She was an enthusiastic investigator of the oral tradition – in fairy tales and elsewhere. And she wanted to write works that could be performed.

When, as her literary executor, I came to look at her papers after her death, I found a characteristic mixture of apparent vagueness and steely grip. The study at the top of her Clapham house was dusty – for the last months of her life Angela had worked in her bedroom and in hospital wards – and dishevelled, but it contained a fairly complete chronicle of a

THE CURIOUS ROOM

Angela Carter was born in 1940. She read English at Bristol University, and from 1976–8 was a fellow in Creative Writing at Sheffield University. She lived in Japan, the United States and Australia. Her first novel, *Shadow Dance*, was published in 1965, followed by *The Magic Toyshop* (1967, John Llewellyn Rhys Prize), *Several Perceptions* (1968, Somerset Maugham Award), *Heroes and Villains* (1969), *Love* (1971), *The Passion of New Eve* (1977), *Nights at the Circus* (1984, James Tait Black Memorial Prize) and *Wise Children* (1991). Four collections of her short stories have been published: *Fireworks* (1974), *The Bloody Chamber* (1979, Cheltenham Festival of Literature Award), *Black Venus* (1985) and *American Ghosts and Old World Wonders* (1993). She was the author of *The Sadeian Woman: An Exercise in Cultural History* (1979), and two collections of journalism, *Nothing Sacred* (1982) and *Expletives Deleted* (1992). She died in February 1992.

The Curious Room: Collected Dramatic Works is the second in a series of three volumes of Angela Carter's collected works. The first volume, already available in Vintage, is *Burning Your Boats: Collected Short Stories*; the third, *Shaking a Leg: Collected Writings*, is published by Chatto & Windus.

BY ANGELA CARTER

Short Stories

Fireworks
The Bloody Chamber
Black Venus
American Ghosts and Old World Wonders
Burning Your Boats: Collected Short Stories
The Virago Book of Fairy Tales (editor)
The Second Virago Book of Fairy Tales (editor)
Wayward Girls and Wicked Women (editor)

Novels

Shadow Dance
The Magic Toyshop
Several Perceptions
Heroes and Villains
Love
The Infernal Desire Machine of Dr Hoffman
The Passion of New Eve
Nights at the Circus
Wise Children

Non-Fiction

The Sadeian Woman: An Exercise in Cultural History
Nothing Sacred: Selected Writings
Expletives Deleted
Shaking a Leg: Collected Writings

Drama

Come unto These Yellow Sands: Four Radio Plays
The Curious Room: Collected Dramatic Works

Angela Carter

THE CURIOUS ROOM

Plays, Film Scripts and an Opera

WITH AN INTRODUCTION BY
Susannah Clapp

EDITED AND WITH PRODUCTION NOTES BY
Mark Bell

VINTAGE

Published by Vintage 1997

2 4 6 8 10 9 7 5 3 1

First published together in one volume by
Chatto & Windus Ltd, 1996

Vintage
Random House, 20 Vauxhall Bridge Road, London SW1V 2SA

Random House Australia (Pty) Limited
20 Alfred Street, Milsons Point, Sydney
New South Wales 2061, Australia

Random House New Zealand Limited
18 Poland Road, Glenfield,
Auckland 10, New Zealand

Random House South Africa (Pty) Limited
Endulini, 5A Jubilee Road, Parktown 2193, South Africa

Random House UK Limited Reg. No. 954009

A CIP catalogue record for this book
is available from the British Library

ISBN 0 09 958621 5

Papers used by Random House UK Ltd are natural, recy-
clable products made from wood grown in sustainable
forests. The manufacturing processes conform to the
environmental regulations of the country of origin

Printed and bound in Great Britain by

CONTENTS

ACKNOWLEDGEMENTS

Vampirella, Come unto These Yellow Sands, The Company of Wolves (radio play) and *Puss in Boots* were first published in 1985 by Bloodaxe Books in an anthology entitled *Come unto These Yellow Sands*.

The Company of Wolves (screenplay) by Angela Carter and Neil Jordan, adapted from Angela Carter's own story, is published here with grateful thanks to ITC Entertainment (copyright 1984, all rights reserved) who presented the Palace Production of the Neil Jordan film starring Angela Lansbury and David Warner. Directed by Neil Jordan.

The Christchurch Murder is published here with grateful thanks to Euston Films (copyright 1988, all rights reserved).

writing life: its small desk and old office filing-cabinet were packed with drafts and final versions of articles and stories; a small red cash-book recorded fees and expenses. It soon became clear that there was no abandoned novel or cache of short stories: Angela's proposal for a book about Jane Eyre's stepdaughter had never got further than a lively page of synopsis. It nevertheless became clear that the office contained a profusion of unpublished and unsuspected work. Drawings and paintings spilled out of these drawers: lusciously coloured pictures of fruits and flowers, a parade of undomesticated cats, sketches of houses and scenery, and a number of studies of her son Alexander as a baby – with round cheeks and bugle eyes, looking more than ever like a picture of the West Wind on an old map; Angela always travelled with a sketch-pad, and one of these pictures provides the cover for this book. There was also an unexpectedly large number of plays for theatre, film and radio. These pieces make up this volume. By their form and extent, they enlarge the scope and alter the contours of a rich body of work.

Several of the plays have not been read before, because several of them have never been performed or published. Angela had considerable success with writing for radio: born in 1940, she was a child of the radio age – as she was a child of Stafford Cripps's England – and grew up hearing both the sweetness of John Masefield's *Box of Delights* and the sepulchral tones of the Man in Black. Her belief that it was 'the most visual of mediums because you cannot see it' served her well in these expansively ambiguous plays, in which she could pit words against tone in operatic fashion, elaborate her cast of characters without losing a narrative line, scatter thrilling sound effects, and continually fade from fantasy to – as it were – fact. She loved her encounters with film (*The Company of Wolves*) and television (*The Magic Toyshop*) but in general was less fortunate with her work for screen and theatre, running into the familiar difficulties of straitened budgets, changing personnel – and some resistance. The capaciousness and dense verbal quality of her plays made them, in the view of some directors, difficult to stage. Angela was not forgiving about this: I remember her white and narrow-eyed with fury at a party explaining: 'The National have just flushed my *Lulu* down the toilet.'

The voice in these pieces is the voice of her fiction and journalism. Sometimes it almost takes the words from their mouths. The fairy pictures of the parricide painter Richard Dadd led Angela to examine what she considered 'a completely twentieth-century great play' by Shakespeare, to look at notions of kitsch and to inquire into the dislocating effects of capitalism. These are among the preoccupations which cluster together in *Wise Children* – in which her original intention had been to replay all of Shakespeare's plays, and which has at its centre a Hollywood *Midsummer Night's Dream* populated by retching pixies, clockwork birds and fairies whose 'bras and knicks had leaves appliquéd at the stress points'. Dadd also enabled her to rehearse an interest in parent-killers. Two years after *Come unto These Yellow Sands* was first broadcast, Angela published the first of two short stories about Lizzie Borden and her murderous axe, which she had hoped to develop into a novel. The novel didn't happen, but she turned again to matricide – and again to expressing the lure of Hollywood – in her most wirily-written screenplay, *The Christchurch Murder*. Behind the most ambitious of her theatrical pieces are years of writing about female icons – about faces and filmstars and fashion: the figure of Lulu was an abiding favourite ('should I ever have a daughter, I would call her, not Simone, nor even Rosa, but Lulu') – as was Louise Brooks, whom she admired for the challenge of her direct look and rumbustious life.

Angela had a gift for making her ideas dance, for making a spectacle out of strenuous thought. The re-imaginer of fairy tales provides *The Company of Wolves*. The socialist dramatises Virginia Woolf's *Orlando* (the only unfinished piece in the volume) and gives the servants more of a say. She is always surprising. *Vampirella* (which Angela and Neil Jordan were talking about making into a film when she became ill) is a reminder that she was an ardent reader of the horror writer Anne Rice. Her cowboy morality play *Gun for the Devil* pays tribute to Daniel Defoe, one of her favourite eighteenth-century writers, in the name of the character Roxana. In her play about the novelist Ronald Firbank, one of the authors she favoured above Dickens for a Desert Island browse, a Ewan McColl song is specified – a nod to her Sixties days of folk music at Bristol University, where she 'developed a respect for the art of the people – through Communist Party propaganda, basically'.

Angela's television examination of the life of Christ, *The Holy Family Album* – which featured Peruvian box shrines, a child's sex instruction book, and angels popping through the wall 'like the cuckoo in a cuckoo-clock' – lost too much without pictures and colour and animation to include here. A scene based on *A Midsummer Night's Dream* was omitted because it exists as a story published in *Black Venus*. I hope that another book will one day be able to accommodate the text of the *Omnibus* programme made about Angela a few weeks before she died – which won its director a prize and Angela the admiration of HM's Chief Inspector of Prisons for England and Wales. This is the second of three volumes of Angela Carter's Collected Works: the final volume will contain her journalism. Together they confirm a bleak truth about a high-spirited writer: that, as Angela put it, 'the fin has come a little early this siècle.'

RADIO PLAYS

Vampirella

Come unto These Yellow Sands

The Company of Wolves

Puss in Boots

A Self-Made Man

Vampirella

(Gently fade in cooing of doves and bring into foreground the song of a lark on interior acoustic.)

COUNTESS: *(Over.)* Can a bird sing only the song it knows or can it learn a new song . . .

HERO: . . . said the lovely, lonely, lady vampire, running the elegant scalpel of her fingernail along the bars of the cage in which her pet bird sang.

(The sound of the COUNTESS's nails against the bars of the cage. The COUNTESS laughs: and her laughter is picked up by a harp which mirrors her laughter – the lark sings; cut short by the screech of a bat.

Fade in doves cooing as before. The lark sings, the COUNTESS laughs, and her laughter, as before, is repeated by the harp and is then crossfaded to her fingers running along the bars of the birdcage – in the same key.)

COUNTESS: *(Over.)* My demented and atrocious ancestors habitually sequestered themselves from the light of the sun in solemn, indeed, lugubrious, heavily curtained apartments; each one, man or woman, was a victim of the most terrible passion.

(A screech from the bat.)

. . . Ah! – scarcely dare to speak its name. Even the meanest fiend in hell shuns the company of my kind. I am compelled to the repetition of their crimes; that is my life. I exist only as a compulsion, a compulsion . . .

COUNT: *(Thoughts microphone.)* In Hungary, in the county of Temesvar, those who fall sick of the fatal lethargy that follows my embraces say that a white spectre follows them, sticking as close to their heels as does a shadow. They track down the dreaded vampire by means of the following ritual. They choose a young boy who is a pure maiden, that is to say, who has not yet known any woman, and set him bareback on a stallion that has not mounted its first mare. The power of these two virgins exists, you understand, only in containment. Like me, like she, they possess the mysterious solitude of ambiguous states . . . they are not linked into the great chain of generation. We are all unnatural. Horse and rider trot towards the village cemetery –

(Bring in exterior acoustic – owls etc. and the clip-clop of a horse – centre.)

– and go in and out among the gravestones while the peasantry follow with spades and scythes and crucifixes and wreaths of garlic. Breathlessly, they creep a little way behind the emissaries of virginity . . . until –

(During above bring in murmurs of villagers which end on a gasp.)

BOY: See! He's stopped! He won't budge an inch! *(Steps.)* Here, here! In this grave, beneath this stone, the vampire lies!

(Shovelling. Clink of spade upon coffin. Creaking: they are opening the coffin.)

Ah!

(The villagers react to what they see.)

COUNT: *(Close.)* There the quarry lies, as ruddy in the cheeks as if I had nodded off to sleep in my shroud. I might have been taking a little after-dinner nap, replete, pacific . . . The priest takes up a heavy sword and . . .

(Sharp blow. Rapid intonation in Greek.)

So they strike off my head and out gush warm torrents of rich, red blood, like melted roses.

(Gasps. Rapid praying.)

BOY: The land is freed from the plague of vampires!

(Cheers and applause. Down behind following and creep in music.)

COUNT: Endlessly, I attend my own obsequies; softly, enormously, across all my funerals, my fatal shadow rises again . . .

COUNTESS: But love, true love, could free me from this treadmill, this dreadful wheel of destiny . . .

COUNT: My daughter, the last of the line, through whom I now project a modest, posthumous existence, believes herself to be a version of the Flying Dutchman – that she may be made whole by human feeling. That one fine day, a young virgin will ride up to the castle door and restore her to humanity with a kiss from his pure, pale lips.

(The COUNTESS sighs dreadfully which cuts music and drily sobs.)

Oh, my little girl, I'd love to see you lie quiet . . .

(Fade in exterior acoustic – bicycle wheels on a track.)

HERO: *(Thoughts microphone.)* Night and silence. I never guessed, here in the Carpathians, there would be no stars. No stars, no moon. I am just a little nervous, although no one is here . . . Is it only a simple twanging of my own nerves that I feel? Yet I am not a timorous man. My colonel assures me I have nerves of steel. But I might almost be prepared to believe this fear no more than a sudden crisis of my own, a revisitation of all the childhood fears of night and silence in my present loneliness, the uncanny dark of this Carpathian tea-time . . . I would be inclined to believe I was so innocently afraid if I did not possess a strange conviction that terror itself was in some sense immanent in these particular rocks and bushes. I've never felt such terror in any other place. The North West Frontier, far more barren, far more inimical . . . damn deserts never scared me so. It is as if terror were the genius loci of the place and only comes out at night. When they told me this morning at the inn I should not stay out beyond the fall of darkness, I did not believe them. But I was not in the least afraid, then.

(Owl hoots, long, lonely sound. The bicycle wheels wobble, click against stone. HERO *exclaims.)*

Ah! ah, nothing but a nightbird. The cry of a nightbird momentarily startled me, so that I nearly fell.

(Bicycle wheels steady on track.)

They say the owl was a baker's daughter . . . not a bird of the best omens.

(Brisker, less introspective tone.)

To ride a bicycle is in itself some protection against superstitious fears since the bicycle is the product of pure reason applied to motion. Geometry at the service of man! Give me two spheres and a straight line and I will show you how far I can take them. Voltaire himself might have invented the bicycle, since it contributes so much to man's well-being and nothing at all to his bane. Bicycling is beneficial to the health. The bicycle emits no harmful fumes and permits only the most decorous speeds. It is not a murderous implement.

Yet, like all the products of enlightened reason, the bicycle has a faint air of eccentricity about it. On two wheels in the Land of the Vampires! A suitable furlough for a member of the English middle classes. My first choice was, the Sahara. But then, I thought, perhaps a more peopled tour would be more fascinating . . .

Nobody is surprised to see me, they guess at once where I come from. The coarse peasants titter a little behind their hands. Le Monsieur Anglais! But they behave with deference; for only a man with an empire on which the sun never sets to support him would ride a bicycle through this phantom-haunted region.

(Pause. Bring up bicycle slightly.)

A bicycle is a lonely instrument.

(Hoot of owl.)

To ride a bicycle involves a continuous effort of will and hence it is a moral exercise. A purposive retention of the perpendicular in circumstances, such as the presence of great fear, when the horizontal – lying flat on the ground scrabbling helplessly with one's fingers in the soil in order to dig oneself a hole in which to hide – would seem to be by far the more sensible thing to do.

Now we approach a rustic bridge.

(The wheels now rattle as they cross the bridge – matching HERO*'s mood.)*

Something atavistic, something numinous about crossing whirling dark water by no moonlight . . .

COUNT: *(Very softly.)* And when he crossed the bridge, the phantoms came to meet him . . .

(Rattle of the bicycle wheels increased.)

HERO: I do believe that now I am so frightened that when the front wheels of my bicycle jolt upon that stone – or is it the skull of a wild beast – that skull or stone I see before me in the tremulous light of my headlamp, I will go flying from my saddle and tumble headlong into the stream, since my fear has so overcome my sense or senses that I can no longer retain the vertical in the face of any unexpected obstacle, however small.

(He gives a sudden cry.
A crash, a splash, a moan: the bicycle wheels run on. One wheel spins round more and more slowly until at last it stops. Crossfade to running water. HERO *moans as he drags himself ashore. Distantly, a babble of rough voices gradually getting louder. The voices speak an improvised language full of Ks and Ts. They come across* HERO *and begin, curiously, inspecting him.)*

HERO: I say, gently does it! Can nobody speak English? Not one word? I say, where are you taking me?

(Kindly, firmly they pick him up, exchanging guttural remarks and occasionally pinching him. Their big boots clatter on the track as they lead him away.)

(Over.) Well, I daresay I'll find out where they're taking me soon enough. Could do with a rest. I could do with . . . a cup of tea. Quite a nasty fall, really – just a little shaken, I must confess. A good, hot cup of tea, now . . . My God, how English I am! It never ceases to astonish me.

Why have they left my bicycle behind, though? Lying where it fell, among the weeds at the side of the bridge, the dew will rust it . . .

(Footsteps now on cobbles.)

Ah, a light before us. We must be going towards that light. A light, a homestead in this abandoned and desolate region. Yet that light does not console me, it does not make me think of home and hearth and fireside. It is a sinister and flickering light, like marsh-fire . . . By God, a castle! And flambeaux at the gates; great, whirling bouquets of gas, darting hither and thither on the wind!

(Hissing of gas-jets.)

COUNT: *(Thoughts microphone.)* . . . a vast, ruined castle, from whose tall black windows came no ray of light and whose broken battlements showed a jagged line . . . like broken teeth. And at my gate I light the visitor a welcome with fireflowers plucked from hell . . .

(Dog snarls: a mournful clanging of a bell. Gate creaks open, melodramatically.)

HERO: The gatekeeper, a horn lantern in his horny fist; lighting up constellations of cobwebs . . . !

(Peasants depart, giggling unpleasantly. Door clangs shut. Footsteps on stone floor.)

I am alone. Dear God, I never heard any portal close behind me with such an emphatic clang. How I'm shivering; these wet clothes . . .

GATEKEEPER: *(Says something incomprehensible.)*

HERO: Good evening. *(HERO sits, with a sigh of relief.)* Must be the concierge's private quarters. Quite clean, quite comfortable . . . a bit Spartan . . . guns on the walls. No spik English, eh?

(Grunt from gatekeeper.)

Well, I dare say we'll get on well enough. My, what a fine fire . . . *(Rubs hands at the crackling blaze.)* Ah, a change of clothes, ready laid out for me . . . why – just my size! A nice piece of worsted, that suit, and a fine silk shirt, monogrammed upon the breast . . . A Cyrillic delta, indeed . . . Ready laid out, as if they were expecting me. And a stout pair of shoes. (HERO *is changing clothes during speech.)* That's better, clean, dry clothes. And judging by the gatekeeper's manoeuvres with that bottle, that glass, I should imagine I'm about to be treated to a little peasant hospitality.

(Bottle emptying into glass.)

Thanks! *(Drinks: coughs.)* Some kind of vodka, very strong . . . warming. I'd certainly not say no to another.

(Another glass is poured. Footsteps and effects in background.)

Now what are you up to! Ah, getting me some black bread, is it? Black bread and cheese. I could do with a bite, I must say. I suppose I'll be lodging here for the night. Only one bed . . . perhaps I'll doss down on the floor, with the dog. Eh, boy?

(Dog barks excitedly.)

COUNT: *(Thoughts microphone.)* Down, boy, down!

(Dog whimpers.)

HERO: Backing away from me, now? Oh, come, the English have a traditional affinity for dogs . . . but not, perhaps, for such dogs as you, you great, slavering, fanged monster! Yes, wild dog, indeed.

COUNT: *(Thoughts microphone.)* Red-eyed devil's whelp, many a witless ancient died a ghastly death at the hands of the inquisition for petting in her bosom such a familiar as you . . . if you are a good dog and don't bite the carpet or foul the floor, my daughter will throw you a juicy bone, a femur with some scraps of flesh still on it, perhaps.

(Door creaks open.)

HERO: *(To himself.)* What have we here, what apparition in black velvet. A valet, by his obsequiousness, the chatelaine's valet? He's gesturing towards me. Why, he's dumb! . . . *(Aloud.)* Taking me off somewhere, are you? Off to meet the king of the castle? No need to clasp my wrist so tight . . . I'll come quietly.

(Footsteps echo on stone floor.)

COUNT: *(Ghostly chuckle disappearing into echoes.)*

(Crossfade to MRS BEANE. *Fire crackling in background.)*

MRS BEANE: *(Baleful, humorous – off microphone.)*

> Fee, fi, fo, fum.
> I smell the blood of an Englishman.

Och, it's only my pawky Scots humour that preserves my sanity!

COUNTESS: I am the lady of the castle. My name is exile. My name is anguish. My name is longing. Far from the world on the windy crests of the mountain, I am kept in absolute seclusion, my time passes in an endless reverie, a perpetual swooning. I am both the Sleeping Beauty and the enchanted castle; the princess drowses in the castle of her flesh.

MRS BEANE: Hush, hush my dearie, don't distress yourself.

(Ripple of larksong.)

COUNTESS: *(Shivers.)* Cold, so cold, Mrs Beane . . . the wind creeps in through the cracks in the old stone and the fire never warms me.

MRS BEANE: *(To a child.)* Now, you just stop feeling sorry for yourself and eat up your egg. Look, I've cut up your bread and butter into soldiers for you . . .

COUNTESS: *(As child.)* Shall I eat up the nice soldiers?

MRS BEANE: Like a good girl, now . . . och, your hands are like ice!

COUNTESS: Since a child, so cold. Always cold. I should like to go to a land of perpetual summer and let the petals of a flowering tree fall upon my face as I lie in the warm shade and sleep without the fever of this eternal shivering. But could even Italian summers warm me, when not all the fires of Hell might do so –

MRS BEANE: *(Angry.)* Countess! Now, just you stop your whining!

COUNTESS: *(Almost sulky.)* Shunned by fiends . . .

COUNT: *(Thoughts microphone.)* Does my beautiful daughter sense her father's posthumous presence or is she indeed a portion of myself . . .

(Door opens, off.)

HERO: *(Thoughts microphone.)* In the dark, luxurious room, I made out two figures beside the little fire, a craggy dame with pepper and salt hair dragged back in an austere bun, upright as a standing stone, and a young lady, seated. *(Out loud; but hesitant.)* Good evening . . .

(Moment's pause.)

MRS BEANE: Good evening to you. May I present you to the Countess –

COUNTESS: *(Breaks in in a tumultuous rush.)* Welcome, welcome to my castle. It is so lovely to see a new face, I rarely receive visitors and nothing – nothing, I assure you! – animates me half so much as the presence of a stranger. The castle is so lonely; only the village people come here to bring milk and eggs and a little fresh meat . . . sometimes they bring me a benighted traveller if they should have happened to have stumbled across one. My castle is famed for its hospitality.

(Faint rumble of the COUNT's posthumous chuckle.)

You must forgive the shadows . . . my eyes. An affliction of the eyes. I can only see clearly in chiaroscuro, a condition my family shares with the cat.

(During the last few lines the COUNTESS sits in rocking chair.
All the following is on thoughts microphone with background continuing.)

HERO: At first, in the heavily shaded lamplight, I could hardly make out her features, only her vague shape as it moved a little backwards, a little forwards in a bentwood rocking chair, inexorably as the pendulum of a giant clock; she wears a white muslin dress, she looks like a trapped cloud.

But as I grew accustomed to the lack of illumination, I distinguished the shocking harmonies of her face.

(In a brisker, more objective tone.)

The young Countess was so beautiful she might just as well have been hunch-backed; her beauty was so excessive it seemed like a kind of deformity. And I thought, her appearance necessitates her seclusion for even, or perhaps, especially, in her nakedness

(Chord of swooning music, continuing during his next sentence.)

– a condition which appalled me even momentarily to contemplate, oh, God, no! not even in her awe-inspiring nakedness!

(Music ceases abruptly.)

No, even were she to wear only the simplest, most unpretentious, most unbecoming of garments, she would, at any gathering, arrive embarrassingly overdressed. Her beauty was like a dress too good to be worn but, poor girl, it was the only one she had.

COUNT: Her beauty is a symptom of her disorder.

HERO: There was about her not one of those touching little imperfections that reconcile us to the imperfection of the human condition.

COUNT: She is a masterpiece of appearance; she is far too fine an imitation of a woman.

HERO: Her visible inhumanity did not inspire confidence. I had been quite unable to rid myself of the terrible unease that had possessed me since night fell on the Carpathians and, in her lyrical and melancholy presence, I felt it increase to an almost unbearable degree.

Too many shadows in the room might conspire to hide she lacks a shadow.

Her hair falls down inconsolably as rain.

COUNT: She would like very much to be human but, of course, that's quite impossible.

HERO: She is so beautiful she is pitiful.

Her stern, tartan governess has a mouth like a steel trap.

MRS BEANE: (*Brisk, objective, autobiographical.*) My name is Mrs Beane. Widowed early in life, in the most distressing circumstances, left to fend for myself in the wide world with only my five wits and moral fibre to aid me, I answered an advertisement in the *Edinburgh Gazette* for a governess to a young lady of aristocratic birth in a far corner of the Carpathians. They offered an unusually high salary; but my attention was particularly attracted by the fact that they offered to pay only the one way fare. That is, the fare out.

My interview took place one winter's evening in the drawing room of a luxurious suite at a sumptuous but discreet hotel. Someone I took to be the Count's personal valet, a deaf-mute in a livery of the most funereal black, ushered me into his presence.

Only a little lamp glowed on a corner table yet, in order to shield his over-sensitive eyes from even those few rays it emitted, the Count had donned a green eye-shade. I was to learn that darkness was the exclusive element of this most unfortunate family.

How pale his face was; livid, I should say. Yet, a perfect gentleman. He offered me a chair, he treated me with extraordinary politeness.

After a few preliminary inquiries, he asked me: did I know the Carpathians well? I answered wi' circumspection.

(*Into drawing room.*
In interview with the COUNT.)

I understand the air is clement. And the mountains generally unfrequented.

COUNT: *(Laughs theatrically.)* Dark, scarcely tenanted forests, a peasantry rooted, rotted deep in the most degrading superstition, vile practices as old as the human race, older . . .

In those rank villages, the Devil himself dances in the graveyards on Walpurigisnacht. A bald mountain, a castle half in ruins . . .

MRS BEANE: *(Thoughts microphone.)* Had I, he asks, rather than an attraction for his phantom-haunted homeland, perhaps, instead, personal reasons for choosing to exile myself so far away from Scotland.

I thought then, och! he must read the newspapers. Maybe he knows more about me than I well ken.

MRS BEANE: *(To the COUNT.)* Well, sir, I must reluctantly confess . . . that I do have personal reasons . . . of the most pressing nature . . . for wishing to leave Scotland at the first opportunity. And destination, you might say, no object.

COUNT: My daughter, your charge, will not grow up to be . . . as other women. Already, by an exquisite irony, she shows signs of unusual beauty and yet her soul is already darkened by the knowledge of her fate; she is the last bud of a great tree of darkness, the final child of the oldest, most deeply cursed line in all the fatal Balkans . . . blood, blood, blood is her patrimony, Mrs Beane!

Father to son, mother to daughter endlessly the taint leaks back in time . . . the silver bullet, the stake through the heart . . . *(He gasps.)* Ohh!

(He pauses to catch his breath and resumes.)

Not one of my house has lain quiet since Vlad the Impaler first feasted on corpses.

MRS BEANE: *(Gasps, recovers herself. Very brisk.)* There's a little taint to every clan, sir. Nobody's perfect. To tell the truth, I guessed there was a snag to the position you have vacant and that's the truth. Such a high salary! And a one-way ticket promised, only the one way. I'd not have answered it had I not been desperate. You see, my husband . . .

COUNT: . . . was recently executed. His crime –

MRS BEANE: I'd never a notion to the nature of his tastes, married so young as I was. He so cold to me. Then that dreadful night when he came back from the graveyard with his fingernails full of earth and a bloated look about him. 'Blood will out,' he said and laughed like a hyena, aptly enough.

COUNT: Necrophagy.

MRS BEANE: Blood will out, the black blood of Sawney Beane, who strewed the beaches outside Edinburgh wi' dead men's bones.

(Skirl of bagpipes. Jaunty. Proud.)

SAWNEY BEANE: *(Over.)* Times was hard, sheep dying in the field for drought, the landlords grasping, bleeding us white wi' taxes. The corn took blight and rotted in the fields; the plague came, and hunger, worse than plague. We poor folk dying for lack of a crust, ditches crammed with the corpses of the poor. So I says to my Jeannie, the outlaw's life for us! And she says, aye, Sawney, let's eat them up the way they've eaten us.

(Bagpipes fade; seagulls, waves.)

So Jeannie and I, she being great with child, took ourselves off to the seashore and there we found a cave as high and wide and handsome as the mansion of the Chief Justice and there we lived in comfort. And every passerby on the highroad, first we killed him, then we robbed him and then we ATE HIM UP!

(Screaming, wild laughter, cheering, bagpipes again.)

And we grew fat and prospered and the bairnies came clustering about my Jeannie's knee, eight fine, strapping sons and six wonderfully blooming daughters. We dressed in silks and satins we pulled off their bodies – skin 'em alive, cried Jeannie! And, oh, she was jewelled like a queen wi' all the gems of the fine ladies whose corpses we subsequently consumed wi' relish, for every night we dined off the fine flesh of earls, barons, marchionesses and so on. The meat had the flavour of excellent pork and you never saw such crackling.

(Sounds of meat roasting; children laughing and eating.)

In due time, our sons turned to our daughters and knew them and cast new coins from the old moulds while our beaches piled high with dead men's bones. We made our chairs and tables from thigh bones and femurs; we played ducks and drakes with the skulls of the powerful. Our bairnies played five stones wi' vertebrae and learned to count till ten upon phalanges. Och, those were fine days! A great clan of Beanes, seed of my loins, fruit of my Jeannie's womb, roared and ranted through our caves and so we lived and prospered even unto the third generation. And not one child nor one of our children's children ever tasted a scrap of anything but human flesh and flesh of the purest pedigree. Oh, I was a great anthropophagic patriarch, I was!

(Fire burning; seagulls; children's voices; the crunching of bones, fade behind following.)

There's nothing to beat the rich flavour of a fat prelate's thigh baked in sea salt over a driftwood fire.

But after five and twenty glorious years, the King's men came for us and there was a mighty battle.

(Sword-fighting; women screaming; but SAWNEY*'s voice rises up almost in triumph.)*

We fought like tigers all day long, until the light began to fade and their reinforcements came and so they overwhelmed us, quite, and I and my Jeannie and the tribe that called me Father were put to death in Edinburgh, after amazing tortures, amidst scenes of wild rejoicing from the populace.

But we'd eaten more of them than they ever killed of us.

We preyed upon the masters like the wolves upon the flock and so we had our furious triumph!

(Screams, shouts, cheers, bagpipes. Fade into child whimpering.)

CHILD: Mama? *(No reply.)*

(Faltering.)

Dada?

SAWNEY BEANE: *(As* MRS BEANE*'s husband.)* The curse of the Beanes. The most insatiable hunger in the world . . .

MRS BEANE: *(Brisk. Thoughts microphone.)* And so I came to take service with the Count, since I was not unfamiliar with the nature of the family's passions. Och! You'd never believe what a pretty wee thing she was, so trusting. How she would cling to me and beg to go out into the garden . . .

(Into drawing room.)

COUNTESS AS CHILD: Just this once, Mrs Beane, just this once before sunset . . .

MRS BEANE: *(Younger.)* Wait till the dark, my pet, and then we'll venture out together just a wee way . . .

(Owl hoots, followed by a high, thin, prolonged, inhuman scream. Sobbing.)

MRS BEANE: *(Thoughts microphone.)* Her condition seemed to me judgement passed on her long ago, before she was born, my poor, pretty dear. My poor pretty . . .

COUNTESS: *(To HERO.)* I am condemned to solitude and dark. I do not mean to hurt you, I do not want to cause you pain. But I am both beauty and the beast, locked up in the fleshly castle of exile and anguish, I cannot help but seek to assuage in you my melancholy . . .

HERO: *(Thoughts microphone.)* A magnificent apartment. Dark tapestries on the walls, a subdued glitter of gold in the ormolu furniture. Here and there a pretty toy, a satin pierrot doll, a figurine of glass, imported from Paris for her, ordered from a catalogue, I dare say. A heavy scent of incense, like a church. Or like a mortician's parlour, for there is something corpse-like about her stillness, as if she were tranced. Her chair moves backwards and forwards but, for herself, she hardly moves at all.

   Velvet curtains heavily shut out the night. The Persian carpets demonstrate luminous geometry upon the floor. In her white muslin dress, with the paisley shawl drawn across her frail shoulders and her long, dark hair in gentle disorder . . . she . . .

COUNTESS: *(Whispers.)* Such a fine throat, Mrs Beane, like a column of marble . . .

MRS BEANE: Hush, hush, child. Calm yourself.

COUNTESS: *(Aloud.)* My ancestors suffered very much from the direct rays of the sun and all lived all their lives in these solemn apartments, shaded from the daylight – so many centuries since one of my family saw the sunshine! I've never seen the sunshine though, when I was little, I wanted to. Now, I cannot even imagine what sunshine might be like. When I try to do so, I see only a kind of irradiated dark.

(The following on thoughts microphone:)

HERO: On her knee a fluffy kitten and on the little table beside her a jewelled cage.

COUNT: I ordered my daughter a jewelled birdcage from Fabergé in Petersburg, for a present on her fifteenth birthday. But when she saw it, she made those signs with her mouth that show how she would like to cry, if only she knew the way.

HERO: In the cage, her pretty bird.

COUNTESS: It is a skylark, its element is morning. But since I've kept it so long in my room, I think it must have grown blind because we keep the curtains drawn all day.

MRS BEANE: You must not give way to self-pity; you are the way you are, a necessary creature of nature, and that's an end to it.

(Skylark sings. Over to drawing room.)

COUNTESS AS CHILD: Can a bird sing only the song it knows or can it learn a new song?

MRS BEANE: *(Younger.)* The skylark's song was written out for it when it was hatched, my dear, and, without the intercession of, let us call it 'grace' for the sake of argument, may not change its tune by so much as a single sharp or flat.

(The following on thoughts microphone:)

COUNT: A chignonned priest of the orthodox faith staked me at a certain Slavonic crossroad in the year 1905.

(Rapid words in Greek. A blow, a cry.)

So end all the line of Vlad the Impaler!

COUNTESS: My destination chose me before I was born. I exist only as a compulsion to repeat it.

(Over to drawing room.)

MRS BEANE: Have you come far today, young man?

HERO: *(Hearty.)* From the village in the valley – I fear I can't pronounce it! How unexpected, how splendid! to be amongst English-speakers again! I so much wanted to give the peasants a message about my bicycle but they couldn't make head or tail of what I was saying, of course.

COUNTESS: Please sit down, there . . . in that deep armchair, beside the fire. Be cosy, please . . . tea . . .

(Chink of crockery.)

You are just in time for tea.

HERO: *(Thoughts microphone.)* A fine silver service, a kettle on a spirit lamp and cups of such fine china her fingernails tap out carillons as she performs the tea ceremony. She is trying to allay my suspicions. She has put on such an innocent look! My suspicions consist only of an apprehension of the uncanny, and are not soothed by her solicitude.

(*Drawing room.*)

Tea. Yes, milk and sugar, two lumps – thank you.

(*Chink.*)

COUNTESS: Will you take a little shortbread? Mrs Beane, my governess, makes it for me herself.

HERO: Shortbread! delicious.

(*Crunch.*)

How delicious!

(*Thoughts microphone.*) So here I am in milady's boudoir, with a cup of tea in my hand – good, strong, Indian tea brewed in a silver teapot, not one of those blasted samovars, and in my hand a piece of home-made shortbread –

(*Drawing room.*)

MRS BEANE: We Scotswomen can boast a light hand with pastry. 'The land of cakes,' they call Scotland. Scones and petticoat tails and flapjacks and I don't know what, such teas! When the winter evenings gather in, we bring out the three-tiered cakestand piled high with melt-in-the-mouth home-baking . . .

HERO: (*Thoughts microphone.*) After the Gothic terrors of the early evening, now I find myself taking late tea in a cunning imitation of an Edinburgh drawing room at five o'clock on a November evening.

How snug. Greenish flames flickering on sweet-smelling apple-logs. How, as the Germans say, gemütlich.

And yet the angel of inquietude stirs her uneasy wings in every corner and I cannot in the least subdue a trembling in my hands. When the tapestry figures shiver in the draught and seem, out of the corner of my eye, to perform the figures of a weird dance, the hairs on my nape helplessly rise . . .

And when she bites her shortbread biscuit –

(*Crunch.*)

– I see how curiously pointed her teeth are. Like the teeth of those Melanesians, or Micronesians, or Polynesian islanders who file their canines to a fine point.

Her teeth are too white, too delicate for human teeth. What little light there is in the room shines through her too white, too delicate fingers . . . what long, what pointed nails!

(More objective tone.)

When I tell you she was the most touching creature I have ever seen, you must realise that this was because her beauty involved the presence of its own absence, implied its own desolating loss, as if it were an uneasy lending.

> She implied her own continuous disappearance.
> Like a haunting.
> A woman is a lonely instrument . . .
> How I'm shaking! Unease. Disquiet. Fear? Yes . . . fear.
> But not yet . . .
> > . . . quite terrified.

(Over to drawing room. Kitten purrs; leaps upon HERO's knee. HERO starts.)

COUNTESS: Oh, puss! What an unexpected honour for you, puss scarcely ever takes to strangers . . .

HERO: *(Recovering his self-possession.)* Pretty pussy, pretty pussy . . .

(Cat begins to purr.)

COUNTESS: I have two pets, my cat and my bird; and Mrs Beane takes care of me. But, most of the time, I sleep. I sleep during the daytime, you have just caught me as I wake up. Usually I wake about nightfall, that is the dawn for me. We have an affliction of the eyes in my family, the eyes are inverted, you understand, and so we see best at night. I have an affinity for the cat, for all night creatures, owls . . . beasts that hunt by night.

(Distantly, a long, high, lonely, inhuman scream of rabbit or stoat.)

HERO: *(Thoughts microphone.)* I thought, perhaps, she was only fifteen or sixteen; but her eyes, the pupils of which were huge as those of all night creatures, contained too much disquiet for so few years. I recognised the high-strung, inbred over-sensitivity, the weakened blood, of an ancient, aristocratic house.

(Drawing room.)

Ah, puss! I see you like having your ears tickled.

(Cat purrs more loudly.)

COUNTESS: Among my terrible forebears, I number the Countess

Elizabeth Ba'thory; they called her the Sanguinary Countess. She used to bathe in the blood of young girls to refresh her beauty; she believed these lustrations would keep old age at bay. Look! there is her portrait on the wall, don't you see how little it is. All gilded. An abstract formalisation of her rank rather than a description of her person, don't you think . . . that was the style of the time. She looks rather like . . . an icon.

HERO: *(Thoughts microphone.)* She spoke the word 'icon' with a cringing temerity, as though the word was usually forbidden her; and her great, sad eyes moved anxiously in her head, as though she were searching for spies in the tapestry, who would be incensed by the word.

I continued to pet the kitten.

(Drawing room. Kitten purring.)

COUNTESS: She looks rather like . . . an icon . . . but an icon of unholiness. It shows her looking in a mirror, do you see; but, of course, she couldn't see her own reflection. She is peering and peering in the mirror for her face but she will never find it, never.

(The following on thoughts microphone:)

Such solitude! to live without one's own reflection.

A genealogy of terror, and of solitude.

MRS BEANE: Her loneliness always tormented her and I could do nothing to console her, only try to convince her, by my continual presence and my resolute inviolability, that she was not indeed inimical to everything human although she'd been born with a full set of teeth, wisdom teeth and all, and every tooth most curiously pointed.

(Drawing room.

Cat purrs more and more loudly; ominous. Suddenly it mews loudly and scratches HERO.)

HERO: Naughty pussy, naughty – aaaaagh!

(Swooping noise, as of wings in an enclosed space.)

Aaaaagh!

MRS BEANE: Naughty, naughty –

HERO: *(Thoughts microphone.)* Like a great, white bird, the girl swooped upon me, she, the Countess, you white nightbird, you white butcherbird, spreading your wings, your muslin sails. She swept across the room to fall at my feet, pressing that delicate wet mouth to the juicy wound with ah! such helpless greed. I felt the needles of her cannibal's teeth. I felt the suction of her tongue.

(Drawing room.)

Aaaaagh!

MRS BEANE: Countess, oh, but you are a naughty wee thing . . . *(Thoughts microphone.)* The poor, pretty dear, she can't help it any more than the kitten could help it. I've grown used to it. At first, I could hardly bear it . . . those nightwalks in the woods. She would bound off and come back in a little while with blood on her dress, making those faces she makes when she wants to cry but can't, poor wee thing.

HERO: *(Thoughts microphone.)* She drinks as deeply as she can. Her face is contorted with avidity. Only now, clenched like a leech to my wrist, does she seem truly alive, truly present. She has come back from wherever it is she goes to and briefly possesses herself.

Then I knew where the fear which inhabits these mountains makes its home; here, in this perfumed boudoir. Lodged in the frail flesh of this beautiful young girl.

She drinks as deeply as she may; then, fainting, slips on to the carpet,

(A gentle moan from COUNTESS and rustle as she falls to floor.)

lapsed into such torpor the Scotswoman can hitch her in her arms as lightly as if the Countess were made all of rags.

(Drawing room.)

MRS BEANE: There, there, my dear. There, my precious.

HERO: *(Thoughts microphone.)* And I, dizzy, sick, can do nothing but clasp my scratched hand protectively with the whole one and gaze at the governess with wide eyes of wonder.

(Drawing room.)

MRS BEANE: It is her passion. Such has been the dreadful passion of her house since Vlad the Impaler founded the line. Now she will sleep a little; she'll return to her almost habitual trance. The valet will show you to your room.

HERO: *(Faintly.)* My . . . bicycle . . .

MRS BEANE: Och, you'll no be needing that. I fear you'll never leave the castle, young man. We'll send home to your folks that you met an accident somewhere in the Carpathians. We've got it down to a fine art, now, providing for her tastes, covering up the traces. Over and over again we've done it. Over and over.

Now you must rest in your room. I shall not wish you sweet dreams. When she feels the need, she'll come to you.

(The following on thoughts microphone:)

HERO: The mute in mute's apparel winds me on the little spool of light he carries in his hand through corridors as circuitous as the passages inside the ear. His flame flushes out demented eyes from family portraits along the galleries; monsters, all . . . Underfoot, worn carpets ripple in the draught . . . a winding staircase of worm-eaten oak . . . I have been here before, in dreams, in nightmares . . .

COUNT: There is no end to the ceaseless cortege of my hospitality.

(Key turns in lock.)

HERO: Securely locked in, eh? Pleasant room . . . good feather bed. A fine candelabra to light my hours of waiting. And a handsome portrait of Gilles de Raie over the fireplace, if you please! Are the whole damn clan related to every vampire that ever lived?

Well, well, here's a to-do. I shall have to call on all my sang froid to deal with the situation.

A species of trance, of course. Interesting medical condition. I wonder what the sawbones back in London would make of it. Haematodypsia, the pathological thirst for blood . . . an exceedingly rare complaint. Where did I read about haematodypsia . . . And a touch of nervous hysteria, too . . . the young girls' disease. I wonder if the family finances could run to a trip to Vienna, to those Jewboy jennies who stretch you out on a couch and let you tell them how you always wanted to murder your father . . .

Wonder what the governess thinks she's up to. Feudal loyalty, I suppose. Stick to the line of Vlad the Impaler through thick and thin, no matter what . . . even do the Countess's pimping for her, in spite of her Edinburgh rectitude.

Seen queerer things on the North West Frontier, and that's the truth!

All the same, a pretty pickle.

Yet what a lovely creature! Poor, reclusive girl with her weak eyes, and so beautiful . . .

And, round about midnight, pale as water, stooping a little beneath her burden of old guilts, the beautiful somnambulist will turn the key

in the door and come into my room on suave, silent feet; she will lay
me down upon that narrow bed and feast upon me . . . ah!

(Chord of swooning music.)

And when I think of that, my shudder is not precisely one of pure
terror, although the rational bicycle-rider at war with the pulsing,
virginal romantic in my heart tells me I must, in my dealings with this
lady, beware, above all else, of masochism.

More things in heaven and earth, Horatio. Do you remember the
fakir who rose abruptly into the air, stiff as a board, flat on his back,
six feet into the air, suspended without visible support . . . and hung
there for fully five minutes, while the crowd wailed?

All to do with breathing . . .

(Moment's pause. Into COUNTESS's *bedroom.)*

COUNTESS: Mrs Beane?

MRS BEANE: Just you lie quiet a while.

COUNTESS: Mrs Beane . . . his kisses, his embraces. His head will fall
back, his eyes roll. Stark and dead, poor bicyclist; he has paid the price
of a night with the Countess and some think it too high a fee while
some do not.

MRS BEANE: I will say this, we shall have to get the kitten put down.
My, oh, my, pussy, you really gave the game away, didn't you, now!
Too soon, too soon . . . she can't resist it, can't resist it for one
moment.

(The following on thoughts microphone:)

COUNT: The sight of blood produces a singular effect on the metabolism
of we unfortunates. Not all the jams of paradise spread out upon a
table could equal the atrocious appetite the tiniest bead of blood
arouses in our febrile senses. Then, only then, do we wake from the
curious kind of waking swoon that passes for consciousness amongst
us. We seize upon the wound and worry it with our pointed teeth
until the liquid life flows down our rabid gullets in torrents, floods
. . . drained, empty as a crushed grape, the victim drops to the floor;
the wineskin of his body has been emptied and we are fat and drunk
upon his life.

ELIZABETH BA'ATHORY: The Sanguinary Countess laved her white,
exquisite body in the blood she tapped from the gross veins of peasant
girls who had too much blood for their own requirements. So she
kept her wrinkles at bay; she knew how much the preservation of her

fabled beauty was worth. Her servants never betrayed her, in spite of torture; they were in such deep complicity with her they urged her to renewed infamies as though her beauty and wickedness were properties of themselves and the more beautiful and wicked she became, the more they, too, were enhanced.

The young girls who became me when they washed me with my awful sponges were as much victims as those whom I immolated. Yet only in their admiring faces could I see the wonderful results of my magic baths for my piercing eye had broken every mirror in the castle.

When I looked at them, I saw how wonderful I was, and how terrifying.

If they had ceased to be afraid of me, I would have ceased immediately to be beautiful.

I was a great lady and my portrait shows me crusted almost entirely in gold.

SAWNEY BEANE: The landlords were eating us alive and I and my Jeannie, why, we set to upon the landlords! But Jeannie and I, at least we had the common decency to kill our prey first before we devoured it . . . oh, nothing equals a fricassée of Justice of the Peace, served up wi' a fine kelp salad.

HENRI BLOT: Chacun à son goût. Moi, je préfère les cadavres.

(Rustle of outrage in court-room; gavel tapped.)

COUNTESS: *(Whispering.)* Sometimes Death comes in an erotic disguise; she is your bride . . . she will sheathe you in lilies, I am the darkness and solitude from which you come, to which you will go . . .

HENRI BLOT: Each to his fancy . . . Myself, I like corpses.

(Rustle of outrage in court-room; gavel tapped.)

Yes, your honour, yes, your magnanimacy, yes, your serene and objective clemency, yes! An honest corpse, with the clean earth still fresh upon her . . . what, you shudder? Your gorge rises?

Hypocrite! When your wife lies beneath your repulsive and importunate body and twists involuntarily away her head so you may not suck upon the open wound of her mouth – immolated alive as she is beneath your judicial weight, my Lord, she who was so young and full of life entombed in your cold house with the children born of no hot passion but only the warmed-over remains of yesterday's unreciprocated lusts, conceived in incidental marital propinquacy alone . . . when you furiously mount the wife whose being you have drained of all fleshly significance, do you not commit a beastly necrophily? A necrophily just as gross as that which I performed upon the dead lilies of the body of Fernande Méry . . .

CLERK OF THE COURT: Professionally known as Carmanio, a ballet dancer.

(Rustle of papers.)

On the night of March 25, 1886, Henri Blot, aged twenty-six years, scaled a little door leading to the graveyard of St Ouen between the hours of eleven and midnight. He went to one of the trenches where persons not entitled to individual graves were buried and lifted up the boards which held up the earth on the last coffin in the row.

The coffin contained the body of a young woman of eighteen years, Fernande Méry, professionally known as Carmanio, a ballet dancer, buried the preceding evening. He removed the coffin from its resting place, opened it, drew out the corpse and carried it to an open space. He removed the paper wrappings from a number of grave bouquets, spread them upon the ground, and rested his knees upon them so as not to soil his trousers.

BLOT: See – what propriety! What concern for appearances! Can't you tell by just this little gesture towards seemliness what a good bourgeois I am?

CLERK OF THE COURT: In this position, he obtained carnal intercourse with the corpse. He then slept and did not wake until nearly dawn. On this occasion, he had sufficient time to leave the cemetery unseen but he did not have time to replace the corpse in its grave.

On June 12, Blot again violated a corpse and subsequently slept. On this occasion, he was discovered drowsing beside the defunct and arrested.

BLOT: Corpses don't nag and never want new dresses. They never waste all day at the hairdressers, nor talk for hours to their girl-friends on the telephone. They never complain if you stay out at your club; the dinner won't get cold if it's never been put in the oven. Chaste, thrifty – why, they never spend a penny on themselves! and endlessly accommodating. They never want to come themselves, nor demand of a man any of those beastly sophistications – blowing in the ears, nibbling at the nipples, tickling of the clit – that are so onerous to a man of passion. Doesn't it make your mouth water? Husbands, let me recommend the last word in conjugal bliss – a corpse.

The perfect wife, your honour. Or so, by what I've seen of your good lady, I take it you yourself believe.

CLERK OF THE COURT: The psychiatrists' reports, your honour.

(Rustle of papers.)

CLERK OF THE COURT: No evidence of insanity . . .

(Rustle of papers.)

No evidence of insanity . . .

(Rustle of papers.)

No evidence of insanity . . .

BLOT: Don't they all agree, I'm perfectly normal? We're all in the same boat together!
    You, you bourgeois husband striking the pointed stake between your loins into the moist, vital parts of the being who is dependent on your being . . . you, you are the necrophile in your clean white graveclothes! And she, then, what is she, who exists only in the shadow of contingency, a little pale spectre who sucks you dry while you perpetrate infamies upon her . . .

COUNT: The shadow of the fatal Count falls across every marriage bed . . .

(Into bedroom.)

MRS BEANE: She stirs.

COUNTESS: How handsome he is . . . how the little pulse in his white throat throbs . . .
    First, I was content with rabbits or lambs. Then one night, walking in the churchyard, my very sensitive nostrils twitched to sniff the fragrance of a new grave.

(The following on thoughts microphone:)

MRS BEANE: Rising from her catafalque, the Countess wraps her negligée about her.
    So delicate and damned, poor wee thing. Quite damned. Yet I do believe she scarcely knows what she is doing.
    Only my bred-in-the-bone, good old Scots hypocrisy keeps me in my position without loss of moral face. I'm secure in my own salvation; I can't alter her destination one little jot.
    Hell's her destination; all roads lead her there. So off you go, my pet, and play.

COUNT: One by one, I shall blow out the candles for her . . .

HERO: The little flames flicker and, one by one, go out . . .

COUNT: The clock whirs . . .

(Clock whirs.)

HERO: Midnight strikes.

(Midnight begins to chime. Continues softly while HERO *speaks.)*

> Only the last little candle left alight, now, bending, dimming yet still not extinguished . . . I do think Milady comes . . .

(Chimes cease. Silence. Key softly in door.)

COUNT: A waft of cold air, like a blast from a freshly opened grave, comes into the room with her. She brings this cold wind in her hair, her garments . . .

HERO: The final little flame is reflected in those woundable eyes, shows them rolled upwards, fixed; she does not see the light, I think that now she sees nothing. But her nostrils faintly quiver, so beautiful, so touching in her blood-stained negligée of very rare precious lace.

MRS BEANE: She smells the blood of an Englishman, you ken. Her wee nose goes, twitch, twitch, twitch.

COUNT: Into the world she slipped, through one of the interstices between reality and imagination, the last little twiglet of that genealogical Upas Tree that sprang from the loins of Vlad the Impaler and cast its poison shade over the Balkans for an entire millennium . . . Even the vilest fiends in Hell shun the company of the vampire –

COUNTESS: Who is dead yet not dead, whose bane is an insatiable thirst for life and yet an inability to live!

HERO: Grinning, she lunged towards me.

(Cry from COUNTESS.*)*

COUNT: Claws and teeth sharpened on several centuries of corpses, sick him, girl, sick him!

(Cry, HERO *grunts.)*

HERO: I swiftly sidestepped her embrace and caught her by her slender wrist. *(Scuffling.)* How we struggled! Her strength was more than human. But at last I flung her upon my narrow bed and slapped her face, once, on each cheek, the remedy for hysteria. *(Two brisk slaps.)* Although it went against the grain to strike a woman.

COUNT: What? Strike her? Raise your hand to my daughter? To the heiress of the regions of ultimate darkness? To –

(But his expostulations are drowned, dwindle away, under the brisk, firm voice of HERO.*)*

HERO: The shock did indeed break her trance. Her shoulders quaked; slowly, slowly, she raised her head and turned those eyes the shape of tears laid on their sides towards me. Her features twisted. Although her eyes were shaped like tears, she could not weep. Nevertheless, she continued to try to do so. Perhaps her whole life had been a balked attempt at crying.

(Bedroom acoustic.)

COUNTESS: I am not a demon, for a demon is incorporeal; nor a phantom, for phantoms are intangible. I have a shape; it is my own shape, but I am not alive, and so I cannot die. I need your life to sustain this physical show, my self. Please give it to me.

HERO: *(Thoughts microphone.)* Her rich lips part; she smiles, she raises herself, she beckons.

I felt myself seized by the most powerful erotic attraction; only the exercise of iron self-control prevented me from throwing myself at her little feet.

Yet I, who love the bicycle and the light of common day, cannot, in the final analysis, bring myself to partake in this grisly charade. My reason forbids it.

(Bedroom.)

COUNTESS: My life depends on yours. I am a woman, young and beautiful. Come to me.

HERO: *(Thoughts microphone.)* And so she folds herself upon the bed with the lace falling about her softly and stretches out her white arms to me, her long hands with those fingernails like mandolin-picks . . . I blessed the cold showers of my celibacy. *(Into bedroom. Addresses* COUNTESS.*)* Countess, keep your talons to yourself.

COUNT: What? What?

HERO: *(Thoughts microphone.)* When I held her wrists together to keep her murderous hands away from me, she made her weeping face and writhed a little, for she was thwarted, poor, spoiled child. *(Into bedroom. Addresses* COUNTESS.*)* When I first saw you tonight, I thought you were an infinitely pitiable creature because of your beauty and your loneliness.

COUNT: *(Thoughts microphone.)* Curious . . . now she seems to wake. Her eyes clear; they settle upon him. How pure and pale his lips are, lips that have never – oh, never! Oh, can it be –

(Bedroom.)

COUNTESS: *(To* HERO.*)* My father loved me and brought Mrs Beane over the sea from Scotland to look after me. He taught me how to suck the blood from the young rabbits and crunch so deliciously their little bones as we crouched in the moist undergrowth of the thickets by the churchyard.

But I grew up and then I was not satisfied with the rabbits and the baby lambs and the little calves still wobbling on their newborn legs. No. Now I must have men. And so they come, but never go. All dead.

All dead.

I know I only lodge within my body; I am I and yet not I, as if I haunted my own shape and am condemned to watch with shame and rage its beastly doings.

HERO: Look! She is trying to cry, again.

COUNTESS: My kith's relations with my kind exiles me from daylight. I am a creature of the night, only.

(In a subtly different tone of voice.)

I belong to the night.

HERO: *(Thoughts microphone.)* One thin, wandering hand muzzles the ribbons of her negligée. She slips succinctly from the garment and relapses upon the coverlet in the most alluring abandon. In my head, I hear all the string orchestras of seduction playing at once together.

So she voluptuously invites me to step into Juliet's tomb.

And I was foolish enough in my rationality to set out upon a bicycle tour of the Carpathians with none of the traditional impedimenta of the vampire hunter about me, no wreath of garlic, no silver bullet . . . But only the conviction this is a poor, sick girl maintains me in the perpendicular stance of reason when common sense tells me the best thing to do in the circumstances is to fling myself helplessly upon her . . .

(Chord of swooning music; which breaks off abruptly in the middle. Bedroom. To COUNTESS, *briskly but tenderly.)*

We should take you away to Vienna, where doctors could examine you. You would stretch out on the therapeutic couch and the stern, quiet, bearded physician would tease from you during the slow intervals of healing time the confused origins of your sickness.

COUNTESS: Why aren't you afraid of me? Why don't you shrink from my murderous fingers?

HERO: What can your governess be thinking of, never to have cut your nails. You fine lady with your Strewelpeter's hands.

COUNTESS: They cripple the feet of Chinese women, as a sign of status. It is the same with me; I may not use my hands as hands. Three inches of horn stick out at the tips, don't you see . . . useless for anything but gouging.

(The following on thoughts microphone:)

HERO: With an infinitely touching gesture, she tucked her hands away behind her back, as though she were ashamed of them, and smiled at me, tremulously.

COUNT: *(Faintly.)* My daughter, oh, my daughter! am I losing you?

HERO: With no thought of passion, heaven forbid! Only of consolation, I took her in my arms.

(Bedroom. COUNTESS cries out in surprise; the cry protracts into a sigh.)

COUNTESS: How warm you are, how you warm me . . .

COUNT: *(Thoughts microphone.)* I find it . . . difficult . . . to breathe. My little girl! Don't you remember me? don't you remember sucking the delicious bones of the baby rabbits?

(Bedroom.)

COUNTESS: I never, in all my life, felt warm till now.

HERO: *(Thoughts microphone.)* She leans her head upon my shoulder with the most moving simplicity and I gently stroke her disordered hair.

(Bedroom.)

COUNTESS: If I sang you my liebestod, you would not understand it.

HERO: I never liked Wagner. Heavy, decadent stuff. Do you think you could sleep, my dear?

COUNT: . . . Choking . . . Airless . . .

HERO: *(Thoughts microphone.)* She's rich enough to pay for treatment, in all conscience. Oh, the poor girl. A ghastly affliction.

(Bedroom.)

COUNTESS: I feel . . . almost a healthy sleepiness come upon me. Will you . . . would you . . . could you give a goodnight kiss?

(The following on thoughts microphone: COUNT moans.)

HERO: I was infinitely moved.
    Softly, with my lips, I touched her forehead, as if I had been kissing a child goodnight.

COUNT: His pure, pale lips on your brow – ah! Fall upon me all at once the consecrated sword, the pointed stake!

(Juicy thud. COUNT screams.)

COUNTESS: I always knew that love, true love would kill me.

COUNT: . . . aaargh . . .

HERO: She felt quite limp in my arms, as if after the crisis of a fever. Soon it will be morning; the crowing of the mundane cock and first light will dissolve this Gothic dream with the solvent of the natural. Yes, perhaps I shall take her to Vienna; and we shall clip off her fingernails and take her to a good dentist, to deal with her fangs.
    Perhaps, perhaps . . . one day, when she is cured . . . mother, want you to meet . . .

(He is growing sleepy, too. The COUNT moans and gurgles.)

COUNT: Is a millennium of beastliness to expire upon a kiss?

HERO: There are some things that, even if they are true, we must not believe them.

(Moaning fades.)

COUNTESS: I existed only . . . as a symbolic formula. I was a woman, young and beautiful.

HERO: A little curl dangles over her forehead and moves with her breathing . . . sweet. So sweet. Oh, I don't believe your silly tales . . . just the hysteria of a young girl. In this isolated place, at the back of beyond, with only the family portraits for company.
    Look, now she sleeps deeply. *(Yawns.)* Could do with a spot of shut-eye myself. Been a heavy day.

(Yawns again. Silence. Sleeping breathing. Last, faint moan from the COUNT. *Cock-crow.)*

When I awoke, refreshed, I found I was clasping in my arms only a white lace negligée a little soiled with blood, as it might be from a woman's menses.

(Over to drawing room. Cage is opened.)

MRS BEANE: Fly away, birdie, fly away!

(Larksong.)

HERO: *(Approaching.)* Why, Mrs Beane, you've opened up the curtains! My goodness, what a view!

(Windows are opened.)

MRS BEANE: Let a breath of fresh air into this mausoleum . . . A glorious morning. I sent a man to look after your bicycle. You'll be wanting to get on with your tour, after you've had your breakfast.

HERO: The Countess . . .

MRS BEANE: I regret most bitterly you should have visited us at a time of mourning. The last of the line, you understand . . . they'll say Mass for her in the chapel. I myself, being a freethinker, will not attend. I am well provided for in the will, of course. I shall return to Scotland as soon as the estate has been wound up and open a girls' finishing school, perhaps. Or a boarding house. *(Pawky humour.)* Not a mutton pie shop, you'll be glad to hear.

HERO: May I see –

(Thoughts microphone.) In the last repose of death, she looked a little older but not much, a good deal uglier since she had lost all her teeth and, because of her loss of allure, for the first time, fully human.

(Bicycle wheels on a stony track. Birdsong.)

So I sped through the purged and rational splendours of the morning; but when I arrived at Bucharest, I learned of the assassination at Sarajevo and returned to England immediately, to rejoin my regiment.

(Drum-beats; above, the COUNT's *dreadful, posthumous chuckle.)*

COUNT: The shadow of the Fatal Count rises over every bloody battlefield.

Everywhere, I am struck down; everywhere, I celebrate my perennial resurrection.

Come unto These Yellow Sands

(Voices, chill, asexual, distant, singing:)

VOICES:

> Come unto these yellow sands,
>   And then take hands;
> Curtsied when you have and kiss'd,
>   The wild waves whist . . .

(An iron door slams to, reverberating: voices cease, a moment of absolute, dark silence.)

FEMALE NARRATOR: The late Richard Dadd! Alas! we must so preface the name of a youth of genius that promised to do honour to the world; for, although the grave has not actually closed over him, he must be classed among the dead.

ANNOUNCER: *Come unto These Yellow Sands*, an imaginative reconstruction for radio of the life and surviving paintings of Richard Dadd.

MALE NARRATOR: Character deposition on Richard Dadd, 1817–1886, from W.P. Frith, 1819–1909, who entered the Royal Academy Schools with Dadd in 1837. Frith became famous as a panoramic painter of Victorian actuality, with canvases crowded with the minutiae of everyday life, 'Derby Day', 'Weymouth Sands', 'The Railway Station', etc. etc. etc.

Dadd himself, painter of poetic reverie, achieved notoriety as a parricide.

FRITH: Dadd was my superior in all respects; he drew infinitely better than I did . . .

MALE NARRATOR: In 1839, Dadd won the painting school's second silver medal for copying in the school of painting, the third medal in the life class. In 1840, the medal for the best drawing in the life class.

FRITH: Apart from his uncommon gifts as draughtsman and colourist, 'I can truly say, from a thorough knowledge of Dadd's character, that a nobler being, and one more free from the common failings of humanity, never breathed.'

The catastrophe was swift, sudden, virtually unheralded. It could be said that, with one fatal blow, he ceased to exist.

And when, as we used, those of us who had been closest to him – myself, Augustus Egg, the doubly unfortunate John Phillip – went to visit poor Dadd in the asylum after his incarceration . . .

(Door unlocks on echo; footsteps on stone.)

DADD: What brings *you* here? Have you killed anyone?

FRITH: He would angrily turn aside from his oldest friends . . .

DADD: *(Derisive.)* Friends!

MALE NARRATOR: And, as the years passed, such visits ceased altogether . . .

DADD: *(Bitter, contemptuous.)* Friends . . .

FRITH: He, who had borne a nature of the noblest stamp, a mind of the most sparkling brilliance . . .

(Fiddle tuning up.)

. . . lost to us. Lost. Amongst that lonely multitude of distracted souls, he crouched over those paintings of his madness that might best be seen with the aid of a magnifying glass, such was the minuscule scrupulosity of their details. Or playing plaintive country airs remembered from his childhood on an old fiddle somebody had given him.

(Fade fiddle.)

When young, Dadd had been very handsome, with his dark hair and his fine eyes. And such a gentle temperament. Gentle as a lamb. Yet full of liveliness and humour. Devoted to his family. A wide circle of friends . . .

(Muttering of hobgoblins.)

. . . kind, generous, talented. A paragon. So much beauty, virtue and genius at twenty! As if the fairies had touched him . . .

(Muttering of hobgoblins turns into rustling of papers, scraping of feet, sounds of a lecture room.)

MALE NARRATOR: Training at the Royal Academy Schools at this time consisted largely of drawing from classical sculpture and casts, until the student was considered proficient enough to enter the life class. Painting itself was confined to copying old masters. The professors of painting, perspective and anatomy each gave a series of lectures every year. Turner, the professor of perspective, rarely put in an appearance at the schools and never lectured; but the professor of painting, Henry Howard, duly took up his place on the podium.

(Bring up coughings; scrapings of chairs, rustling of paper.)

HENRY HOWARD: The genius of the painter, like that of the poet, may ever call forth new species of beings – an Ariel, a Caliban or the Midsummer fairies.

(Fade background.)

FEMALE NARRATOR: The poetic and sensitive Dadd naturally proceeded to summon the fairies to his canvases.

MALE NARRATOR: 'Titania Sleeping', oil on canvas, twenty-five and a half inches by thirty and a half inches, exhibited at the Royal Academy in 1841.

(Fade in fairy music; Mendelssohn's Midsummer Night's Dream.*)*

OBERON: *(Poetry reading voice.)*

There sleeps Titania some time of the night,
Lulled in these flowers with dances and delight.

TITANIA:

(Yawns; murmurs; wakes up.
Bring in tittering of fays.)

I am pictured in a kind of grotto, a recess composed both of flowers and of the tiny bodies of my attendant fays, who are so intertwined and clothed in the cups of bluebells and the horns of bindweed that it is hard, at first, to tell who is the fay, who is the flower.

(Peak tittering of fays slightly.)

These tiny, charming, antic creatures, scarce bigger, some of them, than a dewdrop, contort themselves in all manner of quaint dispositions. Some puff out their cheeks to fill the trumpets of the sweet woodbine with music for my nocturnal serenades, others finger arpeggios upon their own noses, which have whimsically acquired the shape of clarinets. Outside my enchanted slumber, nymphs dance.

(Peak fairy music briefly.)

The tranquil and timeless light of fairyland, the quintessential distillation of moonlight, falls on the bare shoulders of my two attendants and suffuses the white, rosy-shadowed velvet with which my own succulent limbs are upholstered.

My succulent yet immaterial limbs.

(Music distorts.)

Above my grotto, there is a kind of arch formed by an interesting monster with a great many leathern wings.

(Titania yawns; settles back to sleep again; tittering of fays. Fade tittering and music.)

MALE NARRATOR: The same year, Dadd exhibited a companion piece to his Titania at the Society of British Artists. Oil on canvas, twenty-three and a quarter inches by twenty-three and a quarter inches. Puck . . .

(Brisk plucking notes into brisker fairy music.)

PUCK: *(Leaping up from nowhere.)* . . . whom he painted as a plump, white, juicy child seated on a toadstool of a botanically imprecise description with, directly above my head, a bindweed blossom looking not unlike a particularly vulgar satin lampshade, because it dangles a fringe of pendant dewdrops for all the world like glass beads. Around my little pedestal, which looks far too frail to support my Bacchic corpulence, dance dozens of those tiny nudes, dozens of them.

(Fairy music speeds up behind following:)

Dozens of them, jiggering about with positively frenetic abandon, whirling like dervishes, dervishes . . .

And I am bathed in the coolest, purest light, the light of another world.

(Beginning of a rustling and tittering, the sounds of the stirring of a horrid, goblin crowd. Lose music behind them.)

MALE NARRATOR: In the same year, Dadd exhibited 'Fairies Assembling to Hold their Revels', now lost, at Manchester.

(Louder mutterings.)

PUCK: Ravishingly pretty . . . but so much, so very much prettiness suggests the presence of far too many ugly beings gibbering away behind the painted screen where he pushed them –

SCOTS GOBLIN: You may find me in Glen Etive, night coming on, there is my one hand out of my chest, my one leg out of my arse, my one eye in the middle of my forehead, and I bode nae good to nae man, I can tell you.

YORKSHIRE GOBLIN: Sithen tha keeps away from t'marl-pit or raw-head-and-bloody-bones will catch you! I sit on a mound of fresh-gnawed bones and my wounds never stop bleeding and I'm always wi' me weather eye open for fresh meat . . .

WEST COUNTRY GOBLIN: I have gurt horns and gurt claws and gurt red-'ot eyes; when I howl, somebody is dying.

(Fade mutterings behind following:)

PUCK: From all these pictures of fairyland for which young Dadd received so much praise, he chose to leave out the pharisees, the trolls, those shapeless somethings always at your left shoulder that manifest themselves like bad breath, the hags, the shape-shifters, the banshees, the hobs and lobs and all the nasty little demons who exist at the corner of the eye, in the cobwebbed back passages of the mind.

(Sound of footsteps trooping into lecture theatre; squeaks, gibbers, honking – not a normal crowd.)

(Officious.) Settle down, please, settle down . . . emanations of the id to the back of the room, apparitions from the unconscious and preconscious in the gallery. Pre-Christian survivals, fertility symbols, nightmares and ghouls in the pews to the right, death-signs, stormwarnings, to the left. Oedipal fantasies in the front row, please.

(Squeaks, gibbers, objects being thrown.)

And I'll thank you poltergeists to keep a firm hold on your impulses during the lecture.

OBERON: *(Clears throat, rustles papers.*
Chairs squeak, hubbub gradually subsides.)

PUCK: Bugs, long-legged beasties and things that go bump in the night, it is my pleasure and privilege to present to you, summoned here from the vasty deep tonight, Oberon, king of the fairies, fallen angel locked out of both hell and heaven, leader of the wild hunt etc. etc. etc . . .

(Applause.)

OBERON: Thank you, friends, thank you.

(Rustles papers, coughs.)

The vogue for paintings of fairy subjects during the mid-Victorian period might be regarded as the manifestation of a compensatory 'ideology of innocence' in the age of high capitalism, a period when the relations of man with his kind were increasingly under stress and the art which reflected these relations became increasingly fraudulent.

(Hobgoblin chorus of cheers. Hear hear! Well said!)

The primitive superstitions of the countryside, the ancient lore born on the wrong side of the blanket to religious faith, could not survive in the smoke, the stench, the human degradation, the poverty, the cholera, the tuberculosis, of the great cities which the industrial revolution had created.

Here, the poor were stripped of everything, even of their irrational dreads, and the external symbols of their dreams and fears – the wraiths of nightmare – were utilised to provide their masters with a decorative margin of the 'quaint', the 'fanciful' and the 'charming' upon the printed pages of lives that had no imaginative richness of their own.

(Bangings of cans, squeaks, cheers.)

The richly sexual symbolism of aspects of the mythology of the 'wee folk' was buried so deeply beneath the muffling layers of repression and the oppression of women that the fairies were often depicted on these canvases in states of virtually complete undress, of active nudity . . .

(Wolf-whistle; shushings.)

. . . at a period when formal art treated the nude with kid gloves, in the passive mood.

It might be said of these fairy painters, as Hamlet says of Ophelia:

> Death and affliction, even hell itself,
> She turns to favour and to prettiness.

This realm of fictive faery served as a kitschified repository for fancies too savage, too dark, too voluptuous, fancies that were forbidden the light of common Victorian day *as such*. If the reality of the artist could not accommodate itself to that of the world of iron, of steam, of labour, of strife, he retreated to the consolation of the Midsummer fairies without the least idea of the true nature of such creatures in any symbolic schema worth its salt. The enchanting light that bathes these whimsical canvases falsifies not only experience but imagination itself.

Imagination, severed from reality, festers. The beautiful thought in a world of pain is, in itself, a crime.

(Buzzes, groans, shrieks.)

The Victorian fairyland is a place that not only never existed but also served no imaginative function except that of diversion, of the prim titillation of a jaded fancy. It represents a kind of pornography of the imagination.

In this pre-sexual fairyland, dreams may indeed come true. *(He's working up to a lecturer's joke.)* And I hardly need remind our Oedipal friends here in the front row what happens when dreams come true in reality!

(Laughter; applause. A high wind rises, the same wind that will blow when DADD *goes to see the sphinx;* OBERON's *voice is blown away by the wind, gets smaller and smaller from now on, until it fades away altogether.)*

Fairyland, for Henry Howard, and Dickie Doyle, and Arthur Huskisson, and Richard Dadd, was what one might term the 'pastoral exotic', a wilful evasion of the real conditions of life in the insensate industrial towns such as the Manchester of Engels, during the era of imperialist expansion of . . .

(Fade wind.)

FEMALE NARRATOR: In July of the year 1842 Richard Dadd set out on a grand tour of the historic and picturesque ruins of the Middle East as the companion of Sir Thomas Phillips, a former mayor of Newport, Monmouthshire. Phillips, a solicitor, had been knighted for the part he played in putting down the Chartists. Phillips hired Dadd as an artist, to make him an album of watercolour drawings as a souvenir of the trip.

MALE NARRATOR: The last picture Dadd painted before he set sail with his patron was titled: 'Come unto These Yellow Sands'.

(Distant singing, as at opening, faint sound of waves.)

FEMALE NARRATOR: A wild saraband on a deserted beach, at evening.

PUCK: Whirling like dervishes! Like dervishes!

FEMALE NARRATOR: The grand chain of dancers partially conceal their nakedness with swathes of chiffon that drifts to reveal nipples, muscles, sinews that, since they belong to the fairy folk, may be depicted in all the forbidden splendour of authentic flesh because the fairies do not exist. The pleasures of the flesh, rendered insubstantial as dream.

The rising moon applies a coat of mother-o'-pearl to the ambiguously sexed beings. Half the eldritch company float in a great curlicue upon the air, immune to gravity, while the leaders of the dance pass through an arch of rock as through the eye of a needle.

(Music fades; waves rise.)

The waves break on the barren shore.

SIR THOMAS PHILLIPS: All in all, all went splendidly at first. After we had 'done' Europe most comprehensively – I was an indefatigable tourist, I assure you – we left Greece to sail for Smyrna, and, once landed . . .

(Waves recede.)

. . . set out in a caravan across landscapes of most savage splendour.

(Fade in desert; bells, hooves.)

The untamed wilderness spread out for our delight like a glorious picture-book.

DADD: We would stop at some wild, uninhabited place, always in the open, under the stars; we would put down our mattresses, have the mules unloaded, the cook would light the fire . . .

(Crackling of flames, clank of cooking and eating utensils, muttering of men.)

PHILLIPS: Atrocious food, of course. The soup, often, nothing but raw onions in it. And rice, perhaps a stringy fowl boiled to ribbons, a few pots of sour milk . . .

DADD: And the light always gone by the time the caravan halted, dammit, so that my pencil could scarcely keep pace with my impressions by the flickering of our camp fire . . .

(Crossfade back to desert; hooves, bells.)

Then back into the saddle at dawn and jolt, jolt, jolt across another plain of rocks. The sky burning, now blue, now green, above an arid yet sublime terrain . . . and I, accustomed to the sweet English watercolour meadows and the lovely realm of fancy, of poetry . . .

PHILLIPS: From Smyrna to Constantinople to Bodrum to the great ruins at Lycia . . .

DADD: . . . I, all unprepared for the stark light, the wild people, was precipitated into a landscape not dissimilar to that of the infernal regions . . .

PHILLIPS: . . . to Beirut, to Damascus . . .

(Muezzin which brings in background of Damascus.)

DADD: At evening, as we approached the city, the domes and minarets seemed to be embroidered on a sky of flushed satin; a scene of such ethereal loveliness that it lodged in my memory like a kind of grace, amongst much that I found strangely troubling to my spirits. For nothing was as I could have imagined it, all threw my nerves into a state of tremendous agitation. Can men truly live in such a different way to us?

PHILLIPS: When the circumstances of our travels permitted it, I urged my young companion to sketch the picturesque and exotic spectacles of our travels.

(Bring in screeching and wailing of mourners.)

DADD: In Damascus, we chanced to see a funeral procession, I had never seen anything like it, nothing . . . the mourners screeching, the women tearing their clothes, pouring dust from the road by the handful on their veils . . . so that they seemed demented rather than grief-stricken. And then, the dervishes . . .

(Crossfade to dervishes.)

And then, the dervishes – a group of those holy men who dance until they are possessed by their god; they whirled and whirled until they fell, exhausted, lips rimed with froth, a wild saraband.

(Crossfade to hubbub of eastern bazaar.)

In Damascus, walking about the maze of alleys, I came upon a *camel*, poor beast, great, lolloping, starveling brute, who had fallen in the street. Fallen and, I think, broken a leg. Fallen, with all the baggage upon him, in a street so narrow he quite blocked the traffic . . .

(Peak eastern hubbub, cries and down.)

His driver, in his filthy robes, beat the beast but it would not, could not rise. And then, oh horror! they came with axes and with knives and lopped off all its living limbs, as one might lop off the limbs of a tree . . . As it lay there in the intolerable heat of noon, heat so intense it seemed all nature itself might faint with it . . . and the blood sprang out and flowed away down the gutters, mingling with the foul odours of the city . . . and still the wretched camel lived, it shrieked and writhed most fearfully . . .

(*Camel shriekings, cries, blows.*)

. . . and still lived until at last they . . . slit its throat . . . and then they could carry it away piecemeal, you understand, bit by bit. And in that way, the street was cleared.

(*Fade background.*)

Horrible! Horrible!

(*Bring in faint wind.*)

PHILLIPS: In November, we arrived at last in Egypt.

DADD: We had taken a boat to Alexandria. During the brief respite from these savage countries that the sea afforded me, I had felt a lightening of the spirits, the oppression which I had experienced among those intolerable marvels lifted a little. Yet, when we disembarked at Alexandria, although I was consumed by a scarcely tolerable anguish of despair as soon as my feet touched the ancient earth of Egypt, I also felt, at the same time, a sense of *homecoming*, of arriving at a destination that was my destiny, and, in its inescapable quality, this sensation was especially . . . atrocious.

The vast, pitiless, antique land welcomed me as if I was its son.

(*Crossfade to bazaar behind following:*)

PHILLIPS: So we stopped a while in Cairo. Good beds at last, clean linen. The hospitable consul provided decent grub. My young companion browsed about the bazaar, searching out souvenirs, antiquities . . .

(*Jangling of a shop bell – take down bazaar background.*)

SHOPKEEPER: Effendi?

DADD: The meanest merchant in the bazaar looks like a Sultan in an Eastern fairy tale . . .

SHOPKEEPER: I knew immediately I saw him that this young man would buy anything I chose to sell him.

In my little shop in the bazaar in Cairo, I did profitable business with many interesting foreign visitors throughout the entire nineteenth century. Artists of all kinds patronised me; it was no less a one than Victor Hugo himself who gave business a tremendous boost, first of all, with his 'Les Orientales' of 1829.

MALE NARRATOR:

> Ma dague d'un sang noir à mon côté ruisselle
> Et ma hache est pendue à l'arçon de ma selle.

SHOPKEEPER: My dagger drips black blood beside me and my axe hangs from the pommel of my saddle. Exactly. Hugo wished to purchase projections of exotic violence. I supplied them. In the drawing rooms of Paris, Lyons, London, Manchester, the dreams rose up in cursive blue smoke, like incense, from the open pages of handsomely illustrated albums. Pierre Loti, an afficionado of the quaint, a regular customer ... he was pleased to take off my hands a rose-water sprinkler formerly in the possession of the aunt of the Prophet. *(Giggles.)* And I sold one or two particularly succulent trinkets – I especially recall a back-scratcher in the shape of the eyebrow of Ra, removed from the tomb of Queen Nefertiti herself – to Gérard de Nerval, when he stayed in Cairo in 1849 ... de Nerval, another madman.

Ah, you strike a hard bargain, effendi!

(Cash register.)

You would have thought the East had turned their brains.

The English were less flamboyant and more obsessed, preferring the secrecy of watercolour to the privacy of oils. I remember certain furtive visits of a curious fat man, Edward Lear ... Towards the end of the century, Lord Leighton was so struck with the Orient that he went home and built a Moorish hall in Kensington for which I was able to supply a number of tasselled hangings and bead curtains at absolutely cut-throat prices ...

(Cash register.)

What's this? *(To inaudible voice over his shoulder.)* What? You want my lecture on Orientalism?

(Coughs, clears throat. Crossfade to rustling of lecture theatre audience.)

My lecture on Orientalism ... are you attending? Very well.

Throughout the nineteenth century, the Orient exercised a magnetic attraction upon the European middle class, to whom my distinguished visitors purveyed the aesthetic, the sense of style, the taste. Emergent in the seventeenth, rising in the eighteenth, the middle class spent the nineteenth century consolidating itself. It looked at the smoky evidence of the Industrial Revolution that had nurtured its prosperity and turned away its face. These rich dissatisfied men and women saw the world they had made in their own image and they did not like it, although they depended on it to stay alive. They wanted to be taken out of themselves, you understand, but *not for long*.

So tourism was born.

But they soon realised they could hire their artists to do their travelling for them, and so need not hazard the flies, the heat, the diarrhoea and so forth. The European middle class drank deep of the savage splendours of the East, the pious grandeurs of the Holy Land, without stirring a step from their drawing rooms.

OBERON: . . . a compensatory ideology of innocence . . .

SHOPKEEPER: *(Tetchy.)* No, no, no, no! Innocence? Never! These were the lands of the harem, of the assassin, of the naked blonde slave-girl in the market . . . the cult of the exotic was a compensatory ideology of sensuality, of mystery, of violence. Of the *forbidden*, which the customers of my customers could enjoy vicariously, without any danger of their souls.

The Orient held an especial attraction for those uneasy in their spirits.

(Crossfade back to interior shop with distant bazaar.)

DADD: Good morning.

SHOPKEEPER: I gave him a little cup of hot, sweet coffee with cardamom in it; they adored such details.

And now, let me display my treasures . . . objets d'art, curios, little items from the tombs of the pharaohs such as beads of faience and cornelian; rings of jasper, faience and gold; lapis lazuli scarabs blue as the sky, effendi, and mounted in gold . . . tiny figures of the gods . . .

DADD: Gods who ruled the sky before Christ was born . . .

SHOPKEEPER: Or, perhaps, one of these small rolls of papyrus . . .

(Unwraps.)

. . . removed from the grave-wrappings of the dead, inscribed with chapters from the Kitab-el-mayyitum . . .

DADD: The Kitab-el . . .

SHOPKEEPER: We call it *The Book of the Dead*.

DADD: And I saw before me messages from the beginning of time, in an inscrutable script formed of hawks and serpents, full moons and crescents, undulations as of the frozen wave.

SHOPKEEPER: 'The sky burns for you, the earth trembles for you, before the birth of the god.'

DADD: Fearful, wonderful . . .

SHOPKEEPER: . . . 'Hail to thee, O Bull of the Land of the West. I am one of those gods who cut in pieces the enemies of Osiris.'

DADD: (Shuddering sigh.) The West?

SHOPKEEPER: The Land of the Dead, 'Behold, Osiris!'

DADD: And the very mention of the holy name, Osiris, made the hair upon my nape stand upright, a shiver of electric dread and holy expectation ran through me . . .

SHOPKEEPER: Osiris, the King of the Dead, who weighs your heart, effendi.

(Cash register which cuts bazaar and returns us to lecture hall.)

And so we earned our bread by the sale of the mummified remains of antiquity and our customers made of it exactly what they pleased. We were not responsible for their fantasies about us. And could they not turn the pages of the magic book of our lives as soon as they got tired of us?

(Pause.)

PHILLIPS: After so much sightseeing, I yearned for a spot of sport. I would go banging away at crocodiles along the Nile while my young companion took himself off with his easel . . .

(Fade in desert.)

DADD: The desert starts at the gates of Cairo, the desert, mother of mirages, where the light is white as if the sand had scoured the polished metal of the sun white . . .

PHILLIPS: . . . he'd blacken page after page of his sketchbook, zeal enough for a dozen artists, such enthusiasm he'd scarcely take shelter even during the fiercest portion of the noonday sun . . .

DADD: . . . white heat, that pulsed . . .

PHILLIPS: Scribble, scribble as if he were making sketches enough to serve him for the rest of his lifetime!

DADD: And often, after a day's sketching, I lay down at night with my

imagination so full of wild vagaries that I really and truly doubted of
my own sanity . . .

PHILLIPS: Took the boat down to Thebes, good shooting along the
banks of the Nile, our destination – the Sphinx. Memorable spectacle,
truly memorable.

(Thin, high wind rises.)

DADD: The sphinx it was herself who whispered to me what Oedipus
knew. I went to see her, she was crouching in the middle of the dead
sea of sand, attended by three inscrutable pyramids. I saw her lips
move but you had to listen very hard to hear what she was saying and
at first I could not believe what she told me; her message or prophecy
cast me into the pit where terror lives.

(Wind blows through the rest of the speech.)

I prayed to Osiris for his guidance, guidance from this most antique
and therefore most authentic of deities, for the world had resolved
itself around me into weird and dreadful forms.

(Wind fades leaving desert background.)

PHILLIPS: A touch of the sun, poor Dadd, a nasty touch of sunstroke.
Been doing too much; overtaxed himself, out in the sun all day . . .
Delirium; babbling away about I don't know what.

DADD: Visitation of the godhead in a beam of white light . . .

PHILLIPS: . . . asked me to look into his mouth, to see if there was a *green
feather* on his tongue. And then he saw men with heads of dogs and
cow-headed women in the room . . .

DADD: I am come to judgement, I am come to judgement . . .

PHILLIPS: Indeed, I was quite concerned about the poor fellow but,
mercifully, a day's complete rest, a good night's sleep and a good
English breakfast of tea and toast and boiled eggs – thanks to the
British consul! – and he seemed right as rain again.

DADD: Although I recovered from the ghastly hallucinations that my
attack of sunstroke procured me, they left me terribly, terribly fearful
. . . that I might hearken to those voices of the messengers of death,
that I might allow myself . . . to believe in their existence . . .

PHILLIPS: Homeward bound, old boy! From Alexandria, by ship to
Malta –

(Bring in sea and creaking of rigging.)

DADD: And I grew afraid that . . . I might lose . . . my reason . . .

(Creaking of rigging and sound of conviviality, bottles clinking.)

PHILLIPS: A queen and, by jove, an ace!

DADD: And I scrutinised *The Book of the Dead* again and again, and always my eye fell upon those symbols that the merchant had told me signified: 'The Great God aboard the Divine Ship' . . .

(Burst of laughter from Phillips.)

PHILLIPS: My game again, captain!

DADD: *(New, brisk, self-confident voice.)* Under a spare sail slung amidships for a canopy, my worthy benefactor and the ship's captain play all day at cards, sipping thick tumblerfuls of cloudy arak that turn my gut when I try to drink it. Look, he deals –

(Slaps of cards on table; Phillips snorts with glee.)

DADD: He deals the devil's picture books. And I do believe . . . that his tailcoat . . . conceals his tail . . .

(Laughter of card-players.)

PHILLIPS: And it's my game, again!

(Gathers cards together.)

DADD: And as they played and poured more and more arak, I was seized with the conviction that the stake of the game was nothing less than that sea-captain's soul. The point of my pencil snapped in two; I could sketch no more that day! The world burst into fragments of ferocious light and fire whirled about me. With expressions of the most vicious and deceitful concern, my so-called benefactor came to me where I lay struck down on the deck –

PHILLIPS: Dadd! Dadd, I say!

DADD: Take your hands off me, you devil –

(Scuffling which fades behind following:)

PHILLIPS: We got him to his cabin, at last, sponged him down with cool water, left him in a dark room and out he came at sun-down, full of apologies. Delicate constitution, of course, artistic temperament.

(Fade sea.)

So we made our way to Rome . . .

(Fade in crowd noises.)

. . . where, to my consternation, outside the Vatican . . .

DADD: As soon as the Pope, the Holy Father, stepped out upon the balcony, raising his hand in satanic benediction on that obscenely ululating crowd, I understood my sacred duty; I sprang forward –

(Consternation; scuffling.)

But the servants of the Prince of Darkness laid their hands upon me and restrained me.

(Fade scuffling and crowd.)

PHILLIPS: When we reach Paris, I shall make quite certain that Dadd sees a doctor.

DADD: Although he posed as my benefactor and a father to me, this man, this Phillips, all the time wove the ghastliest plans for the perdition of my spirit that would have come to fruition in Paris had I not given the slip to this emissary of the Devil, to post directly home –

(Fade in Victorian London street noises; cab-wheels, street cries.)

FRITH: I must confess to you, sir, that since your son returned from the East, he's been behaving in such an odd way that I hardly like to have him visit my studio.

ROBERT DADD: He is a little overtired from his travels; the exertion, his delicate nerves . . . and is he not painting away in his studio, after all? Has he not sent paintings to the Liverpool Academy? Is he not hard at work?

(Fade street noises.)

MALE NARRATOR: A watercolour from this period, 'Dead Camel', now lost, has been described as 'a ghastly little invention of desert-horror framed in by demons such as his distempered brain alone could devise'.

(Fade in room acoustic.)

LANDLADY: Well, sir, I can tell you that during those three months after the poor young man's return from abroad, he lodged in my house at Newman Street, London, and in and out he would go, about his business, scowling furiously and, sometimes, suddenly grimacing and showing his teeth in such a wild, distracted way that I grew quite frightened of him. And his clothes spotted and dirtied with paint something dreadful; but then, I thought, he is an artist . . .

He told me, did he not, never to set foot in his rooms, neither to clean them up nor to bring him water even for his own ablutions. Never disturb my apartments! he said, with vehemence enough to scare you witless; for, he says, I'm engaged in researches upon the subject of the enemies of the *Almighty*, he says, and my rooms are now sanctuaries for the Great God Osiris, of whom, whilst in Egypt, I was permitted to become a devotee.

Well, I have had strange ones in this house, and, since he paid his rent regular, I thought no more of it.

Indeed, great cases of books and curios now arrived for him that he had purchased in Egypt but I never set eyes on the contents of those chests until after the accident, for he unpacked them in perfect secrecy.

And, yes . . . he said we should give him nothing to eat, for, according to his religion, he must prepare his own diet.

(Cracking of eggshells.)

DADD: Ex ova omnia, all things come from the egg. I shall eat nothing but eggs, the little emblems of eternity, round . . . with a germ of new life in the middle, and I shall eat eggs until I become eternal . . .

LANDLADY: So that, after the accident, we came to clean out his place at last and found eggshells everywhere, ground into the carpet, eggshells in the grate, eggshells on all the tome upon tome of lore about Ancient Egypt and how I pitied his poor solitary meals! But the walls were covered with a tremendous number of drawings of his friends that he had held most dear and all of them, in these pictures, had their throats cut . . .

ROBERT DADD: Rest and quiet. He has not yet recovered from the effects of the sun. Rest, quiet, country air . . .

(Fade in birdsong.)

MALE NARRATOR: *(Cool voice.)* On 28th August Dadd called on his father and asked him to go to the country with him.

(Fade birdsong behind following:)

Out walking in Cobham Park; Richard Dadd kills his father with a spring knife he had brought with him for that purpose, under the delusion that his father was the devil and he himself the incarnation of the god, Osiris.

(Pause.)

FEMALE NARRATOR: He escaped to France, where he was committed to an asylum after attempting to kill a fellow passenger in a carriage. Almost a year later, he was extradited back to England. On 22nd August 1844 he was admitted to the criminal lunatic department of Bethlem Hospital. From that date, Richard Dadd's experience may be termed, posthumous. He was then twenty-six years old.

(Silence.)

FRITH: A catastrophe sudden, overwhelming and absolute. He –

(Voice breaks off, overcome.
Fiddle tentatively tuning up.)

DADD: Far . . .

CRAZY JANE: Far?

DADD: . . . away . . .

(Country fiddle playing old tune.)

CRAZY JANE: You don't want for recreation, then; they let you have your old fiddle, to make a bit of music with.

DADD: Far away from this rock and castle of seclusion . . .

(Fade fiddle; writing noises.)

DOCTOR: As his physician, I feel compelled to report that his delusion remains fixed and immovable, his conversation sometimes exceedingly unpleasant. Colours and canvases have been provided for him.

CRAZY JANE: Watercolours, pastels – oils, even. They let you paint your pictures, then.

FEMALE NARRATOR: He soon resumed painting. But his work suffered a sea change. As if his delusion were an ocean in which he had drowned, full fathom five – or, more deeply still; drowned, fathom upon unimaginable fathom, lost to us more profoundly than if he had been dead in an abyss of loss, the cruellest of all losses, the loss of reason.

In this dreadful isolation, his painting took on an hallucinatory clarity. It underwent a kind of magical petrification. In these strange canvases, the rules of time and space and perspective have undergone a subtle transformation and there is no effect of either depth or movement. As if everything had stopped still, stock fast, frozen in time at the moment that the fatal blow was struck, the crime of Oedipus committed that exiled him forever from the company of those who acknowledge a distinction between inside and outside.

Yet there is an almost miraculous intensification of colour, as if he no longer dipped his brush in natural pigment but in crushed mineral substances, brighter and more shining than those used by painters who inhabit *this* world.

And his work became enormously small, as if the fairies who invaded the most remarkable canvases of his earliest years of solitude were now directing the infinite littleness of the arabesques of the tip of his brush, as if, indeed, he were not painting fancies but, rather, real sitters, from a perfectly material realm of concrete dream.

MALE NARRATOR: 'Contradiction: Oberon and Titania', oil on canvas, twenty-four inches by twenty-nine and a half inches, painted by Dadd between 1854 and 1858 for Dr Williams Charles Hood, physician superintendent of Bethlem Hospital.

FEMALE NARRATOR: He shaped the canvas into an oblate spheroid, like the shape of the world in the Mercator projection. Or the shape of a tear laid on its side.

TITANIA: And he has learned some respect for the Queen of the Fairies. Now I dwarf my court!

(Thumping footsteps; humming, buzzing.)

Here come I, Titania, with my gigantic stride! How big I've grown, since the time he took my picture when I was sleeping in the glade. I tower over my fairy subjects like Gulliver in Lilliput; I trample them underfoot –

(Particularly thumping footstep; tiny fairy scream.)

There! I've flattened her, that winged creature no bigger than my little finger who nestled in the flower bell.

(Insects buzzing, clicking of cicadas etc.)

Fairyland buzzes with the whirr of tiny wings; fays like gnats, like midges, like flies.

He has lost his sense of scale. If this enormous butterfly is as big as I, then it is twice the size of the hairy-chested, horned and bearded fairy centaur who leaps across the violets at the viewer's right, drawing upon me a bow in a fairy assassination attempt that suggests Mr Dadd has left a little signature of murder, almost invisible, in a corner, in order to tease . . .

Such a crowded composition, what overpopulation in fairyland! And the noise, the bustle . . .

(Peak background and down.)

Huge blue trumpets of the hallucinatory morning glory roll round my feet; they have the fragile solidity of painted tin, like the horns of old gramophones . . .

(Tinny sound of cylinder gramophone playing Mendelssohn's Midsummer Night's Dream *music.)*

TITANIA: I have grown very brown, as if my skin had been burned by hotter suns than coaxed his cold kingcups and lilies of the valley out of the earth. The curving petals of these flowers have the waxen and unnatural precision of immortelles, everlasting flowers, graveyard bouquets. They cannot face because they never grew. Flowers the yellowish-white of fangs.

OBERON: He has decided to give to me, Oberon, the fierce, proud air of an Arab chieftain or a Kurdish brigand. No doubt he took my features from some sketch or other of his travels. Observe my eaglish beak of a nose, my fine, crisply curling black beard. And Dadd has dressed me in a fringed tunic of Middle-Eastern provenance and sandals of archaic design. I clasp the arm of my pretty page; horsemen small enough to pass through the eye of a needle ceaselessly parade behind me.

(Tinny horns and drums above the tinny gramophone music.)

The leaves of the plants are flat as palm fans, they might be made of beaten metal, their edges look as if they could cut you. Cruel things occur diminutively in the undergrowth, which is a complicated web of metal vines in which the wee folk are trapped.

No wind stirs or ever could this frozen grove. Time does not exist, here. She and I confront one another in a durationless present.

TITANIA: Dew, dew everywhere. It hangs in lucid drops endlessly about to fall, never to fall, from feathery grasses that curl above us, dew blisters the depthless surfaces of the leaves and flowers, dew like heavy glass beads hanging on the folds of our clothes. But the dew isn't wet; it won't drench us, the dew drips like tears but tears that have dropped from a crystal eye, heavy, solid, mineral, glittering, unnatural. And the earth under the sharp embroidery of the flowers is hard as ship's biscuit.

(During this speech, apart from the tinny Mendelssohn, sounds such as: tweeting of electronic birds; plop of a single raindrop; squeaks; buzzes. The music hiccups and begins to repeat itself.)

OBERON: Ill-met by moonlight, proud Titania!

TITANIA: What, jealous Oberon!

OBERON: Ill-met by moonlight, proud Titania!

TITANIA: What, jealous Oberon!

OBERON: Ill-met by moonlight, proud Titania!

TITANIA: What, jealous Oberon!

(Voices, still repeating themselves, fade. Cackling of hobs rises.)

CHANGELING: There is no time in fairyland. Of his visit there, the changeling remembers nothing but pleasant music and returns, a youth, still, to find his mother dead, his cottage tumbled into ruin, the acorn his father planted for him on the day when he was born grown into an oak and his name forgotten . . .

OBERON: Because time does not pass in these wards of absence, everything acquires the quality of still life –

CHANGELING: Or, as the French say, nature morte.

TITANIA: *(Rich, full.)* Yet what can you imagine lovelier than fairyland?

(Tittering of fays.)

CRAZY JANE: They do say the fairy women have beautiful faces, indeed; but when you look at them from the back, it turns out they are hollow. Quite hollow. Like jelly moulds wi' no jelly in 'em.

LANCASHIRE GOBLIN: Shriker I am, that pads behind thee in the dark night and shrieks –

(Scream.)

FEMALE GOBLIN: Black Annis has a blue face and great teeth and she will come and *gobble you up* . . .

(Fade background.)

MALE NARRATOR: Somebody took Dadd's photograph as he was at work upon this picture.

FEMALE NARRATOR: He turns towards the camera an immense, haunted, shaggy, bearded head.

His eyes, opaque, as if they had been put out by pearls.

(Fade in asylum acoustic.)

DOCTOR: Very charming, very charming, Mr Dadd. And now, perhaps, you could paint one like that just for me – a special commission for your good doctor, who treats you kindly and would like to keep your mind upon the harmless fairies, give you no time to brood upon questions of antique theology.

MALE NARRATOR: The picture usually considered Dadd's masterpiece, 'The Fairy Feller's Master-Stroke', took nine years to complete. Oil on canvas, twenty-one and a quarter inches by fifteen and a half inches.

FEMALE NARRATOR: The texture is as thickly embossed as that of petit point; it looks as though the picture might be read with the fingertips, like braille. The composition is of the utmost complexity, something is going on in every centimetre. And yet a frozen calm holds all the weird actors still. The picture offers a scene from a narrative just before the conclusion; it illustrates a story that has not begun and therefore cannot end, it tells an anecdote the point of which is never made.

(Full in babble of fairy voices.)

RUSTIC GOBLIN: Do 'ee but strike the blow, master! Do 'ee but strike the blow!

CRAZY JANE: See, there's the young man with the gurt axe –

FEMALE NARRATOR: On a wee section of moonlit hill, an innumerable horde of beings have gathered together to witness the fairy feller, our hero, strike a nut with an axe. There are huge daisies above their heads and about their feet. Each petal of the moon-drenched daisies stands out with an hallucinated clarity and the little flowers are white as if made from white metal. Not silver, whiter than silver. And they emit such a luminous gleam they seem of themselves to illuminate this crowded brake where the fairies come.

(Babble rises.)

Each grain of sand is as distinctly visible to the eye as it would be to the eye of God.

FAIRY FELLER: Now I raise my trusty weapon in my good right hand –

(Squeaks; buzzings; chatterings.)

Such a troupe gathered here to see my fatal blow, you can't count them. Here we have, all gathered together, soldiers, gypsies, fiddlers in rags and tags and scarlet jackets, masons and carpenters in their aprons come here a-riding on mice, a deputation of the famous witches of Wales in their pointed hats. Queen Mab herself and all her retinue ride round the brim of the magician's hat.

FEMALE NARRATOR: Our laws of space do not apply to this picture; nor do our laws of being.

None of the plentiful deformities of the swarm of fairy folk astonishes him. He knows each one and welcomes them. And each element in the picture is given the same existential weight. If each ear of corn, each spiked chestnut husk, is rendered with a naturalist's fidelity, so are the spread, fluttering wings and brilliant garb of the crowd, some of whom are so small they are scarcely visible to the naked eye as they glide behind a clod of earth, secrete themselves beneath a blade of grass . . .

And their eyes are full of indifference; a cruel, fierce regard, a fixed grin on all their tiny faces.

FAIRY FELLER: I hold my axe high in the air –

(Squeaks, buzzes.)

And I s'all bring it down upon this here hazel-nut, which I propose to split in half with one stroke –

(Cheers.)

– and so resolve the argument –

DADD: And so resolve the war within me –

(Cheers, applause; which abruptly cease.)

MALE NARRATOR: But the axe cannot fall. Nothing can move.

FAIRY FELLER: And here we are, stuck fast for all eternity, waiting for me to strike. Waiting . . .

DADD: . . . waiting . . . in the rock and castle of seclusion . . .

FAIRY FELLER: And he's too scared of what he did to let on he knows my secret. That the blow I am about to strike, which he prevents me from, is the very blow he struck hisself!

DADD: Osiris defend me!

DOCTOR: Calm yourself, Mr Dadd. Calm yourself; music . . . why don't you play a little?

(Country fiddle plays.)

CRAZY JANE: So then he'd play the old fiddle the doctor gave him, by the hour, see, all the good old tunes such as 'Over the hills and far away' and 'The Devil among the Tailors'. And the music so took him out of hisself that he don't even notice a poor, mad girl who'd like her picture made for her . . .

> *(Persuasive.)* Oh, Mr Dadd, won't you paint the portrait of poor Crazy Jane?

(Fade fiddle.)

MALE NARRATOR: 'Sketch of an idea for Crazy Jane, 1855'. Watercolour.

CRAZY JANE: And since there was not one of the female kind within those walls, Mr Dadd was forced to have a poor, distracted young man stand in for my body, he wrapped the lad in rags, with straw, feathers and little flowers such as daisies and vines of morning glory in my hair. And yet Mr Dadd caught the look of me to a T, for all that, especially about the eyes, my tragic eyes, you might say. And from his memory he recalled a lovely background to my plight, a ruined castle, trees, and, flying across the sky, crows . . .

(Very soft country fiddle; crows.)

Yet, see, how they still be English watercolour crows, not the same crows at all that brought such raucous terror to Crazy Vincent's canvases . . .

OBERON:

> Death and affliction, even hell itself,
> She turns to favour and to prettiness.

CRAZY JANE: *(Laughs.)* Mr Dadd? Still playing your old fiddle?

(Fiddle louder.)

So, hour by hour and year by year, he plays his fiddle, the songs his nursey sang him long ago, whilst around him we pace out our shuttered lives from hour to hour, time measured by mealtimes, by sleeps, by paroxysm . . .

(Fiddle fades.)

MALE NARRATOR: Dadd's delusion remained fixed and immovable, his behaviour unpredictable. When, in 1864, all the criminal patients of Bethlem were sent to the newly opened asylum at Broadmoor, in Berkshire, Dadd went with them, by train. There was never any possibility of his release; yet, as long as no mention was made of those subjects to which his obsessions were sensitive, his doctors described him as a charming companion. In old age, he took on a benign appearance, with a flowing white beard. The doctors liked him, encouraged him, he painted their portraits, was even allowed to paint frescoes on the walls of their private homes.

DOCTOR: Why, Mr Dadd, very fine; a charming figure of the goddess, Flora, bearing fruit and flowers . . . a veritable harvest festival of fruit and flowers! It's good to see you so busy, so absorbed . . .

(Rustling of papers; now he sounds as if he were writing a report.)

And yet my sympathetic scrutiny can find very few clues as to the exact nature of his . . . illness . . . in those of his paintings I have seen, that are all the evidence he ever submitted to the world as to the exact state of his inner life. He would settle for a while with those notebooks he retained, still, from that unfortunate journey forty years before and then commit to watercolour or to canvas some Arab or Greek scene, as if his memory were stuck fast at the point before his delusion took hold of him. And the sea, he retained a great affection for painting seascapes; and he had painted, I remember, a series of little moral sketches in his last years at Bethlem, scenes to illustrate the passions, he called them . . . such as Avarice, and Melancholy, and Ambition . . . My colleagues studied his watercolour 'Murder' for a long time; it shows, I recall, a wild man, dressed in the skins of beasts, with a great club in his hand with which he has just struck down a similar rough fellow . . . no clue, there. As to the visible documentation of the imaginative experience of a man who had – ahem – committed the patricidal crime of Oedipus, it must be admitted that the paintings of Dadd's madness are curiously . . . unsatisfactory. My Viennese colleague, who took such an interest in that kind of thing, did not set up in practice until the spring of the very year that poor Dadd died, in 1886 . . . now, *he* might have been able to extract all manner of meaning from Dadd's pictures; and yet little in them seems, to me, to illuminate his condition, or, indeed, ours . . . for are we not, all of us, residents in the castle of seclusion . . . of the anguished self . . .

(Pushes papers aside.)

But these are the preoccupations of your century, not of my century!

And Dadd, as a madman, had the self-confidence of his period, after all; was he not born of the Age of Assertion?

What would have impressed you most about the poor old boy in his latter years was, what a nice old buffer he was. Prematurely old, of course; institutionalised personality and so forth and quite convinced about this unpleasant Osiris business, wouldn't budge an inch on that. After all, he *had* to believe that or else he'd have realised what it was that he had done, wouldn't he?

FEMALE NARRATOR: The axe never falls, the blow is never struck; self-knowledge, self-realisation remains imminent, never accomplished, the fairies remain fairies, they symbolise nothing ... even the god whom he invented is not made manifest in his painting.

DOCTOR: But nothing *mad* about his paintings, not at all. Not like some of that damn French stuff you see around nowadays ... He'd just gone on painting very much the same sort of thing inside Bethlem as he would have painted outside it, d'you see. Business as usual. Just, the perspective went a bit wonky and all the people in the pictures greet you with an uncommonly disconcerting fixed stare ... And after we all moved to Broadmoor, there was so much to keep him occupied – lantern slides, he painted lantern slides for lectures; and Christmas decorations; and, oh yes, there was a little theatre, where they'd put on plays and shows, don't you know, and he painted a backdrop for that. And some murals. Very nice, little children dancing, that sort of thing. I suppose you could say that the old chap got on with his career as though nothing much had happened.

(DADD sobs; sobbing rises, fades.)

What's that? Repression?

FEMALE NARRATOR: The icy calm of absolute repression, the striving both to justify the actions of the self and at the same time to obliterate the actions of the self –

DOCTOR: *(Bored; dismissing the whole subject.)* Well, wasn't he the product of the most repressed society in the history of the world?

MALE NARRATOR: *(Cool.)* The tragic circumstances of Dadd's life were at length terminated by consumption, in Broadmoor, on 8th January 1886.

FEMALE NARRATOR: 'I am truly thankful to know him at rest, it is less grief to me than it was to think of him in the changed condition in which he has lived for many years past, his life has been to me a living death . . .' Yours faithfully, Mary Anne Dadd, sister of the unfortunate . . .

(Fade in to OBERON, *coming to the end of his lecture.)*

OBERON: The quaint pornography of never-never-land; the infection of the mystic East, as fatal to his spirit as the germ of Asiatic cholera was to the flesh of the inhabitants of the foetid cities of the period; the terrible glamour of parricide, a crime which struck at the very root of the patriarchal order of his time which Dadd yet committed, as it were, in absentia, as if even the consciousness of his actions were denied to him. I submit, therefore, that Dadd, rather than an afflicted poetic genius, contrived in some measure, in spite of or, perhaps, because of, his absolute seclusion from it, to capture the essential spirit of his age. For, you creatures of the dream yourselves, could one of you deny that Dadd was himself, in person, the dream's revenge?

Thank you.

(Applause; fading into reprise of 'Come unto These Yellow Sands'.)

The Company of Wolves

(Fade in cold wind. From the distance we hear the sound of a wolf's cry. It is answered by another then another and another . . . A gust of wind blows the cries away.)

ANNOUNCER: 'The Company of Wolves'.

(Bring up wind and cross to crackling of log fire centre. Ticking of grandfather clock left centre. Click of knitting needles left. Wide spread.)

GRANNY: *(Far left.)* Knit one, purl one, knit two together . . .

RED RIDING HOOD: *(Far right.)* What are you knitting, Granny?

GRANNY: Making some lucky little girl a present.

RED RIDING HOOD: What lucky little girl, Granny?

GRANNY: Lor' love you, my darling, who else would I be knitting a lovely woolly shawl for, if it wasn't for Granny's own pet . . . knit one, purl one . . . a nice shawl to keep her snug, so Granny's darling girl can wrap up warm and cosy, trot through the wood to visit her old grandmother when the winter wind blows and we shall have snow . . . look what a nice colour the wool is, eh? Red to match baby's rosy cheeks!

RED RIDING HOOD: Quite a bloody red. Quite bloody.

GRANNY: Don't think of nasty things, think of *nice* things. Cosy shawl for Granny's precious girl. Who's Granny's precious girl?

RED RIDING HOOD: *I'm* Granny's precious girl!

GRANNY: And I chose a nice, bright red because you need a bit of colour to cheer you up in winter, in the bleak midwinter . . . knit one, purl one . . . when the snow comes . . .

(Fade down domestic noise and overlay with wind.)

NARRATOR: *(Close. Centre.)* It is a northern country; a late, brief spring, a cool summer and then the cold sets in again. Cold, tempest, wild beasts in the forests, under the vaulted branches, where it is always

dark. When the snow comes, it precipitates in this inhospitable terrain
a trance of being, an extended dream that lurches, now and then, into
nightmare. The deer, departed to the southern slopes, the cattle all
locked up in the byre, now is the time the wild beasts come out, now
is the savage time of the year, nothing left for the wolves to eat . . .

(Fade up domestic noise, knitting needles etc.)

GRANNY: When the snow comes . . . red for danger when the wolves
come . . .

*(Clock, fire, knitting needles all as if blown away by a sudden fierce gust of
wind from right to left.)*

GRANNY AND RED RIDING HOOD: *(Flustered.)* Oh! Ah!

(We are left with strong wind. Long, low howl right centre back.)

GRANNY: *(Distant left.)* Lawks a mercy! The wolves are running!

(Peak wind slightly.)

NARRATOR: Now is the season of the wolf, the low part of the year
when the sun has barely the strength to heave himself up over the
horizon. In these days the dire wolf travels in the crepuscular hours –

(Wind.)

WEREWOLF: *(Back centre. Howls.)*

    I pull my pelt around me and go hunting.
    I can be grey as a cloud or I can be tawny.
    At twilight I roam to tear up the world with my huge claws.
    At twilight I roam to devour the world with my cleaving teeth.
    At twilight I travel with eyes in the back of my head.
    My howl deranges the soo–oul.

(Wolf howl. Bring up wind; howling of many wolves from distance.)

RED RIDING HOOD: *(Far left, excited.)* What'll we do, Granny? What
shall we do?

GRANNY: *(Crossing from far left to right.)* Shut the shutters! Bar the door!
Throw more logs on the fire! Make a great blaze! Keep the wolves
outside!

*(As she crosses from left to right so the domestic sounds of fire and clock ticking
spread to the right with her and the wind and howling pan right. At the end of
the speech she slams shutter shut, right, and this cuts the wind and wolves. Fire
rises; clock rises.)*

(Returning to left.)

Fear and flee the wolf, my little one.

(Knitting resumes.)

Purl one . . . knit two together . . . You are always in danger in the forest, where no people are. Oh, my sweet grandchild, whatever you do in the winter weather, never stray from the path through the forest or –

RED RIDING HOOD: *(By* GRANNY.*)* What will happen to me, then, Granny?

GRANNY: You'll be lost, instantly, and the wolves will find you! And always be home by nightfall or the wolves will . . .

RED RIDING HOOD: What will they do if they catch me?

GRANNY: Why . . . gobble you up!

(Making a game of it, she growls at RED RIDING HOOD, *who giggles delightedly.)*

Gobble, gobble, gobble . . .

RED RIDING HOOD: *(Running to right.)* Stop it, Granny, you're tickling!

GRANNY: Grrr!

*(*GRANNY*'s growls get closer and more menacing. Take down background as the growls crossfade to rending sounds. A piercing scream cuts rending sounds and we are left with cold wind.)*

NARRATOR: *(Close. Centre.)* After dark comes, they come, they cluster round the forest path, they track your smell of meat as you go through the wood unwisely late. They are like wraiths, like shadows, grey members of a congregation of the damned . . . the beasts of blood and darkness . . . carnivore incarnate, the eternal predator, the perpetual hunger of the dark wood that encompasses the lighted cottage in the clearing, the village trustfully sheltering in the valley . . .

(Behind first sentence of following speech lose wind and bring up domestic background:)

RED RIDING HOOD: *(Right.)* But I'm not scared of anything. My daddy gave me a big knife – see. Don't I know how to use it? Didn't I see my daddy stick the pig? There's nothing in the wood can harm *me*.

GRANNY: When it gets cold enough, the beasts grow impudent, often I've jumped half out of my skin to see his questing snout under the door and there was a woman once bitten in our village in her own kitchen, as she was straining the macaroni.

RED RIDING HOOD: Straining the macaroni?

GRANNY: Bit in the foot. Purl one, knit one. But the worst thing of all, my dearie, is – some wolves are hairy on the *inside*.

RED RIDING HOOD: What, like a sheepskin jacket? How can *that* be, Granny?

GRANNY: When he be not a natural wolf, my dearie, no wolf at all . . . knit two together.

Near here, just up the valley, when my own granny was alive, bless her soul, there was a wolf, once, in the winter-time, come savaging the sheep and goats. Oh, such a terror as he was! What massacres he made among the flocks!

(Take down fire. Fade up distant baying, baaing, bleating, commotion as from fireplace centre, which through the following sequence becomes a stage for the various backgrounds and action as described by GRANNY. Fade down to be replaced by fire.)

And then this wolf got a taste for man flesh . . .

(Fade in geriatric rendition of a hymn: 'All creatures that on earth do dwell . . .')

It ate up a mad old man that used to live in a hut halfway up the mountain and sing to Jesus all day long, innocent as a lamb, he was . . .

(Hymn broken off by slavering, chewing.)

Once a wolf's tasted human flesh, then nothing else will do.

(Fade chewing.)

When he'd digested the poor old man, just a few days after, the wolf pounced on a poor little girl, couldn't resist her . . .

(Faint girlish scream.)

She so white, so tender, a little girl just as old as you are . . .

RED RIDING HOOD: *(Getting close. Far right.)* Twelve. Going on thirteen, thirteen going on fourteen . . . not such a little girl, for all that you baby me, Granny. Thirteen going on fourteen, the hinge of your life, when you are neither one thing nor the other, nor child nor woman, some magic, in-between thing, an egg that holds its own future in it. An egg not yet cracked against the cup.

I am the very magic space that I contain. I stand and move within an invisible pentacle, untouched, invincible, immaculate. Like snow. Waiting. The clock inside me, that will strike once a month, not yet . . . wound . . . up . . .

I don't bleed. I can't bleed.

I don't know the meaning of the word, fear. Fear?

GRANNY: Just your age or a year or so older and she –

(Bleating of disturbed sheep, centre back.)

was looking after the sheep on the high pasture but she set up such a commotion

(Bleating; barking of dogs; girl shouting centre back, men's voices centre back.)

that the shepherds came running with their dogs and rifles –

(Shouting; barking; shots centre back.)

but this old wolf was cunning and soon gave them the slip, off into the woods he went.

(Shots etc. Fade
Fire, clock, knitting, continued:)

RED RIDING HOOD: So what happened to the poor wolf, then?

GRANNY: Knit one, purl one . . . I was just coming to that. They sent to the town for a man whose trade was putting down such vermin, famous for it, he was.

(Fire effects up.
Fade in digging. Exterior acoustic from fireplace and spread to cover stereo picture. Fade domestic noises.)

And this hunter dug –

HUNTER: *(Centre. Close.)* – a pit, with steep sides. A deep pit. A wolf-trap. And in this pit I stuck a sharpened stake and tied to this stake by a string around its left leg a fine –

(Quacking, fluttering of wings.)

(With fluttering of wings.) Now, you just stop that flapping and hold still! *(Close.)* It dearly grieved me, I can tell you, to give such a fat duck to the wolf when I could have roasted it up for meself but there's no better bait in all the world for a wolf than a duck.

(Rustles etc. moving left.)

So I popped it down the pit and then I covered the pit with branches and settled down in the undergrowth, downwind so he couldn't get a sniff of me, and bided my time . . .

(Last rebellious quack. Pause. Rustling from right.
Mid left and back – whispering.)

Here he comes . . . what a size! Near as big as I am and how his eyes do shine . . .

(Quacking from pit mid right. Crashing sound of branches giving way. Barking of wolf.)

GRANNY: And into the trap went the silly wolf.

(Animal shriek.)

HUNTER: *(Centre.)* So I jumps down and slits –

(Throat slitting from pit and grunts from hunter.)

his throat, quick as a wink. And commenced to lop off his paws, for I had a fancy to mount this brute's great pads, d'you see, to decorate my mantel, along with the boar's head and the moose head and the great carp my uncle caught ten winters ago that he had stuffed *(Thwack; dull thud.)* . . . but only the one paw did I chop off because, so help me, as I stand here –

(From pit.) Mother Mary and all the saints in heaven protect me!

GRANNY: *(Far left.)* Upon the ground the hunter saw there fall no paw at all but –

HUNTER: *(From pit.)* A hand! A man's hand!

(Wind faded out:)

NARRATOR: *(Centre. Close.)* The desperate claws retract, refine themselves as if attacked by an invisible emery board, until suddenly they become fingernails and could never have been anything but fingernails, or so it would seem. The leather pads soften and shrink until you could take fingerprints from them, until they have turned into fingertips. The clubbed tendons stretch, the foreshortened phalanges extend and flesh out, the bristling hair sinks backwards into the skin without leaving a trace of stubble behind it.

(Clock and fire back.)

WEREWOLF: *(Approaching from mid right to* RED RIDING HOOD.*)*

RED RIDING HOOD: Ooh . . .

WEREWOLF: Now my skin is the same kind of skin as your skin, little sister. There! my hand . . . won't you take hold of my hand?

RED RIDING HOOD: *(Gasps.)*

WEREWOLF: See . . . it's just the same as any other hand, only perhaps a little larger . . . didn't you see the enormous prints I left in the snow?

RED RIDING HOOD: *(Close. Far Right.)* Once, one winter when I was little, my father took me out into the wood and we found the track of a wolf, prints as big as dinner-plates, and my father took a good grip of his rifle and peered around but I put my little foot into the print, to match it for size, and I felt all the warmth that lies under the snow swallow me up . . .

GRANNY: *(Far left.)* And now no wolf at all lay before the hunter but the bloody trunk of –

HUNTER: *(Centre.)* So I may never touch another drop, it was a man, with his throat cut, and handless, bleeding, dying . . .

NARRATOR: Dead.

(Bring up and fade domestic background.)

RED RIDING HOOD: *(Thoughtful.)* But I would be sorry for the poor thing, whatever it was, man or beast or some benighted 'twixt and 'tween thing, trapped by a mean trick and finished off without its supper . . .

GRANNY: Knit two together. And worse than that has happened with these vile, unnatural creatures . . . when I was a young thing, about your age, there was a woman in our village married a man who vanished clean away on his wedding night.

(Fiddle music: 'The Hunting Boys'.
Rise subdued babble of voices, fiddle music, sound of party from centre back.
Fade during following speech but do not replace with domestic sounds.)

They made up the bed with new sheets and laid the bride down on it and left them alone together but then the groom said . . .

WEREWOLF: *(From centre back approaching and moving left. Laughs, embarrassed.)* But, ahem, first of all, before I do join you between the covers, it just so happens, my bonnie, how I must slip outside to answer the call of nature.

BRIDE: *(Mid right.)* Why can't 'ee piss in the pot provided, my love?

WEREWOLF: What, on our wedding night, my dear? In the name of decency . . .

(Door slams left.)

GRANNY: So she waited . . .

BRIDE: And didn't he look a lovely man, as he stood there in front of the altar and I come down the aisle in my white frock and he turned his head a bit round to see me . . . *(Yawns.)*

(Rustle of sheets.)

. . . a lovely man, even if his eyebrows meet . . . and he be altogether on the hairy side . . .

GRANNY: . . . and she waited . . .

BRIDE: *(Dreamily.)* and the first, if he be a boy, we shall call after his daddy, but, if she be a girl, why, we'll name her for me mam . . . *(Yawns again.)* . . .

GRANNY: . . . and she waited some more, until she thinks –

BRIDE: . . . surely . . . he's been gone a long time?

(Pause; faint wind; howl left.)

(Sitting up in bed – alert.) God save us all!

NARRATOR: That long-drawn, wavering howl that has, for all its fearful resonances, some inherent sadness in it, as if the beasts would love to be less beastly if only they knew how and never cease, in some wordless, devastating sense, to mourn their own condition.

There is a vast melancholy in the canticles of the wolves, melancholy infinite as the forest, endless as these long nights of winter and yet that ghastly sadness, that mourning for their own, irremediable appetites, can never move the heart, for not one phrase in it hints at the possibility of redemption . . .

(Howl of several wolves off left.)

Grace could not come to the wolf from its own despair, only through some external mediator . . .

(Fade wolves.)

BRIDE: *(Close. Right centre.)* When the rumpus died down a bit and I judged it safe to venture into the farmyard, I got down the lantern and searched among the outhouses all in my nightie as I was and that distressed! Oh, weeping and wailing, I was, to think the wolves had eaten up my bridegroom and left nothing behind to bury. For not a gnawed bone nor hank of hair, even, or yet a rag of his wedding suit did I find, but, in the snow, many huge pawprints, as if the beastly things had been having themselves a bit of a dance. A dance!

(Sobs; blows nose; recovers.)

So then I reckons how he is good and done for so I dried my eyes and went out and found myself another husband not too shy to piss under his own roof and the first boy we named for his father but he would insist the girl be called after me. My bouncing babies, merry as grigs, first they crawl, then they toddle, then they walk, then they run . . . time flies . . . years after, oh, years after, it was one winter's night, one freezing night when the moonlight looks like it could cut you . . . my husband out in the byre tending the cattle, meself in the kitchen with the bairns . . . I just ladling the soup . . . just before Christmas, it was, when night-time lasts longer than daytime . . .

NARRATOR: It is the season of the solstice, the hinge of the year, the time when things don't fit well together, when the door of the year is sufficiently ajar to let all kinds of beings that have no proper place in the world slip through.

BRIDE: . . . one snowy, moony night . . .

GRANNY: . . . her first good man came home again.

(Thump on door, left.)

RED RIDING HOOD: *(Far right.)* He hadn't forgotten her, then. He came home for Christmas.

(Thump on door repeated.)

WEREWOLF: *(Off left.)* Lift up the latch and let me in!

(Latch clicks; indrawn breath from bride by door.)

BRIDE: *(Right centre. Close.)* I knew him the minute I laid eyes on him, though now he was in rags and his hair grown so, not seen a comb for years, down to his backside, alive with lice, and hell-fire . . . yes! hell-fire darting in his look.

WEREWOLF: *(Entering.)* Here I am again, missus! *(Shuts door.)* Fetch me my bowl of cabbage and be quick about it!

BRIDE: *(Right. Back.)* There's changes made in this house, you villain! You been away too long to have a claim on me!

LITTLE GIRL: *(Off centre.)* Mama!

WEREWOLF: Who's this wee tender morsel?

LITTLE BOY: *(Off centre.)* Mama, mama, what big eyes he has . . .

WEREWOLF: What's this? Cubs? Has this wench been playing among the blankets while her lawful wedded husband's out of the way? You bastards, you by-blows –

(Children shriek.)

CHILDREN: Mama! Save us!

BRIDE: Don't you dare lay a finger . . .

WEREWOLF: I wish I were a wolf again, to teach this whore a lesson.

(Sounds of clothes being torn off.)

BRIDE: *(Close. Right centre.)* And then, he flinging off his coat, his shirt, his boots, his trousers . . . a wolf . . . he instantly . . . became.

(Pandemonium; barking; screaming; pots breaking; fire-irons falling.)

But my rightful husband, hearing this commotion –

(Door opens left.)

and hastening in . . .

HUSBAND: What's up then?

BRIDE: . . . seized the axe we used to chop up firewood –

(Thwack; scream; groan; thud; silence.)

HUSBAND: *(Back. Centre left.)* That's fixed him.

BRIDE: So the father of my children made an end of my . . . visitor . . . then and there, such a mess he made, blood and guts all over the kitchen floor, with one blow struck off its head, and the torso twitched a bit, but then –

BOY: Mama, its fur –

GIRL: Its fur is all melting away –

BRIDE: And, indeed, its hairy pelt fell off like snow off a roof in February, when the thaw comes, and you could see how he was nothing but an ordinary man, underneath, and the years since I'd last seen him had scarcely touched him . . . and his head, that had rolled on to the hearth and come to rest just by the kettle, the furry head with the sharp ears and brindled muzzle and dreadful, crushing jaw . . . why, then it turned back into *his* head, and there was my old sweetheart's face . . . with that self-same smile on it that he'd given me long ago, when we were young, when I walked down the aisle towards him, me in my white lace dress, and he'd turned round to look at me, given me a bit of a smile, as if to say, courage, lass . . . and I never did care that his eyebrows met . . . so now I couldn't forbear to . . .

(Bride weeps. Centre right back.)

HUSBAND: Is this the thanks I get for butchering the beast? You harlot, I'll fairly larrup you, I will – take that –

(Thump; cry; renewed weeping; fade out weeping.
Fade in domestic noise of GRANNY*'s kitchen: clock; fire; knitting.)*

GRANNY: Knit two together . . . now. I'm just ready to cast off, see how it's done? Then your shawl'll be ready to slip round your little shoulders . . .

(Pause.)

RED RIDING HOOD: How?

GRANNY: How?

RED RIDING HOOD: Do they let their insides come outside?

GRANNY: It is the devil's reward for long service! For they do say there is a salve the devil gives 'em, hands it out at the Sabbath . . .

NARRATOR: Fat of a cat; camphor; aniseed; opium, all mixed together, rubbed well into the skin.

GRANNY: Or they do sup a drink the devil makes –

NARRATOR: An infusion of mandrake, belladonna, henbane, taken in a glass of wine.

GRANNY: Or else they drink from a stream the devil shows 'em and go ravening off. Or sip the rainwater out of a wolf's pawprint, that is the size of a basin. And some are born so, those that come into the world feet first on St John's Eve and had a wolf for a father . . . and his torso will be a man's but his legs, his privates, those of a wolf . . . and he will have a wolf's heart.

RED RIDING HOOD: A wolf's heart.

GRANNY: Before he can turn into a werewolf, he must always strip stark naked. Peel off all his human concealments, down to the bald, natural buff. If you spy a naked man among the pines, my dearie, you must run as if the devil were after you.

RED RIDING HOOD: A naked man? In *this* weather? He'd have his thingumajigs frozen off, Granny!

(She laughs.)

GRANNY: Well, just watch out!

(But RED RIDING HOOD continues to laugh. Her laughter fades into sound of wind and storm. Wind and storm peak and fade into country-morning sounds — cock-crow, mooing of cows.)

MOTHER: *(Left back.)* Just you watch out.

RED RIDING HOOD: *(Right centre. Close.)* I must and will go to Granny's house today. I've set my mind upon it.

MOTHER: Then don't leave the path through the wood —

RED RIDING HOOD: I've got the big, red shawl my granny knitted me, that'll keep me warm, and my mother is packing a basket —

MOTHER: *(Packing basket.)* — Oatcakes, butter, cheese —

RED RIDING HOOD: Full of good things for the poor old lady.

MOTHER: . . . a little pot of bramble jelly . . . Oh, you spoilt one, oh, you wilful one! But, if off you must go, on such a cold winter's day, the shortest day of all the year, then be sure to keep to the path through the wood and don't —

RED RIDING HOOD: — stay out —

MOTHER: — after nightfall —

RED RIDING HOOD: — or else —

MOTHER: — the wolves —

RED RIDING HOOD: — will gobble me up.

(RED RIDING HOOD laughs.)

MOTHER: If your daddy were here, he'd never let you –

RED RIDING HOOD: But he's out in the forest, picking up sticks.

MOTHER: (*Sighs – aside to audience.*) She being the youngest and, yes, the prettiest, our little bud, our blossom, I can deny her nothing. And she, she's such a high opinion of herself she thinks the snow'll forbear to fall upon her . . .

RED RIDING HOOD: And here I've got my daddy's knife . . . don't I know how to stick the pigs with it?
I shall and will go to Granny's house today.

MOTHER: I'll just slip a bottle of ardent spirits into your basket, to keep the old lady's bones warm . . .

(*Clink.*)

MOTHER: (*Going off left.*) . . . and don't stray off the path for a minute and don't let the sun go down with you still outdoors –

(*Door slams left. Fade up birdsong. Woodland noises.*)

RED RIDING HOOD: (*Right centre.*) If it were summer, I should pick the flowers and chase the butterflies but now it is winter, only last night's snow on the bare boughs, no reason to dawdle . . . how my breath smokes!

(*Robin sings.*)

Well! here's the robin, the friend of man in his bloody waistcoat, perched on a stump to wish me good morning.

(*Fade robin; footsteps on rustic path.*)

And if I walk quiet as I can, then I may spy Reynard the Fox taking home a hen out of my daddy's run so his family can have some dinner . . .

(*Raucous caw.*)

A raven . . . why, Reynard the Fox has been out early, this morning; here's the blood of some poor slaughtered bunny on the snow, the horrid raven pecking it . . . shoo, you cannibal, shoo!

(*Caw; flapping of wings; distant howl.*)

What's that?

(*Rustle of undergrowth; an arrival.*)

WEREWOLF: *(Right.)* Oh, please, young lady, put away that knife! How fierce you look! I never intended to startle you, I would have thought there was nobody in all the wood but me.

RED RIDING HOOD: Well, well, well . . . who's this fine young man, sprung up out of nowhere . . .

GRANNY *(on echo):* *(Repeated from first time.)* If you spy a naked man in the forest, run as if the devil were after you . . .

RED RIDING HOOD: But this one's got all his clothes on, Granny! Such nice clothes, too . . . lovely bit of tweed, that jacket, with the leather patches on the elbows. And a felt hat with a feather in the band. And nice whipcord breeches, and such a shine on his leather boots! It took a gentleman's gentleman to give *this* gentleman's boots that shine. Out after game, he must be out after game . . . doesn't he have his rifle over his shoulder?

WEREWOLF: Here I am, a jolly huntsman.

RED RIDING HOOD: So he makes me a little bow, polite as can be, and –

WEREWOLF: Allow me.

(Takes basket.)

RED RIDING HOOD: What lovely manners, taking the heavy old basket off me to carry himself. Not like those rude clowns in the village who don't know how to treat a lady, let a girl hump the potato sacks all by herself – oh, my knife! I put my knife in the basket!

WEREWOLF: My rifle will protect us both, young lady. You have nothing to fear when you are with me. Permit me –

(Footsteps in undergrowth.)

RED RIDING HOOD: So this fine young gentleman takes my arm and off we go together, as if we were out for a ramble, and soon we're chattering away together as if we'd sucked on the same nipple . . .

(Fade in conversation, burst of laughter. The following four speeches are all faded in/out but background remains constant.)

RED RIDING HOOD: . . . taking a few bits of this and that to my old granny, sir, seeing as she is bedridden –

WEREWOLF: – parted company with my friends in order to bang away by myself and now making for the village –

RED RIDING HOOD: – make haste and speed for the day darkens early, this time of year –

WEREWOLF: – hoping to find some friendly hostelry, a bite to eat, a drink –

RED RIDING HOOD: *(Clean in.)* Should you escort me as far as my granny's house, sir, I'm sure my granny would gladly give you a cup of tea, or maybe something a bit stronger, seeing as how we slipped a bottle of brandy in with the butter and cheese.

WEREWOLF: Delighted. Delighted.

RED RIDING HOOD: *(Close centre left.)* And me all of a flutter, poor simple girl that I am. For he is such a *handsome* young fellow, for all his eyebrows do grow close together . . .

WEREWOLF: *(Close centre right.)* Fifteen going on sixteen, the tenderest age. Under that red shawl, how white her skin must be, as white as breast of chicken, succulent as loin of pork . . .
  Little miss, pretty miss, see what I have in my pocket!

RED RIDING HOOD: Now, this young man had the most remarkable object in his pocket, which he brought forth to show to me. At first I thought it was perhaps some kind of a pocket watch, for it was round and swung on a chain. But *tick* it did not, and then it came to me how it might be a locket with a picture of his sweetheart inside, which made me squint a bit, until he said –

WEREWOLF: This is what we call a compass.

RED RIDING HOOD: It had a round face, much like a clock, but no numbers on it and only the one hand, that moved around in a wavering manner. Wavering as if it were looking for something.

WEREWOLF: Looking for the north.

RED RIDING HOOD: And he told me how this compass had helped him find his way through the trackless forest, because the needle always pointed to the north with perfect accuracy –

WEREWOLF: So, you see, I can never lose my way! I'm always at home in the forest.

RED RIDING HOOD: But I did not believe him. I knew I should never leave the way on the path through the wood or else I should be lost instantly.

WEREWOLF: *(Laughs close.)* Why, I can guarantee you, if I plunge off this winding path directly into the wood, now, at this moment, and find my way by the compass, I will arrive at your grandmother's house a good quarter of an hour before you do. I promise you!

RED RIDING HOOD: I shan't leave the path; I won't leave the path.

WEREWOLF: Then . . . you stay on the path and I'll go through the wood and we'll see who gets to your granny's house first. Is it a wager? Shall we make a little bet on it?

RED RIDING HOOD: You get there how you like; I'll get there how I like.

WEREWOLF: What will you give me if I get there before you?

(Pause.)

RED RIDING HOOD: *(Disingenuous.)* What would you like me to give you?

(Pause.)

WEREWOLF: A kiss. *(Close.)* How she's blushing, like blood leaking into the snow . . .

(Owl hoots – ominous noises.)

RED RIDING HOOD: Look how dark it's getting! Why, I do believe we'll have more snow –

WEREWOLF: A kiss?

RED RIDING HOOD: *(Bursts out laughing.)* You're on –

(Swish – the WEREWOLF *vanishes into the wood.)*

Here, hold on – you've taken my basket with you! And my knife, you've taken my knife!

(Undergrowth rustles at distance.)

Oh, never mind it, I'll soon catch up with him . . . *(Giggles.)* What an adventure, though! Indeed . . . for fear of catching up with him too soon . . . I'll take my time, I will, over this last half mile to Granny's house, although the snow is coming on . . .

(Fade her. Bring up wind. Fade in footsteps in undergrowth.)

WEREWOLF: *(Hums to himself the seduction song from* Don Giovanni.*)*

NARRATOR: Towards the fringes of the forest, nestling in a clearing, a cottage whose ruddy windows beamed with cheerful light as if, in the approaching dark and the whirling beginnings of the snow, that house contained all the human warmth in the world.

Towards the cottage door the huntsman now purposefully directed his footsteps.

(Crossfade background to fire crackling, clock ticking, etc. Rat-a-tap-tap from right.)

GRANNY: *(Crossing from left to right.)* Who's that knocking on my door?

WEREWOLF: *(Off – falsetto.)* Only your granddaughter, come all this way to see you on a cold snowy evening!

(Latch lifted. Door, right, opened. A big wind blows through the house, blows away the domestic noises.)

NARRATOR: And by his incandescent eyes, she knew at once the nature of her visitor, and, clasping her hands together, she besought –

GRANNY: JesuJosephMarySaintAnneSaintElizabethSaint –

WEREWOLF: Call on all the saints in the calendar to speed hot-foot from heaven to help you, Granny, but it won't do you any good. How can you keep the night out, when it wants so much to come in?

GRANNY: *(Screams.)* *(Far left over her own scream 'as heard before'.)* Before he can become a wolf, the werewolf strips stark naked.

WEREWOLF: *(Undressing.)* . . . good . . . to get out of these silly clothes . . .

GRANNY: Under his clothes, he was the colour of goatcheese, and nipples black as poison berries, and a stripe of hair running down his belly, and so thin, he was, that you could count his ribs . . .

WEREWOLF: . . . but I'm not going to give you any time . . .

NARRATOR: And now, as the old lady quivered with dread before him, she witnessed the unimaginable metamorphosis, the coarse, grey, the tawny, bristling pelt springing out from the bare skin of her visitor . . . great jaws slavering . . . his red eyes, now burning with far greater intensity than the coals in her hearth . . .

GRANNY: . . . and his privates, of a wolf, huge . . . he naked as a stone, but hairy . . . he . . . aaaaaaagh! *(Echo.)*

(Fade GRANNY. Hold wind for a moment. Then fade in logs crackle, clock ticks, mastication and lose wind.)

WEREWOLF: *(Right centre.)* Here's a tough old bird, indeed . . . veritable jaw-cracker . . . Not much meat on her, all sinew . . . still, waste not, want not; down the red lane with Granny . . . and isn't dessert trotting through the wood towards me this minute, and she tender as a peach . . . juicy as a wood strawberry . . .

(Swallow. Lip-smacking. Belch.)

NARRATOR: When he had finished her, he quickly dressed himself again, until he was just as he had been when he came through the door. He burned the inedible hair in the fireplace –

(Whizz of flame.)

and wrapped up the bones in the tablecloth.

(Faint rattle of bones centre.)

WEREWOLF: What, Granny, shaking your old bones at me? Playing a tune on your own xylophone *(Moving left.)* I'll put you under the bed, out of harm's way . . . don't you know I've done for you, Granny?

(Rattle of bones thrown under bed, left.)

(As he moves centre.) Oops! here's my rifle; best hide it up the chimney, lest dessert takes a mind to shoot it off at me . . . why, here's her basket; oatcakes, butter . . . cheese . . . nothing fit for a carnivore to eat . . . hello, brandy! How about a little digestive, Granny?

(Pours, drinks.)

Here's . . . to your posthumous health! *(Moving left.)* Now . . . settle down in Granny's chair. Best . . . put on . . . the old lady's nightcap, don't want to scare away the little pretty if she peeks through the window to see if her handsome huntsman got here before her. *(Laughs.)*

(Settles down; resumes humming air from Don Giovanni. *Clock whirs, strikes half hour.)*

Where can she have got to . . .

(Rat-a-tap-tap. Right.)

(Falsetto.) Who's that knocking on my door?

RED RIDING HOOD: *(Off.)* Didn't a young gentleman get here before me, Granny?

WEREWOLF: *(Falsetto, moving to right centre.)* Young gentleman? What young gentleman? I've seen no young gentleman!

RED RIDING HOOD: Oh . . .

WEREWOLF: Lift up the latch and come in, like a dutiful granddaughter!

(Latch lifts, door opens; intensification of domestic noises. Fade slightly.)

RED RIDING HOOD: *(Close centre.)* And then, oh, then, how I did want the big knife my father gave me, to do for him – oh, yes, I did. But as for my knife, I could not get it, it being in my basket, my basket being on the table and him standing between me and the table, tall and wild as if all the wild wood was made into a man and it come into the kitchen and his eyes as big as saucers, flaming –

(Bring up fire, clock, etc.)

What big eyes you have.

WEREWOLF: All the better to see you with, my pretty. You're a sight worth looking at.

RED RIDING HOOD: *(Close centre.)* And there was no trace of my granny anywhere in the kitchen, but for a tuft of white hair caught in an unburned bit of log in the grate, and then I knew I was in danger of death.

What have you done with my granny?

WEREWOLF: There's nobody here but we two, darling.

RED RIDING HOOD: *(Close.)* Then fear of death over me, I who had been afraid of nothing, for, though I knew that he had just eaten, yet I know the wolf is always hungry . . .

And I cannot cry for help because we are a good mile from the village.

(Single howl outside.)

Yet though I am among the wild beasts –

(More howling.)

I must not be afraid because fear is their meat –

(Yet more howling.)

and so I must not suffer it.

(Fade howling until very soft. She takes a deep breath.)

Who has come to sing to us?

WEREWOLF: Those are the voices of my brothers, darling. I love the company of wolves. Look out of the window and you'll see them.

RED RIDING HOOD: *(Moving right.)* How it's snowing! You can't see through the lattice, the pane all caked with snow . . .

WEREWOLF: Open the window . . .

(Lattice opens. Peak wind, wolf-chorus. Take down behind.)

RED RIDING HOOD: *(Close.)* And on the branches of the apple tree outside my granny's window were perched a fruit of wolves . . . it had become a wolf tree . . . they all staring at me with their big, dumb eyes, eyes with such sorrow in the pupils . . . ten wolves, twenty wolves, more wolves than I could count . . . eyes catching the light from the kitchen and shining like candles . . . each beast pointing its muzzle to the moon and howling fit to break your heart . . .

(Lattice slams shut. Cut wind and howling.)

It's freezing cold, poor things, no wonder they howl so.

WEREWOLF: *(Caressing.)* Are you cold, too, my darling? Would you like a glass of brandy, to warm you?

RED RIDING HOOD: Oh, it's warm enough, indoors, by the fire.

WEREWOLF: Then take off . . . your shawl.

RED RIDING HOOD: What . . . shall I do with it, now?

WEREWOLF: Burn it, dear one. You won't need it again.

RED RIDING HOOD: *(Close.)* So I stuffed the shawl in the fireplace, and, seeing the bottle of brandy my mam gave me to give Granny, I dowsed the fire with it, to make the flames jump up.

(Fire crackles.)

WEREWOLF: The light! My eyes!

RED RIDING HOOD: And up the chimney went the red shawl that my granny knitted me, it catching fire on the way, whoosh! Look! Like a bird with flamey wings!

WEREWOLF: *(Groans.)*

RED RIDING HOOD: *(Close.)* And, just as if my granny were angry with me for setting light to her shawl, there came such a rattling of her old bones . . .

(Staccato rattle from left.)

Well . . . I do think, tonight, on such a night, that I should wear nothing but my skin, for why should I go clothed when the poor wolves outside do not . . .

(Rattle of bones.)

my skirt . . . my blouse . . . one stocking . . . two stockings . . . on to the fire! What a blaze!

(Rattling. Flames.)

RED RIDING HOOD: Oh, hush and be quiet, Granny, while your granddaughter entertains your visitor!

(Bones give one last, disapproving rattle.)

WEREWOLF: *(Whimpers.)*

RED RIDING HOOD: There. See? All my clothes burned up. Oh, sir, your eyes – they're watering! Are you in pain? Can't you bear the bright light?

WEREWOLF: *(Sobs and whimpers.)* My eyes . . .

RED RIDING HOOD: Oh, sir, don't turn your head away . . . not from a poor girl like me. Or is it the firelight has got into my skin, too?
Do I *blaze*, sir? Am I too bright for you, sir?

WEREWOLF: I can't . . . I can't . . .

RED RIDING HOOD: What is it, sir? Is it that you're having some difficulty turning into a wolf, sir, because I've had my clothes off first? Is that it?

WEREWOLF: Aren't you frightened of the wolf?

RED RIDING HOOD: Since my fear did me no good, I put it away from me, sir; put it away with my clothes.
Oh, fine gentleman! Fair is fair. If I am to go naked, then you must go naked, too. Let me unbutton that shirt for you . . . Don't struggle, now . . . what does my mammy say, 'Let's skin the rabbit' . . . but *this* rabbit has fur *underneath* his skin . . .
What big arms you have. There . . . put them around me . . . there . . .

WEREWOLF: *(Groans.)*

RED RIDING HOOD: I do believe, since you got here before me, that you owe me a kiss.
What big teeth you have!

WEREWOLF: *(Choking – grabbing at straws.)* All the better . . . to eat you with.

RED RIDING HOOD: Oh, I say!

(She goes into peals of laughter.)

Well, each to his meat but I am meat for no man! Now shall I burn your clothes, just like I burned my own . . .

WEREWOLF: Not that!

RED RIDING HOOD: Why, anybody would think you were scared of being a good wolf all the time . . .

(Flames blaze.)

And now I shall see you as the good wolf you are, the honest wolf, the kind wolf.

    For to their own, the wolves are tender, are they not? If you were truly a wolf, would you not let me climb up on your back and take me home through the forest?

(Bring up fire, wolves and storm outside right.)

WEREWOLF: *(Furry voice.)* Outside's not the place to be, tonight, the snow, the freezing blast . . . stay indoors with me, lie down on Granny's bed . . .

RED RIDING HOOD: What, make ourselves cosy?

(Bed creaks.)

RED RIDING HOOD: There we are . . . lay your head in my lap, there . . . your great, grey grizzled head . . . let me scratch your lovely ears, you can hear the clouds move, can't you, you can hear the grass grow, such sensitive ears, so quick of hearing . . . and I can see the lice move on your fur, poor beast . . .

(Growl.)

And shall I pick the lice out, would that be a kindness to you . . .

(Appreciative growl. Clock whirs – about to strike. Clock strikes twelve – fade down while it is still striking. Distant wind. Fire.)

NARRATOR: Midnight. The blizzard will die down; the door of the solstice stands wide open.

RED RIDING HOOD: *(Yawns.)* She's drowsy, she's sleepy . . . how soft your fur is! Warm!

(Clock out.)

WEREWOLF: When I was a man, I heard a story that, then, I did not believe because I thought that all the wolves were as I.

How there was a woman lived on the mountain and she went into labour in winter, in a storm, and bore her little daughter and died of it, nobody by but her husband. He did what he could but when there was no hope for her, he went off to the village to fetch the priest, the snow falling, the wind blowing, and the ice on the river broke under him, he drowned.

When the storm passed off, this woman's mother went out to see after her and found a corpse but no baby, not a trace, so they all thought the wolves had eaten her. And seven years went by, until another hard winter when the wolves came out of the forest, after the goats, and the dead woman's mother saw a creature with long hair, that might have been a little girl, and she running with them. And they found footprints among the pawprints. Footprints.

So they scoured the mountain and found the child in a cave, with an old, grey wolf they shot when it jumped up at them. Then they took the girl back to the village and locked her in a barn, but she howled; how she howled. She howled until she brought every wolf out from all over the forest, dozens of them, hundreds of them, howling in concert as if demented, and the wolves laid siege to the barn and would let nobody near and the girl ran away with them.

And seven years later, the old woman, she was out gathering mushrooms, she saw a grown woman with two pups, kneeling by the river, lapping up water. But when the old woman called out 'My dear one, my pet, come back to me!' off the other one ran to where her friends were waiting.

Are you listening? Are you sleeping?

RED RIDING HOOD: (*Stirs, murmurs wordlessly in her sleep.*)

NARRATOR: The blizzard died down, leaving the woods as randomly covered with snow as if a clumsy cook had knocked the flour bin over them.

Moonlight, snowlight, a confusion of paw prints under the apple tree outside the window.

All silent, all still.

WEREWOLF: She's sleeping, look, her paws twitch, she's dreaming of rabbits . . .

NARRATOR: Sweet and sound she sleeps in Granny's bed, between the paws of the tender wolf.

(*Fade fire crackling and clock.*)

Puss in Boots

(Fade in Figaro's aria from The Barber of Seville, *take down behind:)*

ANNOUNCER

(Bring up music and fade.
  Dead acoustic.)

PUSS: Ladies and gentlemen, a very good day to you, and I hope you enjoy the show as much as we enjoy – what? what's the big joke? *(He's engaging with an inaudible heckler.)* Never seen a cat before, is that it? Never been addressed *as an equal* by a cat before? . . . and is it any wonder . . .

   Well, I daresay that . . . you've never met a cat like me! Feline and *proud*, ladies and gentlemen. Felis domesticus by genus – that is, for those of you who don't speak Latin, a short-haired domestic ginger. In short, a marmalade cat. Male. *Whole* male. Oh, yes, indeed! This handsome, furred and whiskered person standing here before you tonight has much to be proud of. Proud, for a start, of his white shirt-front, or dickey, dazzling the eye, forming an elegant, formal contrast to the orange, tangerine and amber tessellations of the rest of my coat, my pelt, my brilliant uniform which is as fiery to the eye as is the suit of lights worn by the matador . . . Such a tom as I may well be proud, too, of his bird-entrancing eye and more than military whiskers; proud –

HERO: – to a fault –

PUSS: – of my superbly musical voice. When I break into impromptu song at the spectacle of the moon above Bergamo, my native city, scene of the events about to befall – when I spontaneously serenade the moon above Bergamo, all the windows in the square fly open –

(Fade in exterior, empty square. Cat howling; windows opening; angry murmurs swelling to furious exclamations.)

CITIZEN'S WIFE: *(Off.)* 'eave 'arf a brick at 'im!

CITIZEN: *(Off.)* 'eave it yourself.

2ND CITIZEN: *(Off.)* Shoot 'im!

3RD CITIZEN: *(Off.)* Bomb 'im!

4TH CITIZEN: *(Off.)* Nuke 'im!

(Take cat howling and angry cries down behind following:)

PUSS: When the poor players set up their stage here in the square, they think themselves lucky if the parsimonious Bergamots toss them a few, paltry pence. But I – when *I* start to sing, how liberally my grateful public rewards me with deluges of pails of the freshest water –

(Splash.)

– often they dower me with new-laid – well, fairly new-laid – eggs, and the succinctly ripest of the tomato crop –

(Splatter.)

– sometimes even slippers, shoes –

HERO: *(Off.)* Take that, you caterwauling fiend!

(Crash.)

(Off.) And that!

(Crash.)

PUSS: Boots! A pair of boots! What generosity! What a tribute! What a splendid gift! Fine, high, leather boots polished so brilliantly I can see my face in them . . . hi, there, Puss, you're looking *good*, tonight, good . . . Such boots! I wonder . . . will they fit me?

(Rapturous purring. Take down behind following:)

HERO: *(Narrating.)* When blessed peace fell on the square outside my lodging and all the disturbed Bergamots had gone back to bed, I looked out of the window to see what had become of my boots . . . and there, below me, to my infinite astonishment, the very strangest sight I ever beheld . . .

(Bring up square and purring as heard from window of HERO's room.)

PUSS: *(Off.)* Perfect fit. Purrfect . . .

(Take down background.)

HERO: . . . there was a cat, presumably the perpetrator of the ghastly serenade that had moved me to felinocidal violence, a great big ginger tom of formidable size and length of tail, engaged, of all things, in pulling on, over his hind paws, those very boots that I had just before, in my fury, hurled at him. *(Calling.)* Hey! Puss? What are you up to?

PUSS: *(Off.)* Fit like a glove, sir! Merci!

HERO: Merci? Why does he thank me in French?

PUSS: *(Off.)* It's the only language in which you can purr, sir.

HERO: You strike me as a cat of parts. Let's see how well you can climb in those boots.

PUSS: *(Off.)* Climb?

HERO: Up to my balcony!

PUSS: *(Off.)* Nice rococo façade to the place . . . rococo's a piece of cake for a cat, sir, either booted or barefoot.

HERO: *(Narrating.)* With that, the remarkable creature proceeded to scale the exterior of my lodgings. First, he rose up on his hind legs to his full height, which I judged to be some three or four feet –

PUSS: *(Narrating.)* – three foot eleven inches, call it four foot, not including my tail, that is. You never get it right; let's be precise just this once, for the record, okay? Can we attempt, perhaps, to be scrupulous, tough as it is on you?

HERO: *(Narrating.)* Listen to the way he speaks to me! As though I were a child and he were my nanny! Truly, since I first met him, I could hardly call my life my own; I –

PUSS: *(Off.)* Here! I say! Going to leave me halfway up to the balcony, are you? Going to leave me here all night, are you, while you complain and whinge and moan when all you have you owe to me? Going to abandon me hanging here, are you?

What will happen to your blooming story, then?

HERO: *(Sigh.)* Very well. *(Making amends.)* With a sinuous ripple of marmalade muscle –

PUSS: *(Narrating, approving.)* – nice touch –

HERO: *(Narrating.)* – he sets his forepaws on the carved pate of a curly cherub that decorated the lower part of the façade and, not one whit discommoded by the boots which he had donned, he brought his back paws up to meet them. Then –

PUSS: *(Climbing.)* – first paw forward, hup! to the stone nymph's tit, left paw down a bit, this . . . satyr's bum should . . . do the trick . . .

nothing to it once you know how. I was born to acrobatics, born to them. And very, very often have I performed, in return for a bit of salt cod or the pope's nose off a goose, to the applause of all, a perfect back somersault whilst holding a glass of vino in my right paw and never spill a single drop!

HERO: Not one drop?

PUSS: *(Narrating.)* I see the young man is impressed by my talents. I forbear to inform him, therefore, that, to my shame, I never yet attempted the famous death-defying *triple* somersault that is the greatest trial and test of such ambitious acrobats of the style of I.

   The young man welcomes me in through the window with a friendly chuck under the chin.

(Soft thump of cat jumping into room; purr.)

HERO: Amazing performance . . .

PUSS: *(Narrating.)* . . . and offers me, polite as anything . . .

HERO: A sandwich?

PUSS: *(Narrating.)* Roast beef, just how I like it, lean, moist, pink, easy on the mustard . . .

(Eating noises.)

HERO: *(Narrating.)* But all the time I plied the cat with sandwiches, I pondered how to get my boots back. *(In room.)* A snifter of brandy, perhaps?

PUSS: *(Mouth full.)* Won't say no, sir. I've a great liking for a spot of ardent spirits, picked up the taste in the vintners – I started out in life as a cellar cat, right here, in the city of Bergamo. One fine day, curled up in an empty barrel, overcome with fumes, nodded off, next thing I knew, woke up in Genoa – took service as a ship's cat, learned to roll my r's in Marseilles, to caterwaul in Spain . . .

(Glass filled.)

It's been a full life. Fill the glass right up to the top, sir –

(More pouring.)

Keep out the cold. Chilly, tonight, sir. Winter draws on. *(He downs drink in one, smacks lips.)* Got a drop more of that?

HERO: *(Narrating.)* When I saw the way the cat knocked back the brandy, I realised my plan to render him insensible and then remove my boots was inappropriate. I noticed he was examining my appearance extremely closely . . .

PUSS: By your coat, I see you're a military man, sir. Cavalry, eh?

HERO: *(Embarrassed.)* I – ah. Yes. I –

PUSS: Past tense, is it? *Was* a military man? When was you cashiered, sir?

HERO: Another – beef sandwich. Oh.

PUSS: I ate it already, in anticipation of your invite. Cards, was it? Or women? Or a combination of both, plus, perhaps, duelling and the juice, sir? And how does it earn its living, now?

HERO: *(Narrating.)* I saw I could keep no secrets from this cat . . . *(In room.)* To be perfectly frank with you, Puss, I go in for a little card-sharping, a little gaming, a little bit of this and that, you understand; and I live simply, in these lodgings, here . . . and I have but the one pair of boots . . .

PUSS: Which you so kindly, so very kindly, gave to me. And I shall cherish them always. And, in order to repay you, I shall move in with you –

HERO: What?

PUSS: Don't you ever feel the need of a valet?

HERO: A valet?

PUSS: A valet.

HERO: *(Thoughtfully.)* A valet!

PUSS: A touch more brandy to seal the bargain?

HERO: A valet . . .

(Hero pours drink.)

Do you know, I can see . . . all manner of ways . . . in which you'd make the perfect valet, Puss. Purrfect . . . your health!

(Clinks glasses.)

PUSS: *(Narrating.)* And I daresay the Master and I have much in common, for he's proud as the devil –

HERO: Say that again and smile!

PUSS: *(Narrating.)* – touchy as tin-tacks –

HERO: Swords or pistols?

PUSS: (*Narrating.*) – as lecherous as liquorice –

GIRL: Oh! oh . . . oh! . . . oh!! . . . oh!!!

PUSS: (*Narrating.*) – in short, as quick-witted a rascal as ever changed his shirt.

So Puss got his post at the same time as his boots and then it was busy, busy, busy . . .

(*Fade in Figaro's aria.*)

It was Figaro, here, Figaro, there, I tell you! Figaro upstairs, Figaro, downstairs, and oh, my goodness me! this little Figaro can slip into my lady's chamber smart as you like at any time of the day or night for what lady in all the world of any age, complexion or disposition could say no to my advances, to the passionate, indefatigable yet *toujours discrets* attentions of a marmalade cat . . .

(*Sneeze, which cuts short music.* HAG's *room.*)

HAG: Sod off, bugger off, get the hell out of it, you miserable cat –

PUSS: Get the hell out of it yourself, you old hag – you don't come in till later, anticipated your cue again –

(*Fade on sneeze.*)

HERO: (*Narrating.*) Although I felt that the servant had chosen the master rather than the more conventional way about, I soon found myself wondering how I could ever have managed without him. He was a valet beyond price –

(HERO's *room.*)

PUSS: Is that why you don't pay me, sir?

HERO: Don't I share all that I have with you?

PUSS: Which means, all that I steal.

HERO: So you've brought home some breakfast! Where is it, let's see . . . an orange, a loaf . . . and what's that you're hiding behind your back? Come on, let's have it –

(*Scuffle.*)

A herring!

PUSS: *(Narrating.)* The master chopped up this herring very fairly in order to make two servings, for first he cut the head off –

(Chop.)

and then the tail –

(Chop.)

and popped the meaty bit in between into the frying pan –

(Sizzle.)

for he never could get it into his thick skull that a cat's not choosy as to whether its breakfast is cooked or raw. So, while he was slicing his bread –

(Mew; fish removed from pan; eating sounds.)

HERO: Puss!

PUSS: *(Mouth full.)* Share and share alike, sir! Ain't I left you the head and the tail?

HERO: *(Narrating.)* I could scarcely escape the notion, sometimes, that as soon as my new valet had insinuated his way into my life, I myself had lost complete control of it . . .

(Fade in casino.)

But as soon as we stepped into the casino together, I would forgive him anything; for a cat may move with impunity from one lap to another –

(Purring.)

GAMBLER: Why, whom do we have here? Of all things, a cat – puss, puss, pretty puss . . .

(Purring.)

HERO: *(Narrating.)* I never go anywhere without my mascot, my lucky charm, my portable good fortune . . .

GAMBLER: Why, puss, my goodness me, you do like to be stroked and petted . . . don't you? Yes . . .

(Re-doubled purring.)

PUSS: *(Sotto voce.)* . . . an ace, a king, a ten and a queen, gottit?

HERO: *(Narrating.)* If he was an invaluable extra pair of eyes at a card game, he performed a rather more dramatic function when it was a game of dice –

(*Rattle, cat hunting cry;* PUSS *jumps with a thud on the dice; exclamations of gamblers.*)

Oh! the poor creature can't resist it when he sees the dice roll! Mistook them for mousies, didn't you, you silly old thing . . .

PUSS: (*Narrating.*) And after he scoops me up all limp-spined and stiff-legged as I am, playing the cat-idiot, and he chastises me, then, oh! who can remember how the dice fell in the first place?

HERO: Heaven smiles on me tonight! A double six!

PUSS: (*Narrating.*) And we had, besides, less . . . gentlemanly . . . means of support to which he was forced whenever –

(*Cut casino.*)

HERO: (*Narrating.*) Banned from the tables again, dammit! And my cat, too, my little lucky cat? What do you mean, especially the cat . . .

PUSS: (*Narrating.*) At such times as these, when the cupboard was bare as his backside, when, in short, the pour soul had been forced to pawn his drawers . . .

(*Flamenco guitar.*)

– you must know that all cats have a Spanish tinge –

(*Flamenco singer. Cross to exterior square.*)

– down to the square we'd go and there I'd do the Spanish dance I'd learned in Catalonia –

(*Flamenco; bootheels.*)

– stamping the ground in my boots, olé!

HERO: (*In square.*) Buenas gracias, señora; buenas gracias, señor . . .

(*Chink of money exchanging hands; bootheels; flamenco; conclude with flourish on loud chord and applause. Fade.*)

PUSS: (*Narrating.*) So Puss and his Man rubbed along famously together and all went right as ninepence until –

(*Fade in silent movie* Hearts and Flowers *music.*)

– until, alas –

HERO: *(Narrating.)* . . . with one smile she conjured the heart out of my bosom . . . when I first saw her smile, it was as if this heart of mine, this frequently abused, rarely if ever seriously touched organ in my bosom, my heart . . . my heart sprouted wings that instant and fluttered across the square to hover around her, like a butterfly just out of the chrysalis, tenderly, tremulously . . .

PUSS: – until the man goes and falls in love.

(Fade Hearts and Flowers *music . . .)*

In love!

SEVERAL WOMEN'S VOICES ALL TOGETHER: *(Agitated, astonished, mocking.)* In love? In love! In love . . .

HERO: *(Firm.)* In love.

PUSS: *(Narrating.)* And needs must he chooses to fall in love with the single individual most inaccessible woman in all Bergamo. In love with her at first sight of her smiling face.

And that face, in itself, the most uniquely unlikely sight in the whole city.

HEROINE: *(Narrating.)* I am the wife of Signor Pantaleone. I am young and beautiful and it is my misfortune to have been married against my will out of the schoolroom as payment for bad debts to a bald, gouty miser whose red nose bristles with hairy warts, a grotesque and sinister ancient old enough to be my father – my *grandfather*! A man as jealous as he is incompetent, who keeps me locked up like a holy statue and scarcely lets me see the light of day.

PANTALEONE: *(Narrating.)* Now, now, be fair! Don't I let you have a full hour every evening at your bedroom window? One full hour! What if you *do* have to keep a sack over your head, the while, so, though you can look out, nobody can look in at you – I don't display my prized possessions to the public, I don't waste them on any old Tom, Dick or Harry, oh, no!

(Bring in distant square during following, as heard from heroine's room.)

HEROINE: *(Narrating.)* For one hour, for one hour only, at the tenderest time of dusk, in the obscure light of early evening, then he allows me, half-hidden by the curtains to open the shutters and look down on the busy doings of the square, the dancers on ropes, the women selling cabbages and water melons, the hurly burly of life from which I am in exile. I can look out provided I am securely tied.

PANTALEONE: *(In room.)* Oh yes, I have her on a string. Keep a string round her ankle, tether her . . .

HERO: *(Narrating.)* Sometimes I saw the open window, like the dark mouth of a cave, but I never saw you –

HEROINE: No –

HERO: – not until –

(Bring in church bells.)

PANTALEONE: I even let her go to Mass on Sundays!

HEROINE: *(Narrating.)* Yes; on Sunday mornings, very early, when only the most godly venture out, he allows me out of the house for a brief interview with my maker, although you would think my husband more a Turk than a Christian by the way he makes me parcel up in veils. And, of course, I'm never permitted to venture out alone . . .

PANTALEONE: *(Narrating.)* – Who knows what she might get up to, then? Young women, young women . . . cunning as monkeys. To police my wife's piety, I employ, as her constant companion, a trusted lady of mature years who has been long in my employ.

HAG: *(Narrating.)* I am her governess.

HEROINE: *(Narrating.)* She is my wardress.

PUSS: *(Narrating.)* And so it came to pass as how the lovely wife of Signor Pantaleone was on her way to Mass and my master glimpsed her face by accident, one morning, one Sunday morning, so early of a Sunday morning that, for those of us who go to bed as late as my man and I, it was still night-time . . .

(Bring up bells as heard from exterior street. Footsteps on cobbles.)

HERO: *(Narrating.)* We'd played at cards so late, made such a killing at the tables that the pious ones were already making their way to church through the cold, dark fog as we went home –

PUSS: – our pockets a-chink with ill-gotten gains and our guts a-sweetly-gurgle with champagne . . . *(Hiccups.)* Out of the front door of Pantaloon's mansion comes two women . . .

(Two sets of footsteps approach; rustle of dresses; one woman breathing heavily.)

PUSS: . . . an old woman . . .

HAG: *(In street.)* . . . filthy cold, this morning; filthy fog; black as a bucket this morning, too – filthy, filthy . . .

HERO: *(Narrating.)* . . . the other a tall, slender figure, like a stem of narcissus, but all wrapped up in black . . .

PUSS: *(Narrating.)* . . . she making a graceful and stately progress, though all muffled up in crepe like a mourning doorknocker. And I, having had, I must admit, a couple . . .

HEROINE: *(In street.)* Oh, Puss! Good morning!

PUSS: *(Narrating.)* . . . thinks I'll exercise myself with a game of tag with the dangling fringe of her shawl . . .

HEROINE: Does Pussy want to play?

HAG: Filthy cat! I can't abide – atishoo – get away, you filthy cat! Atishoo! *(She sneezes and continues to sneeze.)*

HEROINE: Take no notice of my governess, Puss. Her nostrils tickle at the flick of a whisker. But as for myself, I'm very fond of cats . . . do you know my Tabs? My stripey Tabs? H'm? Oh my, what a handsome cat you are . . . and so very, very friendly . . .

(Purr.)

Does he like his ears tickled? Just here – is that the ecstatic spot?

(Purr.)

PUSS: *(Narrating.)* . . . And then I couldn't help myself . . .

HEROINE: What a somersault! A double somersault! Well! But – whatever have you got on your hind feet . . .

PUSS: *(Narrating.)* And so she drew her veil aside to see.

HEROINE: Puss in boots!

(Laughter.)

HERO: *(Narrating.)* When she drew back her veil, suddenly, it was May morning –

(Electronic birdsong; few notes on a harp.)

HAG: ATISHOO!

(That puts a stop to the harp and birdsong.)

Drat the nasty beast! Put it down, you don't know where it's been . . .

and down with your veil this instant, don't want any of the rag-tag and bobtail to see you! Quit dawdling – come along!

HEROINE: Don't pull so – oh! you're bruising my arm!

(Rustle of departing dresses; a chill wind rises and blows them away.)

PUSS: *(Shivering.)* Brrr . . . nasty nip in the air all of a sudden.

HERO: How cold it is. And dark. Now that she's gone. She has taken all the promise of spring with her.

(Fade background. Brief pause.)

PUSS: And so my master fell in love.

HERO: Head over heels!

PUSS: Positively the double, nay, possibly even the triple somersault of the heart, eh?

HERO: Without a safety net.

PUSS: Without a partner! She doesn't even know your name.

HERO: She is a princess imprisoned in a tower, remote and shining as Aldebaran, chained to a dolt, guarded by dragons . . .

PUSS: By one dragon. Or, rather, a dragoness.

(Room acoustic. Distant square.)

HERO: *(Moving slightly off to window across bare boards.)* When I sit here, at the window of my room, I can see her house across the square, the locks, the bolts, the barred windows . . . I sit, and sit, and gaze, and gaze . . . oh, the sweet tyranny of love . . . until that moment, once a day, when I can make out her vague shape, like the moon behind clouds –

PUSS: *(Aside.)* Hark at him, babbling on about the tender passions! Has he come to this, he the witty and ingenious lecher who went through all the novices in the *entire convent*, Puss passing in and out the cloister with notes, roses, boxes of chocolates etc. etc. etc. until my very whiskers smelled of incense. Is he reduced to impotent yearning, the notorious rake who had the Mayor's wife under the table at the conclusion of the Mayor's banquet while they served the madeira? This –

HERO: *(Slightly off.)* Cynic.

PUSS: You only want her because you can't have her, you spoiled brat.

The poor girl might just as well live in a bank vault as in the finest mansion in Bergamo, and you don't know the combination to her safe.

And, speaking of money, sir, you should know that we're running a mite short on funds . . . temporary cash-flow problem, sir, which would easily and speedily be resolved by a visit to the gaming tables –

HERO: *(Slightly off.)* No, Puss; not today . . . it's nearly half past four. She'll open her windows presently . . . and perhaps today the Hag will accidentally agitate the curtain as she picks at a pimple, she may even dislodge the curtains sufficiently to let me see the lady's hands, her hands, all that can be seen of her, white hands, like lilac on a coffin . . .

PUSS: *(Aside.)* . . . enough to make you queasy . . .

HERO: And then, an early night; tomorrow, up bright and early – to Mass! Thank God for Sunday!

PUSS: For, would you believe it, the reprobate has now taken to attending church regular as prunes.

HERO: Perhaps, tomorrow, if we sit in the pew behind her, I shall manage, when we kneel, to touch the hem of her dress . . .

(Organ music cuts distant square background. Church acoustic. Rustling; sneeze.)

HAG: *(Angry whisper.)* I could swear there was a cat about; I – atishoo!

HEROINE: Hush, governess, control yourself . . . whoever would bring a cat to church?

HAG: Atishoo!

(Crossfade organ music to congregation leaving church.)

HERO: Look!

PUSS: A glove.

HERO: Hers. She left it lying on the pew.

PUSS: How do you know it's her glove and not the hag's glove?

HERO: Because it's so little, such tiny hands but – see! Long fingers; and it smells sweet . . . her perfume . . . exquisite, scented hands, hands to caress a man, to console . . .

(Fade background behind following:)

PUSS: *(Narrating.)* And all day long he babbled these and similar maudlin sentiments sufficient, as they say, to make a cat laugh, and soon our common purse is flat as a pancake for this new-found unrequited passion of his had suddenly afflicted him with scruples.

(HERO's room.)

HERO: I'll never load the dice nor palm a card again. I'll keep my hands from picking and stealing. She, she'd never look at a cheat, or a thief . . .

PUSS: *(Narrating.)* So my master is in a fair way to ruin us both by neglecting his business due to the unsatisfied ravages that LOVE is making upon his constitution.

Now, since my observation of the human species has led me to opine that love is nothing but desire sustained by unfulfilment, I therefore conclude that . . . if I can by guile and cunning . . . effect a physical consummation of this young man's debilitating passion, he'll forthwith be right as rain in two shakes and next day tricks as usual. And Puss and his Man soon solvent once again.

Which, at the moment, very much not, sir.

(Pause.)

Now, this Tabs to whom the young lady had referred, turns out to be the house mouser her miserable husband employs, a sleek, spry, short-haired domestic tabby of the feminine gender . . .

(Fade in Rossini's Cat Duet – the duet of the two cats singing together; fade slowly, leaving behind heavy, contented breathing. Close acoustic.)

TABS: Well! You are a one and no mistake!

What a hearty greeting from a new-found friend! I tell you straight, the young missus could do with a bit of what you've just given me. Oh, yes, that'd put the roses back in her cheeks, all right.

Poor, lonely lady, as she is, tied for life to that gore-bellied old dodderer, lean and slippered, eyes like a boiled cod only not half so appetising, with his pot leg and his nose going drip-drip-drip like a faulty tap and the hands of his clock always at half past six d'you get my meaning I see you get my meaning and parsimonious! You wouldn't believe. My dear, does he budget for so much as a scrap of anchovy for yours truly! Does he 'ell! Keeps me on short commons for the sake of the mousing, grasping old skinflint as he is.

PUSS: Ma pauvre chérie . . .

TABS: If it wasn't for the young lady, bless her heart, slipping into the kitchen to smuggle me the odd chicken wing, knuckle of mutton, backbone of haddock, I'd be the skinniest tabs in all Bergamo –

PUSS: – instead of the glossiest, plumpest, brightest-eyed little –

TABS: *(Pleased, all the same.)* Go on! I've met your sort. Where was I . . . She's a lovely lady, the missus, lovely; but ooh! that governess of hers!

PUSS: The governess, the hag, the dragoness.

TABS: Apart from her generally unattractive personality and repulsive appearance, she and I never hit it off, not really. See, soon as ever she sniffs so much as a whiff of me, she's off – atishoo! atishoo! Veritable paroxysms.

'Course, I used to love to lie in wait for her behind the parlour door, or curled up on her pillow, if I got the chance, just to tease the old girl, but then she started up such a clamour about her allergies, and the torments I caused her, got to get rid of the cat, she said . . . talked about popping me in a sack and taking me to the river, murderous old cow.

PUSS: She never did!

TABS: She did so. But the young lady put her foot down, told the hag if she didn't give over she'd tell the old one how the hag scrapes the whitewash off the privy wall and uses it to powder her horrible old face with – they're two of a kind, the pantaloon and the hag, mean as hell, he'd have had her out on her arse for chronic thievery for that! Before you could say Jack Robinson.

So then the hag piped down.

Oh, that young lady! She saved my life. But apart from that, many's the time we sneak a game of hunt-the-cotton-reel and jump-on-the-handkerchief together, when we get the chance . . . when she is with me, the hag leaves her alone.

Yes, I would say we are the only ray of sunshine in one another's lives.

Until you popped up out of the coal hole like a good deed in a naughty world, Mr Marmalade!

(Purring.)

PUSS: What say . . . we hatch a plot . . . to antler the old one, darling Tabs?

TABS: You're on! Now you're talking! Do you know, would you believe, that I never, ever heard her bedsprings rattle, not since the poor thing's wedding day . . . not so much as a single twang . . . To him, she is no more than his most prized possession, and a bargain, too, got her cheap off her father due to a mortgage falling in.

But antlering is easier said than done, my old cock, me ginger-winger, me Tim-Tam-Tom. All day and every day, he sits in his counting-house counting out his money and doesn't budge an inch from his securities . . . and he keeps his what you might call *tabs* on her even when she's with me, would you believe he keeps a string tied all the time from his great toe to the lady's ankle so she can't move an inch without him knowing?

(Fade in counting-house.)

PANTALEONE: . . . just check up on the girl . . .

HEROINE: *(Off.)* Oh!

(Back to close acoustic.)

PUSS: He sits in his counting-house all day and every day?

TABS: I tell a lie! Silly old me – Wednesdays! Of course – he clears out just the one day a week. Wednesdays. Then he forsakes his wife and coffers to ride out into the country and extort grasping rents from starving tenants, since he won't trust a bailiff to do the job for him.

But that one day a week he shoots so many bolts on her –

(Shooting bolts.)

and bars so many bars –

(Clanging.)

and chains up the doors he's locked and barred –

(Fugue of locking up noises; **PANTALEONE** *tittering.)*

that the house becomes a veritable impregnable fortress.

(One final bar clangs.)

PUSS: Not to be taken by force, that's for certain! But, perhaps, by guile and stealth, the well-known specialities of the feline kind.

TABS: Even so, inside this maximum security prison, there's the dreadful guardian of the angel . . .

HAG: *(Shattering sneeze.)*

PUSS: The hag. Who is impervious to our furry charms, Tabs.

(Room acoustic.)

HAG: You get out from under my feet, you pestilential feline, or I'll have your horrible striped hide for dusters –

(Blows; squawking of cat; scurrying of paws. Back to close acoustic.)

PUSS: Problems, problems, problems . . . yet, dear Tabs, see how my ingenuity rises to this challenge even here in the coal hole, see how my ingenuity rises to this challenge!

TABS: And not only your ingenuity.

(Purring.)

PUSS: My dearest Tabs . . . do you think . . . if I procured a letter to your mistress from my handsome and charming young master . . . you could . . . slip it to her?

TABS: Watch your language! *(Giggles.)*

PUSS: . . . drat these boots . . .

(Fade rustling, clink of coals, purring.
Fade in HERO's *room, scratching of pen-nib.)*

HERO: 'Since mine eyes were first dazzled by your beauty, as by the rays of the sun, dear lady . . . ' Oh, God!

PUSS: That's not the high road to the rumpling of the bedcovers, sir! She's got one ninny between them already; do you think she wants another?

HERO: When I want your advice, Puss, I shall ask for it.

(Rustle of paper; scribble, scribble, scribble. PUSS *jumps up.)*

Puss – what are you doing on my knee? You're covered in coal dust, too – get down at once! Get down – you're covered in coal dust and you're jogging my arm, you'll make me blot the paper – there! Now look what you've done . . .

PUSS: *(Aside.)* And never did a missive more deserve to be blotted! Poetry. He's descended to *poetry*! Must the prime symptom of love be always softening of the brain! *(To* HERO.*)* I declare, look what you've written: 'Shall I compare thee to a summer's day . . .'
What? Tell her she resembles a wet Bank Holiday? Do you think that will endear yourself to her? No, no, no, no, no! Where's the true voice of feeling, man – speak from the heart! Tell her all about yourself –

HERO: But – Puss, I'm . . . little better than a petty criminal, Puss. A lecher. A –

PUSS: All good women have a missionary streak, sir. Persuade her she's your salvation and she's yours.

(Pause.)

HERO: My past . . . my wicked, wicked life . . .

PUSS: Be fair, sir, 'wicked' is laying it on a bit thick, sir.

HERO: But, if I could win the love of a good woman, the healing, purifying love of a good woman . . .

(Scribble; scribbling fades during following speech:)

'. . . a cashiered officer, a card-sharp, a profligate, a wastrel, a cruel, heartless seducer and, if I never stooped to theft, myself, then I was quite content to let my valet do the thieving for me . . .'

(Crossfade to HEROINE's *room.)*

HEROINE: '. . . but then I saw your face, just for a single moment in the square, and for the first time I knew there was such a thing as forgiveness.

'Your eyes, like holy candles, your mouth as if its shape was formed by prayer . . . and now, can you credit it, I haunt the church and not the brothel. I pass by on the other side of the street from the taverns and the gambling halls. My life has narrowed down to those few sacred hours a week when I can see the veiled angel who will lead me to grace and bliss.'

Well!

Oh, my dear Tabs! I never meant to wreak such havoc with a heart when I first smiled to see a booted cat!

(Sympathetic mew; rustle of letter.)

I'll kiss your signature, you poor soul . . . Lelio . . . can his name truly be Lelio? Fate! Fate! And store your letter . . . here . . . in my bodice; yes, where the hag can't find it . . . next to my heart . . .

(Rustle.)

Oh, the dear, good soul that wrote me such a letter! I am too much in love with virtue to withstand you . . . providing, of course, he's not as ugly as sin or as old as the hills, eh, Tabs, dear?

(They laugh.

Clean in HERO's *room.*)

PUSS: The lady's tabby confidante entrusted me with this.

HERO: Let's have it —

(*Rips open envelope.*)

'... never would have believed ... moved me to the heart...'

HEROINE: (*On slight echo.*) '... yet how can I usefully discuss your passion further without a good look at your person?'

(*Letter clasped.*)

HERO: I'll serenade her this very evening! Puss, off you go and pawn my sword!

PUSS: Pawn your sword? (*Aside.*) What does he want to pawn his sword for? what fresh madness is this ... I knew it! I suspected it! he's going to dress up in costume! Oh, the embarrassment! Oh, unbearable! (*Narrating.*) For would you credit it, the poor, lovesick buffoon went and bought the white, baggy rags off the back of one of the mountebanks that strut and primp in the square ... the zany, moonstruck loon, he thought he'd score a bullseye if he played Pierrot ...

(*Fade in, slowly, during ensuing speech, sounds of a street market.*)

So, when she came out to take her nightly airing at just the hour, the very hour, when they take down the market stalls ...

(*Street market; plus clatter of dismantling; bang, crash, donkeys braying, horses whinnying, wheels on cobbles; fade down sufficient for speech to be heard.*)

... out we set across the square.

HERO: There she is! Do you see her! She looks as if she were dreaming, dreaming of me, perhaps ... what is she looking at? I can't see – I can just see her eyes above her veil but —

PUSS: She's looking at the sickle moon over Bergamo. Strike up.

(*Guitar introduction; bring up street noises; guitar is lost among them. Stops.*)

She didn't hear a note. Try again.

(*Guitar introduction, again.*)

HERO: (*Sings first phrase of song.*)

(*Fade up street noises. Song stops.*)

PUSS: Not heard a word, nor turned her head, never caught hair nor hide of you. She's lost, quite lost, in her own sweet thoughts. You might as well have stayed at home and saved your money. Our money.

HERO: Up you go – tell her I'm here.

PUSS: WHAT?

HERO: Up to her window. 'Rococo's a piece of cake,' you said.

PUSS: That ain't rococo, that's Palladian!

TABS: *(Calling.)* Mr Marmalade! Ginger-winger! Here I am! Up on the gutter! Go on, you can do it! See that bloody great caryatid by the door jamb? Just swarm up her loincloth and take it from there!

PUSS: *(Narrating.)* . . . and since my girl was watching me . . .

(Fade street noises to background and bring up heavy, effortful breathing and scrape of climbing equipment on stone.)

(Effort.) . . . from loincloth up . . . to these massy pects . . . but, oh! that Doric column this caryatid upholds . . . never a handhold nor a foothold on a Doric column, dammit . . .

TABS: *(Slightly off.)* What about a flying leap? Are you an acrobat or are you not! Take a flying leap, like Harlequin on wires! Flex your muscles, tense your thighs, and *spring*! You can make it if you really try, I know you can!

PUSS: Right. For my Tabs I'll do it. Very well.
(Narrating.) . . . and, with one magnificent upward bound . . .

(Whizz of rocket going off.)

TABS: Hooray!

PUSS: *(Narrating.)* . . . I landed on the window-sill.

(Click of bootheels, landing.)

HEROINE: Dear God. What an apparition.

PUSS: Where's the hag?

HEROINE: Sped to the privy, seized with a flux, something she ate . . .

PUSS: What luck.

TABS: *(Sotto voce.)* Luck had nothing to do with it.

PUSS: Quick as you can, cast your eye directly into the square below, ma'am. Him you wot of lurks there in the big hat, in white, ready to sing you an evening ditty –

(Door opens off; sneeze.)

HAG: *(Off.)* What's going on – THAT CAT!

HEROINE: Scram Puss!

PUSS: Discretion is the better part –
Whee!

(Reversed sound of rocket going off.)

(Narrating.) Straight out of the window I jumped.

TABS: I don't believe it. It ain't true. My eyes deceive me. No – he's doing it! he's really doing it! He's DONE IT! THE TRIPLE SOMERSAULT!

(The reversed rocket sound makes three loops, simulating three somersaults – this during TABS's speech.)

Hurrah! Hurrah! Hurrah! What a cat! What a marmalade marvel! Splendissimo!

PUSS: *(Narrating.)* The triple accident, performed during that three-storey drop to the ground – performed, I'm forced to admit, in a not entirely voluntary manner, but not a word to Tabs, the triple somersault left me exhilarated, if breathless.

But did my master so much as witness my triumph, let alone congratulate?

Did he, be blowed.

(Bring up street background.)

HERO: And now I see her eyes turned towards me, how they shine . . .

(Take street noises down as the guitar introduction is played; HERO's song – something suitable (tenor) – perhaps something by Benjamin Britten accompanied by Julian Bream. Pause when the song is over; then murmurs of appreciation, patter of applause.)

HEROINE: *(Off.)* My dear . . .

HAG: *(Off.)* Back in your box!

(Slam – shutters or windows, it doesn't matter; but the slam does: Bang! Pause.

Fade in HERO's *room. Mealtime chink of china.)*

HERO: Bread and cheese? Is there nothing in the house to eat but bread and cheese?

PUSS: Poor pickings, today, sir, but it's weeks since you showed any appetite and I thought –

HERO: Did you hear how she called, 'my dear'? Is there any more of this ... excellent ... gorgonzola? *(Chewing.)* I need to keep ... my strength up, now!

PUSS: *(Huff.)* If you want any more gorgonzola, you can go and pinch it yourself. You know where the grocer's is.

HERO: *(Conciliatory.)* Puss ...

PUSS: Oh, don't mind me, sir. You just get on with your supper, sir. But don't you believe that tonight's successful serenade marks more than Phase One of the strategy of the siege of Casa Pantaleone!

In fact, if you can do without me for half an hour, sir, I think I'll just slip across the square for a tactical conference in the coal hole with my little fifth columnist ...

(Fade.
Clean in close acoustic.)

TABS: Rats!

PUSS: Rats?

TABS: If there's one thing the hag hates more than cats, it's rats. Allergic to cats she may be but with rats she's plain hysterical.

(Fade in, briefly, hag screaming, whimpering, gibbering, on echo.)

Now, my love, if I was to go, we was to go out hunting together and gather up an enormous number of rats, some killed dead, but some we had merely crippled, so they could still scamper, if slowly, and were we to strew some of these rats around the house but assemble still more of them in, under and around the missus' own bed, one Wednesday morning, after the old fool's gone off about his business, and if you and your young man was to ...

(Fade.
Clean in HERO's *room.)*

PUSS: Item one: one houseful of rats;
Item two: one hag in terror of same;

Item three: one young lady confined to her bed for fear of rats;

Item four: one lusty young rat-catcher, to whit, you, sir, in thick disguise, perhaps equipped with a luxuriant and aggressive false moustache so that the hag won't recognise you from church, this rat-catcher plus his intrepid assistant; plying for hire in the square tomorrow morning at just the psychologically precise moment as item two issues from the front door of item one howling, screeching and ululating . . .

(Terrible screams.)

HAG: Help! Assistance! Help!

(Bring in square background behind screams.)

HERO: What seems to be the trouble, my good lady?

HAG: Rattus domesticus dead in bed and worse! Ho, horrors, horrors, horrors! Rats everywhere – black rats, brown rats, little rats, big rats! *(Screams.)*

HERO: Allow me to introduce myself; I am nobody but Il Signor Furioso, professionally known as 'The Living Death of Rats', the sworn enemy of vermin, dedicated to stamping out all the genus of the rattus and the mus variety . . . *(Sotto voce.)* Have I got the patter right, Puss?

PUSS: *(Sotto voce.)* Spot on.

HERO: Lead us directly to the site of the infestation.

HAG: *(Screams. Then sneezes.)* Can't you leave that cat behind?

HERO: What? Venture on an invasion without my assistant, my partner, my pal, my very own ambulant rat trap, my sworn lieutenant in the fight against rattus domesticus, rattus rattus, and last but not least tiny wee mus musculus –

HAG: Oh, stop it! stop it! Just to hear you name the beasts sets me all of a shake – come quick!

(Speeded up footsteps; on flagstones of hall; lose street background; feet stop.)

HERO: *(Sotto voce.)* I say, Puss, haven't you overdone it a bit? The house is like a museum of rats . . .

(Faint squeaking; footsteps up stairs.)

PUSS: Trust your faithful servant, sir . . .

HEROINE: *(Off – calls.)* Have you found a rat-catcher? I daren't get out of bed in case I tread on one of the beasts –

(Bedroom door opens; squeaks! Over to HEROINE's *bedroom.)*

PUSS: *(Aside.)* Rats a-plenty, all alive oh; and there she is, the beauty, up on the bed with the covers up to her chin, and everywhere you look a heaving sea, rattus, rattus, rattus –

(Squeaks; screams; sneezes.)

HAG: Curse the rats! Drat the cat!

PUSS: . . . although, of course, none of the ratti in the best of health, more the atmosphere of a rat casualty ward, in here, than a rat holiday camp . . .

HERO: Good morning, signora! In a moment, all your prayers will be answered. Allow me to introduce myself, Il Signor Furioso and his toothed, clawed, vermin exterminator.

HEROINE: Haven't we met somewhere before, Puss?

HERO: See! Over there, Puss! that big, black beast! Pounce, Puss, pounce!

(Terrified squeak; tearing, rending, gobbling.)

HEROINE: Oh, Signor Furioso, what are you doing under the bed?

HERO: *(Muffled.)* Just . . . taking a look . . . I knew it! Here, in the wainscotting, the biggest hole I ever saw . . . and a detachment, a battalion, an army of the biggest, blackest rats you ever did see lining up behind it ready to storm through!

HAG: *(Shrieks. Then sneezes.)* I'll expire directly!

HEROINE: You go and recover yourself in the kitchen over an infusion of friar's balsam – don't come back until it's over.

PUSS: *(Narrating.)* I can tell the hag is torn between the extreme terror and discomfort of her present situation and loyalty to her employer etc. etc. etc. What? Leave the young lady alone? With her legs unshackled? In a bedroom? With a man? So the hag dithers and shilly shallies until I lob her a little brown mouse, still twitching, with a quick flick of the left paw, it strikes her straight on the chin –

HAG: *(Screams.)*

(Feet run; door slams.)

HEROINE: Just . . . lock the door . . .

(Key turns; squeaks die down.
Fade in, very softly, reprise of HERO's *serenade.)*

HERO: I hardly dare . . . to take your hand . . .

HEROINE: Then I . . . must take yours.

HERO: My darling!

HEROINE: My dearest . . .

HERO: As if we were made for one another . . .

PUSS: *(Sotto voce.)* Come off it, sir; do you think she thinks you've staged this grand charade solely in order to kiss her hand.
　　And get that false moustache off, pronto, love may not consort with the ludicrous . . .

HEROINE: Perhaps . . . we might remove the hairy evidence of Signor Furioso from your upper lip?

HERO: Oh . . . the false moustache . . . there. Is that better?

HEROINE: All the better to kiss me with.

HERO: Too much . . .

PUSS: *(Sotto voce.)* Get a move on, you two! Full speed ahead! Do you want the hag to catch you in flagrante?

HEROINE: Don't you think we'd be more comfortable . . . prone?

HERO: My dearest –
　　Puss! Puss! Mimic the murder of rats immediately! Mask the music of Venus with the clamour of Diana!

PUSS: Tantivvy!

(Squeaks; bedsprings; hunting horns; male voice choir sings 'A-Hunting We Will Go!'; male and female sighing; battering on door.)

HAG: *(Off.)* I say, I say, I say! What's going on? Whyfor the racket?

PUSS: *(Over.)* But did they answer? Did they, like hell.

(Slowly fade effects and mix with gratified laughter of the lovers; bang, bang, bang on door; unlocking.)

HEROINE: See what a victory there's been! The rats are all dead, every one! Oh, Signor Furioso, how can I ever thank you enough? and as for you, you valiant Puss –

HAG: Atishoo! What's all this mess, what's been going on, why are the bedclothes in such a tangle, and the sheet's been ripped . . .

HEROINE: Such deeds as took place on that bed, governess! If the mattress could only speak, it would provide such credentials to the courage and capacity of Signor Furioso . . . and, Signor, how much do we owe you for your singular services?

HERO: Owe me? Why, not a –

PUSS: (*Prompt.*) One hundred ducats. (*Sotto voce.*) What, do it for nothing, would you, you honourable idiot?

HEROINE: Only one hundred ducats?

HAG: That's the entire household expenses for a month!

HEROINE: And worth every penny! Wouldn't the rats have eaten us out of house and home, by then? Go on, go and fetch the money, no need to mention it to my husband; you can easily spare a hundred ducats out of the cash you skim off the housekeeping, hag.
    Can't she, Puss?

(*Purr.*)

HAG: What's this? Atishoo! Get this horrid thing off me, go away –

HEROINE: A hundred ducats. Fetch. Or else the cat will cling on to you like a burr, like a tick, like a succubus –

(*Sneezes diminish as if the babbling hag is running down a corridor; soft laughter and much purring; fade.*)

PUSS: (*Narrating.*) So that night we sat down to a supper for which, for the first time in some months, mere circumstances had not dictated the menu but all honestly bought from the shops . . .

(*Fade in* HERO's *room. Clink of cutlery and china.*)

Eat up, sir. Such a nice escalope de veau and you ain't touched it! Nor the mushrooms, neither, not that I fancy fungi myself, but you've always hitherto relished a –

(*Knife and fork flung aside.*)

Can't fancy it? But you ate like a horse after she smiled at you –

(Aside.) now he picks like a bird after he – I don't understand the human heart, and that's the truth.

HERO: *(Laughs. This has nothing to do with* PUSS; *he is quite preoccupied.)*

PUSS: What's the joke? Share it with Puss.

HERO: *(Weeps.)*

PUSS: *(Aside.)* And now he's burst out crying . . . what's got into him? Is he sickening for something? Could he have picked a germ up from the rats?

Still no point in wasting that bit of veal . . .

HERO: I must and will have her for ever!

PUSS: *(Chokes on mouthful. Aside.)* That fairly put me off my supper, too. I see how satisfaction has not satisfied him. I therefore push my plate aside and fall to grooming myself meditatively. *(Licking.)* Unusually grimy about the shirt-front . . . hmm . . . strong flavour of coal dust about my person . . .

HERO: How can I live without her?

PUSS: *(In the midst of washing himself.)* You've done so . . . for twenty-five years, sir . . . and never missed her for a moment . . .

HERO: I'm burning with the fever of love!

PUSS: Then we're spared the expense of fires.

HERO: I shall snatch her away from her husband and we'll live together, always!

PUSS: What do you propose to live on?

HERO: *(Distracted.)* Kisses . . . embraces . . .

PUSS: Well, you won't grow fat on *that*, sir, though *she* will, and then there'll be more mouths to feed.

HERO: *(Turning on him.)* I'm sick and tired of your foul-mouthed barbs, Puss!

PUSS: *(Huff.)* Sorry. Sorry I spoke, sir. Pardon me for breathing, sir. My apologies for living, sir. Huh. That's gratitude for you. Pshaw!

(Jumps to floor with a thump; imperious mewing.)

Let me out! Open that door!

(Door opens smartly.)

HERO: Good riddance!

(*Door slam. Cut to close acoustic of coal hole.*)

TABS: Had your supper, have you?

PUSS: . . . the merest snack . . .

TABS: Because I've saved you this pig's trotter the missus smuggled me. 'For services rendered,' she said, and tipped me such a wink.

PUSS: I think I could manage a pig's trotter. (*Chewing.*)

TABS: And she was in ever such a funny mood. First she laughed like a mad thing and then all at once she's April, with the showers – how she cried!

   'How can I live without him?' she demands, but does not wait for an answer. 'I must and will have him for ever,' she declares. And the next breath vows she'll leave her husband. Did you ever hear such things?

PUSS: (*Swallows last mouthful.*) I heard them just this minute, Tabs. It's plain enough these two speak with one voice the plain, clear, foolish rhetoric of love.

TABS: (*Sentimental sigh.*)

PUSS: Yes.

(*Pause.*)

TABS: But only *we* are smart enough to bring them together! Scheme, Mr Marmalade, scheme!

PUSS: Tabs, my dearest . . . slowly recapitulate for me the daily motions of Signor Pantaleone, alias old Pantaloon, when he's at home.

(*Fade in church bell ringing four as* TABS *speaks.*)

TABS: (*Narrating.*) They set the clock of the duomo by him, so rigid and regular is he in his habits. Up at the crack –

(*Cock-crow;* PANTALEONE *makes waking-up grunts.*)

   He makes a meagre breakfast off yesterday's crusts . . .

(*Gnawing at stale bread.*)

PANTALEONE: (*In room acoustic.*) Bread's tough, this morning . . .

TABS: . . . which he dips to soften 'em in a cup of cold water –

(Water poured out.)

that he drinks cold, to spare the expense of a fire. Then, bright and early, down to the counting-house –

PANTALEONE: Good morrow to my gold!

TABS: – counting out the money –

(Chink, chink, chink; PANTALEONE *giggles and babbles with glee.)*

until a well-earned bowl of water gruel, that is, water extravagantly *boiled,* served hot –

PANTALEONE: *(Smacks lips.)* That's the stuff!

TABS: – at midday. His afternoons he devotes to usury, bankrupting here –

SMALL TRADESMAN: I'm ruined. You devil!

TABS: – a small businessman; there, a weeping widow.

WIDOW: My starving children! My roofless orphans!

TABS: All this he does for fun and profit, both. Which puts him in the mood for a luxurious dinner prompt at four – more piping hot water, with perhaps a bit of rancid beef in it, or a rubber hen, or some such, he's got an arrangement with the butcher –

PANTALEONE: Tee hee! my old bird for his old bird; take his unsold stock off his hands, fair exchange, on Friday nights he gets the use of the hag . . .

(Affronted noise from hag.)

TABS: From four-thirty to five-thirty, while he airs his young wife at the window –

PANTALEONE: – giving the occasional twitch to my big toe to make sure she's safe and sound the while –

HEROINE: *(Off.)* Oh!

TABS: – he himself adjourns to his strong-room, to check out his chests of gems, his bales of silk, the Persian carpets he keeps well rolled up and out of sight, since, like the missus, they are too beautiful to waste on the eyes of the *hoi polloi.*

*(*PANTALEONE *exclaiming over his treasures. Chinks, rustles, etc.)*

Then – it's early to bed! So as to waste no candles. And sinless slumber in the prospect of another happy today tomorrow.

(PANTALEONE *gives one snore. Fade.*
Back to close acoustic.)

That is his life.

PUSS: Just how rich is he?

TABS: Croesus.

PUSS: Sufficient to support two loving couples?

TABS: Sumptuous.

PUSS: My sweet, pretty, clever one, my soubrette in stripes, Susanna to my Figaro and Columbine to my Harlequin . . . ma chère . . . chérie . . . what if, early some uncandled morning, as the old man, bleary with sleep, descends the staircase blind to all but the peckish anticipation of his bread and water . . . what if, what if then he were to place his foot on the subfusc yet volatile fur of a shadow-camouflaged young tabby cat?

TABS: And topple, topple, topple . . . ? You read my mind, my love.

(*Fade.*
Fade in HERO'S *room.*)

PUSS: Now, sir, you must raid the hagoness's store of ducats and set yourself up in all the gear of a medical man, for we're going to be disciples of Hippocrates.

HERO: What are you up to now?

PUSS: Do as I say and never mind the reasons. Off you go and fully equip yourself. A black bag, a skull cap – and another dose of facial hair, yes; a grey beard, this time. That'll inspire confidence!
      Besides, some sugar pills and bottles of coloured water and jars of goose-grease . . .

HERO: When you've finished with your shopping list –

PUSS: Tomorrow morning, disguised as a doctor, you must stand up proudly in the square for hire, and I, masquerading as your nurse, shall carry the sign. 'Il famoso dottore, aches cured, pains prevented, lovers united, etc. etc. etc.'

HERO: Is she going to play the invalid? Is that the plot? So I can get into her room again? I'll take her in my arms and – jump out of the window with her, we shall perform the triple somersault of love even if we don't outlive it, I –

PUSS: Now, now, now, now, now! Don't let it go to your head, sir. Just leave well alone and do what I say and things will turn out handy dandy, sir. Haven't they up till now?

HERO: *(Grudging.)* I suppose so. May I presume to ask you exactly when we're to have our game of doctors and nurses?

(Church bell rings four times; wind blows through square.)

(Shivers.) ... Another raw, misty, bleak, angular, comfortless morning, the darkness before dawn ... but so dark you think the dawn will never come. And surely this winter has lasted all my life? So cold, here, out in the square, Puss ...

PUSS: Nobody about, yet ... what's that?

(Cough.)

HERO: A client! We didn't prepare for unexpected clients!

PUSS: Let me handle this. No point in passing up a bob or two, is there.

(Cough.)

COUGHER: Got anything for a hacking cough?

PUSS: Rub this on your chest, mate. Ten ducats.

(Tin unscrewed.)

COUGHER: Coo! what a pong! What the 'ell is this? Gone off, 'as it? Ten ducats for this?

PUSS: Oh, no, no, no, my good man! It ain't never gone off! The miraculous substance in this little tin is a triple distilled ointment prepared from the highly refined, ah, lard, of the left thigh of the, ah, exceedingly rare, prophylactically valuable, newly discovered American *armadillo* –

COUGHER: Armadillos? What's armadillos got to do with a hacking cough? And what's more, I don't like the look of your whiskers. Nor, so help me God, of that long red *tail* of yours. I think you've got charlatan written all over you. Take back your lousy unguent!

HERO: Come, come, my good fellow; my assistant, trained in Bologna –

COUGHER: Crooks!

(Door flies open; weeping.)

HAG: *(Off.)* Is there a doctor in the house! Doctor! Oh, doctor, come at once! Our good man's taken a sorry tumble!

(Hag weeps ostentatiously; speeded-up footsteps on to flagstones; lose square background.)

HERO: Where's the patient?

HAG: At the stairfoot.

PUSS: Ah!

HEROINE: Are you the doctor? My husband – a fall –

HERO: Puss, my bag . . .

HEROINE: Puss? You again? Oh –

(Stifles a giggle.)

HERO: Where's my little mirror . . . just hold it to his lips . . .

HAG: Dead, is he? Broke his neck, did he? Where's the keys to the counting-house –

HEROINE: Surely I detect the faintest misting of the glass? Enough to give hope? Oh, doctor, we must carry him up to bed and make him comfortable . . .

HERO: Hup!

(Heaves up a dead weight.)

PUSS: *(Narrating.)* The master, nothing loath, pops Pantaloon over his shoulder in a fireman's lift and the entire party repair to the bedroom in two shakes of a bee's wagger, the young lady pretty as a picture in her morning negligée and keeping, I notice, a weather eye open on the activities of the hag, who's blubbering like a stuck pig to conceal the way she's hovering round the defunct miser and making little darting sallies at his pockets with her thieving hands –

(Clean in bedroom.)

HEROINE: She's after the keys to the counting-house. Take that!

(Slap.)

HAG: Ouch!

HERO: There . . .

(Flop of body on bed.)

Hmm . . . no heartbeat that I can hear . . . and when I tap his knee with my little hammer –

(Tap.)

– no reflex. I hold his wrist and feel no pulse. And when I slip my hand into his wife's bodice –

HEROINE: *(Sighs.)*

HERO: – not the flicker of an eyelid. Dead as a doornail. It's not a doctor you want for this one, madame; it's an undertaker.

HEROINE: Off you go and fetch one, hag. This minute!

HAG: Let's just see how much he's worth, first – go on. Just give me the keys to the counting-house –

HEROINE: I forethoughtfully removed them from his belt while you went to find a doctor, hag.

(Jangle of flourished keys.)

See! We'll check out the counting-house the minute the cover's nailed down on him!

HAG: The minute?

HEROINE: The instant. Undertaker first. *Then* counting-house.

HAG: *(Sneezes.)* Blasted cat back again . . . undertaker, first. Then counting-house. All right. Very well. Undertaker first . . .

(Scuttles off; door slam.)

HEROINE: Darling!

HERO: Dearest!

HEROINE: Get that . . . false beard off . . .

(Embrace.)

The bed –

HEROINE: Occupied.

HERO: The floor –

(They fall down.)

PUSS: *(Discreet cough.)* If a veil were to hand, I would now draw it to conceal the embraces of these two young lovers; but, as it is, I must ask you to exercise the same discretion as Puss himself, who now opened the shutters –

(Shutters open.)

and unbarred the windows –

(Unbarring.)

– and slipped out on to the balcony to observe the rosy fingers of the dawn, for, during the time we had been busy with Signor Pantaleone, those fingers had painted the sky with a veritable herbaceous border.

(Dawn chorus.)

A lovely morning, full of the joyous beginnings of spring; the voice of the turtles . . .

TABS: What'cher, Ginger! Hark at the birdies! Delicious!

PUSS: I do believe at last that winter is over and gone.
Can't you smell a *green* smell, a fragrance of burgeoning things, of quickening –

TABS: 'Burgeoning' and 'quickening' is right, Ginge. For, oh, my love! I do have the most momentous secret to whisper in your ear –

PUSS: A secret?

TABS: Bend down . . .

(Whispers.)

PUSS: Really and truly?

TABS: No more than nature's way. But now your rambling days are over, lad. No more nights on the tiles for you –

PUSS: – no moonlight serenades –

TABS: – sing lullabies, instead. And, henceforward, we two shall sit one on each side of the parlour mantelpiece, as if we were cats made out of china, the household ornaments, Mr and Mrs Marmalade . . .

PUSS: . . . Puss and his Tabby, the genii of the home and the protectors of the hearth. Yes. Well, chérie, my most chérie, few have worked as hard to achieve the tranquil joys of domesticity as you and I. Won't you snuggle up a little closer, Tabs? Plenty of room on the window-sill . . .

(Fade in Rossini's Cat Duet; and, at the same time . . .)

HERO: Dearest.

HEROINE: Darling.

(Passionate breathing.)

PUSS: *(Narrating.)* And, at just this tender if outrageous moment –

(Door bursts open. Bedroom acoustic.)

UNDERTAKER: In comes I, the undertaker, with a brace of mutes –

MUTES: *(Mumble, mumble.)*

UNDERTAKER: – the mutes bearing between them a nice, comfy box of elm, good old, solid elm. And what greets our eyes?

MUTES: *(Excited mumbles.)*

UNDERTAKER: Why, a handsome young couple naked as nature intended, stretched out on the carpet and at it hammer and tongs!
Hurrah!
Magnificent!

(Cheers and applause.
The mutes applaud and make enthusiastic, if inarticulate, cries; torrent of applause and cheers; fade in climax of Tchaikovsky's 1812 Overture, with cannons; shattering climax; thunderous applause.
Pause.)

Spectacular. Spectacular . . . well done, sir and madame.

HAG: Thieves! Murder! Fornication!

HEROINE: *(Firm.)* That's quite enough of your nonsense, hag. New brooms sweep clean. Go and pack your bags.

HAG: What's this? Going to turn me out, are you? After what I did with the butcher to put meat in the pot? Thieves! Murder! Fornication!

HEROINE: Indeed I shall give you the sack, hag, but I'll stuff it with money, first, don't you worry. Yet how can I retain you in my house when your sneezes cause such suffering to my beloved cats?
And, hag, remember . . . it's MY house, now. And my counting-house. For now I am a rich widow and here –

PUSS: *(Narrating.)* – and with a flourish of the counting-house keys she indicates my bare yet blissful master –

HEROINE: – here's the young man who'll be my second husband!

(Renewed applause and cheers; wedding bells; wedding march on organ.)

PUSS: *(Narrating.)* And so I took my master the quickest way to a happy ending; and the young missus rounding out already. But my Tabs beat her to it, since cats don't take half so much lazy time about bringing their progeny into the world as *homo sapiens* does, so almost before they've cleared away the wedding breakfast there's three fine new-minted kittens taking their bows –

(Mew.
  Mew.
  Mew.)

– all as marmalade as might be and each equipped with the snowiest of dickeys, who tumble in the cream pan –

(Splash.)

and tangle up the missus' knitting –

(Sounds of irritation.)

and tumble about the parquet flooring like the born acrobats they are –

(Kitten mewing, skidding – whee!)

– and put a smile on every face, especially those of their proud mother and father.

So, ladies and gentlemen, all is set fair. And may I wish you goodnight and sweet dreams.

And let me wish you, too, in parting, as follows: that all your wives, if you need them, be rich and pretty; and all your husbands, if you want them, be young and virile; and all your cats as wily, resourceful and perspicacious as – PUSS IN BOOTS.

(Fade in conclusion of Figaro's aria.)

A Self-Made Man

(Fade in bells, nightingales, Italian nightingales if possible, if not, then lots of nightingales.)

FEMALE NARRATOR: *(Over.)* In Rome, eternal Rome, in the Protestant Cemetery, where Shelley lies, and Keats . . .

(Nightingales drown out bells.
Fade in the funeral service in the distance.)

ENGLISH VICAR: For a thousand years in thy sight are but as yesterday; seeing that is past as a watch in the night.

As soon as thou scatterest them, they are even as a sleep: and fade away suddenly like the grass.

In the morning it is green, and groweth up: but in the evening it is cut down, dried up, and withered.

For we consume away in thy displeasure: and are afraid at thy wrathful indignation.

Thou hast set our misdeeds before thee; and our secret sins in the light of thy countenance.

FIRBANK: *(Whispering, over.)* 'Say a fragrant prayer for me, child.'

(Fade down VICAR.)

FEMALE NARRATOR: Early on a flawless morning, among the cypresses and roses, and the ecstatic song of the Roman nightingales, who, unlike the sullen Northern ones, sing and sing all day long. On such a day, he was laid to rest where Keats lies, and Shelley, on the fifth of June, nineteen hundred and twenty-six, in the Protestant Cemetery.

(Fade up bells, nightingales and service . . . and fade.
Pause.)

MALE NARRATOR: It turned out he was a Roman himself, of course.

FEMALE NARRATOR: A Roman?

MALE NARRATOR: A Catholic. *(Pronounced with the English High Anglican long a – 'A Caaatholic.')* He'd *turned*, you know.

FEMALE NARRATOR: *(Hearty.)* No peace for the wicked!

(Clean in digging.)

MALE NARRATOR: *(Over.)* When they found *that* out, of course, they had to dig him up and bury him all over again, in more appropriately consecrated soil –

FEMALE NARRATOR: *(Over.)* – even in death, always on the move –

(Stop digging.)

MALE NARRATOR: – under a stone that reads:

FIRBANK:

R.I.P.

PRAY FOR THE SOUL OF

ARTHUR ANNESLEY RONALD

FIRBANK

WHO ENTERED INTO REST

ON 21ST MAY 1926

FAR AWAY FROM HIS COUNTRY

(Sighs.
Pause. Music – 'Lord Berners's polka'.)

ANNOUNCER: *(Over.)* 'A Self-Made Man', an artificial documentary for radio on Ronald Firbank, in which he speaks mostly in the words of his own fiction and letters and his contemporaries also speak mostly in their own words. Written and compiled by Angela Carter. With Lewis Fiander as Ronald Firbank. The two narrators are Frances Jeater and John Westbrook. A Self-Made Man.

(Music out.)

MALE NARRATOR: Firbank (Arthur Annesley) Ronald (1886 to 1926) author of the following novels: V*ainglory* (1915), *Inclinations* (1916), *Caprice* (1917), *Valmouth* (1919), *The Flower Beneath the Foot* (1923), *Sorrow in Sunlight* (1925, published by Brentano in New York as *Prancing Nigger*), and *Concerning the Eccentricities of Cardinal Pirelli* (1926).

He was an aesthete whose work reflects a fastidious and sophisticated mind.

The *Concise Oxford Dictionary of English Literature*, second edition.

FEMALE NARRATOR: The night of his death, from his sick-bed in the Hotel Quirinal, Rome –

FIRBANK: I asked them to telephone Berners, *Lord* Berners, you know.

MALE NARRATOR: – Gerald Hugh Tyrwhitt Wilson, fourteenth Lord Berners, composer, poet, eccentric, wit.

BERNERS: 'I was his only friend in Rome at the time.'

(Clean in room acoustic. Telephone rings. Picked up.)

BERNERS: *(In room.)* Pronto!
    They told me poor Firbank was ill with pneumonia and wanted to see me but it was so very, very late . . . and when I called his doctor –

(Dialling.)

BERNERS: *(In room.)* Doctor Green? About poor Firbank . . . oh? he seems very much recovered? he's sent the nurse away – he said, 'whoever died from a cold in the head?'

(Fade Berners on telephone.)

BERNERS: The doctor reassured me completely. And, besides, it was *so* late . . .

(Schubert: first bars of the 'Death and the Maiden' quartet – this is the 'DEATH' music, and we only need the first bars, then cut cleanly.)

BERNERS: . . . that I decided to wait until morning.

FIRBANK: *(Sigh.)* So there I was, you see: a 'spinster of forty' all alone in an hotel room – such dreadful wallpaper! Alone in an hotel room full of valises . . .

FEMALE NARRATOR: His valises. The Angel of Death apprehended him in an hotel room full of valises, as if he were already ready to move on. He had lived in impermanent lodgings, rented apartments, rented rooms, hotels, for the greater part of his adult life and Rome would have been no more than a wayside halt in the course of his perpetual restlessness . . .
    Imagine his luggage, pasted over and over with the labels of this hotel, that hotel, this steamship line, even, in his last years, of the airways . . . but don't think he thought to travel was better than to arrive! Not travel for the sake of travelling as if the voyage were itself the only home of this traveller without a destination, or, who was eager for *every* destination. Nor travel for the sake of the arrival, either; rather, it might be to travel for the exquisite anticipatory moment when the train brakes alongside the platform and has not yet quite halted, or the ship sidles shyly up to the dock but does not yet dare touch . . . the moment before the aeroplane sets its wheels down on the runway, that fleeting moment when the ecstatic elsewhere of

the imagination is near at hand yet unachieved.

His luggage, his valises, palimpsests of those perpetual voyages that made up the endless gypsying of his life, valises overwritten again and again with the stations of his eccentric pilgrimages, the caravanserais of his wanderings . . . Paris, Madrid, Algiers, Havana . . . Florence, Rome, Tunis . . . London, again, and then onwards . . . his valises, home of his homelessness . . .

MALE NARRATOR: . . . his luggage; it must have looked like the luggage he gave to Mrs Shamefoot in *Vainglory*.

FIRBANK: 'Mrs Shamefoot's portmanteau was a rose-coloured chest, which, with its many foreign labels, exhaled an atmosphere of positive scandal. No nice maid would stand beside it.'

(Railway engine moving off.)

FEMALE NARRATOR: Always on the move!

(Train whistle.)

MALE NARRATOR: This peripatetic life of his could be sustained only by ample private means. Aptly enough, the Firbank fortune itself came from the railways. Almost brand-new money, a very nineteenth-century fortune; a fortune of the Age of Steam and mass transportation.

(Railway engine: puff, puff, puff.)

Sir Osbert Sitwell, baronet, poet, autobiographer.

OSBERT SITWELL: 'He suddenly announced to everyone that I had said the Firbank fortune had been founded on boot-buttons – a remark of which I had never been guilty.'

(During SITWELL*'s following speech, fade in sounds of busy restaurant, clinking glasses, knives and forks, etc. and Firbank muttering to himself with increasing ferocity.)*

'He was enraged about it and would sit in the Café Royal for hours, practising what he was going to say in court, in the course of the libel action which he intended to bring against me. The great moment in it, he had determined, was to be when he lifted up his hands, which were beautifully shaped, and of which he was very proud, and would say to the Judge:

FIRBANK: *(In restaurant.)* 'Look at my hands, my lord: How could my father have made boot-buttons? No, never! He *made* the most wonderful railways!'

(Cut restaurant behind first two words of following speech.)

MALE NARRATOR: No, never! It wasn't your father who built the railways! He *lived* off them, yes; but it was your grandfather built the railways and founded the fortune!

The grandfather, a self-made man –

OLD FIRBANK: *(Thick Durham accent – on echo.)* – and proud of it!

MALE NARRATOR: – who went to work in the mines at Bishop Auckland, County Durham, at the age of seven; and then –

(First line of song, 'Poor Paddy works on the railways', sung by Ewan McColl, on a topic LP 'The Iron Muse'. Line: 'In eighteen hundred and forty-one, my corduroy britches I put on, to work upon the railways' – cut off at this point, sharp.)

– he went to work upon the railways. Soon, by dint of hard work –

(Pick and shovel; cut off.)

– he prospered sufficiently to enable him to contract the labour to build railways for himself.

(Lots of picks and shovels; cut off.)

DADDY: Old Joseph never lost his strong regional accent nor his canny ways. Once, Old Joseph found a hunter stabled by accident amongst the cart horses. Eyeing the slender and delicate creature with his sharp, bright, entrepreneur's eye, he opined:

OLD FIRBANK: *(On echo.)* 'Eh, lad! That woarn't pull a load of muck!' –

DADDY: Laden with wealth and honours, a shining example of self-made success, he died the very year his second grandson, Artie –

FIRBANK: – at home, they always called me Artie –

DADDY: – was born, in 1886. I myself died in 1910, leaving my surviving family with, alas, rather less inheritance than they might have hoped for . . .

FEMALE NARRATOR: . . . and brought up with great expectations of immense wealth, Arthur Annesley Ronald Firbank was put out to find he would be only rather rich . . .

DADDY: . . . unexpected reverses and so on; I did my best but I was not, unfortunately, the best possible steward of Old Joseph's fortune. I had areas of incompetence and a weak heart.

I? Who am I? I am *Sir* Thomas Firbank, knighted in the coronation list of 1902, unionist member of parliament for East Hull from 1895 to 1906.

All my life I strove to do my best. I served my country in the House of Commons. I loved my wife and our four children. I was, as I mention in *Who's Who*, 'very keen on all outdoor sports and athletics, music and objects of art'. I laid my ways as best I could in the undiscovered country of the upper-middle class into which we Firbanks had so lately ventured . . .

OLD FIRBANK: (*On echo – disappearing into silence.*) 'Where there's muck, there's money . . . I values at nowt what I gets for nowt . . . Hard work never hurt no man . . .'

MALE NARRATOR: Plodding, decent, dull Thomas Firbank, as we may characterise him, with all the blinkered virtues of his class and time –

(*Fade in, very faint, 'Land of Hope and Glory'.*)

– Thomas Firbank –

(*Fade out 'Land of Hope and Glory' by now.*)

DADDY: (*Correcting.*) *Sir* Thomas Firbank –

MALE NARRATOR: – who married the beautiful, strong-willed Harriette Jane Garrett, of the Anglo-Irish ascendancy, daughter of the Rector of Kellistown, County Carlow.

(*Fade in, again very faint, 'Believe Me, If All those Endearing Young Charms' sung very beautifully by an Irish tenor, John McCormack if poss; fade down during following speeches.*)

A. C. Landsberg, Firbank's friend at Cambridge.

LANDSBERG: 'I remember that he seemed to be very fond of his mother and to admire her tremendously. I gathered that she was in every way a great and beautiful lady, only too good and fine for his father whom he seemed to consider as rather a vulgarian.'

(*Fade up Baba music; fade in and up Daddy music; allow resulting disharmonies to perpetuate themselves for a moment; fade right down.*)

FEMALE NARRATOR: There were four children born of these always unacknowledged disharmonies.

(*Music faded out by now.*)

First came Joseph Sydney.

MALE NARRATOR: Born, 1884.

BABA: *(Slight Irish accent.)* My Joey. And then, my beloved Artie –

MALE NARRATOR: After Arthur Annesley Ronald, came Hubert Somerset, born 1887.

BABA: Whom we called Bertie. And, last but not least, my little daughter, the baby, my Heather . . .

FEMALE NARRATOR: . . . born 1888 . . .

BABA: . . . who came to be known as Lassie.

(Babble of childish laughter; fade in, very faint, Elgar's 'Dream Children'.)

(Over.) So we all lived happily in our dear home, amongst the beauty I must always have around me; our English porcelain, our Dresden figures, the Sèvres serving dishes, the Gobelin tapestries, everything beautiful surrounding my beautiful children – dear home, a treasure house of objets d'art. The Coopers, near Chislehurst; I called that house our 'little paradise'. And, like paradise, it had the most beautiful garden. With the tulip tree on the lawn, do you remember?

I think of you all, playing in that lovely garden, so long ago . . .

(Fade children's voices and laughter and music on echo; pause.)

MALE NARRATOR: Of those four laughing children playing in the garden of childhood, only two will survive both Daddy and Baba –

FIRBANK: – our pet name for Mama; 'my dearest Baba . . .'

MALE NARRATOR: If dearest Baba will herself die a serene septuagenarian, then her second, most beloved son, Artie, will survive her only reluctantly, by a slender year.

FIRBANK: *(coughs.)*

BABA: And poor Artie never wholly well, all his life, with his weak chest and his fragile constitution . . .

MALE NARRATOR: Of those four Firbank children, only the youngest, Heather, would live long enough to grow old. As if some doom lay upon the menfolk. Doomed –

FEMALE NARRATOR: Doomed to the English upper classes, for one thing, to which they seem to have been constitutionally ill-fitted. There were disastrous experiments with public schools.

('Eton Boating Song', abruptly broken off.)

Bertie spent but eighteen tumultuous months at Eton. No school could contain Joey. As for Artie –

MALE NARRATOR: Register of Uppingham School. Arthur Annesley Ronald Firbank; entered, September, 1900. Left, April, 1901.

FIRBANK: *(Coughs, hollowly – a little affectedly, as if putting it on.)*

BABA: It was poor Artie's health kept him from school, poor little thing! Always coughs and sniffles, bronchial disorders . . . his lungs . . . he needed sunshine to make him well, to keep him well.

MALE NARRATOR: Later, in his own entries in *Who's Who*, Firbank chose to cut a number of corners, exclude the crammers, the private tutors, the special prep schools, and describes his education as:

FIRBANK: 'Abroad.'

FEMALE NARRATOR: . . . beginnings of his gypsyings . . .

MALE NARRATOR: To these childhood traffickings about hot, dry places in search of good health may be attributed the story put about by Osbert Sitwell, that:

SITWELL: 'Firbank was laid low with sunstroke in Egypt when a child, and was thereafter "delicate".'

FEMALE NARRATOR: Egypt!

(Fade in Egyptian sand dance music; fade down and out during following speech.)

He always loved Egypt, visited it often in adulthood, patronised Egyptian fortune-tellers and often wore Egyptian rings on his fingers, surrounded himself with scarabs, sphinxes, Egyptian souvenirs of all kinds.

How he adored that mysterious country where, at the beginning of things, having found just the right way to stand – profile facing one way, feet and torso the other – they stuck in it for two thousand glorious years, a-fixed on their well-shaped lips that permanent smile, as if they always saw the *funny side*; elegant, well-mannered, well-bred people, trapped in an everlasting, unchanging, beautiful frieze . . .

FIRBANK: 'He has such a strange, peculiar style. His work calls to mind a frieze with figures of varying heights trotting all the same way. If one should by chance turn about it's usually merely to stare or to sneer or to make a grimace. Only occasionally his figures care to beckon. And they seldom really touch.

'He's too cold. Too classic, I suppose.

'Classic! In the *Encyclopaedia Britannica*, his style is described as odd spelling, brilliant and vicious.'

MALE NARRATOR: He's talking about a writer he invented for his novel, *Vainglory*.

FEMALE NARRATOR: He might be talking about himself.

Did you always want to be a writer, Artie? Ever since you were little and scribbled away in exercise books?

FIRBANK: 'Miss Raymer the headmistress asked Rachel why she did not eat her beef, and on being told that she did not care for it underdone, Miss Raymer grew angry and said, waste not want not, and eat it up, but Rachel tossed her head. I have quite good enough blood in my family without going to a bullock for more, she said leaving the room and slamming the door . . .'

FEMALE NARRATOR: Scribbled away at a novel called *Lila* in an exercise book, when you were ten . . .

FIRBANK: ' . . . and what did Miss Raymer say, laughed Lila. She said she was "excessively vulgar" and gave us a lecture on the decay of modern manners.'

FEMALE NARRATOR: See, even at that age, the concern with behaviour, with social form; with formalism.

MALE NARRATOR: Perhaps we might even relate that early experience of travelling, which grew to be a lifelong addiction, indeed, his way of life . . . could that early experience of travelling, and the postcards home, have some connection with his legendary habit, in adult life, of composing his novels on postcards?

SITWELL: 'Usually he wrote his novels upon those huge, blue postcards, which we had noticed piled up on his desk, writing on each wide oblong side of them, though each blank face only gave room enough for a few – perhaps ten – words, so much space did his large, regular handwriting take up.'

FEMALE NARRATOR: *(Whispering.)* And where did you start to see the funny side?

FIRBANK: *(Starts to laugh: fade out.)*

MALE NARRATOR: His laughter. His characteristic laughter. Augustus John described it:

AUGUSTUS JOHN: '. . . a long, hollow laugh about nothing in particular, a laugh like a clock suddenly running down . . .'

MALE NARRATOR: Sewell Stokes called it:

SEWELL STOKES: '. . . the most sinister laugh I had ever heard.'

MALE NARRATOR: His characteristic, wild, nervous laughter; the laughter with which he advertised his presence.

FEMALE NARRATOR: The laughter with which he orchestrated his compulsive shyness; he was so shy that once, at a luncheon party, he disappeared under the table out of sheer nerves.

MALE NARRATOR: His laughter, his spontaneous tribute to his own inventions.

SITWELL: 'As for his laughter . . . it would often descend on him just as he was beginning work.'

(*Fade in laughter, fade down and continue throughout next speech.*)

'At the moment when he would be starting to inscribe laboriously one more word on the card in front of him, the essential absurdity of the situation that he was with such care elaborating would overcome him . . .'

(*Fade up laughter; fade out.*)

BERNERS: 'Like the Pope in *Cardinal Pirelli*, he:

FIRBANK: 'often laughed when he was alone.'

BERNERS: 'A man I knew who occupied rooms on the opposite side of a Palazzo where Firbank was living told me that sometimes in the depths of the night he would hear through the open windows the sound of chuckling and laughter coming from the lonely inmate of the apartment vis-à-vis.'

(*Fade up laughter, on slight echo; laughter turns into coughing; fade out.*)

MALE NARRATOR: Nancy Cunard.

NANCY CUNARD: 'If he was really ill, then he was brave and adroit indeed, for one noticed nothing of the kind, save, at moments, a kind of asthmatic conflict between words, breathing and laughter as his quips popped into the conversation.'

(*Bells; same bells as Rome.*)

FIRBANK: 'What is the matter with the bells?

> They're sounding for the sisters.
> Are they ill? Again?
> They died last night – of laughter.'

FEMALE NARRATOR: Where *did* you learn to see the funny side of life, Artie? Was it in Paris, when you were young? In Paris of the 'naughty noughts'?

(Champagne cork pops: bubble, bubble, bubble; fade in, softly, Eric Satie's 'La Belle Eccentrique'.)

MALE NARRATOR: *(Over.)* In Paris of the early nineteen hundreds, the height of the 'belle epoche', polishing up his French in preparation for the diplomatic service –

FEMALE NARRATOR: The diplomatic service?!?

BABA: Since Artie had such a gift with languages, we thought . . . perhaps . . . the diplomatic service . . .

MALE NARRATOR: – polishing his French –

FIRBANK: 'Tell me, do, of a place that soothes and lulls one . . .
The Countess of Tolga considered.
"Paris," she hazarded.'

(Music up and fade; champagne cork pops; bubble, bubble, bubble.)

MALE NARRATOR: Mr and Mrs Elks dancing the cakewalk at the New Circus; and the actress Polaire with her sixteen-inch waist and her equivocal relations with Willy and Madame Colette. Willy and Colette and Willy's *Claudine*; and La Belle Otéro in *Rêve d'Opium* and *L'Aragonaise* and Réjane at the Théâtre du Variété – how he loved the theatre! he kept a big book of actresses' autographs . . . and his friend, his great friend, the actor de Max and the divine Sarah Bernhardt doing Hamlet *en travestie* and the music of Saint-Saëns and Debussy . . .

(Fade in few chords of any Debussy piano piece – 'Fille aux Cheveux de Lin' would do.)

(Over.) . . . in which the century had expired in a delicious ecstasy of mauve . . .

FIRBANK: *(Sighs ecstatically.)*

(Fade out Debussy.)

MALE NARRATOR: Expired in mauve and then got right up again and dances the cakewalk!

(Debussy: 'Golliwog's Cakewalk'; fade down after a few moments; opening a letter.)

BABA: Chislehurst, September 25, 1904. 'I found Joey today very depressed and ill. I feel so sad when I see him and to be unable to do anything for him.'

(Fade in, very faint, first bars of 'Death and the Maiden' – the Death Music; cut off. Pause.)

MALE NARRATOR: Joey, the first to go. He died of 'enteric syncope' on November 22, 1904, at home, in his mother's presence.

BABA: *(Tears.)*

FEMALE NARRATOR: Enteric syncope?

MALE NARRATOR: A polite euphemism for drink and debauchery.

FEMALE NARRATOR: At twenty?

MALE NARRATOR: Just twenty.
   The grandchildren of a self-made man exist, perhaps, at a third remove from reality. Of the four grandchildren of the hard-headed, horny-handed railway pioneer, who built himself up out of his own sweat and labour and the sweat and labour of others, only the very frailest –

OLD FIRBANK: *(Faint – on echo.)* 'Eh lad! That woarn't pull a load of muck!'

MALE NARRATOR: – was sufficiently moved by the will to live to make himself, in *his* turn, as if from nothing, or from the shards of ideas, from brilliant fragments, of illusion, from his irretrievable sense of his own difference – only frail Artie was able to reconstruct out of these intangibles an artificial temperament –

FEMALE NARRATOR: Who was it said: 'The first duty in life is to be as artificial as possible?'

FIRBANK: Oscar Wilde.

MALE NARRATOR: – to construct an artificial temperament durable enough to withstand the buffetings of the world; to create himself a crust, a portable home like that of a jewelled mollusc –

FIRBANK: *(Reproachful.)* Mollusc!

FEMALE NARRATOR: *(Conciliatory.)* Your chrysalis, the beautiful chrysalis of your impenetrable privacy, out of which, from time to time, you would transmit your coded messages to the world.

(Pause.)

MALE NARRATOR: As for Bertie, they sent him to Canada, to –

(Wood chopping.)

– toughen up among the lumberjacks. Bertie at least managed to outlive his father and came home to die in 1913.

FEMALE NARRATOR: At twenty-six years old. Cause of death – cardiac dilation and cirrhosis of the liver.

(Pop; bubble, bubble, bubble.)

Might there have been a family tendency towards excessive drinking?

MALE NARRATOR: *(Softly.)* Briefly resting on his journeyings beside the grave of Keats, on which is written: Here lies one whose name was writ in water . . . Firbank might have convivially cried out:

FIRBANK: Oh! can't we have champagne?

(Pop: bubble.)

In this heat, champagne is so much more refreshing than tea.

(Clink of glasses; fade in restaurant noises. Keep down behind following.)

NANCY CUNARD: *(Over.)* When you fluttered down to rest in London in the Eiffel Tower Restaurant, chez les artistes, Ronald –

MALE NARRATOR: For now, amongst new friends, and upon the covers of those books for whose publication you pay yourself, you have laid aside the homely persona of 'Artie' and tremulously arrived on the world's stage as 'Ronald' –

NANCY CUNARD: – there, in that restaurant on the seacoast of Bohemia, Ronald, sitting alone but among friends . . . Augustus John, the Sitwells, Duff Cooper, Peter Warlock, Walter Sickert, Jacob Epstein, a Vorticist or two . . . sitting alone with your shyness but sometimes we might entice you to us; then you might sit with me, the beautiful and strangely fated Nancy Cunard.

FEMALE NARRATOR: Nancy Cunard, representative of the lost generation, heiress of the Cunard lines, champion of the black races and the red poets.

NANCY CUNARD: If they kept a glass of brandy always filled for you at the Café Royal, at the Eiffel Tower you always ordered champagne. And, perhaps, if you were peckish, a strawberry or two.

FIRBANK: 'I believe strawberries are the clue to my heart.'

NANCY CUNARD: You might, just occasionally, when ravenous, toy with a single chicken liver; or even a spoonful of caviare, a scant spoon.

(Fade up restaurant noises.)

(Restaurant noises.)

WAITER: *(Continental accent.)* 'Mr Firbank is much better. What an appetite he has got now! Yesterday for dinner he ate a whole slice of toast with his caviare.'

(Take down restaurant noises.)

MALE NARRATOR: He ate, as he lived, as he wrote, exiguously but with tremendous style. A minimalist. Impossibly luxurious little nibbles, sketches of meals, vague, idealised outlines of meals . . . so that malnutrition might have helped to hasten his end. All the same, he loved fruit, especially the kind of ornamental fruit featured in still lifes . . . Philip Moeller.

PHILIP MOELLER: *(American accent.)* At dinner, 'all that Firbank ate were peaches and champagne . . . innumerable peaches and a bottle or two of champagne.'

(Pop: bubble. Lose restaurant.)

FIRBANK: 'Life, after all, seemed less raw after a glass.'

MALE NARRATOR: Evan Frederick Morgan, second Viscount Tredegar.

EVAN MORGAN: ' . . . more often than not, Firbank appeared to be under the influence of Bacchus . . . at least, you could never tell, because his conversation was equally wild either way.'

FIRBANK: *(Sharp.)* Is that you, Evan?

MORGAN: *(Cautious.)* Yes . . .

FIRBANK: Of course it is! I saw you just the other day, here in Rome, 'dressed as a priest, with your lunch you said in a paper bag . . .' I have good reason to remember it; we went together to St Peter's . . .

MORGAN: . . . to pray for the repose of your mother's soul. Yes.

FIRBANK: I dedicated my play to you. In nineteen-twenty. My play, that nobody ever acted in. I dedicated it to you.

(Turning pages.)

MORGAN: 'The Princess Zoubaroff . . . To the Hon. Evan Morgan, in Souvenir Amical of a Previous Incarnation' . . . Oh, no!

FIRBANK: Then you made them cut the dedication out of the book. It was already printed. You made them cut it out. It cost a good deal to do that, you know. I'm not a rich man. 'I can't afford a yacht, or to entertain, or to buy pictures. I've just enough for myself.' There are the books to be published, you know. That's an expense. I dedicated my play to you and you wouldn't have it. You said your family wouldn't approve.

MALE NARRATOR: The Hon. Evan Morgan's mother, Lady Tredegar, was said to emulate the birds by building, each spring, a nest. In his youth, her son would entertain guests at the family seat in Wales by going a round or two at fisticuffs against his kangaroo. It was a time of considerable eccentricity amongst the British upper classes.

FEMALE NARRATOR: Then why the fuss about the dedication?

FIRBANK: 'I wonder' . . .

BERNERS: 'The phrase, "I wonder", was constantly on his lips, and uttered in a tone that seemed to evoke all the unsolved riddles of the universe.'

MALE NARRATOR: You took a baroque revenge for the slight; you put him into *The Flower Beneath the Foot* –

FEMALE NARRATOR: – thinly disguised as the Hon. 'Eddy' Monteith, who dies of fright at the sight of a jackal whilst composing a sonnet amongst the excavations of a suburb of Sodom.

(Pause.)

MORGAN: He said I looked like Rameses. Like the mummy of Rameses in the British Museum. When he first met me, he hurried me off to the British Museum to look at my original.

FIRBANK: The reincarnation of Rameses.

(Pause.)

He wouldn't let me dedicate my play to him.

(Pause.)

(*Recitative.*)　I am disgusted with love
　　　　　　　　I find it exceedingly disappointing
　　　　　　　　Mine is a nature that cries for more ethereal things
　　　　　　　　Banal passions fail to stir me
　　　　　　　　I am disgusted with love.

(*Pause.*)

FEMALE NARRATOR: His heart remains an area of absolute privacy.

(*Pause.*)

OSBERT SITWELL: 'One could always, even in his lifetime, see a miniature legend in attendance upon him, hovering round him.'

MALE NARRATOR: As with a medieval saint or any other legendary being, fabulous narratives proliferated around his dandified, powdered, occasionally rouged, inimitable figure as he flitted about the cities of the world or taxied or tottered between the Café Royal, the Eiffel Tower Restaurant, or his club, the Junior Carlton, on those brief summer visits home that were all his precarious health allowed.

　　As with all such narratives, they may be only loosely based on real events and capable of many different interpretations. For example, the anecdote of the steak garnished with violets comes to us in two accounts, which offer us radically opposed versions of Firbank as perceived by his contemporaries.

FEMALE NARRATOR: Both Nancy Cunard and Percy Wyndham Lewis, the butch Vorticist, claim to have personally observed, indeed, to have participated in the incident, but neither mentions the presence of the other.

NANCY CUNARD: In the Eiffel Tower Restaurant, in June, 1922 . . . a charming but at that moment insufferably drunk young man was with me . . .

(*Fade in restaurant noises.*)

YOUNG MAN: Hic.

CONTINENTAL WAITER: (*Heavy continental accent.*) Is m'sieur ready to order?

YOUNG MAN: (*Mumbling.*) Bloody French menu . . . sole Dieppoise; wassat?

CONTINENTAL WAITER: Is a little fillet of fish wiz –

YOUNG MAN: Mucked up with a sauce, what?

(Hubbub of arrival in background.)

MAITRE D: *(Off.)* Mr Firbank, Mr Firbank! Your usual table? The bottle is on the ice –

NANCY CUNARD: *(Calling.)* Ronald, darling!

YOUNG MAN: *(Momentarily – very momentarily – sobered with shock.)* I say, Nancy! You can't possibly know that . . . person? Why, he's wearing . . . hic . . . nail polish!

CONTINENTAL WAITER: *(Patient.)* M'sieur does not wish ze sole Dieppoise?

YOUNG MAN: What? Oh, none of that foreign muck for me. Give me a . . . plain beefsteak – good lord, Nancy, that . . . fairy's waving back to you.

CONTINENTAL WAITER: 'Ow would m'sieur like ze beefsteak? Rare, medium –

YOUNG MAN: Oh, *cooked*, you know – cooked – oh, my God, she's waving back to him . . .

CONTINENTAL WAITER: And vegetables, m'sieur?

YOUNG MAN: Vegetables? I say, Nancy, he's coming over here – you can't possibly expect me to sit with – He's either very, very flushed, or else he's wearing . . . Good God . . . rouge!

CONTINENTAL WAITER: M'sieur –

NANCY CUNARD: How *lovely* to see you, Ronald!

(Kissing; murmurs of ecstatic greeting.)

YOUNG MAN: Her *friends* . . . bloody fairy . . .

CONTINENTAL WAITER: Ze broccoli is very good today, and ze spinach; and perhaps a few potatoes –

YOUNG MAN: *(Distracted.)* Oh, uh, – with – with –

FIRBANK: Try *violets*!

(Firbankian laughter; fade; silence.)

YOUNG MAN: I say, Nancy . . . was that . . . incredible fellow . . . trying to make a fool of me?

NANCY CUNARD: 'May all tipsy, bullying, gross, "he-men" meet with such a neat little swipe as that dealt by Firbank!'

MALE NARRATOR: In Wyndham Lewis's autobiography, *Blasting and Bombardiering*, the scene of this memorable encounter remains the Eiffel Tower Restaurant but Nancy Cunard is written out of the script and we might be in a different world.

(*Restaurant noises.*)

WYNDHAM LEWIS: . . . 'I had dinner with him and a young American "college-boy" who was stopping at the Eiffel Tower Hotel. The presence of the fawning and attentive Firbank put the American out of countenance. He called the waiter.

YOUNG AMERICAN: I guess I'll have something t'eat.

ENGLISH WAITER: What will you have, sir?

AMERICAN: I guess I'll have – oh – *a rump steak*.

ENGLISH WAITER: Yessir.

AMERICAN: Carrots.

ENGLISH WAITER: Yessir. Carrots, sir.

AMERICAN: Boiled pertaters.

ENGLISH WAITER: Yessir.

AMERICAN: What? Oh and er . . .

LEWIS: But with gushing insinuation Firbank burst excitedly in at this point . . .

FIRBANK: Oh, and vi-o-lets!

LEWIS: . . . he frothed obsequiously. Reacting darkly to the smiles of the onlookers, the college-boy exclaimed:

AMERICAN: There seem to be a lot of *fairies* around here!

(*Cut off restaurant noises.*)

MALE NARRATOR: Note how Nancy Cunard celebrates her friend in her version of the story, which might be titled: 'Ronald's Triumph over the Boor'; whereas Wyndham Lewis –

LEWIS: . . . 'the fawning and attentive Firbank' –

MALE NARRATOR: – parodies him.

LEWIS: . . . 'he frothed obsequiously';

MALE NARRATOR: caricatures him; turns him into an offensive cartoon.

FEMALE NARRATOR: But perhaps ... Firbank suggested the violet garnish on two quite separate occasions, after all.

FIRBANK: 'I wonder' ... By the way, 'I wish you wouldn't call me Firbank; it gives me a sense of galoshes.'

MALE NARRATOR: The story about the goldfish is probably entirely apocryphal but, since it was about Ronald Firbank, it might even have been believed.

(Fade in LORD BERNERS's 'Goldfish' music; fade down but not out.)

FEMALE NARRATOR: When Maurice Sandoz visited him:

MAURICE SANDOZ: 'I noticed, as I was about to take my leave, a goldfish, sad and solitary, turning in the traditional bowl.'

(Clean in room acoustic.)

Is he dangerous?

FIRBANK: Not when I'm here! I prefer him to a canary. He's less noisy. Moreover, this animal never drinks the water.

SANDOZ: What does he eat?

FIRBANK: Pearls. He costs me a fortune.

SANDOZ: Have you tried him with artificial pearls?

FIRBANK: He spits them out.

SANDOZ: 'Just as I was leaving Ronald Firbank, my foot slipped on something round and hard, so suddenly that I nearly broke my leg. After looking about for a moment, I found what had caused the misadventure. It was an artificial pearl.'

(Fade up goldfish music, if there's any left; Firbankian laughter.)

MALE NARRATOR: He undoubtedly assisted in the manufacture of his own legend; the legend followed him about like the shadow of his arduously constructed artificial temperament.

FEMALE NARRATOR: But how did he see *himself*, and his project of creating melancholy, facetious and ornamental literature?

FIRBANK: 'I am Pavlova, chasing butterflies.'

MALE NARRATOR: ... he exclaimed to Siegfried Sassoon, then added with 'mock seriousness':

FIRBANK: 'You are Tolstoy, digging for worms.'

FEMALE NARRATOR: However, this diagnosis of himself exists, inevitably, in another version. Sewell Stokes.

SEWELL STOKES: 'I told him how thrilled I was at the thought of being taken to meet Siegfried Sassoon.'

FIRBANK: 'Siegfried is Tolstoy in galoshes, digging for worms, deep, deep . . . I am only a butterfly, waiting to catch caterpillars as they drop from the leaves.'

(Fade in song, 'Poor Butterfly', in a twenties recording if poss. On a cracked gramophone as if wound up – very period; fade down and out.)

FEMALE NARRATOR: But how can one dissect a butterfly?

MALE NARRATOR: Let's try.

(Rustling papers; lecture hall acoustic; scraping of chairs, sounds of audience filing in, sitting, coughing, rustling. N.B. All sound f/a, music etc. heard through a speaker.)

(In hall – clears throat.) Good day. My colleague and myself are delighted to welcome you to the first . . .

FEMALE NARRATOR: *(In hall.)* . . . seminar on modernist literature to be conducted by the literature department of the University of Pisuerga at Kairoulla, held, for reasons of immediate convenience, in a room with dreadful wallpaper in the Hotel Quirinal, in Rome.

FIRBANK: *(Close to mic. Sounds of squirming pleasure.)*

MALE NARRATOR: I and my colleague would like to present a paper entitled: 'Elementary Structures in the Life and Art of Ronald Firbank'.

(Small drumroll.)

FEMALE NARRATOR: 'One: Dandyism.'
Even at school Artie took pride in his numerous collection of waistcoats! And then, in Paris, look at the boy dandy . . . dressed all in black, relieved only by a single pearl in his cravat; linen white as bone and a gold watch chain with one seal . . . or, two. A ring on the little finger. Of Chinese jade, perhaps. Or else Egyptian earthenware. His curly hair tamed to wave just so. And so the boy dandy grows up.

MALE NARRATOR: A. C. Landsberg.

LANDSBERG: *(On speaker.)* 'In appearance, he always reminded me of the portraits of society women by Boldini, as he was always writhing about, admiring his hands etc. His clothes, although made by the best tailors, always looked a little foreign, somehow – perhaps because he wore French ties from Doucet's and from Charvet's, and always had his hair waved in "artistic disorder"' . . .

FEMALE NARRATOR: . . . shirts of colours 'never seen offstage', they say; and 'very Bohemian ties'.

MALE NARRATOR: The bookseller, Cyril Beaumont, recalled he was . . .

BEAUMONT: *(On speaker.)* . . . 'always dressed in a dark, well-fitting lounge suit, and he wore a black bowler, almost invariably tilted far back on his head. He carried gloves and a cane. His hands were white and very well kept, the nails long and polished . . . and stained a deep carmine . . .'

NANCY CUNARD: *(In hall.)* What's that? A bowler? Ronald in a chapeau melon like something out of a painting by Magritte? Come, now! Never a bowler! It was a trilby he wore!

MALE NARRATOR: Nevertheless . . .

AUGUSTUS JOHN: *(In hall.)* '. . . the elegant slanting figure with the exquisitely poised *bowler* . . .'

MALE NARRATOR: It is the exquisite pose that is the thing, rather than the nature of the hat itself; his startling, unerring elegance, so that the painter Duncan Grant said meeting him was like:

DUNCAN GRANT: *(On speaker.)* ' . . . being introduced to an elegant grasshopper in white kid gloves and boots.'

FEMALE NARRATOR: His heroines he dressed to perfection, with the eye of a fashion journalist attuned to the extremes of the decorative, as if the clothes of those self-entranced women were a primary function of their being, as if they were not fully alive until they were dressed.

FIRBANK: *(On speaker.)* 'She was looking charmingly matinal in a simple tweed costume, with a shapely if perhaps *invocative* hat, very curiously indented, and well-cocked forward above one ear.'

NANCY CUNARD: You see? It *was* a trilby!

FEMALE NARRATOR: Examine those precise and unexpected adjectives and adverbs, selected with a gourmet precision, forcing the reader to construct for himself the meaning in the implicit image 'matinal', 'invocative'. Another heroine:

FIRBANK: *(On speaker.)* ' . . . was looking bewitching beyond measure, she believed, bound in black ribands, with a knot like a pure white butterfly under her chin'.

FEMALE NARRATOR: Here the costume coyly hints at bondage and his totemic butterfly; and it is black and white all over, like a Beardsley illustration or himself when young, and similarly intended to be *looked at*. Oh, the quality of *looked-at-ness* of these women like eccentric fashion plates.

FIRBANK: *(On speaker.)* 'One should always be the spectator of oneself, always, dear, a little.'

FEMALE NARRATOR: Dandyism, like drink, ran in the family. Heather Firbank, 'Lassie', ran up enormous dressmakers' bills.

FIRBANK: *(On speaker.)* ' . . . your annuity, which should go towards "Jones" the greengrocer as well as to "Lucille" the dressmaker . . .'

FEMALE NARRATOR: And on her death in the nineteen fifties left her dresses to the nation, where they form a part of the costume collection in the Victoria and Albert Museum, London.

Clothes, as they say, make the man; and the woman, too. The dandy, who creates himself or herself afresh as a work of art each time he or she changes a shirt or a frock, is the perfect 'self -made' person. Yet the dandy's obsession with dress is but a symptom of the disease, not the disease itself. True dandyism is an existential condition.

MALE NARRATOR: Charles Baudelaire, in his essay, 'The Painter of Modern Life':

BAUDELAIRE: *(On speaker. Slight French accent, not too much.)* 'Dandyism is an ill-defined social attitude as strange as duelling . . . dandyism is not even an excessive delight in clothes and material elegance.'

FEMALE NARRATOR: Augustus John drew Ronald Firbank's portrait:

AUGUSTUS JOHN: 'He wasn't really in the least affected, but he did so want to look his best.'

BAUDELAIRE: 'For the perfect dandy, clothes and material elegance are no more than the symbol of the aristocratic superiority of his mind. It is, above all, the burning desire to create a personal form of originality, within the external limits of social conventions. It is a kind of cult of the ego . . . It is the pleasure of causing surprise in others . . .'

CYRIL BEAUMONT: ' . . . we always spoke of him as "the man with the red nails"' . . .

BAUDELAIRE: '. . . and the proud satisfaction of never showing any oneself.'

SEWELL STOKES: *(In hall.)* 'My love of contrasts led me to take him one day into a Lyons teashop . . . There, in an atmosphere of tobacco smoke, eggs-on-toast twice, coffee-with-a-dash, thick cups and strong tea, he wilted like an orchid too long worn. When I asked him what I should order he replied:'

FIRBANK: *(On speaker.)* 'Ask for herons' eggs whipped with wine into an amber foam.'

FEMALE NARRATOR: Dandyism in action is an existential defiance; it is a way of saying, life for art's sake.

(Pause. Muffled drum roll.)

MALE NARRATOR: 'Elementary Structures of Ronald Firbank. Two: Religion.'

FIRBANK: *(On speaker.)*
'Princess. *(Mysteriously.)* I'm in communication with the Vatican, now.
Nadine. So you are actually in touch!
Princess. *(Nodding.)* My prospectus, I may say, is practically approved.'

FEMALE NARRATOR: Ronald Firbank, grandson of an Anglican parson, was received into the Roman Catholic Church on December 6, 1907.

MALE NARRATOR: By the Rev. Hugh Benson, later Monsignor Benson, a Catholic convert himself, one of the three novelist sons of an Anglican Archbishop of Canterbury.

FEMALE NARRATOR: Benson collaborated with Frederick Rolfe, the soi-disant Baron Corvo, author of *Hadrian VII* and *The Desire and Pursuit of the Whole,* on a romantic biography of St Thomas of Canterbury. Corvo also drew up Benson's horoscope.

MALE NARRATOR: Firbank's Catholicism did not so much lapse as learn to parody its colourful beginning.

BERNERS: *(In hall.)* 'I believe that in his early youth, Firbank had thought of taking Holy Orders. But more than once he had said to me:'

FIRBANK: *(On speaker.)* 'The Church of Rome wouldn't have me and so I laugh at them.'

MALE NARRATOR: In Firbank's last novel, *Concerning the Eccentricities of Cardinal Pirelli*, the eponymous Cardinal officiates at:

FIRBANK: *(On speaker.)* 'A christening – and not a child's.'

MALE NARRATOR: A dog's.

FIRBANK: *(On speaker.)* 'And thus being cleansed and purified, I do call thee "Crack!"'

MALE NARRATOR: In the font of the Cardinal's Spanish Cathedral. At last, the Cardinal, whilst in pursuit of a boy –

FIRBANK: *(On speaker.)* 'Olé, your Purpleship!'

MALE NARRATOR: – round and round the great fane –

FIRBANK: *(On speaker.)* 'the great fane (after all) was nothing but a cage; God's cage; the cage of God!'

MALE NARRATOR: – the Cardinal dies.

FIRBANK: *(On speaker.)* 'Dispossessed of everything but his fabulous mitre, the Primate was nude and elementary now as Adam himself. "As you can see, I have nothing but myself to declare," he addressed some phantom image in the air.'

FEMALE NARRATOR: When asked what he had to declare by American customs –

OSCAR WILDE: *(On speaker. Rich Irish accent.)* 'Nothing but my genius.'

MALE NARRATOR: – said Oscar Wilde, converted to Rome on his deathbed.

FEMALE NARRATOR: Aubrey Beardsley, converted to Catholicism on his deathbed.

MALE NARRATOR: In Edinburgh, in 1914, Firbank met Father John Grey, friend of Beardsley and – or so they say – the original of Dorian Gray.
   Therefore Firbank's flirtatious skirmishings with Rome lead us not only to the place of his death but also directly into the mauve and yellow shadows of his fabulous –

(Drum roll – a different one, taps, perhaps.)

FEMALE NARRATOR: 'Elementary Structures of Ronald Firbank. Three: Decadence.'

FIRBANK: *(On speaker.)* 'I hope you'll say I was wicked and interesting.'

MALE NARRATOR: Wyndham Lewis.

LEWIS: *(In hall.)* 'Ronald Firbank – the very genius loci of the "post-war" and the reincarnation of all the Nineties – Oscar Wilde, Pater, Beardsley, Dowson, all rolled into one and served up with a sauce créole.

I shouldn't like to have a grave next to his.

Firbank in his winding-sheet upon a moonlit night would be a problem for the least fussy of corpses in the same part of the cemetery.'

FEMALE NARRATOR: Grant Richards published most of Firbank's novels, upon payment, but did not approve of him.

GRANT RICHARDS: *(On speaker.)* 'I am told that smart young hostesses in New York would give parties at which each guest would be presented with a copy of the same Firbank book and that one who could discover most improprieties therein after an hour's reading would get a prize.'

YOUNG WOMAN: *(On speaker. American accent.)* 'How I envy the *men*, Rara, in his platoon!' 'Take away his uniform, Olga, and what does he become? "Ah, *what* – "'

(Applause; laughter.)

MALE NARRATOR: Harold Nicolson.

HAROLD NICOLSON: *(On speaker.)* . . . epicene giggling . . .

FEMALE NARRATOR: He wore the sign of his decadence upon his face, his powder, his rouge.

OLD FIRBANK: *(Echo, on speaker.)* 'Eh, lad! That woarn't pull a load of muck!'

MALE NARRATOR: *(Accusing.)* What did *you* do in the Great War, Artie?

FEMALE NARRATOR: He was the bravest of the brave. He did – nothing.

Decadence, like dandyism, rigorously embraces the pursuit of the inessential.

MALE NARRATOR: It takes for granted the notion that all pleasure is polymorphously perverse.

FIRBANK: *(On speaker.)* 'Now you're here, I shall ask you, I think, to whip me.'

FEMALE NARRATOR: Forrest Reid, who knew him at Cambridge:

FORREST REID: *(On speaker, pompous.)* 'He was a decadent of the school of Oscar Wilde, but lacking Wilde's intellect.'

FEMALE NARRATOR: He adopted decadence as a pose, another form of artifice, a resolute concentration upon appearances, upon artificial behaviour – a dandyism of the imagination. Harold Nicolson, writing when the memory of Firbank's 'post-war' had been obliterated by another war:

NICOLSON: *(On speaker.)* 'Ronald Firbank is an arresting figure. Most people who were born before 1900 belong to a bygone age. The odd thing about Ronald Firbank was that he belonged to two bygone ages. Emotionally he belonged to the Beardsley period, whereas intellectually he belonged to the Sitwell period.'

FEMALE NARRATOR: But Carl Van Vechten, writing at the time, in that 'post-war' we now know to have been 'between the wars', whose mood seems, now, even more one of defiance of the past and abandonment of the future:

VAN VECHTEN: *(On speaker, American accent.)* 'Firbank is more than up-to-date. He is the Pierrot of the minute. Felicien Rops on a merry-go-round. Aubrey Beardsley in a Rolls-Royce. Ronald in Lesbosland. Puck celebrating the Black Mass.'

FIRBANK: *(Close to mic. Begins to bubble with delight.)*

VAN VECHTEN: *(Getting carried away.)* 'Sacher-Masoch in Mayfair. A Rebours à la mode. Aretino in Piccadilly. Jean Cocteau at the Savoy.'

FIRBANK: *(On mic. laughs. Repeating* VAN VECHTEN *with childlike delight.)* Jean Cocteau at the Savoy!

(Slight pause.)

MALE NARRATOR: The true decadent remains in blissful ignorance of his own social aberrance. He is never aware of his doing or being anything that gets him into trouble. Sewell Stokes:

STOKES: 'I last saw Ronald Firbank on the evening of an unusually warm Easter Monday in London. He had driven the short distance to the Café Royal from Pall Mall, where we had dined late, and all the way Firbank – '

FIRBANK: *(On speaker.)* Hannen Swaffer, Hannen Swaffer . . .

STOKES: ' – kept repeating the name – '

FIRBANK: *(On speaker.)* Hannen Swaffer!

STOKES: – who, having read one of Firbank's novels, wrote in his Sunday paper:

HANNEN SWAFFER: *(On speaker.)* 'It is a piece of decadence which I am surprised to see published. What the censor of books can have been thinking about when he let this pass, I do not know. With pleasure I will show my copy to any policeman who cares to call at the office and see it.'

FEMALE NARRATOR: The American publisher, Brentano's, turned down *Cardinal Pirelli* on 'religious and moral grounds'. Brentano's was afraid that 'the outspokenness of the book regarding the life of the Cardinal and particularly church matters' would offend the general public.

FIRBANK: *(Close to mic. Big sigh.)*

FEMALE NARRATOR: Which put an end to certain dreams Ronald Firbank had lately been cherishing to visit New York, the Rome of the twentieth century, and, perhaps, in some sequestered Harlem bar, to hear at the source:

BLACK VOICE: *(On speaker.)* Take all that and syncopate it!

(Jazz drum roll.)

MALE NARRATOR: 'Elementary Structures of Ronald Firbank. Four: Ragtime.'

BLACK VOICE: This is the new rhythm!

(Ragtime; fade down.)

FIRBANK: *(On speaker. Over.)* 'The latest jazz, bewildering, glittering, exuberant . . . a jazz throbbing, pulsating with a zim, zim, zim, a jazz all verve and abandon . . .'

(Fade up ragtime. Firbank hums along; fade music down.)

BLACK VOICE: *(Over.)* So this white boy thinks he can play the blues?

FIRBANK: *(On speaker. Over.)* Oh yes! yes! just let me join in! show me how it goes!

BLACK VOICE: *(Over.)* Man, if you gotta ask, you just ain't got it.

(Music up; off.)

FIRBANK: *(Close to mic.)* De dum – de dumm dum dum – de dum –

(He hums sadly by himself for a moment, then falls silent.)

FEMALE NARRATOR: So he must syncopate his prose as best he might.

MALE NARRATOR: Think of his syncopated prose as if it were the music, not of Louis Armstrong or King Oliver but of Bix Beiderbecke, Eddie Condon, Mezz Mezzrow, white jazz played by white boys who loved it so much they wanted to simulate, synthesise, make it their own music.

FEMALE NARRATOR: Music of the sweet, self-created Creole which Mrs Yajnavalkya speaks, in *Valmouth*.

FIRBANK: *(On speaker.)* 'We Eastern women love the sun . . . ! When de thermometer rise to some two hundred or so, ah, dat is de time to lie among de bees and canes . . .'

MALE NARRATOR: The Mouth family in *Prancing Nigger*:

FIRBANK: *(On speaker.)* 'Start de gramophone gwine, girls, an' gib us somet'in' bright!'

(Wind up gramophone.)

MALE NARRATOR: *(Over.)* Even, you might say, ragtime with an English accent; composed by someone, in his heart irretrievably committed to high art . . .

(Needle comes down with a click; Constant Lambert: black pieces on white notes; fade down but not out.)

MALE NARRATOR: *(Over.)* An *artificial* ragtime, evidently!

(Fade music up, then down; and out by middle of next speech.)

(Over.) And this *jazz à l'anglaise*, this syncopated high society, the cultivated exoticism that comes to dominate his verbal music, is the exoticism of:

(Not drums, this time, but Afro-Cuban style marimbas.)

FEMALE NARRATOR: 'Elementary Structures of Ronald Firbank. Five: Elsewhere.'

MALE NARRATOR: He tried to live in Harrogate, once, but found it too disgusting.

(Steamship siren.)

Knowing of Firbank's travels, Siegfried Sassoon asked him:

SASSOON: *(On speaker.)* What is your favourite country?

FIRBANK: *(On speaker.)* Lotus Land!

(Close to mic. – Laughter.)

(On speaker.) 'He had been into Arcadia, even, a place where artificial temperaments so seldom get.'

MALE NARRATOR: Raisley Moorsom.

MOORSOM: *(On speaker.)* 'He told me he'd recently come from Carthage where the young men bathing in the sea:

FIRBANK: *(On speaker.)* 'wore diamonds in their navels flashing in the sun.'

(Steamship siren – on speaker.)

MALE NARRATOR: Once he told Aldous Huxley he was going to the West Indies to collect material for a novel about Mayfair.

FEMALE NARRATOR: Osbert Sitwell claims you sent him a postcard.

FIRBANK: *(On speaker.)* 'Tomorrow I go to Haiti. They say the President is a perfect dear.'

FEMALE NARRATOR: The ship is ready.

(Fade in Constant Lambert's 'Rio Grande'.)

(Over.) Some fabulous Indies of the imagination, East Indies, West Indies, either, both; a tropic and utterly exotic elsewhere.

(Fade up 'Rio Grande' until first phrase of singing; fade out.)

FIRBANK: *(On speaker. As 'Rio Grande' fades.)* 'Floor of copper, floor of gold . . . Beyond the custom-house door, ajar, the street of sunrise seemed aflame.
Have you anything, young man to declare?
. . . Butterflies!
Exempt of duty. Pass.
Floor of silver, floor of pearl.
Trailing a muslin net and laughing for happiness,
Charlie Mouth marched into town.'

FEMALE NARRATOR: Who, at customs, had only genius to declare?

OSCAR WILDE: *(On speaker.)* The unfortunate Oscar Wilde.

FIRBANK: *(On speaker.)* 'Charlie Mouth marched into town.
Cuna, full of charming roses, full of violet shadows, full of music, full of love, Cuna!'

FEMALE NARRATOR: The city of Cuna, possibly based on Havana, Cuba, where Firbank stayed for some time at the Ritz in 1922.

MALE NARRATOR: The novel, called *Sorrow in Sunlight* in England, which Carl Van Vechten, perhaps over-presuming on his friendship with Langston Hughes, persuaded him to title, *Prancing Nigger* in the States.

FEMALE NARRATOR: There, elsewhere, in those Gauguin landscapes of fruit and flowers, two elements merge: jazz music and negritude, aspects of a place of perfect, improvisational freedom . . .

MALE NARRATOR: . . . the space in which his ideal fiction unfolds . . .

FEMALE NARRATOR: . . . in the perpetual tension of the knowledge this perfect elsewhere exists only – *as* a fiction, is the forever unattainable, non-existent Eden.

FIRBANK: *(On speaker.)* 'Little city of cocktails, Cuna! The surpassing excellence of thy Barmen, who shall sing?'

(Pop: bubble, bubble, bubble.)

FEMALE NARRATOR: He came to a bad end in Cuna.

MALE NARRATOR: Who did?

FEMALE NARRATOR: Charlie Mouth. He was corrupted by the city. The entire Mouth family fell apart there. They'd come to Cuna to try to enter high society. They paid the dreadful price of failure. Perhaps it *is* a novel about Mayfair?

(Pause; papers being gathered together.)

MALE NARRATOR: To sum up: let us quote, again, from Baudelaire, *The Painter of Modern Life*.
    ' . . . this solitary mortal endowed with an active imagination, always roaming the great desert of men, has a nobler aim than that of pure idler . . . He is looking for that indefinable something we may be allowed to call 'modernity'; for want of a better term to express the idea in question. The aim for him is to extract from fashion the poetry that resides in its historical envelope, to distil the eternal from the transitory.'
    Thank you.

(Applause, fade, end of seminar acoustic. Pause.)

FIRBANK: 'And suddenly the Angel of Death passed by and the brilliant season waned.'

OSBERT SITWELL: ' . . . at the end of each summer (in London) for five or six years it was his habit to drive round in state and say goodbye to my brother and myself; and, each time, he would tell us that he knew there were but a few months more for him to live. These doleful tidings had invariably been conveyed to him either by a Syrian magician or by some wretched drunkard in the Café Royal.

So many times did these final scenes occur that when in truth he came to us for the last goodbye in our house, it conveyed little, being merely part of a regular and ordinary routine.'

FEMALE NARRATOR: Yet that last summer of 1925, to the gloomy forecasts of the fortune-tellers was added the diagnosis of Dr Edward P. Furber, of Welbeck Street. And, after he heard it, Firbank sat all alone in the Café Royal, drunk, crying out:

(Fade in restaurant noises. Restaurant noises.)

FIRBANK: 'I don't want to die! I don't want to die!'

(Fade restaurant noises; Schubert's 'Death and Maiden', again; fade down and out.)

SEWELL STOKES: 'Firbank's last words came in a letter from Rome shortly before he died:'

FIRBANK: 'Have you forgotten a certain laugh? It is growing rarer and rarer, now.'

FEMALE NARRATOR: Alone, in a room with dreadful wallpaper at the Hotel Quirinal, Rome, death surprised him before he'd time to put on some rouge, or change his shirt, or fortify himself with a last glass. Death helped him evade his dreaded fortieth birthday by a few months, and, by a few weeks, forced him to miss the publication of his last completed novel, *Concerning the Eccentricities of Cardinal Pirelli*, whose appearance had been delayed due to the General Strike. The self-made man, unmade; artifice at last put away, packed in a trunk marked 'Not wanted on voyage'.

(Train whistle; the most magnificent 'train' blues that can be found – Ma Rainey or Bessie Smith, at full stretch – Firbank's final black travelling music; or a 'Gospel Train' spiritual, again as magnificent as might be. Fade blues. Music out.)

THE END

LIBRETTO

Orlando: or,
The Enigma of the Sexes

Orlando: or,
The Enigma of the Sexes

PROLOGUE

(Curtain up.
A dark, neutral curtained space. Orlando's tutor, in gown, stock, a Renaissance
figure, stands with an open book at a lectern. Orlando kneels at his feet.)

ORLANDO: When I was a boy, they gave me a tutor
 who taught me Latin, who taught me Greek . . .

TUTOR: I taught him Latin, I taught him Greek,
 I taught him the new learning.
 In those days the ice
 of the old world was breaking,
 the sleeping giants in men's minds were waking,
 the winter of the dark was over.

 We studied Greek, we read together 'The Symposium' . . .

 'Now, Aristophanes banged his wine cup on the table
 and, laughing, swore how no one,
 no man nor woman ever
 had understood Love and all its power
 for, if we had done so,
 we would have built the great god temples
 and sacrificed daily in his honour. And yet we do not.

 But, before we speak of love, said Aristophanes,
 we must speak of the great tragedy of our natures,
 how once we were perfect and are no longer.
 For then, in the beginning,
 there were not two sexes, as there are now,
 but one only – not men nor women
 but one perfected nature, the union of man and woman,
 the double nature, male and female in one being,

contrarieties in harmony,
the resolution of contradictions,

and they were proud, so proud
they fought the gods.

So Zeus, to punish them,
split them all in half,
straight down the middle,
as you slice an apple,
and left us mutilated,
to punish us,
each sex as incomplete
as shadow without substance.

After this cruel division,
bereft, the crippled halves
each one desires the other,
they come together, they throw
their arms about each other,
longing, longing
to grow into one again
as they had been, as once they had been.

So ancient is the desire implanted in us
to reunite our original nature,
to make one of two,
to heal the state of humankind.

And I do believe, said Aristophanes,
that if all our loves were perfectly accomplished,
each one returning to his primal nature,
had his true love, and, reunited, formed
the one, true, perfect being,
why, then our race would be entirely happy.'

ORLANDO: So he read to me
out of the old books
about the great mysteries of our desires.

TUTOR: About the great mysteries of our desires
and the enigma of the sexes.

ORLANDO: But then he closed his book
and said goodbye to me.

(TUTOR *closes book, kisses* ORLANDO's *forehead.*)

>   and the first light
>   that shone on my infancy
>   was quite eclipsed.

TUTOR: Go, little soul, you must go on your journey,
>   you must learn all this again
>   through the years, through the centuries,
>   through the masks, the riddles
>   of your ambiguous being,
>   you child of time
>   and of the imagination.

ORLANDO: And so begins my life in time.

CURTAIN

ACT ONE

SCENE I

(The curtain rises. Darkness. A chinking of keys announces the housekeeper of Knole, Mrs Grimsditch, in decent black with an apron and a bunch of keys at her waist – essentially, her costume is traditional 'servant's' clothes, but more of 1928 than of any other period. (The time is 1928.) The lights rise as Grimsditch switches on a set of electric candelabra.

The stage is a vague space, ready for transformations. It contains only a stylised version of a Great Bed; a night-table; and two enormous gilt frames pendant. In one frame stands ORLANDO, *as an Elizabethan boy, holding a rose. In the other stands* ELIZABETH I, *looking very iconic, the Elizabeth of the last years of her reign. Gloriana, the image of England.*

DUPPER, *the Knole butler, follows* GRIMSDITCH, *carrying a water jug and a glass for the night-table.*

GRIMSDITCH *carries a bundle of bed-linen in her arms.)*

MRS GRIMSDITCH: Getting the bedroom ready, you see.
That's my job – always been my job.
Still my job, in this year of grace
Nineteen twenty-eight, just as it always was.
The others come and go, or change.
But *we* don't change, do we.
Here we stay, the perfect housekeeper –

DUPPER: Here we stay, the perfect butler –
We're part of the furniture,
The fixtures and fittings . . .

MRS GRIMSDITCH: Mrs Grimsditch, the housekeeper –

DUPPER: Mr Dupper, the butler –

*(*DUPPER *strips the patchwork cover off the bed, holds up a sheet that has worn to lace with time.)*

DUPPER: Well, and I will say this, Mrs G. –
You've worn a lot better
Than milady's sheets!

MRS GRIMSDITCH: She said she'd get some new ones.
Said she'd stop off at Marshal and Snelgrove's

And get some new ones,
While she was in town ...

[DUET]

DUPPER: About time, too.
　　　　After all these years ...

GRIMSDITCH: Well I remember
　　　　When these sheets were new.

(She addresses the frame containing ELIZABETH I.*)*

We built this bed for you.
Sheets cost a fortune,
A fortune, in those days ...
Your entertainment!
How much it cost us!
Those were the days,

*(*DUPPER *addresses portrait of* ORLANDO.*)*

DUPPER: Do you remember?

GRIMSDITCH: Do you remember?

ORLANDO: *(Stepping from frame.)* My fathers were noble
since they were at all,
They emerged from the mists of antiquity,
one and all with coronets on their heads.
Then I was young
When I was a young boy,
The age was different.

(Light infinitely rich and golden, now; servants enter, carrying emblematic items to create a richly Elizabethan room; one throws a tapestry over the bed, another hangs a coat of arms above it. They are preparing for a state visit from ELIZABETH I. *The servants, all in Elizabethan costume, take up the refrain.)*

SERVANTS: The age was different ...

ORLANDO: Sunsets were redder, then, the dawn came
Like a white swan out of a dark lake ...
The age is different, the age is Elizabethan ...
There is no twilight, there is no shadow ...

(The servants take off aprons etc. and begin to behave like lords and ladies, forming a formal background for ELIZABETH *in her frame. Her frame vanishes;*

ORLANDO, *a beautiful boy like a Nicholas Hillyard miniature, approaches* GLORIANA, *bows with a tremendous flourish.)*

CHORUS: Vivat, vivat, Elizabeth Regina!
  The golden age, the age of Elizabeth!
  Vivat! Vivat!

(Brilliant, golden light; ELIZABETH *comes forward on her state visit to Knole.)*

ELIZABETH: I am the weary one,
  I am the tired one.
  This is a shell,
  They call it Gloriana,
  I hide inside it.

  In my ears always,
  The sound of gunfire.
  Always before me,
  The blade of the assassin . . .

  I am the weary,
  I am the wary one.

(She turns to ORLANDO.*)*

  Because of my experience, I see his innocence;
  Because of my weariness, I see his strength.
  Because I am withered, I see his freshness.

(She gives him her hand.)

[DUET]

ORLANDO: But I was so shy of her, all that I saw of her
  Was the hand that she offered me, her thin hand,
  Her age-freckled hand, her hand that gifted you
  Death or good fortune,
  Death or the world.

*(*ORLANDO *kneels and kisses* ELIZABETH*'s hand.)*

ELIZABETH: My lovely boy, I shall advance you –
  Fortune's own favourite –
  The child of my heart –

*(*ELIZABETH *takes the ring from her finger and places it on* ORLANDO*'s index finger, where it will remain for the rest of the action.)*

ELIZABETH: I name you my treasurer and my steward, Orlando.

(ORLANDO *rises.* DUPPER *enters, very stately, carrying on high a satin cushion bearing the Order of the Garter.* ELIZABETH *stoops, creaking, and ties the Order round* ORLANDO'S *leg, to his slight embarrassment and the audible wonder of the lords and ladies.*)

LORDS AND LADIES: Such an honour! To be so honoured!
  By the Queen's own hand!

ORLANDO: I was so shy, I saw and heard nothing . . .
  But I knew it was good fortune.

ELIZABETH: When I ride in state,
  You shall ride with me –

LORDS AND LADIES: (*Antiphonal.*) Strength, grace, romance –
  Folly, poetry, youth –

ELIZABETH: The son of my old age
  the limb of my infirmity,
  the oak on which I
  can lean my weariness,
  the child of my heart
  who will sing me to sleep . . .

LORDS AND LADIES: (*Whispering.*) So she can rest, sometimes . . .
  So she can rest, sometimes . . .

(ORLANDO *and three ladies-in-waiting assist* ELIZABETH *to the Great Bed; they arrange her, fully dressed, against the bolster so that she looks more iconic than ever. They place the orb in one hand and the sceptre in the other, to show how the burden of her royalty weighs upon her even at her rest.* ORLANDO, *less shy, now, gently, almost paternally kisses her forehead. Stage slowly darkens.*)

Lullaby for Elizabeth

The moment is brief,
the moment is over
then one long night
we all shall sleep.

The roses fade
the petals fall
pluck the day
the day is all.

> The sun rises
> the sun sets
> we love then
> like the mist we go.

(Stage darkens with ELIZABETH *arrayed in splendour on the bed and* ORLANDO *standing protectively beside her. It is like a lying-in-state. Individual spots on* GRIMSDITCH *and* DUPPER, *standing at either end of the stage, down front, like a pair of pot dogs on either end of a mantelpiece. They are the genii loci of Knole.)*

DUPPER: So the fortunes of the house prospered, you see.
  That was the real start of it.

GRIMSDITCH: The old queen couldn't resist him.
  She with no chick nor child of her own.
  You could say the fortunes of the house were founded
  because he was so shy and tender with her . . .

DUPPER: So shy and tender that she trusted him.
  The fortunes of the house prospered.

(We see that DUPPER *is carrying a large travelling cloak. Now he shakes it out and marches towards* ORLANDO, *who comes down into the light towards him.* DUPPER *wraps* ORLANDO *in the cloak.)*

DUPPER: Now your life has begun, sir!

GRIMSDITCH: It was like the beginning of the world,
  in those days, it was like
  Eden, in those days . . .
  and he had the whole world before him!

DUPPER: The whole world before you, sir!

*(*ORLANDO *flourishes the cloak and laughs triumphantly.)*

  All your life as a man!
  London!

(Gauze descends, concealing ORLANDO, GRIMSDITCH *and* DUPPER.*)*

SCENE 2 GAUZE OF LONDON TOWN

(An Elizabethan London, featuring, say, the Tower of London and the Globe Theatre.)
  ORLANDO, *wrapped in his big cloak, describes the excitement of the great city for a country boy like himself. He explains his love of low company – how he*

always hides his insignia of rank when he goes to Wapping to have a high old time amongst the common people. And how it was, one memorable winter when the Thames itself froze right over, that, for the first time, he lost his heart.)

SCENE 3   THE ICE FAIR

(Gauze vanishes; ORLANDO *exits. The stage is dominated by the frame of the ship of the Russian* AMBASSADOR, *locked in the ice. The ship is black; a huge flag with a double-headed eagle.*

Around the ice-locked ship, a scene of gaiety and tumult not unlike that in the first act of Petroushka – *apple sellers; a roasting pig, off which slices are carved; a puppet booth; ballad singers; a dancer on stilts; a tumbler; pickpockets; whores; a dancing bear.*

Mingling with this throng, the ambiguous figure of the ARCHDUCHESS HARRIET, *though I rather feel we should first be introduced to him as a man. The* ARCHDUKE *enters with a titter of whores and takes part in an Elizabethan dance, perhaps partnered by the bear. At some point, the* ARCHDUKE *catches sight of* ORLANDO, *mingling with the throng –* ORLANDO *also engages in the dance – the* ARCHDUKE *is immediately rapt.* ORLANDO *is flirting with the gypsy girl who looks after the bear.*

The dance is broken up by some dark, Slavonic chords. An EMISSARY *of the Russian* AMBASSADOR *appears on the prow of the ship. He is heavily bearded and furred, like a boyar in* Ivan the Terrible'.*)*

EMISSARY: Where is the servant of the Great Queen
  who has come to bring her greetings to my master?

*(*ORLANDO *flings off his cloak and, a dazzling, Elizabethan gentleman, advances to the ship.)*

ORLANDO: I am he. Welcome.

(The retinue of the Russian AMBASSADOR *file off the ship; the* AMBASSADOR *himself, immense, hairy, ominous, appears on the prow.)*

AMBASSADOR: From the country of snow and perpetual winter
  I bring gifts for the great queen
  From her most suitable suitor, Ivan,
  Ivan, Tsar of all the Russias,
  Ivan, whose name makes all the shadows tremble.

*(*ORLANDO *explains that the* QUEEN *is sick and he,* ORLANDO, *will receive the gifts for her. Russians bring gifts from the ship – an icon; mounds of furs; lastly, modelling one of those 'Ivan the Terrible' crowns that are all fur with lots*

of precious stones and gold round the edge, SASHA, *the Russian princess, appears on the ship, in her Russian tunic and trousers.)*

AMBASSADOR: The Princess Marousha Stanilovska Dagmar
  Natasha Ilian Romanovitch, my niece, no,
  my daughter, no, my niece, no, my daughter . . .

(SASHA descends from the ship, makes an Oriental kind of obeisance, very ironically, to ORLANDO; ORLANDO *raises* SASHA *to her feet. There follows a scene between them culminating in this aria:)*

ORLANDO: Sasha. I shall call you Sasha.
  It was the name of a fox,
  a white Russian fox,
  that my father gave me
  when I was a boy.

  It was soft as snow, that fox,
  oh, how I loved it!
  but it bit me so badly
  My father killed it . . .

  Sasha. I'll call you Sasha.

(Darkness falls upon the ice fair behind them, among which the Russians have adopted still, hieratic poses. SASHA *and* ORLANDO *are alone in a pool of light. They sing a love duet, a winter love duet, the words of which I haven't yet assembled.)*

[LOVE DUET]

SASHA: I must give you a present,
  I know the perfect present –
  something you can only possess
  in the moment of giving,
  the perfect love gift . . .

*(She runs back into the ship.
  Lightning; a lurid light – and a tremendous crack.)*

VOICES: *(Off.)* The ice! The ice! The ice has broken!

(SASHA appears on the prow of the ship with a white falcon on her wrist. She releases the bird as the ship begins to move away, to the right, amidst a tumult of splintering wood and shrieks. All the relics of the ice fair float away, off to the right. Tumult. Chaos.

The falcon flies away. Sasha stands on the prow with her arm flung out, as it was when she let the bird fly from it; the Russian AMBASSADOR, *her uncle, her father, or her lover, stands beside her, now engulfing her in his great fur.)*

ORLANDO: The ice is broken! My heart is broken!

SCENE 4 THE BEDCHAMBER AT KNOLE

(The notional Great Bed rolls on and comes to a halt in its position stage centre. Coat of arms descends from above, likewise two portraits, now real portraits, of ORLANDO *as Elizabethan boy and* ELIZABETH I.

ORLANDO *flings himself on the bed, weeping.*

DUPPER *comes in and helps him off with his cloak and boots.*

Rain and tears; SASHA'*s voice, offstage, sings about Russia.*

ORLANDO *sleeps. When the absolute quintessence of romantic melancholy had been reached, suddenly bells ring out.* ORLANDO *does not stir.* DUPPER *rushes in.)*

DUPPER: Milord! The Queen! The Queen is dead! Long live the King!

(ORLANDO *stirs drowsily but does not wake.)*

CURTAIN of English country house gauze.

End of Act One.

No intermission. Musical interlude.

ACT TWO

SCENE I THE BEDCHAMBER AT KNOLE

(ORLANDO *is engaged in changing the furniture.* DUPPER *organises servants filling the stage with heavy, oak, Jacobean furniture; a portrait of King Charles II, with spaniel, descends from the flies to join the portraits of* ORLANDO *and* QUEEN ELIZABETH. *Servants carry in a large, heavy wardrobe; they swear and curse as they do so. The servants retire, leaving* ORLANDO *to admire his fashionable, new surroundings.*

The door of the wardrobe opens. Out steps the ARCHDUCHESS HARRIET, *a tall, stately matron in a crimson satin dress with lots of patches on her rouged cheeks.*

The ARCHDUCHESS HARRIET GRIZELDA OF FINSTER-AARHORN *introduces herself.*

ORLANDO, *startled but graciously composing himself, calls for madeira.* GRIMSDITCH *brings a tray of madeira and glasses, with an ill grace; she does not think the* ARCHDUCHESS *has made a lady-like arrival in* ORLANDO'S *bedroom. She exits, with a flounce. The couple sit on* ORLANDO'S *new chairs. The* ARCHDUCHESS *flirts more and more outrageously;* ORLANDO *is flattered, embarrassed and soon a little tipsy.*

At last the ARCHDUCHESS *rises to her full height, which is not inconsiderable. She swoops in for the 'kill', like an enormous crimson bird.*

Carrying ORLANDO *in her arms, like a sacrifice,* ORLANDO *protesting, but only limply, she bears him towards the Great Bed.*

Blackout.)

SCENE 2 THE BEDCHAMBER AT KNOLE

(*The lights come on to find* ORLANDO, *in considerable disarray, shirt undone etc., pacing about a room that is also in considerable disarray – overturned chairs, etc.*)

ORLANDO: I must leave the country; compromised!
　By a woman old enough
　to be my mother!
　Ruined!

(GRIMSDITCH *enters and begins, primly, to tidy up, muttering antiphonally about 'that terrible woman', how* ORLANDO *'mustn't take on so', etc.*

ORLANDO *lists the countries to which he could go; to Virginia – glance at the portrait of* ELIZABETH I; *to the Virgin Islands, unless this is a weak joke; to burning Africa and the incorruptible sands; to Turkey, where all the women go veiled and there is no temptation –*

DUPPER *enters self-importantly, carrying* ORLANDO'S *letters patent on a silver salver and announces King Charles's intention to send him to the Sublime Porte as his ambassador to Turkey.*

To Constantinople, where the women are all locked up together, out of harm's way, and ORLANDO *will be safe from temptation!*

The servants enter and begin to remove the furniture of the bedchamber. DUPPER *takes a caftan out of the wardrobe that held the* ARCHDUCHESS *and* ORLANDO *slips it on. Now he is ready for the Orient.*)

SCENE 3 CONSTANTINOPLE

(ORLANDO, *as Ambassador from the Court of Saint James, sits behind the large desk, signing documents. His secretary brings in another box of documents. As* ORLANDO *signs them, he comments on the beauty of the distant mountains and the exoticism of the court.*

The secretary, meanwhile, discusses the instability and xenophobia of the Ottoman regime, the notorious propensity of the Turks for treachery and the stories in the bazaar of plans for a pre-emptive putsch against the foreigners, who are not sons of Islam.

ORLANDO *ignores all this; he muses on the difference between the Golden Horn and Tonbridge Wells.*

The muezzin is called as twilight descends. A team of purple-plumed janissaries run in, pulling a carriage containing His Britannic Majesty's emissary, SIR ADRIAN SCROPE, *who emerges pompously to announce that* ORLANDO'S *sterling work as Ambassador to the Sublime Porte has earned him a dukedom.*

Rockets explode. ORLANDO *says this calls for a very special celebration.*)

SCENE 4 EMBASSY INTERIOR

(*The Turks assemble a tent of silken hangings around* ORLANDO *and close the flap, concealing him. A theatrical atmosphere is present.*

European lords and ladies, in flamboyant costume, take up their places; the Sultan, the veiled Sultana and the entire harem, fill up the stage on cushions, as spectators.

ORLANDO's *secretary, looking very uncomfortable in a brief, neo-classical toga, announces the presentation of a masque in the classical style to be performed in celebration of* ORLANDO's *elevation to the highest rank his country can afford.*

A brief overture; three white-robed female figures, PURITY, CHASTITY *and* MODESTY, *pick their way through the crowd towards the silk tent.* MODESTY *is carrying* ORLANDO's *ducal regalia on a satin cushion.*

CHASTITY *peeps inside the tent-flap, emits a squeak and drops the flap back in place.* PURITY *sternly opens the tent-flap and pins it back, to reveal* ORLANDO, *in a toga, lying as if asleep on a dais inside the tent.*)

PURITY: I am our Lady of Purity,
   the guardian of the sleeping fawn,
   the snow is dear to me,
   and the moon rise,
   and the silver sea.
   I cover the speckled hen's egg
   with my silver robe,
   I cover vice and poverty.
   On all things frail or dark or doubtful
   my veil descends.
   Sleep, my Adonis, in your purity . . .
   ought Purity hide you from fame?

CHORUS: No! no! never! never let Purity hide him from Fame!

(Purity retires.)

CHASTITY: I am our Lady of Chastity,
   whose touch is snow,
   whose glance is cold water.
   I live in the chaste air
   of the mountains, lightning
   flashes in my hair.
   Shall I wake Orlando
   to the promiscuity of fame?

MODESTY: Our Lady of Modesty, they call me.
   My voice is only a little whisper.
   Virgin I am and ever shall be.
   Not for me the fruitful fields
   – ever I shun the fertile vineyard.

I veil myself with my abundant hair
so that I shan't see the vain,
the fleeting shadow of fame.
Never must Orlando wake!

(They join hands and sing.)

PURITY, CHASTITY AND MODESTY: Never awake! Never awake!
Never awake!

(Trumpets.)

ALL: Who is here? Who can this be? What goddess rises?

(And perhaps she does indeed rise; or, rather, make an extraordinary entry, on a litter borne by Nubians in a huge cloud of rosy smoke. VENUS PANDEMOS, *all covered with fruit and flowers.)*

VENUS: My Adonis! Yonder he sleeps!
He must know the truth!

(Now, while all this has been going on, the Turks in the audience have been growing increasingly restless. And, as VENUS *cries out: Truth! the Sultana rises and drops her veil. We see it is the* ARCHDUCHESS HARRIET, *all the time.*
At this signal, the veiled ladies rise, throw off their robes and reveal themselves as fully armed janisseries, who fall upon the Europeans, waving scimitars. ORLANDO's *secretary dashes stage front –)*

SECRETARY: What a to–do! What a bother! Guessed it all along!
Treachery! Black treachery! England expects –

(and is cut down. Screaming. Fighting. Only VENUS *continues to loll, laughing, in front of the dais on which* ORLANDO *continues to sleep.*
Trumpets.)

VENUS: The truth! Avaunt ye, you weird sisters,
you Purity, you Modesty, you Chastity!
What have you to do with my Orlando?
The truth!

*(*PURITY, MODESTY *and* CHASTITY *make themselves scarce. Above the wild scene of mayhem,* ORLANDO *slowly wakes and, slowly, rises from his sleep.*

VENUS, *laughing, pelts him with roses.*
A shaft of white light transfixes him.
The riot is stilled as all present take in the fact that ORLANDO'*s toga has
slipped from his shoulders; he is naked.*
Awe, wonder, amazement.
Orlando is a woman!)

CURTAIN

End of Act Two.

Intermission.

ACT THREE

SCENE I SHIPBOARD

(Rough tars shanty, pulling ropes to set the scene. A bluff sea-captain enters, telescope under his arm, escorting an elegant lady. Stumbling over a coiled halyard, the lady, ORLANDO, reveals a glimpse of stocking and is amused by the rough tars' reaction, the sea captain's blushing embarrassment.

He assists her to a comfortable seat on a barrel. ORLANDO flirts gently with the sea captain and reflects on her changed state. She is getting used to being a girl. The sea-captain announces they are now nearly home, are sailing up the Thames; he points out the new sights of London. There has been a plague, there has been a fire. Now we have Saint Paul's. There is a new spirit abroad; it is the age of wit and wisdom, it is the eighteenth century. He mentions ADDISON, SWIFT, POPE. Then invites ORLANDO below to take tea with him.

Tea? What is this tea?

The sea-captain explains how the new refinement of the times is not compatible with the hearty ale of Old England. In these days, an infusion of the Chinese leaf is said to clear the palate and make the brain dance. She must try it. ORLANDO, nothing loath, goes below with him to partake of a farewell dish of this curious beverage.

The ship docks. The tars start unloading tea chests.)

SCENE 2 KNOLE

GRIMSDITCH: The house goes badly when the master is away.

DUPPER: The tiles want mending.

GRIMSDITCH: The towels want mending.

DUPPER: The drains want seeing to,
the trees need planting.

GRIMSDITCH: There's moth in the curtains
in the chaplain's parlour;
shall we darn them or shall we replace them?
Who makes the most important decisions
when the master is away?

DUPPER: And it's high time we had some
little masters and mistresses,
why, the master must be thirty
if he is a day –

(ORLANDO, *in sumptuous travelling dress, enters to greet them.*)

ORLANDO: Dupper! Grimsditch! my good and faithful servants!

DUPPER AND GRIMSDITCH: Milord! milady! milord! milady!
Milady!
Milady!
Welcome home . . . well I never . . . welcome home.

GRIMSDITCH: If Milord is Milady now, I've never
seen a lovelier . . .

DUPPER: Like as two peaches both on one bough . . .
she hasn't changed, has she; not
what you'd call changed . . .

BOTH: Welcome milady!

(ORLANDO *kisses them both.*)

SCENE 3 THE DRAWING ROOM

(*As the servants bring on a round Georgian table,* ORLANDO *announces her
intention of holding a tea party, as a tribute to the elegant and refined spirit of the
New Age, and intends to invite some of the Age's finest flowers.* GRIMSDITCH
*helps her off with her travelling cloak to reveal an informal gown of the kind
called, I think, a 'sac', and* ORLANDO *sits at the tea table.* DUPPER *brings a
silver pot, milk jug etc., and announces* POPE, ADDISON *and* SWIFT, *all
looking like caricatures of themselves.*
   They sit down. ORLANDO *pours.*)

POPE: 'Whether the Nymph shall break Diana's Law,
   Or some frail China Jar receive a flaw,
   Or stain her Honour, or her new Brocade,
   Forget her prayers or miss a Masquerade,
   Or lose her Heart, or Necklace, at a Ball – '

(*All applaud.*)

ORLANDO: What brilliance. What wit.

(POPE *sips his tea.*)

ADDISON: 'I consider woman as a beautiful, romantic animal
that may be adorned with furs and feathers,
pearls and diamonds, ores and silks.
The lynx shall cast its skin
at her feet to make her a tippet,
the peacock, parrot and swan shall pay
contributions to her muff;
the sea shall be searched for shells,
and the rocks for gems,
and every part of nature furnish out its share
towards the embellishment of a creature
that is the most consummate work of it . . .'

ORLANDO: *(Aside.)* What a wonderful piece of work is a woman!
How well he puts it!
Strange how I never think of myself
in this way!

ORLANDO: *(Aloud.)* Bravo, Mr Addison!

(ADDISON, *his party piece over, sips tea.* SWIFT *looks furiously misanthropic.*)

ORLANDO: Yet, for all this brilliance, I feel such emptiness . . .

SWIFT: Ah, but when my Gulliver was living among the horses!
Then, ah, then, he knew greatness of mind!
How did I write it in my book? I said:
'I enjoyed perfect Health of Body
and Tranquillity of Mind;
I did not find the Treachery or Inconstancy of a Friend
nor the injuries of a secret or open Enemy.
I had no occasion of bribing – '

[ENSEMBLE DEVELOPS]

(DUPPER *enters; coughs.*)

DUPPER: The Archduchess Harriet asks to be admitted, madame.

ORLANDO: *(Starting, spilling tea.)* The Archduchess Harriet?
Oh, let her come in!

(*The poets, affronted, rise as one man and take a brisk leave.* ORLANDO *rises to greet the* ARCHDUCHESS, *who looks tremendous in a great hooped skirt.*

ORLANDO, *having trouble with her gender body language, strides forward to kiss the* ARCHDUCHESS*'s hand, remembers her sex, converts the stride into a curtsey and takes a slight tumble. She is righted by the firm hand of the* ARCHDUCHESS. ORLANDO *is in a pleasant state of confusion. She believes the* ARCHDUCHESS *will prove a sympathetic friend who will be able to initiate her into some of the more arcane mysteries of femininity.*

Flustered, she peers into the teapot and rings the bell for more hot water. GRIMSDITCH, *deeply suspicious of the* ARCHDUCHESS, *brings it.* ORLANDO *busies herself with the teapot.*

While her back is turned, off comes the ARCHDUCHESS*'s tremendous dress; off comes her high-piled, powdered wig (that might have a ship in full sail on top of it?).*

When ORLANDO *turns to offer her visitor a cup of tea, she finds the* ARCHDUCHESS *has turned into the* ARCHDUKE.

She screams and drops the cup.

The ARCHDUKE *explains how he was always in love with* ORLANDO *since that first moment at the ice-fair, how he pursued her through the centuries and the sexes, how Venus herself snatched her away from him in Constantinople yet now has brought her to him in her most perfect self, a woman, so that he can reveal himself as simply a man.*

ORLANDO *busies herself picking up the broken pieces of china. She is deeply embarrassed.*

The ARCHDUKE *grows more ardent; he falls on his knees to press his suit.)*

ARCHDUKE: Marriage! the two of us! always together!

(He explains how he will make their home a shrine for ORLANDO; *she will sit in the nursery, rocking the cradle, waiting for him to come home . . . she will jump up for joy to hear his foot on the step . . . her little home, her world . . .)*

ORLANDO: What has all this to do with love?
With the fierce teeth of the white fox?
With passion?

(But the ARCHDUKE *becomes almost pathetic in his celebration of conjugal joys. He pleads.)*

ORLANDO: If *this* is love, I'm afraid there is
something inherently ridiculous in it . . .

ARCHDUKE: My heart, my soul!

ORLANDO: I should like most of all
in some quiet spot
to run him through with a rapier –
God! how he embarrasses me!

(She explains that she does not want to marry; that she is rich, has a lovely home of her own, does not need another one. Does not need a husband. A husband is the last thing she wants.

Infinitely crestfallen, the ARCHDUKE *clicks his heels together, bows, goes stoically off.* ORLANDO *is left alone. Surely, she soliloquises, there is more to life than this house, though? Or possibly, he asks* ORLANDO *to run him through if she cannot accept him, and this she obligingly does.)*

> I am alone . . . alone . . .
> sometimes I'm lonely . . .
> I'm often lonely . . .
> I'm always . . . lonely . . .
> and . . . bored . . .
> I want life!
> Life and a lover!
> Never a husband!
> I want life and the world!
> Society! London! the world!

(The bells of London ring out. GRIMSDITCH *enters, carrying* ORLANDO*'s travelling cloak. She wraps her up in it.)*

GRIMSDITCH: Now post-haste to London.
> You've got all your life in front of you.
> Pretty girl like you, why shouldn't you have some fun!
> Your whole life in front of you!
> Your life as a woman!

*(*GRIMSDITCH *waves* ORLANDO *offstage with her handkerchief as servants remove the tea-table and the portraits fly away. A huge chandelier drops from the flies.)*

SCENE 3 BALLROOM

(A small orchestra, conducted by a little boy, MOZART, *with* NANNERL, *a year or so older, at the keyboard, is assembled on stage. Mirrors drop from the flies; a buffet, with hams and turkeys.*

This ball scene is a pageant of the Age of Scandal, peopled by famous eighteenth-century heroes. ORLANDO, *the belle of the ball, dances with* CASANOVA. ROUSSEAU, *in a caftan, puts in an appearance.* KIT SMART, *the mad poet, escaped from Bedlam, rushes in and invites everybody to pray;* DR JOHNSON *prays with him.* ORLANDO *slaps* CASANOVA *with her fan.*

Then the PRINCE REGENT *enters, to denote the passage of time, accompanied by a bevy of rouged whores.* NELSON *and* LADY HAMILTON *make a grand entrance, too, and are dancing together. All grows more ominous. Discordantly, in the distance, the sound of the 'Marseillaise'. All stand to attention. The French wars!* NELSON *kisses* LADY HAMILTON *and, with a grand gesture, bequeaths her to the nation. The* PRINCE REGENT *tittups off, in a state of quivering cowardice. Gradually, the ballroom empties. All the men go off to fight Boney, the women sorrowfully depart, leaving* ORLANDO *once more alone.*

ORLANDO *opines that she has scandalised the Age of Scandal but it has all turned to dust and ashes for her. She will try being a boy again. She will go off to war.*

The stage band, yawning, packs up. Rag-pickers and beggars invade the ballroom. Servants come to remove the debris of the ball.

A gauze of London – but, this time, an early nineteenth-century London – drops.)

SCENE 4 LONDON

(A tart, about twenty, not of the most reputable type, enters, bedraggled, down-hearted. Trade isn't brisk. She's tired. Rag-pickers pass, carrying relics of the ball.

ORLANDO, *as a boy, enters; the tart accosts her; eventually* ORLANDO *reveals herself as a woman.*

The prostitute laughs; she says she will gladly settle for just a chat with another woman, she feels she needs a friend, she doesn't know why. A vague sense of oppression is overcoming her . . . perhaps the weather is changing.

Both come to the footlights, scan out over the audience.)

ORLANDO: *(Pointing.)* Is that a storm-cloud? Do you see? Over there!
   A black cloud no bigger than a man's hand.
   But growing –
   I see a cloud, a cloud spreading over London –

(The stage darkens.)

ORLANDO: I do believe . . . that cloud . . . is the
   NINETEENTH CENTURY!

PROSTITUTE: Oh, my gawd! the Age of Respectability!
   Better repent, hadn't I!

(A troupe of repentant harlots, carrying signs advising repentance for all, crosses the stage, sweeping ORLANDO'S *new friend along with them.* ORLANDO *is left alone, on the steadily darkening stage.)*

ORLANDO: Nothing for it, now, but
    to go home . . . home
    where you go when nobody
    else will have you . . .

(She wanders disconsolately off.)

CURTAIN

End of Act Three.

No intermission. Musical interlude.

ACT FOUR

SCENE I KNOLE

(The portraits have added PRINNY *to their number; otherwise the Knole space is Victorianified, crammed with antimacassars, petit-point footstools and stuffed owls.* GRIMSDITCH, *dusting with a feather duster, sings the 'Song of the Damp', how England has suddenly got damp, how you can't keep the damp out . . .*

ORLANDO *comes in, shivering. She is still wearing her eighteenth-century boys' clothes but* GRIMSDITCH *tells her how much more cosy she would be if she put on three or four red flannel petticoats. All the maids are wearing them, even if it is only August. And, really, it isn't right — it isn't respectable — for* ORLANDO *to show her — cough, blush — legs. Indeed, a dressmaker, summoned by* GRIMSDITCH, *is waiting outside in order to fit* ORLANDO *for a crinoline, such as the Queen herself wears.*

What Queen? No. Not Queen Elizabeth. Victoria.

A portrait of QUEEN VICTORIA *drops to join the other royals.* GRIMSDITCH *exits.*

The dressmaker enters and fits the reluctant ORLANDO *for a crinoline.* ORLANDO *examines herself nervously in a looking glass and sings how nothing is changed . . . The dressmaker takes the crinoline off her and puts it on a tailor's dummy; she says the crinoline is a cage, a cage for her body, they are forcing her body into ever more and more ridiculous clothes . . . Even* GRIMSDITCH *is in the plot, too. Alone,* ORLANDO *weeps.*

A busy knock. GRIMSDITCH *re-enters with* DUPPER, *hand in hand, both laughing and blushing. They confess, that after all these years, they've decided to get married, regularise their union, although* GRIMSDITCH *will keep her own name, for professional purposes . . . 'Time to make an honest woman of her!' But* GRIMSDITCH *stops laughing at that and gives* DUPPER *a brisk rap across the knuckles for his lewdness.*

And, feeling they can presume on the fact that they have known ORLANDO *intimately for several centuries, they feel they can make so bold as to say that perhaps it is time she herself thought — for hasn't everything in the castle got a mate but* ORLANDO?

ORLANDO *congratulates and kisses them. But, left alone, she cries: 'lonely . . . lonely . . . I need love . . . and a husband . . .'*

As she grieves, servants remove the Victoriana and replace it with a single tree to denote the garden. The portraits vanish.)

SCENE 2   THE GARDEN

(In her kimono, ORLANDO *contemplates hanging herself from the oak tree.)*

ORLANDO: I looked for happiness all through the ages
  but never found it.
  Love sailed away when the ice broke.
  The good times never lasted.
  The best I can do
  is hang myself,
  hang myself – with the order of the garter
  the old queen gave me –

(As she tests the strength of a low hanging bough, a shadow as of that of a great bird falls over her. The shadow is followed by a hurtling body and a great, billowing mound of silk. Offstage, an enormous crash. Marmaduke Benthrop Shelmerdine Esq., in natty aviator's garb and goggles, has parachuted out of his bi-plane and engulfed ORLANDO *in his fall.*

  SHELMERDINE *struggles out of his harness and parts the waves of silk to find* ORLANDO.*)*

SHELMERDINE: Madame, you're hurt!

ORLANDO: I'm dead, sir!

SHELMERDINE: Will you marry me?

ORLANDO: I already have!

SHELMERDINE: Are you positive you aren't a man?

ORLANDO: Is it possible you're not a woman?

(She emerges from the cocoon of silk wearing a Poiret wedding dress in white satin. They love-duet. He describes his castle in the Hebrides, how he had been a soldier, once, and then a sailor, but now has taken to the air, like a bird. She tells him he reminds her of a bird.)

SHELMERDINE: Orlando.

ORLANDO: Shelmerdine.

(They kiss. While they are doing so, the servants troop in, giggling, wearing flowery hats, the men with flowers in their buttonholes. GRIMSDITCH *will be matron of honour.)*

GRIMSDITCH: Oh, ma'am, I never thought I'd live to see the day!

(Enter DUPPER, *in clerical gear, carrying an ostentatious prayer book.)*

ORLANDO: Neither did I.

(DUPPER marries them. Wedding bells. Confetti. Above the sounds of epithalamium rises the whirr of a bi-plane. Kentish folk push in SHELMERDINE's bi-plane, its propellers spinning, all mended. It is wreathed with flowers and covered with streamers. SHELMERDINE announces how the wind governs him and he must go where the wind blows, to all the corners of the earth; and yet the winds will blow him back again.

They embrace, again. He climbs aboard.

With the entire household waving and cheering, ORLANDO weeping and laughing, the plane rises up. Flowers, ribbons, confetti fill the stage.)

CURTAIN of English country house gauze

End of Act Four

EPILOGUE

(1928. The bedlinen department of Marshall and Snelgrove.
A mahogany counter; a pile of sheets. ORLANDO, *very elegant in a Chanel suit, is at the counter; an assistant stands behind.)*

ORLANDO: Sheets for a double bed, please. A very large double bed.
  You could call it a king-size double bed.
  No wonder the sheets have worn out
  after all these years.
  But I don't feel a day older,
  just the same as I did long ago,
  when the Kentish hills looked as if
  they had sheets thrown over them, such snow!
  and the Thames froze over . . .
  and the Russians came . . .
  and I fell in love . . .

*(*SASHA, *now a blowsy, overfurred, overjewelled forty, enters and demands, rudely, in bad English, the way to the fancy goods dept.* ORLANDO *starts forward: 'Sasha!')*

SASHA: You must be making some mistake!

*(*SASHA *gives* ORLANDO *a look of gratuitous contempt and sails out.* ORLANDO *smiles; shakes her head to get rid of the memories. The counter-jumper interrupts them, anyway: 'Any towels, napkins, dusters, today, madam?')*

ORLANDO: Nothing, no, thank you, nothing – only the past.

COUNTER-JUMPER: It isn't for sale, ma'am. Here are the sheets, ma'am.

ORLANDO: Ah!

(She sinks down on a chair by the counter while the shop assistants transform the bedlinen department into the Knole bedroom; the counter rolls off, the Great Bed appears, the night-table, the electric candelabra. The portraits come down from on high. There is no new royal portrait but, instead, a silver-framed photograph of the Prince of Wales on the night-table, signed flamboyantly.
  The shop assistants tiptoe off. GRIMSDITCH *and* DUPPER *come in.* GRIMSDITCH *takes the parcel of sheets out of* ORLANDO's *hands.)*

GRIMSDITCH: There you are, see? I told you she wouldn't forget
  That the bed needed new sheets.
  A mistress is better at details than a master,
  and I do say that as has had them both.

(The couple make up the bed together. DUPPER kisses his wife and departs. GRIMSDITCH gently wakes ORLANDO and helps her off with her town clothes, into her pyjamas, ready for bed. Perhaps they duet.)

GRIMSDITCH AND ORLANDO: Here I/you came as boy and woman,
  here I/you lay as the west wind's bride,
  the years passed lightly over,
  here in this great bed you'll die . . .

(ORLANDO kisses the photograph of her husband that she keeps under her pillow while he is off cutting the airy wave. She climbs into bed.

  SHELMERDINE, *off, sings her a lullaby; perhaps a reprise of the 'Lullaby for Elizabeth'.*

  GRIMSDITCH *switches off the light.)*

GRIMSDITCH: Goodnight, milady. Milord, milady.

(Her keys chink. Darkness. Midnight strikes.)

CURTAIN

SCREEN PLAYS

The Company of Wolves
(with Neil Jordan)

The Magic Toyshop

Gun for the Devil

The Christchurch Murder

The Company of Wolves

(1. *Exterior. Countryside. Day.*

A country road, with forest all around. There are threads of heat mist around the trunks of the trees. The road isn't tarmacked, so there is a sense of period. A dog, a big German shepherd or Alsatian, comes lolloping down the road, past hedgerows of wild flowers.

A car – a new Volvo estate – roars into view, past the dog, tooting its horn. Seen from the dog's eye-view, the driver is invisible. But the dog recognises the car. The dog runs barking after the car, which slows in order to turn in at an ornate gateway, with griffins on the gatepost, and a wrought-iron gate standing open.)

(2. *Exterior. Country House. Day.*

A formal shot of a Georgian house, neither big nor small, standing in grounds in front of a background of gently wooded hills. Again, the sense of period, on a quiet summer evening. The house is well-kept, though no longer in the original style – the garden, especially, has been adapted to a twentieth-century lack of gardeners and there is a lot more grass than there would have been. Shrubs somewhat overgrown.

A garden statue or two, left over from former grandeur, green with moss. One is a cupid. Another is a satyr, with a girl's school-hat – a round panama, with badge – on its head. A dry fountain, with a marooned toy boat in the basin.

A tennis-net is stretched across the lawn in front of the house. Thrown down beside it are a pile of racquets and sweaters.

The car draws up the driveway and stops in front of the portico. We see it again from the dog's point of view as he bounds towards it.

A WOMAN *gets out of the car. She is elegant, and matches the house. The dog leaps on her and licks her face.*)

WOMAN: Careful, boy – careful –

(*Behind her, her husband can be seen getting out of the other door.*

A young GIRL *of about ten comes to the front door, wearing shorts, a T-shirt and sneakers, eating a slice of bread and jam from her hand.*)

WOMAN: Hello, darling.

(*Her husband opens the hatch-back, takes out bags of groceries and parcels.*)

GIRL: Any presents for me?

WOMAN: A surprise.

(*The dog pads through the doorway behind the girl. We see a dark hallway within. The* WOMAN *glances at the dog, then lifts her eyes to an upper window.*)

WOMAN: Where is she? Did she miss tea again?

(*The* GIRL *looks away.*)

WOMAN: Is she still sulking in her room?

(*The* MAN *comes up behind the* WOMAN *and puts his arm around her. He has a solid face, like someone from a working-class background who made good.*)

MAN: Now, darling. It's a difficult age.

(*He lifts the young* GIRL *up, who kisses them both in turn.*)

(*3. Interior. House. Day.*

The dog pads through a discordantly grand hall, which now serves as a reception room. There is a huge chandelier, family portraits on walls, a television and a grand piano. The dog crosses the carpeted floor and makes for the marble staircase.

On the first landing, he noses a discarded sweater. He pads up the second flight of stairs. This second flight is less grand. There are marks of damp and mildew on the walls, traces of moss growing in the joints of uncarpeted steps.

He comes to a corridor. It is gloomy here, there are bubbles and cracks in the ceiling plaster. There is a potted plant on a stand which has gone lushly to seed. A sycamore seedling sprouts from a crack in the wall. He startles a pigeon in a niche in the wall, which beats its way to the ceiling.

The dog stops outside an attic door. He whines and scrabbles at it.)

(*4. Interior. Attic Bedroom. Day.*

The thin curtains, loosely drawn, flap a little.

It is a young GIRL'*s room, very disordered. There is a dressing-table, loaded with make-up of all kinds. Camera lingers on an open lipstick and a pile of paper tissues marked with red lipstick blottings, on deodorants, perfume, blusher. By the mirror is a framed photograph of a small girl holding the same dog who is scrabbling at the door outside. There are posters on the walls. One is a picture by Douanier Rousseau, 'Carnival Night', showing two figures in a winter wood, by moonlight. The other is an old horror film poster, Lon Chaney as a werewolf.*

The whining of the dog increases, and we glimpse its nose, thrust under the door. On the bed, ALICE, *a young girl, shifts in her sleep. She's been practising with cosmetics, and her face is covered with smudged mascara, eyeshadow and lipstick, which has stained the pillowslip. Her face is flushed, her mouth slightly open. She is a troubled sleeper. Her hair comes loose from a pony-tail tied with a red ribbon. She wears only her knickers, white cotton, possibly part of her school uniform. Her T-shirt and shorts lie tangled in the blankets at her feet, among a litter of teen magazines and pulp romance novels, one with a gothic 'woman in peril' screaming from the paper cover. An alarm-clock ticks from a chair, a discarded brassière beside it, and a white fancy dress hanging over the armrest. A gold chain with a neat golden cross lie beside the alarm-clock. An open cupboard reveals a mix of school uniform garments and teenage high style. There is a bookshelf above it with Enid Blyton books and school stories. Among them a sex-instruction manual – Jane Cousins's* Make It Happy, *and dog-eared copies of fairy-tale books.*

The GIRL *shifts on her pillow. There is a sense of oppressive heat, oppressive and unfocused sensuality, adolescent turbulence.*

A breeze comes through the curtains and stirs her hair.

Outside, the dog whines louder.

The breeze stirs the pages of Iona and Peter Opie's The Classic Fairy Tales *which lies on the window-sill, beneath the flapping curtains. The room has darkened subtly. We glimpse fairy-tale illustrations through the shifting pages, until the illustrations by Doré for 'The Little Red Riding Hood' are reached.*

Outside, the dog scrapes at the door, whines again.

The GIRL *shifts in her sleep. Her hair is blown over her face, as the breeze strengthens.*

The breeze turns into a wind, blows the curtains wide open.

Through the window, we see a forlorn, abandoned garden and the margins of the mysterious forest of the European imagination, under a sky darkened with storm, or approaching night. It is a brooding, Disney forest. One huge gust of wind blows through it, through the open window into the room, filling the room with whirling leaves.

The GIRL *stirs uneasily in her sleep.*

Footsteps can be heard on the stairs outside. The dog growls. Then, the WOMAN's *voice.)*

WOMAN: *(Off.)* Darling? Are you feeling better? Shouldn't you come downstairs?

(The girl clutches at the pillow in her sleep and begins to pant and moan.)

(5. Exterior. Forest. Night.

Boughs of trees wave across the full moon. An owl hoots from a tree, then shoots towards the camera and out of sight, startled by movement in the undergrowth. ALICE *bursts through the undergrowth, breathing heavily, fear in her eyes, as if she is being followed by something she cannot see.*

She walks forwards hurriedly, as if trying to contain her fear.

The wood around her is strange. Toys, larger than lifesize, a teddy bear, a sailor doll, stretch their arms out from the undergrowth. Leaves that detach themselves from the trees and whirl towards the camera are made of pages of books.

ALICE walks on faster, past a dolls' house covered in ivy, the front doors open, revealing the little room within; past the statues of the garden we have seen, wreathed in strange flowers; past a cuckoo-clock that whirrs and hoots at her; past huge, phallic-shaped mushrooms, toadstools, jacks-in-pulpits etc.

There is a rustling of deadened leaves. ALICE gasps as a clockwork mouse whirrs across her path. She hurries on faster.

The more she hurries the more the wood becomes a real wood – although the animals that watch her pass – a rabbit, a fox, a frog – are huge soft toys. They turn their heads as she passes, and their eyes flash red. Behind them, there is the glimpse of something larger, of huge padding feet.

The howl of a single wolf echoes under the moon.

ALICE breaks into a run. A bramble catches at her clothing. She tugs desperately at the garment, ripping the fabric to free herself, leaving a rag on the bramble.

She runs on, stumbling. Now she is really frightened and we are in a real wood, no more toys nor possibly harmless animals.

There is, instead of a plush bunny, a wolf in the undergrowth. He looks perky and alert. He sniffs the air.

Wisps of cloud drift over the moon. We hear the howling of several wolves, the panting of the hurrying GIRL.

The WOLF lopes off through the undergrowth in her pursuit.

Close-up of ALICE with moon behind her. She pants and sobs as she runs.)

ALICE: No, oh no, not yet . . .

(ALICE trips in the undergrowth and tumbles down an incline. She falls by the root of a large tree.

The WOLF's feet pad through the leaves. They gain speed.

ALICE struggles to her feet by the roots of the tree. Her knees are scored with blood from the brambles. She clutches the cross round her neck. The WOLF's feet, running fast. Then, slowly, they stop.

ALICE stands. She fingers the cross. There is a sudden silence all around her. Her panting slowly subsides. Was it all just a dream?

She edges round the tree. She sees a moonlit clearing before her. A slim poplar, a mossy, overgrown rock. Silence, as before. She steps forward. Then behind her, into the foreground of the frame, steps a huge WOLF. He stands absolutely still, observing her. ALICE drops her hand from the cross. She breathes easily. Then, the worst of all fears comes upon her. She turns, slowly, her face setting into that expression of female terror we saw on the cover of the pulp romance.

The WOLF *leaps.)*

(6. Interior. Attic bedroom. Night.

Moonlight seeps in through the curtains. The sleeping ALICE *is now quiet, her face turned to the pillow, her beautiful hair spread out in a fan around it.)*

(7. Exterior. Graveyard. Day.

A graveyard, in the forest. A tumbledown church can be seen near it, and a road, tracing a path through the trees.

A coffin stands beside a freshly dug grave. Around it are a group of peasants, standing in the hard, crisp, winter daylight. Their clothes and their attitudes are those of the peasants out of any number of fairy-tales, redolent of the late-eighteenth century, perhaps, the world of the Brothers Grimm, but much else besides.

MOTHER *walks to the coffin, helped by* FATHER. *She bends down to it, and we see* ALICE *inside it, white and ethereally dead. She kisses* ALICE's *lips and removes the gold cross and chain from around her neck.* ROSALEEN *comes up behind her.)*

MOTHER: Kiss goodbye to your sister now, dear.

*(*ROSALEEN *looks down curiously at* ALICE, *and bends and kisses her lips — then withdraws her mouth quickly.* MOTHER *places the locket she has taken from* ALICE *around* ROSALEEN's *neck.)*

MOTHER: So you never forget her . . .

(Tears well up in MOTHER's *eyes. They fall on* ALICE's *face.* FATHER *and the sexton — who is dressed in black clothes, with white ruffs at the sleeves and throat, place the lid on the coffin, covering* ALICE's *face.* MOTHER *begins to weep copiously.* ROSALEEN *still stares, with her child's curiosity.*

A hand slips into ROSALEEN's *and draws her backwards, away from the grave. It belongs to* ROSALEEN's *granny — an anachronistic old lady with wire-rimmed 'granny' glasses, a blue costume, lisle stockings and 'sensible' shoes, a fox-piece round her neck with glittering eyes.)*

GRANNY: Stay with me, child.

*(*GRANNY *digs into the big handbag which she carries and takes out a gingerbread man. She slips it to* ROSALEEN.)*

GRANNY: Chew on that, pet. It'll keep yer mind off things.

*(*ROSALEEN *nibbles the leg of the gingerbread man, as the coffin is lowered into the grave. Around her, an ancient peasant and a man with an eye-patch murmur.)*

ANCIENT: Poor pretty one, nobody to save her.

EYE-PATCH: It's the parents I feel sorry for.

(ROSALEEN *chews away. Among the peasants round the grave, a young boy stares at her.* ROSALEEN *sticks her tongue out at him, then bites off a huge lump. The boy turns away, blushing.*)

ANCIENT: They got three sheep and a lamb in the village over.

EYE-PATCH: No . . .

ANCIENT: And bit a good wife in the leg in her own kitchen . . .

(*Earth is shovelled into the grave. The* PRIEST *begins to intone.*)

PRIEST: Man that is born of woman hath but little time . . . Ashes to ashes, dust to dust. The Lord giveth and the Lord taketh away. Blessed be the name of the Lord.

(*8. Exterior. Road by graveyard. Day.*
    GRANNY, ROSALEEN, MOTHER *and* FATHER *sit in a small trap which is being driven towards the village by the* SEXTON. ROSALEEN *polishes off the last few pieces of the gingerbread man.* GRANNY *talks softly to her.*)

GRANNY: Your only sister. She all alone in the wood, and nobody to save her, poor little lamb.

ROSALEEN: (*Swallowing.*) Why couldn't she save herself?

GRANNY: You don't know nothing. You're only a child yet.

(*A small, fairy-tale peasant village comes into view. Cluttered peasant hovels, ringed around a single water-pump. A stork stands on one leg on one of the chimneys, etched against the blue wintry sky.* FATHER *dismounts, and lifts* MOTHER *down. He then picks up* ROSALEEN *and gives her a big hug. At long last,* ROSALEEN *herself begins to cry.*)

DADDY: There, there pet . . .

GRANNY: (*Undertone.*) Shall I take her home with me tonight? Her mother's in no fit state . . .

DADDY: If only you would!

(*He thrust* ROSALEEN *into* GRANNY'S *arms.*)

GRANNY: Come, pet.

(GRANNY *begins to dry* ROSALEEN'S *eyes with a handkerchief.* ROSALEEN *squirms in her grip.*)

ROSALEEN: I want to stay with Mammy –

DADDY: Your mother isn't fit. Just for tonight.

(GRANNY *strokes* ROSALEEN's *hair, till she quietens. Her voice is quite hypnotic.*)

GRANNY: It's a long way, through the wood. But safe in daylight. Safe if you keep to the path, with me . . .

(*9. Exterior. Forest clearing. Day.*
ROSALEEN *and* GRANNY *walk hand in hand through the clearing, with the mossy rock and slim poplar, where* ALICE *encountered the* WOLF.)

GRANNY: And nowhere as safe as your Granny's house.

(*It is a perfectly normal forest – no giant plants or toadstools. Just the ordinary sounds of birdsong.*
GRANNY *pauses under a large beech tree. She reaches up and pulls down a handful of beechnuts. She plucks out a nut, cracks it between her teeth and offers it to* ROSALEEN. ROSALEEN *eats it.*)

ROSALEEN: Mmmmm!

GRANNY: Plenty more in the forest, if you know where to look.

(ROSALEEN *glimpses berries in the thickets beyond the path.*)

ROSALEEN: Berries –

(*She pulls free of* GRANNY's *hand and makes towards them, through the thickets. She picks a big clump and is about to eat, when* GRANNY's *hand reaches in, pulls her abruptly from the thickets on to the path once more.*)

GRANNY: But don't stray from the path girl. Didn't you hear what I told you? Once you stray from the path, you're lost entirely. The wild beasts know no mercy. They wait for us in the wood, in the shadows. And once we put a foot wrong, they pounce.

(ROSALEEN *looks up into her* GRANNY's *face with frightened eyes. The discs of* GRANNY's *glasses reflect the sunlight, hiding her eyes.*)

GRANNY: There, there. Don't take on so. It's a lesson you have to learn . . .

(*She takes* ROSALEEN's *hand and walks forward briskly once more.*)

GRANNY: Or you'll end up like your poor dear sister . . .

(*10. Exterior.* GRANNY's *house. Evening.*
They walk on down the path, hand in hand till they come to a clearing, where GRANNY's *house is. It is a small detached cottage set in a walled garden with a*

gated path. There is an apple tree in the garden laden with lush red fruit. The house sits snug in the forest clearing, all on its own. There are some late flowers, dahlias, gladioli, round the apple tree, and the beginnings of several rows of late winter cabbages.

GRANNY *opens the gate, walks down the path towards the cottage with its lace curtain windows, its faint curl of smoke from the chimney.* ROSALEEN *stops by the apple tree, dragging on* GRANNY'S *hand.)*

ROSALEEN: Granny –

GRANNY: *(Impatiently.)* Yes, child?

ROSALEEN: Can I have one?

GRANNY: I don't see why not.

*(*ROSALEEN *picks a windfall from the earth at the tree's trunk.* GRANNY *busies herself with the door key.* ROSALEEN *is about to sink her teeth into it, when she sees a worm curling round in a hole in the apple. She throws it away with disgust.)*

ROSALEEN: Ugh!

*(*GRANNY *sighs and strides over to her. She plucks a luscious red apple from the tree itself.)*

GRANNY: You've a lot to learn, child.

ROSALEEN: What have I to learn, Gran?

GRANNY: Never stray from the path, never eat a windfall. Never trust a man whose eyebrows meet . . .

*(*ROSALEEN *is hardly listening, though. She sinks her teeth into the apple and follows* GRANNY *who lifts up the latch and enters the house.)*

(11. Interior. GRANNY'S *house. Evening.*

It is neat and homely inside. A tiled floor, a rag rug, a big brass bed in one corner with a patchwork quilt, a rocking chair by a crackling log fire, a pair of pottery spaniels on either side of the mantelpiece above. A rocking chair to one side of the fire, a small child's stool on the other. ROSALEEN *goes straight to the stool and sits on it, chewing the apple. She watches her* GRANNY *busy herself stoking the fire, placing a large black kettle on the ring above it.)*

GRANNY: A tidy hearth is a tidy home. I fear that's a lesson your mother should learn.

ROSALEEN: *(Chewing.)* Nobody's perfect, Granny.

GRANNY: Who told you that?

ROSALEEN: Mammy did.

GRANNY: Mammy would.

(ROSALEEN *stares at the gently steaming kettle.*)

GRANNY: The watched kettle never boils, child. Help me with the tea things.

(ROSALEEN *rises, goes over to the china cabinet, begins to take out the cups.*)

(*12. Exterior.* GRANNY's *house. Night.*)
(*An almost fairy-tale moon shines over the chimney of* GRANNY's *house. An owl sits on the apple tree, among the apples, turning its head this way and that. Through the window we can see the figures of* GRANNY *and* ROSALEEN, *flickering by the light of an oil-lamp.*)

(*13. Interior.* GRANNY's *house. Night.*
   Tea is over. There is a big black missal on the table beside the tea-things.
ROSALEEN *sits on the rug at* GRANNY's *feet, eating a slice of bread and jam.*
GRANNY *is rocking on the rocking chair, knitting a shawl with bright red wool.*)

GRANNY: The best winter wool, pet. Woven in the far valley. It was so good, so soft, I thought I'd weave a shawl for your sister. But now do you know what I'll do?

ROSALEEN: What, Gran?

GRANNY: I'll make one for you. A very special shawl for a very special lady!

(ROSALEEN *reaches out to touch the wool.*)

ROSALEEN: Soft as a kitten . . .

(GRANNY *rocks as she knits. The firelight reflects on* ROSALEEN's *face.*)

ROSALEEN: Knit one, purl one . . .

(GRANNY *glances at her quizzically.* ROSALEEN *catches her glance.*)

GRANNY: There's something I should tell you –

(ROSALEEN's *ears prick up.*)

GRANNY: But maybe you're too young.

ROSALEEN: Tell me, Gran, please –

GRANNY: Too young to understand . . .

ROSALEEN: I'm nine and three quarters –

GRANNY: But then maybe no child is ever too young – for the Devil has his way of working his will amongst even the purest of hearts. And amongst the pious, child, he needs must be subtle. He must come in many disguises.

(She knits on for a moment, as if thinking to herself.)

GRANNY: A wolf . . . may be more than he seems.

ROSALEEN: What's that?

GRANNY: The wolf that ate your sister was hairy on the outside, but when she died, she went straight up to Heaven. But the worst kinds of wolves are hairy on the inside and when they bite they drag you with them to Hell.

ROSALEEN: What do you mean? Hairy on the inside? Like a sheepskin jacket?

(She giggles.)

GRANNY: Hush that, foolish child! Listen.

(The fire glows brighter. The clicking of GRANNY's needles becomes rhythmic and hypnotic. ROSALEEN stares at her face.)

GRANNY: Once upon a time there was a woman in our village and she married a travelling man . . .

(We dissolve from a close-up of GRANNY's clicking needles to . . .)

(14. Exterior. Church by graveyard. Day.
Two FIDDLERS stand among the gravestones playing soaring gypsy music. They are recognisable from the crowd of peasants at the funeral. One is blind, the other lame. It is a bright day in high summer.

A village wedding party emerges from the church in a burst of cheers and laughter. The BRIDE and GROOM pause on the steps to kiss. She is in normal peasant dress, but decorated with ribbons and flowers. He is dressed differently from the rest of the villagers, in once elegant cast-offs.

The villagers pelt the COUPLE with rice and flowers, then make an arch for them to walk under. A couple of dogs frisk around, barking.

The COUPLE emerge from the arch laughing, shielding their eyes from the rice and flowers, making their way down the path towards the village. The villagers follow them, in procession behind both of them.)

(The BLIND and LAME FIDDLERS follow, more slowly.)

BLIND FIDDLER: What does she look like?

LAME FIDDLER: Whiter than a spring lamb . . .

(15. Exterior. Village street. Day.)

GRANNY: *(Voice over.)* And the new bride was brought to her new home.

(The BRIDE, GROOM, *villagers and* FIDDLERS *arrive at a freshly built house at the end of the village. The* GROOM *picks up the* BRIDE *and lifts her over the threshold. The* BRIDE *clings to his neck, laughing, wild flowers in her hair and ribbons and bows, the image of happiness and abandon.)*

(16. Interior. Cottage. Night.

A poor but clean room. Not much in it besides a bed set into a wall in peasant fashion, a chair beside the bed with a lighted candle on it, an alarm clock on a small stool.

The BRIDE *sits on the bed, combing her long hair. The* GROOM *stands in the shadows, watching her.)*

GROOM: They've all gone now.

BRIDE: It's a shame your people missed the wedding.

GROOM: Maybe it is and maybe it isn't.

(The BRIDE *picks up the alarm-clock. She gives the* GROOM *a coy look and stows it away under the pillow.*

Some sixth sense makes her pull back the bedclothes. Nestling in the sheets is a young hedgehog. She bursts out laughing.)

BRIDE: My pestilential little brother's idea of a joke!

(She picks up the hedgehog tenderly and watches it run across the floor. Then she turns to the GROOM. *He is still in the shadows, watching her.)*

BRIDE: Why are you staring like that?

(The GROOM *smiles nervously.)*

GROOM: Because I've never seen anything like you before.

BRIDE: Don't they have girls where you come from?

GROOM: None like you.

(His voice is deep and reverberant. The BRIDE, *as if in answer to him, begins to take off her clothes. She smiles at him as she does so. He takes off his clothes too, but more slowly. He is handsome, but his eyebrows meet. When he is naked, he stays in the shadows, covering his privates with his white shirt.)*

BRIDE: Come out of the shadows and let me see you, my love.

(The BRIDE looks at him as he approaches. Her eyes travel up his body and come to rest on his face and glowing eyes.)

BRIDE: Are all travelling men as handsome as you?

GROOM: So you think I'm handsome?

BRIDE: The first thing that struck me about you was the way your eyebrows meet.

GROOM: Doesn't it spoil me, then?

(The BRIDE smiles at him. The candles flicker softly over her half-dressed body.)

BRIDE: Come to me and I'll tell you.

(He moves forward. He trips on the hedgehog.)

GROOM: What the hell –

(He scoops up the hedgehog, furious, and opens the door. He throws the hedgehog into the yard.
He is just about to close the door when the moon comes free of clouds. The pale light shines on him, making him look most strange. He lingers on the threshold.)

BRIDE: *(Suddenly anxious.)* My dear?

(The GROOM is gazing at the enormous full moon. Now the GROOM gives her one last look. His eyes flash red, but it could be the effect of the moonlight.)

GROOM: *(Strangled voice.)* My dear, I must just go out into the yard for a minute –

BRIDE: Why ever –

GROOM: The call of nature –

(He slams the door behind him. A reverberating slam. The bride lays her head on the pillow and sighs.)

GRANNY: *(Voice over.)* So she waited.

(The BRIDE shakes the pillow, settles down again.)

GRANNY: *(Voice over.)* And she waited.

(The BRIDE's eyes close. Then she wakes up with a start. She looks round her, as if she isn't quite sure where she is.)

GRANNY: *(Voice over.)* And she waited again.

(The BRIDE gets out of bed and walks towards the door.)

BRIDE: Surely he's been gone a long time!

(*She reaches for the door-handle, but before she touches it, an anguished howling starts outside. She stays her hand, frozen with horror. Then another wolf howls – then a chorus of wolves. The* BRIDE *runs to the window terrified, presses her face against it.*

Outside she sees moonlight, the forest and a movement of vague, grey shapes among the trees.)

BRIDE: No – No – it can't be –

(*17. Exterior. Forest. Dawn.*

There is the gleam of flickering lamps in the early morning mist. It is a search-party, made up from the villagers we saw at the graveyard. They come to a clearing in the forest, with a wide meadow.)

EYE-PATCH: Look –

(*There is a ripple through the long grass.*)

ANCIENT: That's no wolf, that's the wind.

MAN WITH RED NOSE: She swore that she heard them –

ANCIENT: Wolves, indeed. He upped and ran, that's all. He had it in his blood. Wasn't he a travelling man?

(RED NOSE *takes out a bottle and drinks from it, hands it to* ANCIENT, *who drinks in turn.*)

ANCIENT: Home –

(*They turn and walk homewards.*)

(*18. Exterior. Farmyard. Dawn.*

A busy scene, with disturbed ducks and hens flapping round as the BRIDE'*s family search round the duckpond. Her* FATHER *throws a rope tied round a heavy stone into the pond and drags it towards him.*

The BRIDE *herself stands above a huge paw-print in the mud. She watches the search-party approach.*)

BRIDE: Anything – ?

EYE-PATCH: Not a hair nor a hide of him. Not a footprint –

BRIDE: And what's that, might I ask?

(*She points at the paw-print. She grows hysterical.*)

BRIDE: I told you I heard the wolves last night! They came and took him while he was making water, when a man is at his most defenceless. Oh, the murderers! The murderers!

(She begins to weep. She buries her face in her apron.)

GRANNY: *(Voice over.)* But she was a young thing, and cheerful by temperament.

(She takes her face from her apron, blows her nose and wipes her tears away. She looks down and sees the hedgehog scurrying towards her. She smiles.)

(19. Interior. Cottage. Night.)

GRANNY: *(Voice over.)* And found another husband not too shy to piss in a pot.

(There is a chamberpot in the middle of the floor. The hedgehog stands on his hind legs, looking into the chamberpot.

There is a chair above the pot, with a candle on it. Next to it is the bed, with agitated covers, much muffled laughter, no sign of the young couple themselves, who are hidden beneath the jiggling quilts.

The alarm-clock jumps out from under the pillow with a metallic twang.

A man's hand extends out from under the bedclothes, gropes round, snuffs out the candle, knocks candle and candlestick to the floor.

Laughter and sighing, then, in the darkness.)

(20. Interior. GRANNY's house. Day.

ROSALEEN sits wide-eyed, as GRANNY knits on.)

ROSALEEN: So then they lived happily ever after?

GRANNY: Indeed they did not!

(Her needles click on rhythmically, knitting the shawl.)

(21. Interior. Cottage. Day.

A baby bawls in the cradle, beside the freshly made bed. Nothing else in shot.)

GRANNY: *(Voice over.)* But at first the time passed happily enough.

(Dissolve to . . .)

(22. Interior. Cottage. Day.

More things in the room. Table, chairs, dresser. The BRIDE, more dishevelled, hair spilling out from a bun on top of her head, stands at the table peeling potatoes. A toddler peers over the edge of the table, stretching out to play with the potato peelings. BRIDE slaps his hand. The cradle stands beside the fireplace and from it another baby bawls.

Dissolve to . . .)

(23. Interior. Cottage. Day.

The BRIDE sits on a chair by the fire. A small child hangs over the arm of the chair, eating a slice of bread and jam. The BRIDE feeds an eighteen-month-old baby on her lap with a bottle. Yet another new baby bawls in the cradle she rocks with her foot. GRANNY's voice-over comes in over this vignette of domestic life.)

GRANNY: *(Voice over.)* Time passed, and she gave him children, and it was a bad time for wolves, those years, oh yes, not a sheep nor a cow was safe . . . but for herself, all went right as a trivet until . . .

(24. Exterior. Farmyard. Night.

Snow. Moonlight. Silence. The BRIDE's house is covered in gleaming icicles.)

GRANNY: *(Voice over.)* One winter's night . . .

(A figure picks its way through the yard, disturbing a chicken that flies up, squawking. The figure makes for the cottage window, from which a light shines. The figure breaks the window free of icicles and views inside . . .

A woman bent over a pot by the fire . . . a table set for a meal . . . children . . . a picture of warmth and comfort, blurred by the frosted window.

The figure walks to the door and bangs on it.)

(25. Interior. Cottage. Night.

The BRIDE makes for the banging door, wiping her hands on the apron. She opens it.)

BRIDE: My God!

(We see the figure from the BRIDE's point-of-view, the cold winter moonlight behind him. He is instantly recognisable as the GROOM from the wedding, but has suffered a profound change – long wild hair, lean filthy cheeks, rough mangy clothing.)

GROOM: I'm starving.

(He walks inside as if he had just left yesterday. The BRIDE draws back from him as he enters. The table is laid with bowls and spoons for five people. Three children sit there, napkins tucked under their chins, soup in front of them, spoons in their hands. They look at the wild man curiously. The BRIDE stands there searching for words.)

BRIDE: You want something to eat?

GROOM: Didn't you hear me the first time?

(The BRIDE ladles soup into the HUSBAND's bowl out of the pot on the fire. She glances at the GROOM, then away again.

She opens a drawer in the table to look for a spoon. Her hands shake so much that all the cutlery rattles.

The GROOM *walks towards the ready-made place at the head of the table. He sits down. He eyes the children suspiciously.)*

GROOM: Where did these three spring from?

(The BRIDE *looks at the children, then at him. She takes a breath.)*

BRIDE: *(Defiantly.)* Out of my belly.

(The GROOM *bends the spoon in his hands.)*

GROOM: Your children, but not my children!

(He rises wrathfully, knocking over the table. The children scream and scatter. The BRIDE *backs towards the fire, takes the ladle from the soup-pot as the* GROOM *comes towards her.)*

GROOM: Whore – adulteress – you hoped I'd never come back –

BRIDE: I thought the wolves took you –

GROOM: Better wolf than whore – if I were a wolf once more, I could
   teach this whore a lesson –

(He strips off his jerkin as he advances towards her. His body beneath it is hairy and muscular. The BRIDE *screams and dips the ladle in the soup-pot, throwing it over him. The* GROOM *screams and clutches his skin where the hot soup scalds him. Hair sprouts from his scalded skin. His cheeks ripple, as if they are transforming. He stretches a hand out towards her, and the skin on it is bulging, as if from thrusting muscles underneath.*

The BRIDE *screams, grabs the pot from the fire and flings it at him.*

The GROOM *staggers backwards, in the mess of scalding soup. He falls on the floor, howling in pain, dragging the table with him.*

The CHILDREN *huddle in one corner, staring in horror.*

The BRIDE *stands by the fireside, searching for a fresh weapon.*

The GROOM *howls in anguish and raises his head. The skin is peeling from his face to reveal the head, now of a wolf. He rises to his feet as –*

The door flies open. The burly figure enters of the second HUSBAND, *silhouetted in the doorway, obscured by the wind and flying snow from outside. He looks aghast at his wife. The* GROOM *snarls and makes for him as –*

The second HUSBAND *grabs an axe from a woodstack against the wall –*

The GROOM *flails with his hands towards him –*

The HUSBAND *swings the axe –*

The CHILDREN *scream –*

The WIFE *screams in protest – moves forwards –*

Blood spatters the wooden walls and the severed, half-transformed head of the GROOM *falls in a vat of milk at her feet.*

The shrieking of the CHILDREN *changes to whimpering.*

The HUSBAND *drops the axe, staring at the decapitated body of the* werewolf/GROOM, *in a mess of soup, broken cutlery and shattered table.*

The BRIDE *looks down at the vat of milk. It is slowly turning red. Very slowly, a shape rises to the surface. It is the head of the* GROOM. *Now it is no longer a wolf's face – it is the face of her first husband, very human, very beautiful and very young.*

She crouches down and closes the eyes. One, two.

The second husband comes up behind her.)

BRIDE: He looks just the same as the day I married him.

(She looks up at the second HUSBAND. *His face is very ugly. He slaps her with his hand.)*

HUSBAND: Whore – adulteress –

(26. Interior. GRANNY's *house. Night.*

ROSALEEN *stares wide-eyed at her* GRANNY, *who continues to knit. She has been enthralled by the story, but has not understood it.)*

ROSALEEN: I'd never let a man strike me. I'd not permit it.

GRANNY: Oh they're nice as pie until they've had their way with you. But once the bloom is gone, the beast comes out.

(Her needles click away.)

ROSALEEN: When wolves, though, the real wolves, the hairy–outside wolves – when the real wolves mate, do the dogs beat the bitches afterwards?

GRANNY: Animals. All wild animals.

(GRANNY looks at the fire. It is dying down.)

GRANNY: That's enough knitting for tonight. Bedtime! Come and give your granny a big kiss.

(GRANNY takes off her glasses. Without them her eyes are cold and steely. ROSALEEN, *still thinking of the story, stays looking vacantly into the fire.)*

GRANNY: Don't I deserve a kiss for my story?

(ROSALEEN looks at GRANNY and hesitates, as if her eyes are off-putting. Then she brings her lips to GRANNY's cheeks and softly kisses her old wizened skin. GRANNY gazes at her, rocking and smiling, but her old eyes do not smile.)

GRANNY: The best of all girls!

(*27. Exterior.* GRANNY's *house. Night.*
    The owl rises from the apple tree and flaps off through the night. In the house, the light from one window dims.)

(*28. Interior.* GRANNY's *house. Night.*
    GRANNY *and* ROSALEEN, *in long nightdresses, very prim, kneel by the bedstead, a dim oil-lamp beside them.*)

GRANNY: . . . and from the perils and dangers of this night, good Lord deliver us. Amen.

ROSALEEN: Amen.

(ROSALEEN *hops quickly into bed.* GRANNY *heaves herself up more slowly.* ROSALEEN *sleeps against the wall,* GRANNY *on the outside. They settle down.*)

GRANNY: Sweet dreams, pet.

(GRANNY *turns over on her pillow, closes her eyes and begins to snore.* ROSALEEN *closes her eyes, but after a time opens them again. She glances round the room. It is full of moonlight.*
    There is a faint howling, as if blown on the wind from a far distance, faint and very far away.
    ROSALEEN, *slowly, very carefully, raises herself on one elbow to listen.*)

(*29. Exterior. Forest. Day.*
    ROSALEEN *and* GRANNY *walk back towards the village. As they pass through the trees, exaggerated natural forms reveal themselves among the forest growth. Huge mushrooms and toadstools, jacks-in-pulpits. And once again, animals, much larger than life – a rabbit, a fox, a frog – turn their heads to watch as they pass.*
    They walk under the boughs of a eucalyptus tree – they are tiny, dwarfed by the immense vegetation.)

GRANNY: You won't stay a young girl much longer . . .

(*A snake uncoils itself from the branches above them. They walk beneath, without noticing it, but the head of* GRANNY's *fox fur, hanging over her shoulder, twirls its bright eyes to gaze at it, and cocks its head.*)

GRANNY: And your Mammy and Daddy will need all the help they can get. You must work hard, grow wise! Now that your sister's gone . . .

(*The village comes into sight ahead of them, small and homely in the distance.*)

(*30. Exterior. Village. Day.*

GRANNY *and* ROSALEEN *walk down the village street. A group of village children are in a circle round the boy whom* ROSALEEN *stared at in the graveyard. He has a blindfold on his eyes and is being twirled round.)*

CHILDREN:
Wolfie wolfie can't catch me
I have a wife and family
How many children have you got
Twenty-four and that's a lot –

(The CHILDREN *give the* BOY *a last twirl and scatter. The* BOY, *stumbling round blindfolded, bumps into* GRANNY *and* ROSALEEN's *path. He grips* ROSALEEN.)*

BOY: Caught –

*(*GRANNY *whips the blindfold from him.)*

GRANNY: Caught who, you snotty-nosed ragamuffin?

BOY: Caught Rosaleen –

(He looks at ROSALEEN *in an amorous way.* GRANNY *suddenly twirls him once more and boots him up the transom.)*

GRANNY: Nobody catches my little princess! Come on, child –

*(*GRANNY *marches* ROSALEEN *towards her mother's house.)*

(31. Exterior. Farmhouse. Evening.
Rosaleen washes clothes with her MOTHER *by a large tub and a washboard.* ROSALEEN *fills the tub with water, while her* MOTHER *kneads the linen off the washboard.)*

MOTHER: Your granny shouldn't fill your head up with stories. Old wives' tales. Lies.

ROSALEEN: You mean what she says isn't true?

MOTHER: Aren't the real wolves bad enough?

ROSALEEN: Granny says that the worst wolves are hairy on the inside. There's a beast in all men.

MOTHER: You'll find out all in good time.

(Suddenly two arms lift them from behind. It is FATHER. *He has a bunch of dead rabbits slung over one shoulder, a gun over the other.)*

FATHER: There's two lovely armfuls now . . .

(ROSALEEN giggles. Her MOTHER protests. His hands are bloody and have stained the linen.)

MOTHER: Watch what you're doing – after all our work –

FATHER: That's the supper Daddy's caught for you –

(He carries both of them into the house, one in each arm.)

(32. Interior. Farmhouse. Night.

Dinner table. The fire crackles, and a lamp flickers from among the plates. ROSALEEN and FATHER sit down. MOTHER sets down a big pot, lifts the lid and ladles out the rabbit stew.)

MOTHER: There's too much for three people.

FATHER: Stop grieving, would you? Least said, soonest mended.

(He begins ladling out the stew.)

(33. Interior. Farmhouse. Night.

MOTHER *piles the dishes in the sink. She stares out the window at the large moon.* FATHER *comes up behind her and slips his arms around her. He buries his face in her neck and mumbles something we cannot hear.* MOTHER *stares at the moon through the window, then turns and kisses him.)*

(34. Interior. Farmhouse. Night.

ROSALEEN *is in bed sleeping. She is woken by the fluttering of a moth, against the window-pane. She reaches out her hand and touches it. It flutters off again.*

She hears the sound of her MOTHER*'s murmurs from the parents' bed. She looks around. The room is lit by the glow of the dying fire. Her eyes come to rest on her parents' bed. The quilt on the bed is moving.*

ROSALEEN *props herself up on her elbow and watches. Her parents' bed begins to shake.* ROSALEEN *continues to observe, in horrified fascination. She begins to shake her own bed in time to that of her parents.*

Then the agitation abruptly ceases. MOTHER*'s face can be seen, sighing, turning on the pillow.*

ROSALEEN *drops her face and turns away, sighing like her* MOTHER. *She hears the sound of her* FATHER*'s feet on the floor. She closes her eyes.*

She hears the click of the latch. She opens her eyes. The moth hovers just over her face.

She turns her head then, very slowly, and sees her FATHER, *silhouetted in the doorway. He walks outside, out of view.* ROSALEEN *stares, as if in terror, that, like the* GROOM, *the wolves will get him.*

Then she hears the sound of running water. She relaxes. She closes her eyes

once more, curls up to sleep, to the sound of running water and of her FATHER
whistling a tune.)

(35. Interior. Farmhouse. Morning.

ROSALEEN *wakes up in her bed. Her* MOTHER *tidying the kitchen table,
alone.)*

ROSALEEN: Mammy –

MOTHER: Yes pet?

ROSALEEN: Does he hurt you?

MOTHER: Does who hurt me?

ROSALEEN: Does Daddy hurt you when he –

MOTHER: No. Not at all.

ROSALEEN: It sounds like –

MOTHER: Like what?

ROSALEEN: Like the beast Granny talked about –

MOTHER: You pay too much attention to your granny. She knows a lot,
    but she doesn't know everything. If there's a beast in men it meets its
    match in women too. Now get up and fetch some water for me.

(36. Exterior. Village pump. Morning.

ROSALEEN *walks down to the village pump, with a pail in her hand. The
stork that we saw on one of the chimneys is now sitting on the arm of the pump,
gazing at her.)*

ROSALEEN: Good morning –

*(She goes to work the pump, and the stork hops off, on to the ground some
distance away.* ROSALEEN *works the pump to fill the bucket. After a while she
hears a giggle behind her. She turns and sees the* AMOROUS BOY, *feeding the
stork with a handful of corn.)*

AMOROUS BOY: Can we play now, Rosaleen?

ROSALEEN: Play what?

AMOROUS BOY: A game.

ROSALEEN: I know a good game. Close your eyes.

(The AMOROUS BOY *closes his eyes.)*

ROSALEEN: Come to me.

(The AMOROUS BOY *walks towards her, gingerly, his eyes closed.)*

AMOROUS BOY: Now what?

*(*ROSALEEN *empties the bucket over his head. The stork flaps into the air, alarmed.* ROSALEEN *runs off laughing.)*

ROSALEEN:
   Wolfie wolfie can't catch me
   I have a wife and family –

(The BOY *chases her in rage.* ROSALEEN *runs to the safety of her house.)*

(37. Exterior. Graveyard. Day.

   ROSALEEN, *now somewhat older, kneels in front of her sister's grave. She takes a bunch of faded daisies out of the jam jar and replaces them with a bunch of roses.* GRANNY *sits some distance from her, on another gravestone. She is knitting away furiously. The red shawl is quite large now, spreading all over her knees and on to the graves around her.)*

GRANNY: They're the best of all roses. Fit for the grave of a princess.
   They came off my best rose-tree.

(Her needles click away, hypnotically, as she talks.)

ROSALEEN: Why can't Mammy grow roses like that?

GRANNY: It's a question of the green thumb. She lacks that. No hand at
   pastry either. Good morning, Father.

(The old PRIEST *walks through the gravestones towards the church, carrying a large ladder.)*

PRIEST: Good morning –

(He passes out of earshot. GRANNY *whispers conspiratorially.)*

GRANNY: They say the priest's bastards often turn into wolves as they
   grow older.

ROSALEEN: What's that?

*(*ROSALEEN *cocks her head, intrigued. She sits down on her sister's grave, looking up into* GRANNY*'s face.)*

GRANNY: If the child is born on Christmas Day, if he's born feet first,
   he'll be the one.
      If he's born feet first and his eyebrows meet in the middle, yes.
   That's a bad sign.

*(*GRANNY*'s needles click on. The wool unravels . . .)*

GRANNY: And one day he'll meet the devil in the wood . . .

(38. Exterior. Forest. Dawn.

A clearing in the forest. A thick blanket of mist covers the trunks of the trees. A young BOY *of about fourteen or fifteen cycles through the mist and props his bike against a tree. He gazes around him anxiously – and we see that his eyebrows meet. He shivers in the freezing mist, waiting anxiously. Then two lights appear in the distance, glowing like eyes. The* BOY *backs against the tree, doubly nervous. The lights grow brighter. The* BOY *stares, as if hypnotised. The lights grow even brighter.*

The lights grow larger and more brilliant until they dominate the screen, like truly monstrous eyes. We then see that they are the headlights of a large, old-fashioned white Rolls-Royce glimmering in the mist, moving forwards in utter silence.

The BOY *looks in wonder. The Rolls-Royce glides to a halt beside him. At its wheel sits an albino version of* ROSALEEN, *wearing an impeccable chauffeur's costume, but all in white satin. She steps out, smiles at the boy, then opens the rear door.*

The DEVIL *sits inside. A small, but perfectly normal man, dressed like a provincial doctor. He pulls back a cabinet in the upholstery before him. A series of glazed pots and bottles are revealed. His fingers ripple over them, and we see that he has no fingernails. He extracts one small pot, gestures to the boy and hands it to him.)*

DEVIL: Now use it wisely . . .

(The BOY *takes the pot and gazes into the* DEVIL's *eyes.)*

DEVIL: Waste not, want not.

(We see the DEVIL's *eyes in close-up, strangely distant and cold, like* GRANNY's.

The BOY *strips off his shirt, and spreads the ointment on his chest. Hair begins to sprout, weaving curlicues over his skin. His eyes glow red.*

The CHAUFFEUSE *closes the door, slinks into the front once more. The* BOY *gazes at her, hair sprouting all over his chest now. A terrible rending sound is heard. He looks down at his trousers and sees the seam has split.*

The front door magically closes. The car begins to glide off, slowly.)

BOY: Wait –

(He runs after the car, ripping his trousers from him as he does so.
The car glides on, faster than him.)

BOY: Wait – please –

(The BOY *runs after the vanishing wraith of the white car. His stride has*

become crouched and animalistic. He runs on, desperately, as the car vanishes from sight.)

(39. Exterior. Graveyard. Day.
  GRANNY *knits on placidly.* ROSALEEN *is disturbed.)*

ROSALEEN: That's a horrid story. I didn't like it at all.

GRANNY: Not a story, child, but God's own truth. And that is why, if you spy on a naked man in the wood, you should run as if the Devil himself were after you.

(The PRIEST *comes back with the ladder, and props it against a nearby tree. He now has a gigantic pair of clippers in his hand. He begins to climb the ladder, exposing his spindly legs.*
  ROSALEEN *looks up at him.)*

ROSALEEN: *(Whispering.)* The Devil is one thing, but a priest making babies is another. I don't think our priest would have it in him.

GRANNY: You can't trust anyone, least of all a priest. He's not called 'father' for nothing. And there's no need to whisper. He's as deaf as a post!

(She casts off the last stitch of the shawl.)

GRANNY: Isn't that lovely? All we need now is the border and the fringe. See how soft it is?

(She holds it up to ROSALEEN. *A cascade of leaves falls down on* ROSALEEN *from the tree above.)*

ROSALEEN: Soft . . . as snow.

GRANNY: And red as a berry.

(More leaves fall. The PRIEST's *head appears in the tree, looking down at the results of his handiwork. Then he disappears among the foliage again.)*

ROSALEEN: Red as blood.

(She wraps the shawl round herself and smiles gloriously at her GRANNY. GRANNY *smiles benignly. Then suddenly, a branch of the tree falls from above, knocking* GRANNY *on the head. She is immediately diverted from* ROSALEEN.)*

GRANNY: Does the old fool want to brain me? What's he up to in the tree, the old monkey?

(She peers upwards shouting.)

GRANNY: Father, Father, are you climbing up to Heaven and chopping the rungs of the ladder after you? Watch what you're doing!

(The PRIEST's *benign old beard reappears, beautifully tinted by the autumn leaves.)*

GRANNY: Can you hear me?

PRIEST: Don't make so much clamour in the garden of God's house, you irreverent old woman! I heard every word.

GRANNY: What's your silly game, then?

(The PRIEST *clips again. More leafy twigs fall to the ground.)*

PRIEST: Someone's got to do it. Someone's got to cut away the old wood so the new branches can flower next spring.

(He retreats among the foliage again. A creaking. Now an entire branch falls, over ROSALEEN's *sister's gravestone, obscuring it completely.)*

(40. Interior. ROSALEEN's *house. Day.*

ROSALEEN, *now perceptibly older, is combing her hair in front of a square of cracked mirror, propped up against a jar full of buttercups.*

Chickens walk in and out of the open door, scrabbling under the chair she's sitting on.

She combs her hair and sings a song to herself (song from 'Night of the Hunter'). She smiles at herself in the mirror.

She puts down the comb, takes out a red lipstick from her skirt. She looks around to make sure she is alone, then she draws in a big, red mouth over her own mouth. She smiles at herself in the mirror with her new, red mouth.

Close-up of her smiling, voluptuous mouth.)

(41. Interior. Attic bedroom. Day.

We pull back from the red lips in the mirror. They now belong to ALICE, *the girl who was sleeping, in the present-day attic bedroom. She is sitting in front of her cluttered dressing-table in her party dress. She gives her freshly made-up face a last, dreamy, satisfied look, then stands up and twirls round, so that the dress flares beautifully around her legs. She goes to the bedroom door, and hesitates for a moment, as if preparing herself for a spectacular descent down a big staircase. When she opens the door, however, she finds no corridor or staircase, but the terrifying moonlit forest through which she ran, pursued by the wolf at the beginning of the story. A huge wind blows through from outside, whipping her skirts about her. She struggles with the door as the wind whips through her room, tearing the sheets off her bed and whirling them about her. The wind drives her backwards on to the bed, where the white sheets whirl around her like a shroud. She falls on the bed, to the sound of the whipping sheets.)*

(42. Exterior. ROSALEEN's *yard. Day.*

The sound of whipping sheets continues, but now it belongs to freshly washed sheets billowing on a clothes-line. ROSALEEN *is pegging out the sheets, but the wind is so strong that she is having great difficulty.*

Her blouse is pulled tight into a belt, improvised with a piece of rope, showing off her new breasts. The sheets whip into her face, obscuring her vision. When the sheets whip away again, we can see that the entire village is hung with sheets, outside every house, all flapping in the breeze.

The AMOROUS BOY *is moving towards her, from his own house, through the flapping sheets. He stands there, watching her, as if gathering the courage to speak. Then he plunges.)*

AMOROUS BOY: Rosaleen, I –

ROSALEEN: Yes?

(He looks at her face, then takes a breath.)

AMOROUS BOY: I brought you a little present, Rosaleen.

*(*ROSALEEN *peers round the sheets to look at him. He has his hands behind his back.)*

ROSALEEN: What kind of present?

(He takes a bunch of leaves, flowers and berries, made into a bouquet from behind his back. A sad, clumsy little love-offering.)

AMOROUS BOY: I thought maybe you'd take a walk with me. In the woods, on Sunday, after service. Just a little walk, Rosaleen.

*(*ROSALEEN *looks from the flowers to him.)*

ROSALEEN: Why should I?

AMOROUS BOY: I thought – maybe you'd want – to –

*(*ROSALEEN *pauses. She self-consciously makes sure her blouse is properly tucked inside her belt. She is half-puzzled, half-touched by this demonstration. She holds out her hand and takes the posy.)*

ROSALEEN: I'll have to ask.

(The AMOROUS BOY *grins. He takes one step forwards.)*

AMOROUS BOY: Tell your mother I'll be with you. We won't stray from the path –

(43. Interior. ROSALEEN's *house. Day.*

ROSALEEN *sits by the window. She is looking at an elaborate spider's web strung across the pane, with a large, whey-coloured spider weaving a cocoon inside it. The* AMOROUS BOY's *flowers are by the window-sill. Her* FATHER *can be seen outside the window, chopping blocks of wood. Her* MOTHER *is behind her, by the table. She has a round of cheese in a gauze and is squeezing the whey from it.* ROSALEEN *seems lost in a dream.*

FATHER *enters, and drops the wood by the door. He sees* ROSALEEN, *chuckles, and takes a flower from the* AMOROUS BOY's *bundle. He sniffs it, then eats it.)*

MOTHER: Daddy, don't laugh –

ROSALEEN: All he wants is to take a walk with me – on Sunday after service.

MOTHER: All the same, I don't know. It's not as if –

FATHER: What harm can there be in it? The neighbour's son. She's known him since she was a baby. She *still* is a baby!

(*He leans down and tickles* ROSALEEN's *cheek. She squirms. She doesn't like to be teased.*)

MOTHER: To lose . . . another daughter . . .

DADDY: This one will be gone soon enough. So pretty! And besides, what is it they say? It's not losing a daughter, it's gaining a son. Ha! ha! ha!

(ROSALEEN *looks hurt and affronted.*)

ROSALEEN: Stop! You're going too fast. He only asked me to walk with him.

(FATHER *drinks the whey* MOTHER *is squeezing from the cheese. He smiles at* ROSALEEN *mischievously.*)

FATHER: One thing leads to another!

(*44. Exterior. Church. Day.*

The village walks en masse down towards the church, all dressed in their Sunday best. ROSALEEN *is wearing her red shawl.* GRANNY, MOTHER *and* FATHER *walk alongside her. The* AMOROUS BOY *walks behind them, all fresh and scrubbed, with his parents.* FATHER *has his arm around* ROSALEEN *and* MOTHER. *The sun is bright and sparkling, and all's right with the world.*

FATHER *glances back at the* AMOROUS BOY *and pinches* ROSALEEN.)

FATHER: Young people!

(GRANNY *throws her eyes around disapprovingly.*)

GRANNY: The neighbour's son? That scabby little farmer's boy walking out with my little princess?

MOTHER: Now – she promised –

(GRANNY *snorts and looks behind her with disapproval.*
They approach the church. The stork is standing on the bell-tower on one leg. The SEXTON *is pulling the bell-rope, sending pealing ripples out over the village and the forest around it.*)

(45. *Interior. Church. Day.*
The whole village is gathered in congregation. The kindly, eccentric old PRIEST *stands on the lectern, reading the lesson.*)

PRIEST: Isaiah Two, verses six to eight.

(ROSALEEN *glances at* GRANNY *beside her. Her eyes are closed and she is snoring slightly. The sun streams in the window on the scrubbed congregation. The* AMOROUS BOY *darts his eyes towards her and away.*)

PRIEST: The wolf shall dwell with the lamb and the leopard shall lie down with the kid; and the calf and the young lion and fatling together and the little child shall feed them.

(*He glances down at his congregation as he reads.*
We see the congregation has changed. ROSALEEN *is sitting alone now, among a congregation of animals. A row of sheep crowd the front pews, a wolf amongst them. A calf noses its way round the altar. A deer stands in the open doorway, framed by the sunlight outside. It walks slowly, gracefully in.*
The PRIEST *reads on.*)

PRIEST: And the cow and the bear shall feed. Their young ones shall lie down together. And the lion shall eat straw like the ox and the suckling child shall play in the hole of the asp and the weaned child shall put his hand on the cockatrix den . . .

(ROSALEEN *listens avidly to the* PRIEST'*s words. Next to her a bear kneels devoutly, and an ox next to that. A kindly lion, like the lion from* The Wizard of Oz *raises its head in the pews in front of her, its mouth filled with straw.*
By her feet is a large Victorian china doll, with holes for eyes. Out of its empty eyes an asp emerges, tracing a path down its neck.
The PRIEST'*s words continue through all this.* ROSALEEN *glances from him up to the ceiling, where a shower of spiders falls down on her lap, from a large web . . .*)

(46. *Exterior. Church. Day.*
ROSALEEN *walks out the church doors. The* AMOROUS BOY *is standing there. He glances at her, smiling shyly, then away again.*

Behind ROSALEEN, *we can see a flock of sheep coming down the aisle towards the door, the lion and the bear and the deer visible among them, crowding the doorway.*

ROSALEEN *steps past the* AMOROUS BOY, *and slowly down the steps. He follows her, walking slowly. Behind them, the animal congregation emerges.*

ROSALEEN *pulls at the tassles of her shawl. Then she stops and looks back. Now she sees the villagers crowding round the church steps, as if on any normal Sunday. The villagers watch them both, as with one eye.* GRANNY *waves her finger.)*

GRANNY: Don't stray from the path!

(They walk on, the whole village standing on the church steps, observing them benignly, but for GRANNY, *who looks strictly through her gimlet eyes.)*

(47. Exterior. Forest. Day.

ROSALEEN *and the* AMOROUS BOY *walk through the forest, along the path.* ROSALEEN *is restless, the* AMOROUS BOY *is nervous.)*

AMOROUS BOY: When have you to be back, Rosaleen?

ROSALEEN: Soon.

(She walks on moodily.)

AMOROUS BOY: Why are you so crabby? I thought you wanted to come.

ROSALEEN: And what if I did?

AMOROUS BOY: Well, you should –

ROSALEEN: What should I?

(The AMOROUS BOY *slides his arm around her waist.* ROSALEEN *looks at his hand, as she walks, leaving it there for the moment.)*

AMOROUS BOY: You know –

ROSALEEN: I don't know!

(His arm slides more around her. A gaily coloured clockwork bird flies past.)

ROSALEEN: Look –

AMOROUS BOY: Pretty. But not as pretty as you –

(He edges her towards a tree-stump.)

AMOROUS BOY: We can sit here.

ROSALEEN: So we can.

(He kisses her. He is nervous and his lips are wet. He draws his lips away and looks at her.)

AMOROUS BOY: Wasn't that nice?

ROSALEEN: No.

AMOROUS BOY: You're terrible.

ROSALEEN: I know something nicer.

AMOROUS BOY: What?

(ROSALEEN suddenly darts off through the brambles.)

AMOROUS BOY: Rosaleen –

(He follows her through the brambles. He finds her by a bush full of berries – the one she found on the walk with GRANNY.)

AMOROUS BOY: You shouldn't stray off the path –

ROSALEEN: Neither should you.

(She eats the berries, reddening her lips. She hands a bunch to him. She watches him as he eats.)

ROSALEEN: Adam and Eve and Pinch Me went down to the river to bathe. Adam and Eve were drowned, now who do you think was saved?

AMOROUS BOY: Pinch Me.

(ROSALEEN pinches him. He cries out in pain.)

AMOROUS BOY: I'll get you for that –

ROSALEEN: No you won't –

(She runs off through the brambles again. He follows her, calling.)

AMOROUS BOY: Rosaleen –

(She runs, enjoying the experience of being chased.
As she runs, the sunlit forest grows increasingly strange.
The exaggeratedly large mushrooms and the phallic flowers and seed-heads appear. A huge crow flaps out of a tree into her face, going: caw! caw! very loudly, startling her. She stops, panting. Looks over her shoulder. There is a thrashing about in the undergrowth.)

AMOROUS BOY: *(Faintly.)* Rosaleen! Wait for me!

(ROSALEEN giggles. She looks up at a tall, easy-to-climb pine tree, spits on her palms, rubs them against her thighs and starts to climb it.

When she gets high enough for the branches to hide her, the AMOROUS BOY comes running through the long grass below her.)

AMOROUS BOY: Rosaleen! Where have you got to!

(She stays up in her tree, chuckling delightedly to herself until he disappears. Then she continues to climb. There is a large, untidy nest in the crook of a bough. As she approaches it, there is a loud flapping of wings and the stork rises from it, vanishing into the tree tops. She gazes at the vanishing stork, then climbs to the nest. It contains four eggs and a small gilt mirror with a handle. The mirror catches the sunlight and flashes. She wedges herself securely in the tree, takes her lipstick out of the pocket of her skirt, stretches her lips and starts to paint her mouth in the mirror.)

(48. Exterior. Forest. Day.

The AMOROUS BOY runs through the real forest. He has lost his cap. His face is scratched with brambles. He is hot, sweaty and grubby.)

AMOROUS BOY: Rosaleen!

(49. Exterior. Forest. Day.

ROSALEEN smiles at her freshly painted mouth. When she does that, the birds' eggs in the nest all burst open with a musical little exploding noise and reveal tiny babies in them. ROSALEEN, enchanted, stretches out her hand to touch.)

(50. Exterior. Forest. Day.

The AMOROUS BOY bursts through the barrier of the undergrowth on to the cultivated land. He stops short.)

AMOROUS BOY: Jeeeeezus!

(Close-up AMOROUS BOY's aghast face. He wipes sweat off face with the back of his hand.)

(51. Exterior. Meadow. Day.

The meadow lies in the lee of the wood. It is full of the bitten and mangled bodies of cattle. One or two surviving cows stand helpless, lowing.)

AMOROUS BOY: *(Voice over at top of his voice.)* Wolf! Wolf!

(52. Exterior. Forest. Day.

ROSALEEN is back on the broad path through the wood. She is cradling something in her cupped hands as though it were very precious. Her head is bent over her cupped hands. Her red shawl glows in the dusk. Rustle in the undergrowth. A huge wolf raises its head and watches ROSALEEN *as she passes by.)*

(53. Exterior. Village. Day.)

AMOROUS BOY: *(Voice over.)* Wolf!

(The doors of all the houses open. All the men come out carrying shotguns. The AMOROUS BOY *now appears from the direction of the meadow.)*

AMOROUS BOY: Wolf!

He is on the village street, still running. By now he is utterly dishevelled and his clothes are in tatters due to the thorns etc.

The door of ROSALEEN's *house opens. The* FATHER *storms through the farmyard, carrying his shotgun, followed by the* MOTHER *weeping and wailing.*

The FATHER *makes for the* AMOROUS BOY, *seizes him by the collar, shakes him like a dog shaking a rat.)*

FATHER: Where is my daughter? What's happened to my daughter?

(The MOTHER *grabs hold of the* AMOROUS BOY's *arm.)*

MOTHER: We've lost one girl to the wild beasts.

(The other village men run past, along the street past the church, towards the meadow.)

AMOROUS BOY: She ran away from me! I couldn't stop her!

(Their dogs follow, barking.)

FATHER: Take that!

(The FATHER *punches the* AMOROUS BOY *on the jaw. The* AMOROUS BOY *staggers backwards. The* AMOROUS BOY's FATHER *runs towards them with his shotgun. He threatens* ROSALEEN's FATHER *with the shotgun.)*

AMOROUS BOY'S FATHER: Don't you hit my boy.

FATHER: Your precious boy left my only daughter to the mercies of the wolves!

AMOROUS BOY'S FATHER: A daughter is one thing but a heifer is another. They've killed all my cattle – you can get a daughter for nothing but it takes hard cash to get a heifer.

(The FATHER *can't take this. He punches the* AMOROUS BOY'S FATHER *on the jaw. The* AMOROUS BOY'S FATHER *drops his shotgun and punches* ROSALEEN's FATHER. *The* MOTHER *screams. The* AMOROUS BOY *hits at*

both men, weakly and indiscriminately. The village street is now deserted. In the distance shouts, banging of shotguns.

Dusk is coming on.

The MOTHER *goes off up the village street towards the water pump. She walks with determination. A pail stands beside the pump. She fills the pail with water.)*

MOTHER: I'll cool you off!

(She empties the pail of water over the fighting men. They separate cursing and gasping, wiping their faces. Suddenly, ROSALEEN *is there, arrived out of the dusk in her red shawl with the precious something in her hands.)*

ROSALEEN: Mammy?

MOTHER: Oh, my darling! Where've you been? You're in such a state –

*(*ROSALEEN's *face is smeared with dirt from her tree-climbing. Her hair is stuck with pine needles. The men look at her with relief and joy.)*

FATHER: Rosaleen . . .

*(*ROSALEEN *holds out her hands towards her parents.)*

ROSALEEN: Look at the wonderful thing I found in the forest.

(Close-up ROSALEEN's *hands opening round the fragment of bird's egg with the baby in it. Two large tears drip out of the baby's eyes.)*

(54. Interior, Rosaleen's house. Night.

FATHER *loads his shotgun.* ROSALEEN, *still grubby from her tree-climbing brings him his sleeveless leather jacket and his cloth cap.)*

MOTHER: Take care, won't you. And take this –

(She takes something out of her pocket. She goes to hang it round his neck, and we see that it is a silver crucifix.

He pushes her away, not unkindly.)

FATHER: It's lead and cold steel those beasts understand. Kill 'em before they kill you, that's the way.

(55. Exterior. Forest. Night.

FATHER *and the other villagers course through the undergrowth, all heavily armed. The* AMOROUS BOY *follows behind, carrying a large duck.)*

ANCIENT: There was once a village so plagued with the beasts that they drew one up in the bucket of the well . . .

FATHER: Hush your antique gossip, unless you want the wolves to hear it.

(*The duck quacks. The* AMOROUS BOY *holds its beak.*)

AMOROUS BOY: Will you keep your beak still?

(*56. Interior.* ROSALEEN'*s house. Night.*
Candlelight, firelight. MOTHER *has* ROSALEEN *draped in a towel. There is a wooden tub next to the fire, a three-legged stool with a saucer containing soap and a flannel laid ready, a pitcher on top of it.*)

MOTHER: You need a good scrub, you do. Straying away from the path after all we told you!

ROSALEEN: I came to no harm!

MOTHER: More luck than judgement. Rosaleen, promise me –

ROSALEEN: Never again?

MOTHER: Promise!

ROSALEEN: I promise.

(MOTHER *is satisfied. She takes the kettle off the hook and pours hot water into the tub. She tests the water with her elbow and jumps.*)

MOTHER: It'd take the skin off you . . .

(*She adds cold water to the tub from the pitcher and tests it again.*)

MOTHER: Ready when you are.

(ROSALEEN *takes off the towel and drapes it over the back of the chair. She quickly hops into the tub. The* MOTHER *begins to soap her thoroughly.*)

(*57. Exterior. Forest. Night.*
The hunting party is digging a pit in the middle of the wood, by the light of lamps and torches. The AMOROUS BOY *stands a little apart, stroking the duck to calm it. Snow begins to drift around them now.*)

(*58. Interior.* ROSALEEN'*s house. Night.*
MOTHER *washes* ROSALEEN'*s back with the flannel.*)

MOTHER: My my, but you're getting to be a big girl now.

(ROSALEEN *covers her breasts with her hands. We see she is still wearing the locket* MOTHER *gave her at the funeral.* MOTHER *soaps* ROSALEEN'*s hair.* ROSALEEN *squeaks as the lather gets into her eyes.*)

MOTHER: Hold still – big girl. Have to watch out for the boys. I should never have let you walk out with –

ROSALEEN: Boys! What boys? Clowns is what the village boys are! Clods!

(MOTHER *pours water from the pitcher over* ROSALEEN'*s head, to rinse off the soap.* ROSALEEN *splutters, quenched.*)

MOTHER: Your granny spoiled you. Made you think you were something special. That cashmere shawl –

(*59. Exterior. Forest. Night.*

The hunting party covers the pit they have dug with freshly made branches. The AMOROUS BOY *settles the duck carefully on top of the branches, which bears its weight. The duck is tethered to the* BOY'*s hand by a string. The* BOY *scatters corn around it, which the duck pecks. Then he retreats with the other hunters into the bushes.*)

(*60. Interior.* ROSALEEN'*s house. Night.*

ROSALEEN *stands beside the fire now, draped in the towel.* MOTHER *peels off her woollen stockings and puts her feet into the hot water.*)

ROSALEEN: When will Daddy have done with the killing?

MOTHER: When the beast is dead. Not until the beast is dead. We won't live quiet until then.

(ROSALEEN *looks out the window. She sees through it the poor village, with the forest in the background in the thin moonlight. A few snowflakes are drifting around.*)

ROSALEEN: Now that the snow has started . . .

(MOTHER *slowly washes her feet.*)

MOTHER: Early, for snow. Hard winter. The hard winter brings out the wolf. Thank God we're safe indoors . . .

(*61. Exterior. Forest. Night.*

A wolf comes loping through the undergrowth. All around in the bushes, we glimpse the faces of the villagers. But the wolf sees only the pinioned duck.

The duck quacks. The villagers draw breath.

The wolf tenses and pounces on the duck.

The branches break under the wolf's weight and they both vanish into the pit.

FATHER *rushes out from the bushes, shotgun at the ready, other villagers behind him. In the pit, the wolf snarls and leaps but cannot escape. The hunters blast the pit with their shotguns, a crescendo of fire.*)

(62. Interior. ROSALEEN's *house. Night.*

ROSALEEN *is now in a nightdress, with the red shawl around her shoulders. She crouches by the fire, combing her hair.*

MOTHER *takes her feet from the tub and dries them slowly on the towel* ROSALEEN *has discarded, first the right foot, then the left.)*

ROSALEEN: *(Looking into the fire.)* Granny says –

MOTHER: Granny says!

ROSALEEN: *(Undeterred.)* Granny says the wolves might not always be what they seem.

*(*ROSALEEN *drops the comb from her hair, looking at her mother.)*

MOTHER: But how can a wolf be worse than it is?

ROSALEEN: Not worse, but different. Maybe it's not the wolf's fault, Mammy! Maybe . . .

*(*MOTHER *continues to dry her feet, looking into the fire.)*

ROSALEEN: Maybe, once upon a time –

*(*MOTHER *turns around, smiling.)*

MOTHER: Are you going to tell me a story?

ROSALEEN: Maybe I am . . .

*(*ROSALEEN *enunciates the words as clearly as* GRANNY *does.)*

ROSALEEN: Once upon a time, there was a woman in the valley and the son of the Big House did her a terrible wrong, so she came to his wedding to put wrong to right –

(63. Exterior. Country house. Day.

The same country house as in the opening sequence but in its full, former glory – shining new paint, manicured lawns, formal gardens with topiary, peacocks, statues all new and unchipped, and the fountain playing.

Formal presentation of the house, as in an old engraving.

Peacocks on the lawn; cries of peacocks.

On this front lawn, where the tennis net was, an enormous pink-and-white striped marquee open at the front, the flaps drawn back and arranged in swags like curtains in a theatre to reveal, as in a tableau, a magnificent wedding party seated round three sides of a long, mahogany table.

To the left of the marquee a dais with a string trio on it performing light classical selections.

A stream of servants are processing back and forth to the big house laden with dishes.

Peacocks strut around, cawing. One stops, spreads. Pan to the marquee.

The guests are seated round three sides, à la Leonardo's 'Last Supper', so that a full view may be obtained of them in all their splendour. They are magnificently dressed in elaborate mid-nineteenth-century fashion-plate styles, with appropriate hairdos; not one hint of an anachronism, here, but every detail, feathers, flowers, jewellery, lace, crinolines, monocles, decorations of male guests, perfect.

The only slightly surreal touch is the chandelier we have already seen in the hall of the house, hanging over the table from the ridge-pole of the marquee, and the family portraits hung along the back of the marquee, behind the guests.

One female wedding guest has a little lap dog on her knee, which she is feeding with petits fours.

Buzz of contented laughter and chat.

The meal is almost over, fruit and dishes of petits fours, all that is left on the table. The moment for the Cake is at hand.

The BRIDE and GROOM, the central focus of the table – sitting in Christ's place in Leonardo's 'Last Supper' – rise up to stand behind a huge wedding-cake, a really huge one, a monstrously excessive one. Five or six tiers. As magnificent as a wedding-cake may be, all white icing and silver balls and God knows what.

Right up at the top, on the highest tier, in the middle, are the traditional miniature figures of bride and groom.

The BRIDE, in a white wedding dress of most extravagant cut and style, orange blossom wreath, veil thrown back, pearls round her neck, is clasping a regimental sword, raised in order to cut the cake.

The handsome GROOM stands solicitously at her elbow, his hands guiding her hands on the sword.

Pop!

Close-up butler, rapidly filling glasses on a tray from a foaming champagne bottle.

Waiters whisk round champagne.

The guests take glasses, rise to their feet in a wave motion following the progress of the waiters.)

(64. Exterior. Gates. Day.

A young peasant woman, very poorly dressed, with bare feet, in the last stages of pregnancy, drags herself through the gates and along the drive.)

(65. Exterior. Marquee. Day.

The BRIDE and GROOM bring the sword down on the cake.

Cheers, applause.

The little dog jumps up from its owner's lap on to the table, yapping excitedly. It is slapped, and scooped up.)

(66. Exterior. Drive. Day.

The PREGNANT WOMAN *pauses, panting, wiping sweat from her forehead. Now she can see the marquee. She sees the* GROOM *kissing the* BRIDE, *while the guests applaud.)*

(67. Exterior. Marquee. Day.

The GROOM *draws back from the kiss. The guests raise their glasses towards them, in a babble of congratulations.)*

GUESTS: I say! Good health! A long life and a merry one! May all your troubles be little ones. . . . !

(The GROOM *smiles at his blushing* BRIDE. *Then he sees in the distance behind her, the* PREGNANT WOMAN *standing by the ornate gates, arms akimbo, staring directly at him. He looks aghast.*

The babble of talk ceases as the wedding-party follows the GROOM's *look and sees the other* WOMAN.

The trio stops playing. The BUTLER *drops a tray of glasses, starts to move towards her, then thinks better of it.*

Alone among the party, an old and deaf DOWAGER *cuts a side of ham and eats it voraciously, oblivious to the change in mood.*

The PREGNANT PEASANT WOMAN *walks forward. Her eyes are terrifying. The little dog yaps.*

The more she approaches, the more the awful hush descends.

But the DOWAGER *chews on, unconcerned, pince-nez dangling now above her plate of meat.)*

PEASANT WOMAN: You prey on us and you take from us. You grab what you need and discard the rest. The wolves in the forest are more decent.

(She takes her hand from her smock. It contains a small mirror. She glances in it, and sees the wedding-tableau perfectly framed. The mirror starts to crack.

We see the wedding-party, frozen by her words.

A male, jewelled hand, holding an elegant glass begins to transform. Hair sprouts along knuckles, the hand bunches till the glass cracks.

The DOWAGER *eats on voraciously. She grabs the side of ham in both hands and sinks her teeth in it, teeth and jaws now quite wolf-like . . .*

Underneath the table, we see the wedding-party's feet . . . Each foot is elegant and overdressed. The sides of the shoes are beginning to split, wolf-like joints sprouting through the apertures . . .

The PEASANT WOMAN *begins to laugh . . .*

We see the tableau of the wedding-party, as it was before but now instead of overdressed humans there are overdressed wolves, in crinolines, feathers, flowers, jewellery, frock-coats, striped trousers, monocles.

The little dog scrambles out of its wolf-mistress's arms, yapping furiously, and runs out of frame.

For a moment, they seem almost like a wedding-photograph.

The PREGNANT WOMAN *laughs again, without bitterness now, with honest amusement.*

The BRIDE'S *trousseau is now a squirming mass, from which a she-wolf struggles towards its mate, which squirms out of the* GROOM's *monkey-suit . . .*

The other wolves snap at themselves, trying to get rid of their clothes until they're covered in splendid rags.

They scramble over the table, dive beneath it, come out the other side, and race off through the garden. One has an orange blossom wreath still on its head, but she catches her pearl necklace in a rose-bush, the string breaks and she scatters pearls this way and that, bouncing across the garden.

The wolves howl as they run, first one, then the others . . .

They leave behind a litter of broken glass, crockery, champagne bottles, a mess of wedding-cake . . .

The musicians on their dais shrug and quietly begin to pack away their instruments. The servants, first silent and impassive, then softly chattering and laughing, come forward and start cleaning up, pocketing bits and pieces of jewellery and fob watches as they do so.

The peacocks strut, as before.

Pop! The BUTLER *uncorks another bottle of champagne. There is a soft, appreciative murmur from the rest of the servants, who collect glasses and gather round.*

The PREGNANT WOMAN *watches the wolves scatter. She begins to pick up the pearls from the rose-bush.*

She glances at the servants, who raise their glasses in unison towards her. She curtseys, and smiles.)

(68. Interior. ROSALEEN's *house. Night.*

MOTHER *is staring at* ROSALEEN, *as gripped by the story as* ROSALEEN *was by* GRANNY's.)

MOTHER: And where did you hear that story?

ROSALEEN: Not a story, but God's honest truth. Granny was a servant at the wedding!

MOTHER: Never!

ROSALEEN: And, after that, the witch-woman made the wolves come and serenade her and the baby, at night. Made them come and *sing* for her.

MOTHER: What pleasure would there be in that? Listening to a lot of wolves? Don't we have to do it all the time?

(69. Exterior. Forest. Night.)

ROSALEEN: *(Voice over.)* The pleasure would come . . . from knowing the power that she had . . .

(The WITCH-WOMAN, *now delivered, is standing upright in the same pine tree where* ROSALEEN *perched, on the same branch. Her baby lies chuckling in a cradle hanging from another branch. The baby has a string of pearls round its neck. The moon is behind them.*

We see the WITCH-WOMAN's *point-of-view shot, the wild forest at night, under the moon. A fugue-like howling comes from the forest.*

The WITCH-WOMAN *laughs and laughs with pleasure; the baby laughs.)*

(70. Interior. ROSALEEN's *house. Night.*

The door suddenly bursts open, letting in wind and snow. FATHER *enters, stamping his feet, leaving snow on the floor. He carries a blood-stained bundle, and his shotgun.)*

MOTHER: Praise be!

(She runs to greet him. She throws her arms around him, but he thrusts her away. He props his shotgun by the wall. He throws the blood-stained bundle on to the table. ROSALEEN *goes to the table to have a look. He gestures her away.*

He unfastens the bundle, but does not open it.)

FATHER: When I chopped it off the carcase for a trophy, it was a forepaw. The forepaw of the biggest wolf I ever saw. The forepaw of the wolf that killed the sheep, the heifer –

MOTHER: That killed –

FATHER: Maybe.

(He stops for a moment, looks at the bloody bundle.)

FATHER: I cut it with my knife and it was a forepaw, I swear it. A grizzled, giant wolf. And then, before my very eyes . . .

(He opens the bundle to reveal a man's hand, severed at the wrist. There is a ring on the finger.

MOTHER *goes into hysterics, but* ROSALEEN *looks at the hand with unmoved curiosity.)*

ROSALEEN: Whose is it, Daddy? Is it someone you knew once?

FATHER: What do I know, whose hand it is? All I know is what I see.

MOTHER: Get it out of here!

(ROSALEEN *edges closer to the bundle.*)

ROSALEEN: Was it a wolf or a man you killed, Daddy?

FATHER: I killed a wolf. Then it turned into a man. Seeing is believing.

ROSALEEN: Is it? What about touching?

(*She reaches out to touch it.* MOTHER *screams.*)

MOTHER: Get it out!

(FATHER *slaps* ROSALEEN's *hand away.*)

FATHER: Whatever it was, now it's dead meat.

ROSALEEN: Do we bury it, or burn it, Daddy?

(FATHER *answers her by picking the bundle up and throwing it in the fire. As the flesh begins to burn, the room fills up with human sobbing.*
   ROSALEEN *stares, listening to the sound.*)

(*71. Interior. Attic bedroom. Night.*
   The sound of sobbing continues. ALICE *is cowering on the now very much disordered bed, in a room whose original untidiness has been rendered even more chaotic by the wind that broke in from the forest – clothes, books and cosmetics higgledy piggledy everywhere, posters hanging by one drawing pin.*
   ALICE *is knuckling her eyes. When she hears the sound of sobbing, she lowers her knuckles, looks up. (Her make-up is now very much smeared.)*
   A fat, multi-faceted tear seeps out from under her right eyelid, rolls down her cheek, falls off the bed on to the bare floorboards and shatters.)

(*72. Exterior.* ROSALEEN's *yard. Day.*
   ROSALEEN *wrapped in the red shawl scatters corn from a basket for the chickens.*
   Midwinter. Shots of snow all around. Icicles hang from every eave.)

MOTHER: (*Calling from inside the house.*) You can only go if you keep on the path!

(ROSALEEN *empties the basket of corn, turns towards the house.*)

(*73. Interior.* ROSALEEN's *house. Day.*
   ROSALEEN *comes into the house.* MOTHER *is at the table piling freshly made oatcakes in a dish.* ROSALEEN *goes to a dresser, takes out a couple of pots of jam.*)

ROSALEEN: I'm . . .

ROSALEEN/MOTHER: . . . a big girl now! I'm not a baby any more!

(MOTHER *smiles.* ROSALEEN *returns to the table, takes oatcakes from the dish, starts packing them, plus jam and bottle into the basket that has held the chickens' corn.*)

MOTHER: You're besotted with the old lady! The old lady and her old wives' tales.

(ROSALEEN *ignores all this, goes on packing the basket.*)

ROSALEEN: We must take her some Christmas cheer, poor old thing!

MOTHER: Poor old thing! Her with her nice house and her pet dogs. Maybe you shouldn't go.

ROSALEEN: Didn't Daddy kill the great wolf? Nothing to fear in the forest now!

MOTHER: Don't you stray from the path, mind! Isn't there something you can take to protect yourself –

(ROSALEEN *opens cutlery drawer in table. Takes out carving knife. Tests sharpness of blade against her thumb. Slips it into the basket.*)

ROSALEEN: There's power in a knife.

(*She takes a tea-cloth from the drawer, tucks it over the contents of the basket.*)

MOTHER: You're not afraid, are you. You're a fearless child, I'll say that. She'll make you stay the night, the old lady. You were always her favourite, she never cared for –

(*She still can't mention the name.* ROSALEEN *knows the danger signs; she hurries in with:*)

ROSALEEN: Of course I'll stay the night, if she asks me! It'd be rude not to. She *is* my grandmother, Mammy. She's Daddy's Mammy and you took her beloved boy away from her, didn't you, so she's not got a kind word for you. But she's always been good to me. And she's nobody else, just us.

(MOTHER *listens thoughtfully; then goes to the dresser, takes out a green bottle of home-made liquor, adds that to the contents of the basket and tucks the cloth tidily round the contents again.*)

MOTHER: Maybe you're right, maybe you're not. But give her that from me. And don't stray, now. I trust you, Rosaleen. Don't stray, even if nothing happened last time.

ROSALEEN: I promise.

(ROSALEEN kisses her MOTHER, picks up the basket.)

(74. Exterior. Village street. Day.
  MOTHER *watches* ROSALEEN *from the yard gate. She walks down the village street past the* AMOROUS BOY *who is standing outside his house.)*

AMOROUS BOY: Where are you going, Rosaleen?

ROSALEEN: Off to see my granny. Why?

AMOROUS BOY: It's a long way through the wood. Let me go with you, Rosaleen, make sure you're safe. Let me –

ROSALEEN: No, no, no and no again! Go into the woods with you again? Anyhow, I've got this to look after me.

(She takes the knife out of her basket and waves it at him.
  He flees.
  Chuckling, she replaces the knife in her basket.)

(75. Exterior. Forest. Day.
  ROSALEEN *walks through the forest, a lyrical, midwinter, woodland scene.*
  ROSALEEN *looks very much alone, in her red shawl which glows against the predominantly white background, but she is utterly sure of her knowledge of the wood, which is the perfectly real wood it sometimes is. Swish of bracken as rabbit darts through;* ROSALEEN *smiles. A robin perched on a stump begins to sing. She stops to listen.*
  She slips her hand in her basket, takes out an oatcake, crumbles it, kneels, spreads crumbs on snow. The robin stops singing, flutters down from stump, pecks up crumbs.
  ROSALEEN *takes a few crumbs on the palm of her hand, offers them to the robin. The robin hops across and pecks crumbs from her hand.)*

(76. Exterior. Forest. Day.
. *Further down the path.* ROSALEEN *rests, sitting on a fallen tree. She takes the little mirror out of her pocket; looks at herself in it; smiles at herself; digs in her pocket again and brings out the stub of lipstick. She stretches her lips showing her teeth and gums in an expression like a snarl, which is supposed to help you put on lipstick smoothly.*
  Snarling, she paints in a huge, red mouth.
  Distant howling.
  Instantly alert, she puts down lipstick and mirror. The undergrowth rustles. She snatches her knife from the basket, stands up. Menacing attitude.
  The undergrowth rustles again. She backs away from the noise and the movement, with her knife ready.

Close-up ROSALEEN, *reacting – surprise, laughter.*

The undergrowth is still quivering from the exit of a tall, handsome young man, so handsome you do not notice his eyebrows almost meet. He is wearing full, nineteenth-century hunting gear, almost to excess – like a Victorian fashion plate of a sportsman. Hat with feathers of game birds in the ribbon; Norfolk jacket; breeches; boots. Gun over his shoulder, a brace of pheasants dangling from his hand.

He has emerged like an apparition of grace and elegance.

He takes off his hat.)

HUNTER: Miss –

ROSALEEN: *(Laughing.)* Where did you spring from?

HUNTER: Did I scare you? I'm sorry –

ROSALEEN: At least you've got your clothes on!

*(*HUNTER *is momentarily bewildered by this. She leans forward, pokes the pheasants with her knife.)*

ROSALEEN: Tantivvy, is it? A-hunting we will go? Have you lost your horse, that you're trudging through the wood on foot?

HUNTER: Lost my horse and lost my companions, young lady.

*(*ROSALEEN *puts the knife back in the basket. It chinks against the bottle.)*

ROSALEEN: And lost your way, too.

HUNTER: *(Laughing.)* I do believe I just found it. I say, d'you think you could spare me a drink out of that –

(He smiles at ROSALEEN *seductively.)*

HUNTER: I know the very place up the way for a picnic –

(77. Exterior. Clearing in forest. Day

ROSALEEN *has spread the cloth that covered the basket on the ground and arranged the oatcakes and jam on it, with the bottle of liquor in the middle. She dips the blade of the carving knife in the jam, smears it on an oatcake and offers it to the* HUNTER.*)*

HUNTER: I have the most remarkable object in my pocket, that means I never lose my way in the wood.

ROSALEEN: In your pocket, you say.

(The HUNTER *accepts the oatcake, but picks up the bottle in the other hand and takes a quick swig. Her forgotten mirror catches the light and flashes.)*

HUNTER: This object goes everywhere with me. Whenever, that is, I wear my trousers.

(He takes a bite out of the oatcake in his left hand, then offers it back to ROSALEEN, *holding it towards her mouth.)*

HUNTER: Go on! Take a bite! Bite it!

*(*ROSALEEN *tries to dodge away but he pursues her with the jammy oatcake until she is forced to open her mouth and take a bite. They both collapse, laughing. He offers her the bottle he still holds; she shakes her head. He drinks again.*

ROSALEEN *snatches away the bottle, holds it up to the light to check the level of the contents, shakes her head, corks the bottle firmly and puts it back in the basket.)*

ROSALEEN: Don't you know how strong that stuff is? A man in our village keeps the still . . . He's the reddest nose you ever saw . . . It's the drink talking! That's a tall tale you tell, I don't believe in the existence of such an object.

(She picks up a jammy oatcake, consumes it firmly.)

HUNTER: Seeing is believing.

(The HUNTER *takes a compass out of his pocket and displays it to her on the flat of his hand.)*

HUNTER: The little needle always points north, no matter where I go. So I always know exactly where I am.

ROSALEEN: And I still don't believe it, although I see it.

HUNTER: It was this compass that brought me safe through the wood.

ROSALEEN: But you got lost in the wood.

HUNTER: But I found you.

(Pause.)

HUNTER: Are you sorry?

(Pause.)

ROSALEEN: I'm not sorry. They're clowns, the village boys.

HUNTER: Well then.

ROSALEEN: But don't you know you should never leave the path?

HUNTER: I've only just got on to the path. I was perfectly safe before.

ROSALEEN: Aren't you frightened of the wolves?

HUNTER: Why should I be frightened of the wolves?

(*The* HUNTER *taps the butt of his rifle.*)

ROSALEEN: The wolves kill for pleasure – just as you do.

(ROSALEEN *kicks at the shot pheasants.*)

HUNTER: I'll tell you a story about wolves, about the tenderness of wolves.

(*Half-unwilling, she draws closer, attracted by the idea of a story even if she is arguing with the story-teller.*)

HUNTER: Many years ago, before you were thought of or your granny was thought of, there was a couple who lived . . .

(*78. Exterior. Mountain. Day.*
Panorama of barren mountains under storm clouds.)

HUNTER: (*Voice over.*) . . . way up a mountain.

(*On the mountain, a stone hovel, washing on a line outside, smoke coming from the chimney.*)

HUNTER: (*Voice over.*) And this woman was near her time.

(*Scream issues from hovel.*)

HUNTER: (*Voice over.*) So her husband went down to the village to fetch his wife's mother to help her.

(*Hovel door opens,* MAN *exits in a hurry. He runs down the stony mountain path.*
Thunder, lightning, torrents of rain. Water pours down the stony track. The MAN *is buffeted by wind and rain. He loses his footing, falls. Rolls a little way. He tries to rise, in the wind and the torrential rain. He falls forward on his face and rolls, bumping, down the track.*)

(*79. Interior. Hovel. Day.*
Stark poverty of hovel interior. Chickens roost under the eaves, on the roofbeams. A WOMAN *lies on a heap of straw. Her face is covered with sweat. She screams. She is in labour.*
The door of the hovel blows open, letting in the storm, the wind and the rain. The WOMAN's *prone form is lit by lightning. She screams again.*
Fade up howling of wolves.)

(*80. Exterior. Mountain. Day.*

An OLD WOMAN *is clambering up the mountain path. No wind, no rain, now – just pale sunlight on soaking grass.*

Crows rise up from the side of the path.

The OLD WOMAN *sees the crows and apprehensively goes to inspect whatever it is they have risen from. She finds the corpse of a* MAN, *contusions on his forehead, lying under a bush at the side of the path. A stream created by the heavy rains trickles across him, his clothes are soaked and his hair floats this way and that.*

The OLD WOMAN *puts her hand on his forehead, draws it back. She shakes her head sadly.)*

(81. Exterior. Hovel. Day.

The OLD WOMAN *approaches the hovel. No smoke issues from the chimney. The washing-line is blown down, the wet clothes trampled in the muddy grass. The muddy grass and the wet clothes are covered in huge paw-marks.*

The OLD WOMAN *bends to look at the paw-marks. Straightens. The door of the hovel bangs open on its hinges, this way, that way. The* OLD WOMAN *pauses, as if to gather strength, before she goes into the hovel.)*

(82. Interior. Hovel. Day.

Inside the hovel, there is a great mess. What furniture there is, a table, two chairs, is overturned. A flour barrel has been upset. Gnawed chickens lie around, and lots of feathers. Muddy paw-prints cover the floor, and also paw-prints that have tracked the spilled flour around.

The straw upon which the WOMAN *in labour was lying is scattered about but the corpse of the* WOMAN *lies on the ground, untouched.)*

OLD WOMAN: So the wolves never touched you, did they, my dearest. But they must have taken the child . . . They spared the dead but took the living. Took the living.

The OLD WOMAN *kneels beside her daughter, looks at her untouched body, gently closes her staring eyes.*

Then she looks around the hovel.

Close-up OLD WOMAN's *still, stoic face as a tear trickles down her cheek from one eye only.*

Then she begins to keen.)

(83. Exterior. Forest. Day.

ROSALEEN *sits with her arms round her knees, utterly absorbed in the* HUNTER's *story.)*

HUNTER: Seven years passed. And then, one summer's day . . .

(84. Exterior. Mountain. Day.

The same mountain-side, but this time under brilliant sunlight. There is the tinkle of a little bell.

A white goat with a bell round its neck comes frisking into view.

The goat frisks ahead of the OLD WOMAN, *who follows on, leaning heavily on a stick.*

The goat stops in its tracks, bleats with terror.

The OLD WOMAN's *point-of-view shot. A wolf and cubs, at play among the boulders and rocks on the mountain side.*

Very innocent and lyrical scene. The cubs are rolling over and round the wolf-bitch. Among them is another small figure, not at first distinguishable from them.)

OLD WOMAN: Hey!

(The OLD WOMAN *shouts and brandishes her stick. The mother wolf scrambles up and runs off, the cubs dashing whimpering behind her.*

The other figure gets up on its knees more slowly, looks in the direction of the OLD WOMAN.

Close-up WOLF–CHILD. *(Suggest same child as* ROSALEEN-as-a-small-girl.)*

WOLF–CHILD, *on knees and forearms, looking curiously towards the camera.*

Long, brown, tangled hair with burrs, leaves, grass and flowers of broom stuck in it. She is bright brown all over but otherwise completely naked, except for her hair.

Very wild, very beautiful – very shy, but responding to something in the OLD WOMAN.

OLD WOMAN *a few yards from* WOLF–CHILD.)

OLD WOMAN: Darling! My granddaughter!

*(*OLD WOMAN *stumbles forward, dropping stick, holding out her arms.)*

OLD WOMAN: Come to me!

*(*WOLF–CHILD *wavers, undecided. She takes a few uncertain steps towards the* OLD WOMAN.

Howling from distance.

WOLF–CHILD *ups and whisks off, running, bent low, very gracefully. She disappears across the sunny mountain-side.)*

OLD WOMAN: Come back!

(Great, triumphant howling.

The OLD WOMAN *struggles to the crest of the hill. She sees the* CHILD *below, running towards a waiting circle of wolves.*

The OLD WOMAN *covers her face with her hands. When she emerges again, she is smiling wistfully.)*

(85. Exterior. Clearing in forest. Day.)

HUNTER: . . . And the old woman knew her grand-daughter was safe with those who found her wailing beside her mother and rescued her from the storm.

(Pause.)

ROSALEEN: But those were *real* wolves.

HUNTER: What's that?

(He's suddenly uneasy.)

ROSALEEN: Don't you know the worst wolves are hairy on the inside?

HUNTER: Old wives' tales! Peasant superstitions! What! A bright young girl like you – pretty, intelligent girl like you – believes in werewolves?

(He laughs.)

ROSALEEN: My granny said –

HUNTER: For believing in old wives' tales, you deserve . . . to be . . . punished –

(The HUNTER pounces on her, knocking her backwards, and starts tickling her.)

ROSALEEN: Stop that – stop it!

(ROSALEEN writhes this way and that way, giggling delightedly. The HUNTER straddles her.)

HUNTER: I'll show you I'm not afraid of the wolves, Rosaleen, I'll make a bet with you.
   I'll bet you – anything you like! – I'll get to your granny's house before you do. Because I'll use my compass to help me across the country while you trudge along the dreary path.

ROSALEEN: *(Laughing.)* Bet me your compass?

HUNTER: Bet you . . . your heart's desire.

(ROSALEEN's eyes twinkle.)

(86. Exterior. Big house. Day.
   ROSALEEN, *in a white lace ball-gown, not a nineteenth-century one, hair up, diamonds in her ears, diamond necklace, sits on porch of Big House as it was in its nineteenth-century heyday.*

This time, the crystal chandelier hangs from the portico above her head. She's eating an enormous ice-cream sundae with a cherry on top, out of a cut-glass dish. Gold spoon.

What kind of chair she sits on is immaterial but – her feet are propped up on the back of the HUNTER, *whom she is using as a footstool. Beside her sits the big, wolf-like dog from the opening sequence, with a red ribbon bow tied round its neck.)*

(87. Exterior. Clearing in forest. Day.)

ROSALEEN: And if I lose?

HUNTER: You can give me . . . a kiss.

(Terrific erotic charge between them.
Then ROSALEEN *gets to her feet, packs basket.)*

HUNTER: Here – take my hat, as a token of good-will. Wear it until we meet again.

(He pops it on her head at a jaunty angle.
The HUNTER *slips the carving knife into the basket and gets up. He takes the basket from her hand. Then with an elaborate bow, he walks backwards into the thickets, smiling all the time, until he vanishes.*

ROSALEEN *listens to his retreating steps. Then she begins to walk, smiling to herself, forgetting to take her mirror, which lies among the crumbs in the grass behind her.)*

(88. Exterior. Clearing in forest. Day.

Flurries of snow blow across the clearing now. Crows peck at crumbs of oatcake. The forgotten mirror glints from the snowy ground. We see it in close-up. It still retains the image of ROSALEEN's *smiling face. Gradually it is covered with large snowflakes.)*

(89. Exterior. Forest. Day.

It is darker than it was. A wind is building up. ROSALEEN, *alone, dawdling along, smiling. Snow flurries.* ROSALEEN *ignores them.)*

ROSALEEN: *(To herself.)* And what does it matter to me that he took my big knife away with him? I know I'll see him soon. But not *too* soon!

(Big, red, smile.)

(90. Exterior. GRANNY's *house. Day.*

Day, but darkening. Snow flurries. The HUNTER *opens the garden gate. The pheasants he is carrying have a gnawed look. There is blood round his mouth. He walks past leafless apple tree, past winter cabbage, up path to door.*

He is changed. His hair is long, more unkempt. He still carries ROSALEEN's

*basket, swinging it carelessly. His bootheels click on the path. He raises his hand
to knock at the door.*

There is hair on his knuckles. He knocks.)

GRANNY: *(Inside the house.)* Who's there?

(He hurriedly slips off his jacket, then unbuttons his shirt with his hairy hand.)

HUNTER: *(Falsetto.)* Only your granddaughter!

GRANNY: *(Inside the house.)* Lift up the latch and walk in!

(He puts his hairy hand on the latch.)

(91. Interior. GRANNY's house. Night.

GRANNY *sits in armchair by the fire, wire-rimmed glasses on her nose, missal
open on her knee. Fire burns. Lamplight.*

*The latch lifts. GRANNY's eyes are on the door, watching happily. Her fox-
piece hangs on a hook at the back of the door.*

Door opens. GRANNY's happy expression changes to horror.)

GRANNY: God save us!

(The VISITOR is reflected perfectly in each frame of her wire-rimmed glasses.

*He has not yet changed into a wolf but now looks terrifying – lean, fierce,
wild, with blood streaked face, matted hair.*

*His eyes are just red discs of light, no pupils visible. He has ROSALEEN's
basket of goodies in his hand, the dead pheasants on top of them. He walks
towards GRANNY slowly, something of his old courtesy still evident.*

GRANNY *rises up, holding the missal in front of her like a shield.)*

GRANNY: Back with thee to hell, from whence you came.

*(The fox-piece's eyes dart from the hook. Its mouth opens and a strangled cry
comes from it. The HUNTER silences it with a blow from his gun.)*

HUNTER: I don't come from hell. I came from the forest.

*(He drops ROSALEEN's basket on the table. The contents spill out. He props his
gun in a corner. He gazes around at his surroundings, as if he has arrived for
dinner.)*

GRANNY: What have you done with my granddaughter?

HUNTER: Nothing she didn't want.

*(Granny throws her missal at him. It hits him a glancing blow on the forehead,
and falls to the ground, spilling out dried texts and flowers. The HUNTER rubs
his bruised forehead and glares at GRANNY.)*

HUNTER: No –

(His eyes glower with rage. GRANNY snatches a broom and hits him a solid blow. He falls to the ground, howling with pain. The howls are quite wolf-like. We see his face beginning to transform, the skin splitting away to reveal the wolf beneath.

GRANNY screams in horror. She backs away towards the fire. We see the transforming HUNTER reflected in her glasses.

The transforming HUNTER gives a long-drawn-out howl of pain. His head is now almost wholly wolf. The skin of his hands is splitting, revealing the wolf-hands underneath.

GRANNY grabs a red-hot poker from the fire. She swings it. The HUNTER, rising, stops the poker with his wolf-hand.

Close-up of the wolf-hand, gripping the poker. It sizzles and burns. The HUNTER howls once more, in real pain now. He swings his other hand with huge power towards GRANNY's head.

The wolf-hand strikes GRANNY's head. It spins off her body.

GRANNY's head flies across the room, face set in an expression of outrage. It is very like a china doll. It hits against the wooden wall and shatters, into shards of china.

Close-up of the wolf-hand, dropping the poker. The poker falls beside GRANNY's headless body. There is no blood, though, and GRANNY's body is very much like an overdressed, headless Victorian doll.)

(92. Exterior. Forest. Night.

The snow has covered the forest now in a white blanket. A fairy-tale moon is rising. A single wolf howls.

ROSALEEN walks through the white landscape, pulling her red shawl around her more tightly. She hums a tune to herself to keep her spirits up.

When she comes to the gate of GRANNY's house, she sighs with relief. She opens the gate, and sees the moon over the apple tree. The moon slowly colours over red, as if with blood. The blood drips down on to her hand, and spatters the snow.

ROSALEEN shivers, and makes for the door. She knocks at it, rapping it loudly with her knuckles.)

HUNTER: *(Falsetto.)* Who's there?

ROSALEEN: Only your granddaughter!

HUNTER: *(Inside, falsetto.)* Lift up the latch and walk in!

(93. Interior. GRANNY's house. Night.

ROSALEEN comes in, bringing a gust of snow with her.

The HUNTER stands behind the door, hidden from her as she enters.)

ROSALEEN: Cold as hell, outside, tonight, Granny. And have you seen a young man – ?

(She realises that GRANNY *is not sitting, as usual, in her rocking chair. She realises something is wrong. There is a click as the* HUNTER *closes the door gently behind her.)*

ROSALEEN: Granny?

*(*ROSALEEN *turns. She sees the* HUNTER.*)*

ROSALEEN: So . . . you got here before me, just as you said you would.

(The HUNTER *smiles. For all his feral look, he is patently the same person.* ROSALEEN *is bewildered but half-reassured.)*

HUNTER: I did.

ROSALEEN: Where's my granny?

HUNTER: Gone out to the woodpile to fetch more logs.

ROSALEEN: A *real* gentleman would never let an old lady go out for logs on a night like this.

(But this is an attempt at badinage. She is still almost reassured and goes towards the fire to warm herself.

But, as she does so, something crackles beneath her feet. She sees GRANNY's *broken glasses there.*

She takes a deep breath. She sees a circle of splinters of porcelain, that bewilder her. Now she is scared, but brave. She sinks down in the rocking chair and glances at the fire. She sees a tuft of grey hair, caught on a log.

As she watches, the hair catches fire and flares up.)

ROSALEEN: Was that all you left of her? Your kind can't stomach hair, can you? Even if the worst wolves *are* hairy on the inside.

(She takes off his hat and turns it round and round in her hands.)

HUNTER: What do you know about my kind?

ROSALEEN: My granny told me plenty.

(With a sudden, purposeful gesture, she throws the hat into the fire.

She sees the carving knife among the remains of the oatcakes. She edges towards the knife, her eyes on the HUNTER. *He lets her stretch out her hand almost to the handle of the knife before he brings his own hand down on hers, stopping her grasping the knife. He bends down over her, trapping her in the rocking chair.)*

HUNTER: Are you very much afraid?

ROSALEEN: *(Deep breath.)* It wouldn't do me much good, to be afraid.

(His eyes glow very red.)

ROSALEEN: *(Deep breath.)* What big eyes you have!

HUNTER: All the better to see you with!

ROSALEEN: They say seeing is believing but I'd never swear to it.

(He lets go her hand. As she snatches at the knife, he takes hold of it himself, leans forward and touches her breast with the tip of the blade. Which is still covered with strawberry jam.)

HUNTER: *(Normal voice.)* You must be wet through. Won't you take off your shawl?

(He nudges at her shawl with the blade of her knife. She takes off her shawl. She's wearing peasant blouse and skirt underneath. She holds the wet shawl in her hand.)

ROSALEEN: What shall I do with it?

HUNTER: Into the fire with it. You won't need it again.

ROSALEEN: *(Deep breath.)*

(She crouches in front of the fire, poking the shawl into a blaze with a poker. The damp fabric darkens the fire and produces an abundance of smoke. This makes the HUNTER cough. The knife point wavers. ROSALEEN turns on the HUNTER, the poker raised to strike. He traps her hand, again, twists her wrist so she drops the poker.)

ROSALEEN: *(Angry gasps.)*

(ROSALEEN is furious.)

HUNTER: Now your blouse.

(The HUNTER twitches at her blouse with the point of the knife.
    She opens her blouse. First, she hides her breasts from him. Then, with a defiant gesture, she suddenly displays them to him. It is obvious that she gains a kind of confidence from doing so.
    The HUNTER looks her over. Now she blushes furiously and covers herself up with the blouse again.)

HUNTER: You must take off all your clothes, my darling.

ROSALEEN: Do you think they give colic then?

(A terrible howling starts up outside.)

ROSALEEN: Who has come to sing us carols then?

(ROSALEEN cocks an ear to the howling; she is playing for time.)

HUNTER: Only my companions, darling. I love the company of wolves.
    Look out of the window and you'll see them.

(ROSALEEN goes to the window, raises the curtain.)

(94. Exterior. GRANNY's garden. Night.
    ROSALEEN's *point-of-view shot through the window.*
    *The kitchen garden is full of wolves, wolf upon wolf, variously sitting,
standing or weaving about among the rows of winter cabbage.*
    *Some sit on the branches of the apple tree, sit there like fruit, except they
howl.*
    Howling, snow, wind.)

(95. Interior. GRANNY's house. Night.
    ROSALEEN *drops the curtain. She sees the shotgun propped by the window
against the wall.)*

ROSALEEN: It's perishing cold; poor creatures, no wonder they howl so.

HUNTER: What? Are you sorry for them?

ROSALEEN: Yes. And for you, too.

*(She snatches the shotgun and turns round, taking him by surprise. She
threatens him with the shotgun. He chuckles, softly.)*

HUNTER: You're a bold, fearless girl, aren't you! And now you must
    give me back my gun, my dear, after your little game.

(He creeps a little closer to her, chuckling, deceitful, wary.)

ROSALEEN: Stop!

*(The HUNTER, chuckling, comes closer. She releases one barrel of the shotgun,
blasting the pot dogs off the mantel with a crash.*
    *He drops the knife and cowers, whimpering and beginning to howl. The
wolves outside pick up the howling.*
    ROSALEEN *keeps the shotgun pointed at him. She is frightened but putting on
a very brave show.)*

ROSALEEN: Are you our kind or their kind? Tell me truly.

HUNTER: Not one nor the other. Both.

ROSALEEN: Where do you live? In our world or theirs?

HUNTER: I come and go between them. My home is nowhere.

ROSALEEN: Are you only a man when you dress like one, like Granny said?

(*The* HUNTER *growls. He slips off his shirt, revealing a human chest.*)

ROSALEEN: (*Ironic.*) What big arms you have!

HUNTER: (*Sardonic.*) All the better to hug you with!

(*Nursery tale motif introduced here with ironic intent.*
    Shirtless, he lunges at ROSALEEN *but she knocks him in the belly with the gun, winding him. He lurches back, breathing heavily.*)

ROSALEEN: Well, perhaps . . . after all, perhaps . . . you *did* win your bet, didn't you, you gentleman, you fine gentleman.

(*She looks at him in wonder and ironic appreciation. He is still human, but magnificently strange – cheekbones more prominent; jutting eyebrows; hairier; and his eyes shine more. His pectorals gleam.*)

ROSALEEN: They say the Prince of Darkness is a gentleman, and, as it turns out, they're right . . . fine gentleman . . .

HUNTER: Gentlemen always keep their promises. Do ladies keep their promises, too?

ROSALEEN: What do you mean?

HUNTER: Indeed I won my bet, so now you owe me –

ROSALEEN: – I remember –

HUNTER: – a kiss. Will you be honourable and pay me, or will you not?

(ROSALEEN *looks at him. Apprehensive, first she raises the shotgun as he comes towards her, then lowers it. She shivers, closes her eyes. He kisses her.*
    ROSALEEN *opens her eyes, breaks out of the embrace. Now his face is covered in lipstick.*)

ROSALEEN: Jesus! What big teeth you have!

HUNTER: All the better to eat you with . . .

ROSALEEN: Ha! ha! ha! You silly old thing!

(*Laughing, she rapidly bends down, scoops up his shirt and jacket from the floor and throws them into the fire. The fire blazes up brightly. The* HUNTER *snatches at the burning clothes in the fire trying to get them back but only succeeds in burning himself. He falls back on the floor, whimpering.* ROSALEEN *looks at him, the firelight glinting on her face.)*

ROSALEEN: I'm nobody's meat, not I!

(We cut back to the HUNTER. *His hands are clawing at his face, as if to stop the transformation. He howls, piteously this time.*
  We cut back to ROSALEEN. *She is staring at him with wide-eyed curiosity. She speaks slowly, like a child repeating a lesson.)*

ROSALEEN: And now you must be a wolf for good and all. Never be a man again. Not gentleman nor prince of darkness. But an honest, good wolf . . .

(We cut back to the HUNTER. *Now his head and torso are those of a wolf. He crouches by the bed, howling as if his heart would break.)*

ROSALEEN: What? Hurt yourself, have you? Burned your poor paw?

*(*ROSALEEN *slowly approaches him, dragging the gun behind her.)*

ROSALEEN: I never knew a wolf could cry . . .

(She sits on the bed, takes his head in her arms and cradles it gently, maternally.)

ROSALEEN: Oh come on now, don't make such a fuss. Come on, old fellow, old dog. Good boy, good . . .

(The wind rises outside. The howling can be heard more distant. The HUNTER/WOLF *raises his head, as if longing to join his companions.)*

ROSALEEN: Leaving you, are they? You'll be all alone.

(She croons her little tune, like a lullaby.
  The howling dies away altogether, as does the wind, slowly, gradually.)

ROSALEEN: I'll tell you a story, you pitiful creature, though you showed my grandmother no pity, did you. Yet now you're worse off than she . . .
  I'll tell you a story about love between wolves . . .
  There was a priest, once, down the valley, and he was a good and honest priest.

(96. Interior. Chapel. Night.
  Interior of a primitive stone chapel. Just an altar. The old eccentric PRIEST *kneels. There is a candle lantern on the floor beside him, so that the shadows are odd.)*

ROSALEEN: And, once winter's night, as this priest was saying his prayers —

(A whining, a scrabbling at the closed chapel door.
The PRIEST *continues to kneel, silently praying.*
Whining and scrabbling increases.
The PRIEST *looks over his shoulder.*
A questing snout appears under the chapel door.
The PRIEST *gets up, opens door, lets in an old dog wolf. The* PRIEST *backs away from the wolf.*
The wolf follows the PRIEST, *tugs at the* PRIEST's *soutane, pulling him towards the door.)*

PRIEST: So you want me to go with you? Is it a question of a death?

(The wolf whines and pleads.
The PRIEST *picks up a candle lantern, exits chapel accompanied by the pleased wolf.)*

(97. Exterior. Forest. Night.
Wolf trots through the frost-stiff, snow-caked bracken, the PRIEST *following with more difficulty. The light of the lantern bobs and sways.)*

(98. Exterior. Clearing in forest. Night.
A clearing in the undergrowth, with a shelter formed by a fallen tree. On a mound of dead leaves lies an old bitch wolf. When she sees the dog wolf and the PRIEST, *she feebly wags her tail.)*

PRIEST: I fear she's not long for this world.

(The PRIEST *puts his hand on the bitch's forehead. The dog wolf whines, crouches down, lays his head on his forepaws, the picture of misery.)*

PRIEST: Are you that attached to her, old chap? I never knew the wolf kind observed the sacrament of marriage . . .

(The PRIEST *keeps his hand on the bitch's forehead; now he looks startled. When he raises his hand, the furry pelt comes away with it, revealing human skin on a human forehead. The* PRIEST *begins to mutter a prayer.*
Very slowly, very gently, he begins to pull away at the wolf skin. The wolf skin slowly peels off, revealing beneath it more and more of a human face. Face of an OLD WOMAN *near death.*
Now not a wolf but an OLD WOMAN *lies on the bed of leaves, breathing feebly, her eyes closed, the* PRIEST *kneeling beside her. Rustle. He looks up. The male wolf has disappeared; rising up from where he lay is an* OLD MAN, *in rags. The* OLD MAN *comes and kneels beside the* PRIEST. *The* OLD MAN *and*

the OLD WOMAN *are tramps, outcasts, the rejected ones. The* OLD MAN *kisses the* OLD WOMAN's *forehead very lovingly.*

Snow blows over them all.)

(99. Interior. GRANNY's *house. Night.)*

ROSALEEN: So then the priest knew what any wise child could have told him, that there are no devils, except the ones we have invented.

(The transformation is now complete. The HUNTER, *now completely a wolf, lies sleeping in the* GIRL's *arms. She strokes his head.*

She yawns. She leans forward and sticks in the fire-shift. The head in her arms rubs itself against the table. The lamp burns.

Outside the window, the wind has died down completely and the wolves are all gone. All white and silent under the moon.)

(100. Exterior. Forest. Dawn.

The grey light of dawn, outside GRANNY's *house. The* FATHER, *with his shotgun primed bursts through the undergrowth. Behind him can be seen* MOTHER, *and others of the villagers.*

He is tracking the prints in the snow. He sees they lead towards GRANNY's *gate. He breaks into a run.)*

(101. Exterior. GRANNY's *house. Dawn.*

FATHER *rushes up the garden path to the door. He cocks his gun. He hears a snarl from inside. He raises his hand slowly to the latch when the snarl grows into a roar. He glances to his right.*

Crash! The window shatters under the impact of a leaping wolf. The shards of glass fly everywhere and the magnificent creature bounds past the apple tree, leaps over the wall and vanishes into the forest.

FATHER *stares, aghast.* MOTHER, *now beside him, looks after the wolf with wild sorrow. Then she reaches out her hand and lifts the latch.)*

(102. Interior. GRANNY's *house. Dawn.*

The latch lifts and the door opens. MOTHER *stands there, looking at the wild disorder inside. She stares, numbed. Her eyes course slowly over the room and finish on the bed. She hears a purring growl.*

There is a she-wolf curled on the patchwork quilt. The she-wolf raises its head and looks directly into MOTHER's *eyes.*

MOTHER *walks forward, as if mesmerised by the wolf. Round its neck dangles a cross and chain.*

The wolf's eyes are beautiful and serene. Then they perk, as if sensing danger. We hear the click of a shotgun-catch.

FATHER *is now behind* MOTHER, *the shotgun raised.* MOTHER *turns, on instinct. Screams.)*

MOTHER: No – no –

(She swings her arms and strikes the barrel of the gun, deflecting it. The gun explodes, blowing a hole in the wooden roof. Snow cascades inside.

The she-wolf whines, terrified, then leaps in one magnificent bound through the window.

MOTHER *runs to the shattered window. She stares in anguish outside.)*

(103. Exterior. GRANNY's *house. Dawn.*

We see, in a frigid tableau, GRANNY's *house,* MOTHER *at the window,* FATHER *at the door, the villagers crowded round the path and garden, all staring at something outside our vision.)*

(104. Exterior. Forest. Night.

The she-wolf is bounding through the forest, in magnificent slow-motion, as if she is running through time.

The forest makes the change from real to imaginary, giant toadstools at first, then toys and statues.)

(105. Exterior. Magic forest. Night.

Now two wolves run through the magic forest. Past the Doll's House, covered in ivy, the teddy-bears, the clockwork animals etc.)

(106. Interior. Attic room. Day.

ALICE *is sitting on her bed, her knees propped up beside her. She has taken her party-dress off and is in her knickers as before. She is smoothing the dress on the bed before her, folding it neatly.*

The door is still open and the tangle of the forest can be seen sprouting through it.

ALICE *stands up on the bed. She looks down at the floor below the bed. She bounces a little on the bed, as if testing its springs. A long howl can be heard – this time from somewhere beyond the open door.*

ALICE *suddenly springs off the bed, up into the air, as if off a diving-board. She curls, in a graceful jack-knife and plummets towards the floor. The floor parts. It is in fact water. She vanishes beneath it.*

The floor ripples, with the aftermath of her dive. Gradually it settles back into plain floor again.

We see the room, for a beat, half-forest, half-girl's bedroom. There is a whining at the door. It opens, under the pressure of one wolf's snout. First the he-wolf enters, then the she-wolf. They nose their way around ALICE's *things.)*

END

The Magic Toyshop

(*1. Exterior. A London square. Night.*

But a shabby square. Wet and misty, creating a halo around a street lamp – an old-fashioned, gas one, the period is circa *1954/55. The mist partially obscures the surroundings. Out of the mist emerges a man, gaunt, raw-boned, in a soiled trenchcoat open over a shabby, ill-fitting suit. His five o'clock shadow is just showing. His thoughts are worlds away from his surroundings. His age is indeterminate, anything from mid-twenties to mid-forties.*

He is heading towards the row of shops on one side of the square: fog hides the square itself but the outlines of one or two trees are visible – the diffused light from the street lamp illuminates some leaves.

The shops comprise a greengrocer's – as FRANCIE *approaches, a woman in a blue overall reaches out and pulls down a blind, hiding the piled fruit; and a butcher – closed, nothing in the window but greaseproof paper hanging from meathooks and enamelled metal trays, on which sits a black and white cat. There is also a toyshop.*

The toyshop is old-fashioned, quaint, in fact, almost pastiche. It has a slightly bowed window and above, a very ornate sign in gold on green: Philip Flower, Toys and Novelties. *The window itself, closed off from the interior of the shop by shutters, is lit only by the street lights, but we can make out inviting outlines of the toys with which it is crammed – rocking horses, elaborately dressed dolls, a huge Noah's ark.*

As FRANCIE *arrives at the door, a light goes on inside the shop. On the door hangs a sign:* Closed: *stuck into the frame – the top section of the door is panelled in glass – a visiting card,* Francie O'Connor, Jigs and Reels, *in Irish lettering.*

We glimpse a red-haired woman running through the shop just before she flings open the door. She is tall and skinny, in shabby black dress and lisle stockings, with, around her neck, a barbaric-looking silver necklace as tight as a dog collar. Her very bright red hair is untidily pinned on her head. She is carrying a fiddle case.

Cut to:)

(*2. Interior. Toyshop. Night.*

MARGARET *ushers* FRANCIE *into the shop, registering joy and relief.*

A parrot, brilliantly coloured red and yellow, flies up from its perch squawking: No sale, no sale. *Then subsides, with a faint clank. We see the chain that chains it to the perch.*

Down one side of the shop runs a long, mahogany counter: behind it, shelves stacked with many inviting cardboard boxes; the lower shelves display a selection of bright and beautiful, mostly wooden, toys. Other toys – masks, hobby horses, jumping jacks etc. – hang from hooks or are propped against the shelves. The shop has a musty, old-fashioned air; lit by a single bulb hanging from the middle of the ceiling, the upper shelves are shadowy, dusty, cobwebby, their contents enticing, mysterious, possibly sinister.

There is a wooden chair on the customer's side of the counter, no chair on the service side. A huge, ornate metal cash register, registering pounds, shillings and pence (this is pre-decimalisation) dominates the counter.

Behind the counter, a blackboard, '7s 6d' is written on it.

At the end of the counter, in the side wall, is a doorway, that opens on to the stairs down to the basement workshop. The sound of furniture being moved issues from this doorway.

MARGARET *gives* FRANCIE *a quick hug and kiss. She mouths:* 'quick! quick' *and thrusts the fiddle case in his hands, then dives down the stairway to the workroom. The door to the passage is open. In comes a white bull terrier with pink eyes, it registers* FRANCIE's *presence with a wag of the tail.* FRANCIE *takes off his trenchcoat and hangs it over the back of the chair.* FINN *rushes through the same door.* FINN *is a slight, red-haired boy, sixteen or seventeen, in paint-stained overalls. He is pleased to see* FRANCIE, *but agitated.*)

FINN: Get a move on, man!

(He vanishes.
  Cut to:)

(3. Interior. Workroom. Night.
  The workroom is a whitewashed cellar running the entire length of the building. Very little is visible of the front end of the workroom. But there are bunches of what appear to be severed limbs hanging from hooks in the ceiling, also figures hanging from hooks.
  There is a scuff of sawdust and woodshavings on the floor.
  The main focus of the workroom, tonight, however, is a very very large toy theatre which is situated at the back garden end.
  This is a square box, curtained all round in red plush, with an elaborately carved and gilded proscenium arch and red plush curtains in front. From behind the curtains come knockings and bangings. The curtains bulge and part, to reveal a single, glaring eye peering out.
  In front of the theatre, a wooden upright chair, in which sits MARGARET, *craning round anxiously. She looks relieved when* FRANCIE *comes in.* FRANCIE *takes up his position in front of the little theatre. Removes fiddle from case.*

Tucks fiddle under chin. Tunes up. The curtains part further to reveal PHILIP
FLOWER's *face; it is still shadowed, but the eyes and teeth gleam.)*

PHILIP: Now you've deigned to arrive, Mr Fiddler, we can begin.

(FRANCIE *plays. The curtains glide open, revealing a marionette, about three
quarters life size, dressed as Coppelia in the ballet, occupying the centre of the
stage.*

MARGARET *applauds.* FRANCIE *starts to play again.*

As FRANCIE *plays on, the puppet gets up en pointe. The puppet takes a
moment or two to absolutely synchronise itself with the music; then begins to
dance stiffly, but rather well, culminating in an unstoppable pirouette – she spins
like a top.*

Cut to:)

(4. MELANIE's *bedroom. Day.*

MELANIE, *fifteen, is pirouetting ferociously to music she hears in her mind.
She has tied her long, dark hair back and is wearing a sort of improvised ballet
dress, an outgrown liberty bodice over a petticoat, somewhat like a Degas.*

*It is a pretty, rather luxurious young girl's bedroom, featuring a dressing table
with silver-backed hair brushes. On the single bed, with candlewick
counterpane, a teddy bear with a protuberant paunch looks on. By his side, a
glossy art book, open at the reproduction of a Degas ballet dancer. The curtains
are pulled to, the sun shines through them, making a vague, dreamy light. The
dressing-table mirror reflects the room, the bed, the teddy bear.*

MELANIE *glances at herself in the mirror, unbalances and topples forward.
The bear watches. A draught from the window blows the pages of the book
over.)*

MRS RUNDLE: *(Voice over.)* Melanie!

MELANIE: *(Automatically.)* Coming!

(MELANIE *reaches up, unfastens her hair from its elastic band and, watching
herself in the mirror, lets it stream around her face. She pulls the bedspread off
the bed, dislodging the bear, and drapes herself. She turns slightly from the
mirror, so that she's only three quarters reflected. There is a pre-Raphaelite
quality to this image. She watches herself perform that Janey Morris pouting
frown. A faintly anxious expression crosses her face as her hands slide up and
cup her own breasts.)*

Physically, I've reached my peak. From now on, I can only
deteriorate.

MRS RUNDLE: *(Voice over.)* Melanie! Dinner's ready!

(MELANIE, *looking rather vague and unpremeditated about it, slides into a vague simulation of the pose of Botticelli's Venus – she pulls forward one lock of black hair, lowers her right hand to crotch level. She irritably shrugs off the bedspread, to reveal the liberty bodice and petticoat business underneath. She giggles a little and starts unfastening the liberty bodice. Furious banging on the door.)*

MRS RUNDLE: *(Outside.)* Melanie! Your dinner's getting cold! Whatever are you up to!

(MELANIE, furiously embarrassed, snatches up shirt and shorts from the floor, clutches them to her.)

MELANIE: Sorry, I'm coming – sorry!

(Cut to:)

(5. Interior. MELANIE's kitchen. Day.
The country-style kitchen/dining room of a discreetly luxurious house. Sitting at table are MELANIE's brother, JONATHON, nine, flannel shorts, short-sleeved shirt, sleeveless pullover, a characteristic small boy of the period, wearing thick glasses, and her sister, VICTORIA, a fat, cheerful three-year-old. MELANIE, rumpled and childish in aertex shirt and shorts, has just slipped into her place.

JONATHON eats steadily, eyes on plate. VICTORIA makes a mess. MELANIE looks at her food with distaste. MRS RUNDLE, the housekeeper, stately, aproned, very conscious of her aspirates. She takes a postcard out of her apron pocket.)

MRS RUNDLE: I thought your dad was supposed to be a writer, but he hasn't written much here.

VICTORIA: Let me see!

(MELANIE tweaks the card from MRS RUNDLE's fingers.)

MRS RUNDLE: Melanie! Manners!

(MELANIE reads the postcard out loud.)

MELANIE: 'Have ploughed the stormy seas – '

JONATHON: Storms?

(As MELANIE reads on, his glasses begin to reflect, not the kitchen but a stormy sea.
Close-up JONATHON's glasses; reflected within them, a three-masted barque riding huge waves. Sounds of storm and seagulls etc. In the background, MELANIE continues to read.)

MELANIE: *(Voice over.)* 'Very rough weather, good to be back on terra firma.'

(Storm and noises fade. JONATHON's glasses clear. He cocks his head to get a good look at the picture on the postcard. It shows an ocean liner of the period. He sighs, bends his head. Begins to eat again.)

MELANIE: 'The New York lecture went quite well, now on to Chicago. Daddy. P.S. Be good chicks and lots of love, Mummy.' Do you want the card, Jonathon?

(JONATHON shakes his head.)

JONATHON: Wrong sort of boat. Almost as bad as an aeroplane.

(MELANIE moves her cottage pie about on her plate.)

MELANIE: They're going to fly everywhere. Mean things. They should have taken us.

JONATHON: We're too young.

MELANIE: I'm not too young. Juliet was my age.

JONATHON: Juliet who?

MELANIE: In the play. She was married, by my age. And Mummy. Mummy wasn't much older than me when *she* got married. Well, not *that* much older.

(Cut to:)

(6. Interior. MELANIE's house. Parents' bedroom.

Close-up a bride, in monochrome: it is a bride in a black-and-white photograph, an extravagantly dressed bride in a white-lace crinoline wedding dress and a veil surmounted by an orange blossom wreath. At first, it would seem the bride is MELANIE but the hairstyle – early Forties and the faded condition of the photograph tell us this is MELANIE's mother.

The camera pans back to show the rest of the photograph – a groom, in tails and topper: and a huge, stern, somehow incongruous man in a suit and a bowler hat.

The photograph, in a silver frame, stands on a dressing table that otherwise holds a silver box and a jar or two of cosmetics, in front of a casement window. The curtains are not drawn and moonlight floods through, bleaching the colours out of the plushly glamorous bedroom, with its fitted carpet and period touches of Regency stripe wallpaper and Redouté rose prints. A big, white moon hangs directly outside the window.

The bed is stripped: the pillowcases lack pillows. The room is not in use.

MELANIE *is reflected in the photograph as she opens the bedroom door. Somewhere a grandfather clock finishes striking midnight.*

MELANIE, *looking nervous and audacious at the same time, slips into the bedroom.*

Cut to MELANIE *holding the wedding photograph in her hands, inspecting it closely.*

She is wearing plain, practical striped pyjamas, a little too tight across the chest. Her hair hangs over her shoulders.

Looking at the photograph, she absent-mindedly scoops up her hair and holds it on top of her head, in a loose knot. It looks something like the bride's hairdo.

She sets the photograph tenderly down on the dressing table, briefly glancing at her reflection with its piled-up hair in the dressing-table mirror. Then, even more nervous and audacious, she tiptoes to the wardrobe. Tiptoes, although there is nobody to hear her, because she is in a place that is out-of-bounds.

She opens the wardrobe door. A huge, sheeted shape looms within the depths of the wardrobe, among the empty metal hangers.

Nervous, audacious, aware she is handling one of her mother's treasures without permission, MELANIE *reaches inside the wardrobe. The metal hangers jingle. She takes the dress off its hook.*

The hooped skirts erupt from the sheet and engulf her in lace.

Cut to:)

(7. Interior. Parents' bedroom. Night.

The room is deserted, although the wardrobe door is swinging open and the sheet in which the dress was wrapped, and a drifting spoor of tissue paper, lie on the floor, shifting in the draught. Also MELANIE*'s discarded pyjamas lie on the floor, too, where she has dropped them.*

The wedding photograph is once again propped up on the dressing table. As we watch, a breeze shivers the lace frills on the bride's gown. She raises a hand to clutch her veil.

Just for a split second, this is not *a photograph but a fragment of monochrome actuality.*

Cut to:)

(8. Exterior. Front of house. Night.

MELANIE *lives in a stockbroker Tudor kind of house, set in a big garden. The front door opens.* MELANIE, *in the wedding dress, the veil on her head secured by a wealth of orange blossom, stands on the doorstep, an ecstatic smile on her face. The dress is too long; she has difficulty manoeuvring the elaborate skirts. We see her feet are bare as she steps on to the gravel path, wincing slightly.*

Cut to:)

(9. Exterior. Garden. Night.

Huge garden, huge moon overhead, rosebushes with huge roses and huge thorns. And a lily pond.

She catches sight of her reflection in the moonlit water and stops, rapt. Very lyrical and romantic shot of MELANIE, *looking bridal, reflected among the moonlit water lilies.*

As she gazes at herself, the peace is shattered by the ripping roar of an aeroplane overhead. A wind blows across the pool, shattering her reflection. The same wind whips the trees this way and that and blows the petals off the roses in drifts. It lifts up the veil and blows it and the orange blossom wreath up and away. MELANIE *makes an ineffectual grab after them.*

Bang! Big, reverberating bang.

Cut to:)

(10. Exterior. Front of house. Night.

A gust of wind; the front door slams shut. (This is what has made the bang.) Melanie swoops up and wrestles with the shut front door, but cannot open it.)

MELANIE: *(Under her breath.)* Drat and bother and drat, drat, drat and bother and drat . . .

(She lifts up the knocker, she looks down at the wedding dress ruefully and sets the doorknocker down gently on the door. She gathers up her unwieldly skirts and makes off.

MELANIE *looks up towards the open casement of her bedroom window through the gnarled boughs of the old apple tree. High on an out-of-reach bough have lodged the orange-blossom wreath and the wedding veil, hanging drifting down.*

MELANIE *is tense and nervous. The garden is beginning to frighten her. Silence, except for* MELANIE's *agitated breathing. Nightingale starts to sing. She swings herself up on to a lower bough of the tree. A big moth briefly batters her face, disorienting her. There is a ripping sound; the bodice tears under the arms.* MELANIE *makes a face of woe, but raises herself up on the bough, clutching at a higher one. A lace flounce catches on a twig and tears. She looks down again; but another flounce has caught somewhere else. Sharp intake of breath.* MELANIE *swings herself further up, in a cascade of ripping lace. Small, unripe apples, leaves and twigs bounce off her on to the ground. The nightingale continues its serenade. She scrambles up the tree, apple tree debris tumbling round her. The tree itself seems to be against her. A branch catches at her arm.)*

MELANIE: Aagh!

(She inspects her arm. It is badly scratched and bleeding. A drop or two of blood plops on to the white satin bodice of the dress.)

Oh, no!

(She looks up towards the open window, then back down the way she has come. It seems miles to the ground.

She reaches up towards the window ledge. A whole section of the dress rips with a rending sound.

Cut to:)

(11. Interior. MELANIE'S *bedroom. Night.*

The open casement, the flapping curtains, the branches against a now darkening sky.

MELANIE *launches herself from the tree and flings herself forward into the room. Her hair is full of leaves and twigs. Her face is streaked with dirt and tears, scratched and torn; her hands and arms are scratched and the dress is in tatters and streaked with blood and dirt. The only sound is her laboured breathing.*

Cut to:)

(12. MELANIE'S *front hall. Day.*

MRS RUNDLE *in black cloth coat, smooths black gloves over her fingers one by one. On the hallstand, a wicker shopping basket contains a leather purse.* VICTORIA, *neatly dressed waits.* JONATHON *scuttles out of the open front door, with a model ship in his arms, looking out into the garden.* MRS RUNDLE *calls after him:)*

MRS RUNDLE: Don't fall in the pond is all I ask, Jonathon, dear. *(To* VICTORIA*)* We'll give Madam one last chance. *Melanie! (A call to raise the dead.)* Victoria and I are going to the village! If you want breakfast, you get it for yourself! And clear up after you!

*(*MELANIE, *in shorts and blouse, sulks behind the banisters, close behind* MRS RUNDLE *and* VICTORIA. *She is carrying a basin of water with a flannel draped over the side.*

The following shots succeed one another very rapidly.

Cut to:)

(13. Exterior. Lane. Day.

MRS RUNDLE *and* VICTORIA *walk down the lane.* VICTORIA *stops to pick a flower from the hedge. Peaceful summer countryside; sunshine. The peace is interrupted by a motorcyclist, early Fifties vintage, with goggles, in black on a black bike. He is visibly reminiscent of one of Maria Cesare's motorcycle escorts from Cocteau's* Orphée. *He rips down the country lane.* MRS RUNDLE *and* VICTORIA *are forced to jump aside on to the verge.* MRS RUNDLE *grumbles and mutters.*

Cut to:)

(14. Interior. Parents' bedroom. Day.

MELANIE, *rubbing at the bloodstains on the dress with a moistened flannel, is*

startled by the sound of a motorbike and knocks over the basin of water, which spills over both dress and bed, making a big, wet puddle that starts to drip on to the floor.
    Cut to:)

(15. Interior. Hall. Day.
    A loud knocking on the door. MELANIE *opens it.*
    Framed in the doorway is the motorcyclist, holding a yellow telegram envelope out towards MELANIE.
    Cut to:)

(16. Exterior. Drive. Day.
    JONATHON *launches his boat on the pond. He blows lightly and a breeze takes hold of the boat's sails. It skims across the pond. He sits back on his heels, looking pleased.*
    There is a swan swimming languidly on the distant reaches of the pond.
    Abruptly, for no good reason, the boat keels over. JONATHON *rises from his knees, agitated.*
    Cut to:)

(17. Interior. Kitchen. Day.
    VICTORIA, *kneeling on a chair, is unpacking the basket of groceries on to the kitchen table.* MRS RUNDLE, *still in coat, hat and gloves, casts an eye around the kitchen, looking for evidence that* MELANIE *has got up. She finds none. She is irritated, but not with* VICTORIA.*)*

MRS RUNDLE: You be a good girl, Victoria, and don't stir out of that kitchen.

(Cut to:)

(18. Interior. Landing. Day.
    MRS RUNDLE, *panting, irritable, has arrived at the top of the stairs.*
    MELANIE*'s door is wide open; the curtain blows in the draught from the open window but the room is empty.*
    MRS RUNDLE *looks around, puzzled. She sees a feather blow out from under the door of the master bedroom. Followed by another feather. She puts her ear to the door. No sound inside.)*

MRS RUNDLE: Are you in there? Melanie?

(She opens the door.
    Cut to:)

(19. Interior. MELANIE*'s parents' room. Day.*
    A gale of white feathers whirls round and round, a maelstrom and, sitting cross-legged on the bed, in the middle of the trashed room, the bolster, empty of

its feathers, the wedding dress, jars from the dressing table etc. scattered round
her, sits MELANIE, *consumed with grief, clutching the yellow telegram envelope*
in one hand.

As MRS RUNDLE *watches, the feathers subside.* MRS RUNDLE *plucks the*
unopened telegram from MELANIE'S *fingers.* MELANIE *makes no attempt to stop*
her.

MRS RUNDLE opens the telegram. She reads it. She shakes her head sadly.
She folds the telegram, puts it in her pocket. She awkwardly clambers on to the
bed and clumsily puts her arms round MELANIE.)

MRS RUNDLE: You poor things. All on your own.

(Close-up wedding photograph. Nobody remains, now, but the figure of the
man in his bowler hat.
   Cut to:)

(20. Exterior. Garden. Day.
   Two months later. Autumn. Mist in the bushes, mist in the branches of the
apple tree, from which leaves and ripe fruit are falling. High in the branches can
still be seen the orange-blossom wreath and the wraith-like remains of the veil.
   On the lawn is a tableau; all the glamorous furniture and pictures (Redouté
rose prints, old maps, hunting prints) sofas, beds, lamp standards, the kitchen
furniture, the parents' four poster bed, MELANIE'S *dressing table, everything.*
All draped in dustsheets. Pots, pans, cups, saucers, everything.
   Before this, as if posed for a photograph, the orphans. MELANIE, *in school*
raincoat, kneesocks, sensible shoes, with her hair in very, very tight plaits,
looking much younger than fifteen. JONATHON *in school cap and blazer.*
VICTORIA *in what is known as a 'Princess Anne' coat. All with black armbands*
stitched round their upper arms. JONATHON *carries a boat.*
   Beside them, a pile of strapped-up suitcases.
   MRS RUNDLE *stands a little to one side, in front of her strapped trunk. She is*
in coat and hat too.
   She coughs to hide her emotion. The tableau comes to life.)

MRS RUNDLE: Families should stick together. Your uncle and his missus
   are going to look after you.

(MRS RUNDLE and the children move closer to one another.)

MELANIE: We didn't even know Uncle Philip got married. Mummy
   never said. He didn't like Daddy. He never visited.

(VICTORIA runs to MRS RUNDLE and butts her head against MRS RUNDLE'S
knees, weeping furiously. MRS RUNDLE picks her up. Hugs her. Feels in her
pocket for a bar of chocolate. Gives it to VICTORIA. VICTORIA begins to open
it. MRS RUNDLE puts her in MELANIE'S arms.)

MRS RUNDLE: You look after your sister, Victoria.

JONATHON: If they'd stayed on the boat, none of this would have happened.

(Cut to:)

(21. Exterior. Railway station. Day.

Puffs of smoke; hissing of steam engine – we are still in the age of steam. A train has just pulled in, a crowd mills along the platform, disembarking and meeting. Pigeons strut and flutter.

FRANCIE *and* FINN *are briefly visible through the drifting smoke, leaning against a pillar.* FRANCIE *wears his trenchcoat,* FINN *wears a threadbare donkey jacket over paint-stained corduroy trousers. They both look rough, not English, not middle class, hence possibly dangerous or criminal or Irish (which they are).*

FINN *is smoking a cigarette. He moves with great grace and elegance.*

JONATHON *still clutching his boat, gets out of a third-class carriage far down the train. He is followed by* MELANIE, *very flustered as she helps* VICTORIA *down the steps.*

MELANIE *looks around the platform helplessly;* VICTORIA *slips away from her, chasing a pigeon.*

FINN *spots* MELANIE *and puts out his cigarette.* FINN *and* FRANCIE *start towards her just as* VICTORIA, *intent on chasing her pigeon, topples over and sets up a howl.*)

FINN: There, now . . .

(*He stops, kneels, takes out a packet of chewing gum, offers a stick to the crying child.* MELANIE, *unsure of what is going on, starts after* VICTORIA. *She comes up short against the monolithic figure of* FRANCIE *and stares upwards.*)

FRANCIE: You'll be Miss Melanie.

MELANIE: I thought our uncle was coming to meet us.

FRANCIE: I'll get your bags.

FINN: (*With courtly grace.*) He was called away suddenly on business and sent us in his place, even going so far as to give us the necessary taxi fare, an unaccustomed attack of generosity on his part.

(*He heaves cases. The party moves off down the platform. The children are nervous and confused.* FINN *keeps up a babble of chatter.*)

You'll need to know who we are, we're the brothers of his wife, which makes us in an unsanctified kind of way, your uncles. Me name is Finn, me brother is called Francie –

MELANIE: But you're Irish!

FINN: *(Gently.)* There's no law, as I know of, to prevent it.

FRANCIE: As yet.

(The brothers chuckle, to MELANIE's *bewilderment. The crowd swallows them up, the three children looking very child-like in the company of the two men, although we register that* FINN *is about the same height as* MELANIE.
    Cut to:)*

(22. Exterior. Square. Night.
    Taxi *draws up outside toyshop. While* FRANCIE *unloads the cases,* FINN *pays the taxi driver.* JONATHON *gets out of the cab, followed by* MELANIE, *more slowly. Assisting the yawning* VICTORIA. FINN, *having paid, goes to help* MELANIE *with the baby. She flinches away.*
    JONATHON's *glasses flash with light as they reflect the light from the toyshop, which is dazzlingly lit up, this time. And there is a big toy boat in the window.* JONATHON's *face lights up.* VICTORIA *springs to life.)*

VICTORIA: Toys!

(The taxi drives away. The doorbell jangles. The door opens. MARGARET *stands in the doorway, arms extended in welcome, hair tumbling out of its bun, smiling – she looks very lovely.* JONATHON *stares.* VICTORIA *takes a first few steps towards her, then stops, puzzled.* MARGARET's *face falls a little. She looks anxiously over the children's heads at* FINN *and* FRANCIE.)*

    Are you our Auntie? *(*MARGARET *nods.)* What's your name?

*(*MARGARET *opens her mouth; closes it again. She looks helpless.* FRANCIE *moves round and takes her by the arm.)*

FRANCIE: Didn't they tell you your Auntie Margaret was dumb?

(Cut to:)

(23. Interior. Kitchen. Night.
    MARGARET *is nervous and embarrassed, the children anxious. The bleak room looks as festive as it can. A white cloth on the table is laid with an enormous tea – laid for only six places. There is a carving chair at the head of the table, with no place in front of it.* MARGARET *kneels in front of* VICTORIA, *unfastening her coat.* VICTORIA *puts her hand on* MARGARET's *mouth. They look at one another for a moment.* VICTORIA *smiles.* MARGARET *goes on unfastening* VICTORIA's *coat.* JONATHON *looks for a place to put his boat; stands on tiptoe to prop it carefully on the mantelpiece. The white bull terrier noses open the door.* VICTORIA *extends her hand to it joyfully.* FRANCIE *seats himself in one of the chairs by the fire.* FINN *sees the boat.)*

FINN: That's a stylish craft.

JONATHON: I made it from a kit.

FINN: Did you now?

(MELANIE *stares vaguely, holding her coat. She feels lost.* FINN *takes her coat away. She is wearing a plain, grey pleated skirt and a V-necked pullover – almost school uniform.*)

FINN: We'll get your things upstairs, settle you in.

(MELANIE *pulls herself together with an effort.*)

MELANIE: Uncle Philip isn't back yet.

FRANCIE: One thing at a time.

(*Cut to:*)

(24. *Interior.* JONATHON's *room. Night.*

An attic, with sloping ceilings; it looks like an upturned boat. Plain floorboards, a plain little bed, a table, a chair. One lamp bulb dangling from centre of room. Plain, bleak.

The dormer window, at which the curtains are not drawn, gives a view of the lights, it would seem, of all London. JONATHON *runs to look at the view.* FINN *sets his suitcase down beside the bed, gestures to the window.*)

FINN: In daytime you can see St Paul's.

(JONATHON's *point-of-view shot, the city, all brilliantly lit, lying in a scoop of dark.*)

JONATHON: It's like a crow's nest.

(*He turns round with a radiant face. From where* MELANIE *and* FINN *are standing, the floorboards look like those of the deck of a ship.* JONATHON *spreads his feet, so that he looks as if he is standing on the deck of a ship. The deck sways from side to side.*

Cut to:)

(25. *Interior. Girls' bedroom. Night.*

Wallpaper with red roses and green leaves. A big brass bed, with a chamber pot under it. A chair. FINN *opens a cupboard, revealing a few coat hangers.*)

FINN: You'll put your clothes here.

MELANIE: There's no mirror.

FINN: There's not.

(She gulps.)

MELANIE: Excuse me.

(She heaves at her suitcase. FINN *leaps forward.)*

(Vehemently) I can manage.

FINN: *(Heavy irony.)* Excuse me.

(He backs away, leans against the chest of drawers, watching with a touch of irony as she heaves her suitcase on to the bed, opens it, takes out Edward Bear, puts him on her pillow. She smiles, tremulous, defensive, at FINN.*)*

MELANIE: He's a pyjama case, really.

FINN: Do you know you've lovely hair, even if you torment it in those braids.

MELANIE: *(Stiff.)* I like plaits.

FINN: You're spoiling your pretty looks. Come here.

(She tries to take a step backwards but can't because of the bed. So she takes a step forward. He puts his hands on her shoulders. He smiles reassuringly. Very gently, he takes hold of one of her plaits and starts to unplait it.
*   With an effort,* MELANIE *becomes admirably self-possessed.)*

MELANIE: Don't you ever wash your neck?

*(*FINN *chuckles and starts on the other plait.)*

FINN: Give me your comb.

(Cut to:)

(26. Interior. Kitchen. Night.
*   View of kitchen through the open kitchen door – the remains of that enormous tea, and* JONATHON, *yawning enormously.* MELANIE, *her hair sprayed out around her face, is clumsily holding a big, heavy tea cup in both hands, in a way that suggests she isn't used to such coarse crockery; she looks tired out.*
*   Cut to:)*

(27. Interior. Staircase. Night.
*   MARGARET, very tenderly, is carrying sleeping* VICTORIA *upstairs to bed.*
*   Cut to:)*

(28. Interior. Girls' room. Night.
*   VICTORIA sleeps sweetly on the side of the bed next to the wall, but* MELANIE, *on her side of the bed, sits up in the dark, crying very, very quietly –*

we only know because we see the tears on her cheeks glistening. She is holding Edward Bear.

She sits up, reaches under the pillow for her handkerchief. Faintly, in the distance, she hears fiddle music.

She blows her nose on the handkerchief. The music starts again. Fiddle and flute.

Cut to:)

(29. Interior. Kitchen landing. Night.

The music is now very loud; it comes from the kitchen. MELANIE *stoops to peer through the keyhole.*

MELANIE's *point-of-view shot:* FRANCIE *and* MARGARET *are playing,* FRANCIE *the fiddle,* MARGARET *the flute. They are playing a jig.* FINN *sits in the armchair; he gets up and starts very casually to dance.*

The dog sits down on the rug. MELANIE *kneels down, in order to look more comfortably.*

Cut to:)

(30. Interior. Kitchen. Night.

The fiddle and flute piece ends.

MARGARET *sits in the armchair, idly holding the flute.* FINN *sits at her feet. She strokes his hair, smiling at* FRANCIE. FRANCIE *rosins his bow and begins to play a slow air.*

Cut to:)

(31. Interior. Kitchen landing. Night.

A shadow of a large man in a bowler hat falls over MELANIE *as she lies asleep on the floor. Music is still being played in the kitchen. The bowler-hatted man looks thoughtfully down at the sleeping girl; it is her uncle,* PHILIP FLOWER, *recognisable at once from the wedding photograph.*

Close-up UNCLE PHILIP's *impassive face.*

He bends over her and opens the kitchen door. The music dies away.)

PHILIP: She ought to be in bed.

(Cut to:)

(32. Interior. Girls' bedroom. Day.

Roses; red roses, fat and rich and blowing on the tree and wet with dew – red roses and green leaves and bristling thorns, rustling in the breeze, drenched with sunshine. MELANIE *is waking up in a bower of roses.*

Close-up MELANIE's *face, as she wakes up, opens her eyes.*

She sits up; the roses retreat, flattening out and becoming two-dimensional. She rubs her eyes. The roses are back on the wallpaper, again.

Cut to:)

(33. Interior. Bathroom. Day.

Close-up a pair of false teeth, in a glass of water, on a smeared glass shelf.
MELANIE, *in her pyjamas, stares fascinated at this apparition. There is a mysterious dripping noise.*

The bathroom is a masterpiece of beastliness; a deep, old-fashioned basin, with a crack in it. A cake of household soap, with fingerprints on it. A grubby roller towel.

The lavatory chain has broken and been replaced with string, to which the original handle – ceramic, inscribed with the legend: Pull *– has been reattached. No toilet paper, but, hanging from a loop of string, a number of sheets of the Daily Mail ripped into squares.*

The bath stands on four clawed feet. Above the bath, a large geyser, ·the exposed metal of which has turned green, dripping greenish water, the source of the dripping noise. Beside the geyser, a box of matches. MELANIE *picks up the matches; puts it down.*

She puts the plug in the washbasin; the basin fills; a long red hair waves out on the water. She puts her hand in the water. She shivers. It is cold.

Cut to:)

(34. Interior. Kitchen. Day.

The kitchen door opens: FINN *comes in, carrying a couple of bottles of milk. He wears his habitual paint-stained trousers, plus an unbuttoned pyjama jacket. He is accompanied by the bull terrier who, barking furiously, leaps up at* MELANIE, *who has been furtively exploring the kitchen. She jumps. The bull terrier barks and leaps up at her and licks her. She retreats behind the table, which is ready laid for breakfast.*

Her hair is in tight plaits again.)

FINN: You're the early bird! After the late night you had.

(He clatters the milk bottles down on the table.)

Curled up on the landing like love locked out!

MELANIE: *(Shy.)* I did like the music.

FINN: I carried you up to your bed.

*(*MELANIE, *embarrassed, averts her eyes from his naked breast; her eyes meet those of the painted dog hanging above the mantelpiece. She edges round the table to get a better look at it. The dog winks at her. She jumps again.*

Now FINN *can see she is wearing trousers – black corduroy trousers and a brown polo neck sweater, just what she'd wear for an autumn day at home. She looks gently, youthfully pretty. But* FINN *is horrified to see the trousers.)*

FINN: Oh no, no, no! You must go and change your clothes. Now, this minute.

(MELANIE *turns round, startled, inquiring, scarcely believing her ears.*)

He can't abide a woman in trousers. He says a woman in trousers is a sin against nature.

MELANIE: A sin against *what?*

FINN: Slip up and change into a skirt, else he'll create something terrible. Don't you want to make a good impression on your first day?

(MELANIE *pauses with her hand on the doorknob. She is frosty and affronted, but anxious too. She* does *want to make a good impression.*)

MELANIE: Is there anything else I should know about him?

FINN: Speak when you're spoken to. He likes his women quiet.

(MELANIE *glances at the blackboard.*)

MELANIE: (*Crisp.*) Yes.

(FINN *crouches, setting a bowl of chopped meat down for the dog.* MELANIE *reappears in the doorway, looking mutinous but wearing the same pleated skirt she was wearing the previous night. She used to wear it for school. She no longer looks like a teenager but like a schoolgirl.* FINN *takes in her appearance.*)

FINN: I see you've plaited your hair again.

(*She ignores this.*)

MELANIE: I saw his teeth in the bathroom.

FINN: He can take out his smile and keep it on a shelf, but, his bite is worse than his bark, isn't that so, old fellow?

(*The bull terrier barks briefly.*)

MELANIE: Mummy was scared of him, I think. He went to her wedding but he was *furious*, you can see it in the photograph.

FINN: *She* got away.

(*The hands of the cuckoo clock now stand at half past six. The cuckoo clock whirs and emits a stuffed cuckoo. A real cuckoo, stuffed. It goes 'cuckoo' once, then it disappears behind its front door.* MELANIE *is startled and entranced.*)

He made that. In his off hours.

MELANIE: It's as though he'd trapped a real cuckoo inside.

FINN: Didn't you know he made things?

(*Melanie shakes her head.*)

He's forced to sell the toys, to feed us all. But he keeps the other stuff to entertain himself.

(He looks at her assessingly, comes to a sudden decision, catches hold of her hand and pulls her towards the door. She is startled.)

Come and see.

(MELANIE tugs her hand away but goes with him all the same.
Cut to:)

(35. Interior. Toyshop. Day.
   The parrot sits drowsily on his perch as FINN and MELANIE dash through the toyshop.)

PARROT: Gooday! Gooday!

FINN: Gooday to you, you old bugger.

(They disappear down to the workshop. A big doll on the counter turns its head sharply, as if to look after them, or perhaps its head has just fallen forward by chance. A clockwork mouse, its mechanism probably activated by a sudden change in the atmosphere, comes to life and scoots along the counter, squeaking; it falls off and lies on its back, its wheels whirring.
   Cut to:)

(36. Interior. Workshop. Day.
   FINN throws a light switch. MELANIE blinks in the sudden light.
   The basement workshop is a long, white-washed room running the entire length of the house. At the far end, a window, caked with grime and cobwebs, gives on to a coal hole; a little daylight could filter in at an angle from an iron grating in the pavement above it.
   Underfoot, on the bare concrete floor, woodshavings.
   A carpenter's bench runs along one wall, covered with a huge variety of pieces of wooden toys and also of limbs and so on in the process of being carpentered. A selection of wood-turning tools, planes etc. A decapitated head, hairless, eyeless, featureless, is immediately noticeable. Next to it, a jar of eyes.
   There is a painting bench, splattered with paint, holding tins of paint, brushes in jam jars, etc. Above it, a shelf of freshly painted toys waiting to dry. FINN picks up a painted bird and hands it to MELANIE.)

FINN: I'm the sorcerer's apprentice in this establishment.

(MELANIE takes hold of the bird, caresses it.)

I paint the feathers and the fur and the skin but Himself breathes the life in.

(From the walls hang jumping jacks, dancing bears and bunches of carved painted limbs – arms and legs, also puppets, either fully completed or partially assembled, some almost as tall as MELANIE *– they hang from both walls and from hooks in the ceiling. Some are armless, some legless, some headless, some fully painted with wigs, some only partially painted without wigs. It is a strange sight. Also from the walls hang many brightly coloured masks of wild animals and birds.*

There are also several kinds of curious machines with wheels and pulleys, and other, archaic-looking machines – planes, saws, etc.

There is also a log of wood, with a hatchet stuck in it. The atmosphere is that of a toy-maker's shop in a somewhat sinister fairy story.

FINN *takes her arm and draws her down the room, away from the window, towards a flat, large, box-like construction, hitherto concealed in the murk; it reaches nearly to the ceiling. He flicks a switch in the wall and the lights in the back part of the workroom come on, revealing the theatre.* FINN *lets go of* MELANIE*'s arm and advances towards it.*

Unbeknown to her, he has donned a mask – the mask of a bird with a fierce beak, a bird of prey. She jumps once again to see it.

The bird-man stands before the theatre and bows.)

FINN: Ladies and gentlemen, boys and girls, welcome to Flower's Marionette Microcosm.

(He pulls a cord and the curtains open. No scenery except curtains at the back; on the floor of the stage is collapsed, in a tangle of strings, the ballerina doll from the pre-title scene; but the doll is naked, all bare wood and visible joints and dishevelled black wig. MELANIE *is upset by this spectacle but tries hard to conceal it.* FINN *notices, however.*

The bird-man cocks its head to one side; it pulls the cord and closes the theatre curtains again.)

FINN: Don't fret. It's only his dream. Dreams aren't catching, not like measles.

MELANIE: I didn't know about the puppets. It's a lot to take in, all at once.

(He turns off the light in that part of the workroom. They retreat back to the benches of dismembered limbs.

Suddenly, FINN *streaks off down the workshop in a series of wonderful cartwheels.* MELANIE, *amazed, looks up; he lands on the painting bench, takes off the mask with a flourish. She tries to smile but cannot. Her face crumples.)*

MELANIE: I want to go home.

FINN: *(Heavy irony.)* Home is where the heart is.

MELANIE: I can't go home because there's no home left.

(*A great booming overhead; the gong.* MELANIE *jumps.* FINN *is halfway to the stairs already.*)

FINN: Shift yourself, girlie!

(*Cut to:*)

(*37. Interior. Kitchen landing. Day.*
A man blocks the head of the stairway, with the light behind him, so only a great block of shadow is visible. He is holding a round watch. The stair lights come on. UNCLE PHILIP *is visible, a big, big man, impassive of face, in white shirtsleeves, a waistcoat.*)

PHILIP: Improperly dressed, young Finn.

(*He makes as if to aim a blow with the back of his hand at* FINN. FINN *seizes his jacket from the coat rack, hastily buttons it up.* PHILIP *looks over* FINN*'s shoulder at* MELANIE.)

MELANIE: I'm Melanie.

PHILIP: You're late for breakfast.

(MELANIE*'s point-of-view shot through the door, in the kitchen, everybody else*
— MARGARET, FRANCIE, *even* VICTORIA *— sit stiffly around the table, waiting, looking like waxworks, in a terrible morning silence.*
Cut to:)

(*38. Interior. Kitchen. Day.*
Breakfast is just coming to an end; knives and forks are being set together on plates greased and curded with bacon and fried eggs. UNCLE PHILIP, *a vast, moustached, impressive figure at the head of the table, has a huge white linen napkin tucked into his collar; he seizes this napkin, tears it off, throws it in his plate.*)

PHILIP: This morning's plan of action, is as follows: the big girl to stay with her auntie in the shop, to learn the price of things and where they're kept, the child to stay with them and occupy herself whilst getting into as little trouble as possible and —

(JONATHON *scrapes his chair.*)

JONATHON: (*Greatly daring.*) May I go and work on my boat, please?

(PHILIP *casts his eye upon the boat on the mantelpiece.*)

PHILIP: That's plastic. You made it from a kit. Not your own creation. Try harder.

(JONATHON *sits back, shamed.*)

PHILIP: He'll come with me. See how a real craftsman works. Downstairs in five minutes.

(PHILIP *exits. The door slams.* FINN *lights a cigarette, Sweet Afton.*)

JONATHON: He didn't ask our names.

FINN: He knows your names.

(VICTORIA *dissolves in tears.* MARGARET *cuddles her.*)

MELANIE: She's not accustomed to being ignored.

FINN: She'll have to learn.

MELANIE: (*Faintly.*) What about school?

(*The elder brother and sister exchange troubled looks.*)

FRANCIE: (*Gently.*) Too late in the term to start.

(*Cut to:*)

(*39. Interior. Shop. Day.*

Montage of selected toys – clockwork toys; painted horses on wheels, elaborately dressed dolls; dolls' houses.

MARGARET *turns the key that sets in motion a cage of clockwork singing birds.*

More toys – a jumping jack, a tambourine. MARGARET *produces a wooden model of two men hammering at an anvil. She activates it for* VICTORIA. VICTORIA *activates it for herself, laughing.*

MELANIE *climbs on a chair, to dust the high shelves with a feather duster.*

A jumping jack hanging from a nail is activated by her activities, or activates itself; at any rate, the grinning wooden figure contrives to hitch her skirt up over her knees. Although there is nobody to spy on her, MELANIE *is discomfited.*

Cut to:)

(*40. Interior. Workroom. Day.*

PHILIP *lifts down the jar of eyes from the shelf and selects a brown one. Holding it in his right hand, he inserts it in the wooden head he holds in his left hand.* FINN, *at the painting bench, is painting spots on a wooden bird.*

JONATHON *has been sweeping up; he props the broom against the wall.*)

PHILIP: Come here, young feller.

(JONATHON *edges towards him.* PHILIP *puts down the head and picks up a chisel.*)

PHILIP: Ever seen one of these?

JONATHON: No, sir.

PHILIP: Sir is it? Mark that, young Finn. Here –

(PHILIP *gives* JONATHON *the chisel. He gestures to the carpenter's bench.*)

PHILIP: Here's a bit of wood. Try it!

(JONATHON *nervously attacks a piece of wood with a chisel.*)

PHILIP: There. See? Wood's got life in it. Not like plastic.

(JONATHON *gingerly makes his first incision.* FINN *watches with a touch of irony. The chisel slips and cuts* JONATHON *a little. He doesn't cry out but says 'oh' soundlessly.* PHILIP *looks smug.*)

PHILIP: Butterfingers. Wood's got life in it. Look.

(*He takes hold of the wood and gently touches it with his chisel. It sprouts a twig from the incision; the twig sprouts a leaf.*
    Cut to:)

(*41. Interior. Toyshop. Day.*
    The doorbell rings as customer leaves. Next to the blackboard lies the hammering men toy; a hammer has been damaged. MELANIE *rings up seven pounds and ten shillings on the till. She looks down at the counter, which is a mass of toys removed from their boxes and tissue paper.*
    She starts packing up; she begins with the gigantic and beautiful Noah's ark, with all the animals displayed round about it – lions, tigers, zebras, kangaroos, etc., two of each. The ark itself is beautifully and brightly painted, too. She picks up the animals, stows them away inside the ark, smiling and laughing at their charm. Her hands look very big.
    She peeks at the price tag on the mast and is startled to see it reads: 'Seventy five guineas'.)

MELANIE: Gosh!

(PHILIP *emerges from the doorway.*)

PHILIP: It's a fair price for the work. A man must charge a fair price. That's economics.

(*He walks round the front of the counter.*)

PHILIP: And you be careful with them things. They're your bread and butter now.

(*He picks up the damaged toy tenderly.*)

PHILIP: Did you do this:

MELANIE: Victoria –

PHILIP: What? Did you let that child play with one of my toys? I don't like children playing with my toys.

(*He addresses the broken toy.*)

Have to fix you up with another hammer, won't we. Give her a saucepan to play with, that'll do.

(*Cut to:*)

(*42. Interior. Bathroom. Night.*
VICTORIA *stands expectantly beside the bath as* MARGARET, *equipped with a taper, carefully lights the geyser. Bang!* VICTORIA *squeals, applauds.* MELANIE *watches.* MARGARET *turns on the spigot, hot water trickles out. She turns to* MELANIE, *as if to say: it's easy!*
MELANIE *starts to unbutton* VICTORIA'*s dress.*)

VICTORIA: Auntie undress me!

(MARGARET *looks at* MELANIE *with inquiry in her eyes.* MELANIE *laughing, gets out of the way.*
  Cut to:)

(*43. Exterior. Front of Toyshop. Day.*
  Close-up a card hanging on the shop door. It reads: 'Half day closing, Wednesday'.
FRANCIE *and* MARGARET *stand at the first-floor window looking out, smiling down at the street below, as* FINN *and* MELANIE, MELANIE *in her school raincoat but with her hair flowing down her back, walk off together along the pavement – a considerable amount of pavement between them, but all the same, together. The bull terrier follows them for a little way.*
FRANCIE *and* MARGARET *turn away from the window, towards one another, still smiling.*
  Cut to:)

(*44. Exterior. Park. Day.*
  As woodsy, neglected and romantic a park as may be. Uncared-for bushes and shrubs; tall grass, bracken, gorse.
FINN *takes* MELANIE'*s hand, helps her over a fallen tree-stump blooming with yellow fungi.*)

MELANIE: I didn't think London would be like this.

(She jumps. A stone Pan, with pipes in hand, is leering at her through the brambles. She drops FINN'S *hand as if stung.*

The wood is full of statues – dryads, nymphs, Egyptian figures, Victorian philanthropists – any and every kind of statue, overgrown with moss, ivy and lichen, standing among the brambles.)

FINN: A hundred years ago, the Queen of England threw a big party and everyone who was still there at cockcrow turned to stone.

(They pass beneath the boughs of a scrubby tree (hawthorn, covered with red berries) and find themselves on a relatively open hillside, where the mist is gathering. It is already growing dark. Out of the mist and shadows emerges a rococo plinth, daubed with vandals' initials and pierced hearts, etc. The plinth is surrounded by stinging nettles, and bushes and it is empty of its statue.)

FINN: Now she's the Queen of the Waste Land.

(Fallen from the plinth, among the nettles, is a largish statue of Queen Victoria, broken in two at the waist, overgrown with lichen, muddy. FINN *kneels beside the top half, takes out a grubby handkerchief, wipes away some of the mud from Queen Victoria's face. A little stream of water runs out of her eye.)*

MELANIE: She's a fallen woman, poor thing.

(They look extraordinarily lyrical and romantic in the misty park, surrounded by bare trees, the red-haired boy and the dark-haired girl. MELANIE *looks at* FINN *in contemptuous challenge.)*

MELANIE: What are you waiting for?

*(*FINN *kisses her.* FINN *puts his tongue in her mouth.* MELANIE *leaps backwards. She slaps his face. Hard.)*

FINN: *(Genuinely puzzled.)* What was *that* in aid of?

MELANIE: Get away from me . . .

(She thrusts her hands in her pockets, stamps off across the park.)

FINN: You don't know the way home!

*(*MELANIE *tosses her head, strides onwards without a backward look.*

FINN *follows the rapidly departing* MELANIE *across the field, more slowly, crestfallen. He kicks a tuft of nettles.)*

FINN: Damn . . . damn . . .

(Cut to:)

(45. Interior. Girls' bedroom. Night.

MELANIE *flings her coat on the bed. She hasn't bothered to turn on the light. She throws herself down on the bed, thrusts her face into the pillow. Her shoulders start to heave.*

She is laughing. She digs Edward Bear out from the covers.)

MELANIE: Do you think he did it right, Edward Bear? Do you think he knows . . . how to do it?

(*Having cheered herself up, she now sits up.*

At the heart of one of the roses on the wallpaper, something gleams.

Holding the bear, MELANIE *leans forward. She sees a hole in the wall. She applies her eye to it.*

MELANIE'*s point-of-view shot: the two, neat beds. The square of carpet. A chair, with an open fiddle case on it.*

A painting, hanging on the wall.

She squirms, to get a better view.

Close-up the painting. It is of MELANIE, *it is a nude, done with an emblematic stiff chasteness; she is hung about with black hair and has a black ribbon tied round her upper arm. She holds a red apple on the outstretched palm of her hand.*

FINN *comes into* MELANIE'*s field of vision, walking on his hands.*

She gets up soundlessly, pushes the chair against the wall and hangs her cardigan over the back, thus concealing the hole.

She is half-furious, half-amused, muttering vague admonitions under her breath.

Cut to:)

(*46. Interior. Kitchen. Day.*

The bull terrier nudges the kitchen door ajar.

PHILIP *and* MARGARET *are alone.* MARGARET'*s hair is pinned up.* MARGARET *wears the same drab black dress she wore in the opening sequence. She bows her neck submissively before* PHILIP *and he ceremoniously places round her neck the silver collar she wore in the opening sequence. Her head jerks up; the collar is so tight and so constricting she has to hold her head high while she is wearing it. It is a barbaric-looking object, studded with precious stones. It looks very old.*

Cut to:)

(*47. Interior. Workshop. Night.*

A poster advertises 'Performance Tonight'.

MARGARET *descends the ladder last. She wears her black dress and the collar. The children stand in a subdued group, all very neat, clean and smart. Three extra chairs have been provided in front of the theatre, whence emerge bangs and thumps.* MARGARET *shepherds them to their places.* FRANCIE *stands in front of the theatre, fiddle under chin.*

FINN *emerges from between the curtains tense and preoccupied. He turns off the main lights. Now the workshop is lit only by the footlights of the theatre.* FINN *ducks back between the curtains.*

FRANCIE *tunes up: then waits, fiddle under chin. Bow extended.* PHILIP *opens the curtains and steps out. He wears a dinner jacket.)*

PHILIP: Ladies and gentlemen, boys and girls, welcome.

*(*MARGARET *applauds; she gestures to* JONATHON *and* MELANIE *to applaud. They do so.)*

Tonight we celebrate the grand opening of the winter season of Flower's Marionette Microcosm. We present an original drama entitled 'An Artist's Passion'.

(He disappears backwards through the curtains.
FRANCIE *begins to play something very romantic.*
Cut to:)

(48. Interior. Theatre. Night. 'Living Statue.'
FRANCIE *is playing beautifully.*
When the curtains open, it is as though a window has opened on to another place – an enchanted place.
On the stage, it is a night of radiant moonlight. The backcloth is painted with the flowers of a magical garden, the most glorious and unlikely flowers; FINN *has had a field day – blue roses the size of cabbages, purple tiger lilies.*
Centre stage is a cupola, in white, fancy, lace-like ironwork, twined with glorious roses, on which hover a couple of gauzy butterflies. The cupola contains a plinth on which stands the figure of a young woman in a romantic white dress, white stockings, white ballet slippers – a garden nymph out of a ballet; and she is covered in wet white, to simulate marble or plaster. She is a puppet pretending to be a garden statue.
The only thing wrong with her is, she has no face; it is a blank.
Applause over.)

(Interior. Auditorium. Night
MARGARET *applauds furiously. She nudges* MELANIE *and* JONATHON *to applaud, too.* MELANIE *is confused and upset by this faceless girl in the garden but, at* MARGARET*'s urging, she applauds, without enthusiasm.)*

VICTORIA: Why hasn't the lady got any eyes?

*(*MARGARET *hurriedly pops a piece of chocolate into* VICTORIA*'s mouth.)*

(Interior. Theatre. Night.
A young man enters, wearing a white smock and a floppy bow tie; he scares

the butterflies, they flutter away. He is an artist and carries a big palette in one hand, a paint brush in the other.)

PHILIP: *(Out of vision.)* The creator adds the last vital tints to his masterpiece.

(The ARTIST *is tall enough to be able to pass his hand lightly over the nymph's empty face; when he draws his hand away, she has eyes, nose, a rosebud mouth – all complete. A real face – but everything is still white and stiff, like a death mask.*

The ARTIST *dips his brush in the red on his palette and applies the tip of his brush to her lips. Then he stands back. He releases hold of the palette and brush, which whisk off up into the flies.* (FINN *is operating the artist, whose movements are somewhat clumsier than the nymph's.)*

The face of the nymph and her exposed limbs flood with colour and her eyelashes flutter; but then are still again. She makes no movement.

Hand on heart, the ARTIST *mimes adoration.)*

PHILIP: *(Out of vision.)* How can the Artist transmit life to that which is his own Creation and expresses the very depth of his being?

(The ARTIST *takes the statue in his arms, lifts it bodily from the plinth and kisses it on the lips.*

Her eyelids flutter. Her bosom heaves. Her lips part. She awakes.

She runs her fingers through her plaster or marble hair – it turns back into black ringlets that she shakes out delightedly. She stretches out her arms, flexes her fingers; she stretches her legs, points her toes.

The ARTIST *sets her down lightly on the ground, to a renewed wave of applause from the auditorium; they begin to dance, an ecstatic pas de deux among the moonlit flowers.*

The gauzy butterflies return.

Close-up MELANIE *watching, childishly sucking her thumb; she is obscurely distressed by this girl in white, in the moonlit garden.*

The pas de deux concludes in a tremendous arabesque for the nymph; there is a tumult of applause. As the applause dies away, the ARTIST *turns to his creation and sinks to his knees. He raises his hands; he beseeches her. She hovers en pointe, unsure of his intentions; she retreats, prettily confused. He turns.*

FRANCIE *strikes a moving chord. The* ARTIST *plucks, out of the air, a golden ring – a big, thick, chunky wedding ring.)*

(Interior. Auditorium. Night.

MARGARET *coughs; she hastily covers her mouth with her hand, revealing her wedding ring.)*

PHILIP: *(Out of vision.)* The Artist offers his creation his heart, his hand, his very being.

(Interior. Theatre. Night.

The ARTIST *offers the nymph the ring.*

She laughs musically. She shakes her head flirtatiously. He rises. He stamps his foot and beseeches again. She shakes her head emphatically, pulls a rose off the pergola and throws it at him. It strikes him in the face. She laughs soundlessly, then runs off and crouches behind the plinth. The ARTIST *follows; she darts off, to crouch in a corner of the stage, still laughing.)*

PHILIP: *(Out of vision.)* Each man kills the thing he loves.

(The ARTIST *reaches beneath his smock and draws out a knife.*

The blade of the knife catches the light and flashes.

FRANCIE *plays a menacing phrase.)*

(Interior. Auditorium. Night.

The flashing blade reflects on JONATHON*'s glasses, that flash with that light, too.*

VICTORIA *whimpers and buries her head in* MARGARET*'s lap.* MARGARET *strokes her hair.*

MELANIE *is sitting up very straight, her hands clenched in her lap; her eyes glisten with tension.)*

(Interior. Theatre. Night.

Knife raised, the ARTIST *runs towards the nymph. The nymph mimics fear almost too well: there is a sense of real danger.*

FRANCIE *repeats the menacing phrase.*

The nymph runs round the stage; the ARTIST *traps her with his arms. She throws herself at his feet, pleading for mercy.*

He raises the knife. He brings it down.)

(Interior. Auditorium. Night.

Close-up MELANIE, *involuntarily closing her eyes.)*

(Interior. Theatre. Night.)

FINN: *(Out of vision.)* Whoops!

(The knife, which is perfectly real, perfectly sharp, has, by bizarre accident – and FINN*'s clumsiness – cut through one of the strings that uphold the nymph.*

What happens next happens in slow motion as the girl turns back into a doll.

First, one arm drops to the floor with a dull, wooden thud – the hand splats out and disarticulates.

She jerks about on her strings; PHILIP *is trying to get her away, but her dress is tangled up in the pergola.*

The ARTIST *jerks around on his strings;* FINN *is trying to disentangle the artist – and, in doing so, he slices through another string, so that the other arm drops. Then – Bang! The torso; and, as the puppets wrestle, her head falls, too. And shatters. It turns out the head is made of porcelain.*

There are fragments of shattered porcelain all over the stage floor; a pair of blue marbles, the eyes – pearly false teeth – a delicate little ear – masses and masses of silky black hair.

The ARTIST's *arms drop to his sides. He sags forward on his strings, completely inhuman looking, a doll once more.*

From aloft, clear and irrepressible, comes the sound of FINN's *laughter.*

The tension eases immediately; the audience rustles with relief.)

(Interior. Auditorium. Night.

MELANIE *has opened her eyes, unclenched her fists, smiles.*

VICTORIA *removes her head from* MARGARET's *lap.*

Then MELANIE's *smile is replaced by a look of pure horror.*

FINN's *laughter modulates into a scream. He falls down from the flies, seems to fall endlessly, his long red hair drifting after him as if he were falling through water, somersaulting as he falls.*

He lands with a crash, on top of the dismembered puppet and lies there, looking completely dislocated. The only sound is his terrible sobbing attempt to breathe.

FRANCIE *and* MARGARET *both knew that something like this was inevitable one day, but are as if transfixed.*

Except that tears flood soundlessly down MELANIE's *cheeks. The children are very distressed.* VICTORIA *wails.* JONATHON, *jerked into reality, claps his hand to his mouth.* MELANIE *half-rises.*

MARGARET *tries and tries but cannot bend her head down to comfort* VICTORIA *because of the collar. Tears splash on to* VICTORIA's *face.* MELANIE *turns towards them as* FRANCIE *puts his arm round them both.* PHILIP *comes on stage, in dinner jacket and bow tie. He is straightening the bow tie. He looks down at prone* FINN.)

PHILIP: Won't use him to work the puppets again.

*(*FINN *remains motionless.* PHILIP *looks out at the audience; suddenly he points to* MELANIE.)

I'll use you instead of a puppet, Miss.

*(*MELANIE *is startled but doesn't appreciate fully the implications of this.* FRANCIE *and* MARGARET *are horrified and distressed.* FINN *is the most horrified of all. He moans loudly. He struggles to sit half-upright, blood trickles from the corner of his mouth. He collapses again.* PHILIP *almost to himself.)*

After all, why shouldn't the girl do something for her keep. God knows she eats enough. She's not too big, she won't be out of scale. *(Out loud; firmly.)* That's settled.

(Cut to:)

(49. Interior. Girls' room. Night.

VICTORIA *is having a bad dream;* MELANIE *is cuddling her in her arms in bed. She wears her cardigan round her shoulders. As* VICTORIA *quietens down,* MELANIE *sees a glimmer of candlelight through the hole in the wall.*

MELANIE *settles* VICTORIA *down and tiptoes to the wall.*

MELANIE*'s point-of-view shot:* FINN, *very pale, lies on the bed, looking like 'The Death of Chatterton'.*

FRANCIE *in shirtsleeves has just lit a candle and is cupping the flame with his hand to protect it as it flickers into life. After a moment,* FRANCIE *dribbles melted wax from the candle on to the floorboards and fixes the candle into it next to* FINN*'s bed.*

FINN*'s bed is banked by many, many lighted candles. He hasn't moved.* FRANCIE, *now fully, rather elaborately dressed in his best suit, stands at the foot of the bed, tuning his fiddle.*

We see MELANIE *watching through the spy-hole.*

Cut to:)

(50. Interior. Brothers' bedroom. Night.

FRANCIE *begins to play.*

At first, FINN *does not move. Then he shudders convulsively jerking and twisting. The candle flames shiver, creating grotesque shadows.* FRANCIE *goes on playing.* FINN *quietens down, stops struggling, rolls over, knuckling his eyes.*

The fiddle music comes to an end.

Cut to:)

(51. Interior. Kitchen. Day.

The entire family are assembled around the table, having tea. PHILIP, *especially, is making a hearty meal from the spread – shrimps, a bowl of mustard and cress, bread and butter . . . and drinking enthusiastically from his tea cup.*

MARGARET *wears her black dress and the big, heavy, jewelled collar and can only eat with the utmost difficulty. She looks wonderful, beautiful and strange as some pagan deity, but one shrimp alone lies on her plate and she pulls off its whiskers one by one. She tries a swallow of tea, and chokes.* FINN *darts up, pats her on the back.*

PHILIP *watches her, relishing her discomfort.*

MARGARET *finishes peeling her shrimp, then slips it to* VICTORIA.*)*

PHILIP: Ain't you having a bite more to eat, Margaret?

(She looks at him with wounded eyes. There is a terrible silence. FINN *is deathly pale.)*

Pour us more tea, Margaret.

(MARGARET quivering with nerves, slops tea into the saucer of the cup she passes to PHILIP.)

Live with the Irish; live like pigs.

(MARGARET makes a wild, conciliatory gesture that knocks over a cup. It spills tea all over the tablecloth. PHILIP clicks his tongue against his teeth.)

Tut, tut.

FINN: Excuse me.

(He gets up, limps out, in very bad shape, still. MELANIE watches him leave. Her face is full of anguish.
Cut to:)

(52. Interior. Toyshop. Day.
A very elegant woman, who looks like Barbara Goalen, the great Fifties model, in a winter white-tweed suit and hat, a startling apparition in the cobwebby shop, is having the Noah's Ark packed in a box.
She is leaning on a furled umbrella; she looks bored. MELANIE, packing the Noah's Ark, steals the elegant woman a sidelong look; her mother looked like that. The elegant lady does not like to be looked at by MELANIE, who is lank-haired and grubby, in her worn, grubby skirt and sweater, her knee socks, her lace-ups.
MELANIE ties the string and strikes the cash register with a clang. It shows seventy-five guineas.)

MELANIE: There!

(The lady takes the huge parcel in her arms; she balances on her high heels, opening the door while grubby MELANIE watches ironically. So does the parrot. JONATHON is lurking in the basement doorway, waiting for the lady to be gone, full of suppressed excitement.)

LADY: *(Ironically.)* Thanks!

(The doorbell clangs behind her; JONATHON rushes into the shop. He hands MELANIE a beautiful toy boat, not a three-master but a very reasonable sailing boat. He is bursting with pride. MELANIE admires the boat.
PHILIP looms up behind them.)

PHILIP: Put it in the window. It ought to fetch at least ten guineas.

JONATHON: I'm earning my keep, sir!

PHILIP: Not yet, you're not.

(He brushes JONATHON aside and descends into basement. JONATHON

lingers, hurt. He picks the boat up, doubtfully. MELANIE *scribbles* Fifteen Guineas *on a price ticket and ties it on to the mast.*

JONATHON *reads the ticket, looks up, smiles at* MELANIE.

Cut to:)

(53. Interior. Kitchen. Night.

MELANIE *is unfolding lengths of white chiffon from a paper bag on the table. Other paper bags lie on the table.*

MARGARET *dips into a paper bag, produces an armful of flowers – real flowers, roses and carnations – and throws them over* MELANIE. MELANIE *spins round and round, unfolding the chiffon, flowers whirling, and emerges in a chiffon tunic, crowned with flowers, her black hair flowing everywhere, laughing. Looking wonderful, and like a Victorian painting of a nymph. In soft focus.*

We see JONATHON *standing in the doorway.)*

JONATHON: Uncle Philip wants Melanie downstairs straightaway.

*(*MELANIE *comes back into hard focus. The crown of flowers is obviously artificial.* MELANIE *is sulky.)*

MELANIE: Can I keep my shoes on? I'll need my coat to go downstairs, it's freezing away from the fire –

(Cut to:)

(54. Interior. Workshop. Night.

The entire workshop is brightly lit. The curtains of the theatre are open; FINN *is onstage, in overalls, surrounded by paints, painting a backcloth showing a brightly coloured sunset over the sea.*

On the carpenter's bench, a big, ominously sheeted shape. PHILIP *squats on the floor with a mound of white feathers on a spread sheet before him. He is sorting the feathers into smaller piles. There are feathers and down caught in his moustache.*

MELANIE, *flowers in her hair, huddled in her school raincoat, bare feet in sensible shoes stands sullenly in front of him.*

JONATHON *goes and stands beside* PHILIP. PHILIP *ignores him.)*

PHILIP: Take off that wrap.

(She does so. The only sound is the slap, slap of FINN*'s paint brush as he fills in an area of the sky.)*

You're well built; how old are you?

MELANIE: Sixteen. Well, nearly sixteen.

PHILIP: I wanted my Leda to be a little girl. Leda and the swan. See?

(He gestures towards the sheeted shape on the carpenter's table.)

Big swan, little Leda. But you're a big girl. Do you have periods?

(MELANIE is aghast. FINN continues painting, but mutters:)

FINN: What's that to do with swans?

(JONATHON moves away from PHILIP, scared, anticipating blows.)

PHILIP: *(Equably.)* Keep your mouth shut, Finn. I'll talk to her how I please.

(FINN suspends painting.)

FINN: I can say what I like.

(PHILIP looks at him thoughtfully, stroking his moustache.)

PHILIP: Oh no you can't. Get on with the painting.

MELANIE: It's all right, Finn.

(PHILIP looks smugly at FINN. FINN looks mutinous, then defeated. FINN picks up his brush and carries on painting.)

PHILIP: *(To MELANIE.)* I suppose you'll do. Turn round. *(MELANIE turns round.)* Smile. *(MELANIE smiles.)* Not like that. Show your teeth. *(MELANIE smiles and shows her teeth.)* You've got a bit of a look of your mother. None of your father, thank God. Should have seen his face when I turned up at the wedding. Thought I'd come to drag her away with me. But I knew she was gone for good. You've got a fair bit of your mother in you, though.

(Momentarily, he seems almost sentimental and MELANIE is bewildered, a little scared, but he soon snaps out of it and orders briskly.)

Walk up and down.

(MELANIE clumps up and down in her tunic and her lace-up shoes.)

Not very graceful, are you. Finn O'Connor! *(FINN looks around.)* Teach her how to shift herself.

(FINN stops painting, staring at PHILIP.)

You used to fancy yourself at the light fantastic. *(FINN stares.)* Get on with it.

(MELANIE looks from PHILIP to FINN, puzzled: she starts to move towards the theatre.)

Not down here. You'll spoil the set. Upstairs.

(He goes back to sorting the feathers. FINN *lays his paint brush across the tin of paint.*

Cut to:)

(55. Interior. Brothers' bedroom. Night.

They are shy and nervous with one another.

FINN *opens a drawer in the chest of drawers, takes out a shell – a beautiful, rosy pink, tropical shell.)*

MELANIE: Where did you get that?

(She looks in the drawer. It is crammed with precious shells, lumps of coral, pieces of glittering minerals.)

FINN: We brought them with us from over the sea.

(He sets the shell down on an empty strip of linoleum.)

That's your beach. This is the story. Leda walks by the shore, gathering shells. *(He indicates the shell.)* Night comes on. She hears the beating of great wings and sees the approach of the swan. She runs away but it bears down and casts her to the ground. Curtain.

MELANIE: Is that all?

FINN: *(With irony.)* Ah, you should see the swan! His masterpiece. Now, walk along the beach and stoop to pick up the shell.

*(*MELANIE *takes her shoes off. As she does so, a wave breaks on the linoleum, swishing round the legs of the furniture.*

Cut to:)

(56. Interior. Beach. Dusk.

The furniture remains, huge and outlandish, on a desolate expanse of wet sand. MELANIE, *watched by* FINN, *walks along, bends down, retrieves the shell. She is nervous and walks clumsily.*

Neither she nor FINN *give any indication they are not still in the bedroom.)*

FINN: That won't do. Make it flow.

(He walks along the imaginary beach, but he is no longer graceful; he hobbles. He stops short.)

Try again. *(She walks a little more gracefully.)* That's a bit better. Now do it again. I'll be the swan.

(She walks gracefully along the imaginary beach. He stands on tiptoe, raising and lowering his arms. He is purposefully grotesque.)

Swish, swish, that's the beating of my wings. When you hear that, you put a spurt on.

(*He limps along, beating his arms in the air. She looks behind her, runs a few steps. She can't help giggling.*)

He'll turn you out if you don't do what he wants, Melanie! (*Sobered, she runs.*) You run, you stumble and I bear you to the ground with my enormous pinions.

(*She runs, she stumbles, she falls on the sand, she opens her arms to receive* FINN *as he does a neatly choreographed dancer's fall on top of her. She welcomes him.*

FINN *lies with his face pressed into* MELANIE's *shoulder, so that we cannot see his expression. His hand lies on the sand. She picks it up, examines it — calloused, paint stained.*

She caresses and kisses the hand, very tenderly.

Cut to:)

(*57. Interior. Brothers' room. Night, as before*

FINN *has vanished.*

MELANIE *slowly sits up, angry, hurt and puzzled. She looks round the room. She looks under the bed. Smoke drifts out of the keyhole of the cupboard.*

She opens the cupboard door. A suit hangs on a hanger; some white shirts on a shelf on top of the cupboard, his head and body concealed by the clothing. His hand comes out and taps ash on to the floor from his cigarette. MELANIE *inspects the soles of his feet.*)

MELANIE: Finn, there's a splinter in your left foot. (*Silence.*) If you don't let me take the splinter out, it will fester.

FINN: (*Muffled by clothing.*) Go away.

MELANIE: (*A wail.*) What did I do wrong?

(FINN *parts the shirts and looks out. He is angry and mutinous.*)

FINN: I won't do it because he wants me to do it, even if I want to do it.

MELANIE: Do what? (*Pause.*) Oh, I see.

FINN: You're only a young thing.

MELANIE: (*Stung.*) You're not so old yourself!

FINN: Living with him put years on me.

(*He pulls the shirts together again, hiding himself. The agitation of the coat hangers disturbs the paintings on the top shelf; they slither to the ground.*

A formal portrait.

It shows PHILIP, *naked but for his bowler, sitting in the same pose as the white bull terrier in the picture in the kitchen, wearing* MARGARET'S *silver collar round his neck.*

A leash is attached to this collar. MARGARET *stands, holding the leash, looking spectacular – brilliant green cloak around her shoulders, on her head, a spiky crown.* MELANIE *directs a remark at the smoking wardrobe.)*

MELANIE: Wishful thinking.

*(*FINN *makes no response. She stows the picture away on top of the wardrobe. She picks up another; it is the nude of herself that she once glimpsed through the spy-hole. It remains unfinished.)*

You never finished it.

*(*FINN *parts the shirts again, not angry now, but melancholy.)*

FINN: That was wishful thinking, too.

*(*MELANIE *touches her own painted breast.)*

MELANIE: All the same, I'd like to keep it . . . in my room . . . if you don't mind . . . There aren't any mirrors in the house.

*(*FINN *looks at her directly and, after a moment, he smiles.*
    There is a sudden flurry of rain on the bedroom window.
    Distracted from one another, both glance at the window, the incipient tenderness between them evaporates.
    Cut to:)

(58. Exterior. Square. Day.

It is raining. Rain lashes against the shop window. In the shop window, fireworks are piled in decorative piles: also many more masks than usual are hanging.

In the square garden, a huge bonfire is under process of construction; chairs, tables etc. stick out from the pile of rubbish.

Two shouting kids trundle past the window with a limp, floppy guy dragging behind them in an orange box fitted up with pram wheels. They hold newspapers over their heads to keep the rain off.

PHILIP, *rain dripping off the brim of his bowler, crosses the road to reach the shop. The kids accost him.)*

FIRST CHILD: Penny for the guy, guv –

*(*PHILIP *brushes past brusquely, jangling the shop-door bell.)*

SECOND CHILD: Mean bastard.

(Cut to:)

(59. Interior. Kitchen. Night.
The blackboard reads 'Special performance. Tonight. MELANIE*'s debut.'*
Towels are warming over the fireguard. MARGARET *removes them.*
Cut to:)

(60. Interior. Bathroom. Night.
MELANIE *sits in the bath. She scrubs her elbows vigorously with a nail brush;*
then she raises her left leg and scrubs the hard skin behind her heel. Then the
right leg. Then she plunges right under the water and comes up streaming and
gasping. She has brought her portrait with her and propped it against the geyser.
She scrutinises nude image earnestly – there isn't a hint of her earlier, dreamy
self-obsession; now she really wants to know what she looks like. The geyser has
done its work well. The window has misted up with condensation.

MARGARET *brings in the towels. She holds a towel open for* MELANIE *to step*
into, as if she were a little girl. MELANIE *raises herself in the bath; the portrait*
tips up and tumbles into the water. MELANIE *snatches it up; the colours are*
running, her features are already blurring. She looks up at MARGARET *with a*
frightened face. MARGARET *quickly scrawls with her finger in the condensation*
on the window: '– Silly –' She envelops MELANIE *in a towel and rubs her*
briskly, hugging her at the same time, tickling her to make her laugh.
Cut to:)

(61. Interior. Theatre. Night
We are inside the curtains, onstage.
The stage is heaped with real sand, shells, starfish etc. The backcloth is
painted with a lugubrious sunset.

PHILIP *and* MELANIE *are onstage. She is dressed and ready, with flowers in*
her long, loose hair. PHILIP *nods. He climbs the ladder to the catwalk.*

MELANIE *kicks at the sand with a bare foot. She looks upwards; she sees*
FINN, *foreshortened, squatting on the catwalk above the stage. He does not smile*
at her. Next to him, resting on the catwalk, is a huge bundle, wrapped in a
sheet.)

PHILIP: *(Voice over.)* Music!

(Outside the curtains, FRANCIE *begins to play selections from* Swan Lake.
The stage lights go off, leaving a brownish gloom. Then MELANIE *is*
transfixed by a brilliant spotlight; she blinks and jumps.)

PHILIP: *(Hissing.)* Get started!

(The curtains open but MELANIE *can see nothing beyond the stage because of the*
lights. PHILIP, *overhead and unseen coughs.* MELANIE *spreads out her skirt,*
bends, picks up a shell, puts it in her skirts.)

PHILIP: *(Reciting over.)* 'Leda gathers shells by the shore in the approaching dusk. Little does she know that Almighty Jove has picked her out to be his mate.' *(Applause.)*

(Aloft, PHILIP beats on the metal gong which has been transferred above. Startled, MELANIE drops her shell.)

'The sound of thunder announces the presence of the majestic visitant.'

(Enter the swan, lowered down from above. MELANIE giggles in spite of herself; then clamps her hand over her mouth.

MARGARET smiles, to encourage MELANIE. MARGARET's point-of-view shot: from the audience, it looks as though a beautiful, very stylised swan is descending in a piece of clever stage magic. But, from MELANIE's point-of-view shot, there is no illusion.

The swan is an egg-shaped sphere, painted white, coated with glued-on feathers. The neck lolls comically. The wings are like those of model aeroplanes, again coated with glued-on feathers. Its black, rubber legs are tucked up underneath it.

MELANIE remembers to mime astonishment.

The swan's feet come down and it lands on them with a thud. Its head points towards MELANIE. MELANIE is frozen in her mime of horror; she is fascinated by the ingenuity and vaguely suggestive ugliness of the swan. The swan's wings beat steadily up and down, disturbing MELANIE's hair. A rose blows away.)

PHILIP: *(Voice over.)* 'Leda attempts to flee her heavenly suitor but his beauty and majesty bear her to the ground.'

(The swan's beating wings blow the sand around. MELANIE remembers to run a few steps; she looks back – splat, splat! on its rubber feet; the swan is following her.

Up above, PHILIP, smiling narrowly, is directing the swan's movements.)

PHILIP: 'The innocent girl's thighs tremble. Her loins melt. She falls.'

(MELANIE's point-of-view shot: a white, monstrous shape is advancing upon her in the floury glare of the spotlight. The light is in her eyes and she cannot see it properly. The swan's head rears up and towards her.

MELANIE tries to run and falls. The screen is filled with the image of the great, beating wings.)

PHILIP: *(Voice over.)* 'Almighty Jove in the form of a swan wreaks his will.'

(MELANIE screams. Roaring of the beating wings. No other sound – the music has stopped, no sound from the audience.

Cut to:)

(62. Interior. Theatre. Night.

From aloft, PHILIP *is looking down with satisfaction at the girl lying on her back, dress dishevelled, eyes closed. The swan dangles beside her harmlessly, on its strings. The stage curtains are closed, again.*

FINN *has covered his eyes.*

The applause from the outside begins. MELANIE *slowly sits up and looks around.*

FINN *looks down from the catwalk as* PHILIP, *the swan and a shaken* MELANIE *take a bow.* PHILIP *puts his arm proudly round the swan. The little audience applauds mechanically.*

JONATHON *whispers to* MARGARET:)

JONATHON: I didn't like that play.

*(*MARGARET *passes him a toffee. Her eyes do not leave* MELANIE, *who still looks stunned.*

Close-up MELANIE, *looking stunned.*

Cut to:)

(63. Interior. Girls' bedroom. Night.

A nightlight is burning. VICTORIA *is asleep;* MELANIE *lies still but wakeful, open-eyed unable to sleep. A withered geranium falls off the plant in the window.*

There is a scratching at the door. Renewed scratching. MELANIE *sits up.)*

MELANIE: *(Sharp.)* Who's there?

FINN: *(Voice over.) (Whisper.)* Let me in.

*(*MELANIE *is visibly relieved.)*

MELANIE: *(Whisper.)* The door's not locked.

*(*FINN, *haggard, sidles in.)*

FINN: Can I come into bed with you for a little while, I feel terrible.

MELANIE: Well . . . yes. All right. But –

FINN: Ah, come on now!

(He kicks off his shoes. MELANIE *moves* VICTORIA *over to the wall, to make room for* FINN.*)*

Would you mind holding me in your arms for a little while?

MELANIE: Finn –

FINN: I'm cold.

(She puts her arms round him, clumsily. His teeth are chattering.)

MELANIE: You *are* cold. Where have you been?

FINN: I finished it off.

MELANIE: You did what?

(Cut to:)

(64. Interior. Theatre. Night.)

FINN: *(Voice over.)* I chopped it into little pieces.

(The swan hangs by its strings in the middle of the stage. The scene is lit by a huge, ominous-looking yellow moon; night has arrived on the beach, with moon and stars on the backcloth. The swan looks huge, ugly, ridiculous and malign, with its neck rolling a little from side to side.

FINN, *with one blow from a hatchet, strikes off the head at the base of the neck. It falls to the floorboards which are still covered with sand, where it writhes like a snake.*

FINN *stamps on the swan's neck and head, trampling it until it stops writhing.*

Now the wings open and beat frenziedly, the swan's body agitates itself dreadfully on its strings.

FINN *lops off a wing. It drifts to the ground. The other wing beats and beats on the air; he grabs hold of it, lops that one off too.*

The little rubber feet are still going up and down. More and more slowly.

FINN *raises the hatchet, splits the swan open down the back with a rending sound of chopped wood. The little feet stop moving.*

With one blow of the hatchet, he slices the mutilated swan away from its strings. It falls to the ground with a thud.

FINN, *surveying the wreckage, begins to laugh.*

Cut to:)

(65. Interior. Girls' bedroom. Night, as before.)

MELANIE: He'll murder you when he finds out.

FINN: He'll be looking for another apprentice.

MELANIE: I hope he doesn't pick on Jonathon.

FINN: Can you move over a wee bit?

*(*MELANIE *gently nudges* VICTORIA *towards the side of the bed.)*

MELANIE: The swan was so ridiculous. All the same, it did scare me.

FINN: *(Derisively.)* Almighty Jove in the shape of a swan.

(The bed begins to shake. MELANIE rears up.)

MELANIE: Stop it!

FINN: I've got a present for you . . .

MELANIE: *(Warning.)* Finn . . .

FINN: In my pocket.

(He hands her a painted egg, with a pair of naked lovers painted on it in the naive style. MELANIE cups it in her hands, wondering.)

It's a swan's egg.

(He yawns, his eyes close, open again. He smiles at MELANIE. Hesitant at first, she smiles back. They hug. FINN's eyes close again, he sleeps. MELANIE stows away the egg safe under the bed.
Close-up MELANIE's face, on the verge of sleep.
Cut to:)

(66. Interior. Jonathon's bedroom. Night.
Close-up JONATHON's glasses, lying on his chair beside the bed. These reflect MELANIE's face.
MELANIE in her pyjamas, is standing by JONATHON's bed, looking down at him.
JONATHON stirs and murmurs. JONATHON opens his eyes.
JONATHON's point-of-view shot: the room is blurred and myopic. He reaches out for his glasses, puts them on; the image clears.)

MELANIE: I think you should go, now, Jonathon.

(Jonathon sits up in bed.)

JONATHON: What do you mean? Run away to sea?

(A seagull flies in through the bedroom door. JONATHON looks up.
Cut to:)

(67. Interior. Workshop. Night.
The workshop is full of the crash of breakers. The theatre is a square box glowing with light. MELANIE and JONATHON run towards the theatre. JONATHON is fully dressed, MELANIE in pyjamas. The curtains fly open; the light of brilliant day floods into the room from FINN's painted seashore, which transforms itself into a real beach under JONATHON and MELANIE's eyes.
LEDA's shell, and a pile of splintered wood and feathers lie on the stage, but they look like silly stage props, now.

It is brilliant early morning on the beach, now.
Cut to:)

(68. Exterior. Beach. Day.
JONATHON *and* MELANIE *run along the beach until they come to a small rowing boat with a pair of oars ready in the rowlocks beached on the sand.*
Cut to:)

(Exterior. Sea. Day.
JONATHON *in the rowing boat, sculls out to sea; his blazer bothers him; he slips it off.*
JONATHON'*s glasses mist over with spray. T'sking with irritation, he snatches them off and throws them into the sea.*
JONATHON'*s point-of-view shot:* MELANIE, *clear and distinct, stands waving on the beach.*
Cut to:)

(69. Interior. Staircase. Morning.
MELANIE, *very anxious, races upstairs to* JONATHON'*s bedroom.*
Cut to:)

(70. Interior. Jonathon's bedroom. Morning.
Window open, curtain flapping; the wind blows through the room. The bed is rumpled and empty. A pair of cracked spectacles trailing a little seaweed lies on the floor.
MELANIE *rushes in and looks round. She sees the spectacles and picks them up. She looks first puzzled, then oddly reassured.*
Cut to:)

(71. Interior. Bathroom. Morning.
MELANIE *enters, turns on the tap, splashes her face with cold water. As she looks up, she sees* PHILIP'*s tooth glass empty, except for cloudy water.*
Cut to:)

(72. Interior. Girls' bedroom. Day.
FINN *is sitting up in bed, smoking meditatively, while* VICTORIA *attempts not without difficulty, to put on her own sweater.* MELANIE *comes in, bearing aloft* PHILIP'*s tooth glass. She offers it to him with a flourish.)*

MELANIE: Philip's gone and taken his teeth with him.

(She empties the contents of the tooth glass into the geranium pot.)

FINN: Reprieve.

MELANIE: I know for a fact he didn't take Jonathon. Jonathon went off by himself.

(FINN *looks sharply at* MELANIE, *as if she's stumbled on something important she doesn't understand;* MELANIE *doesn't notice.* VICTORIA *has begun to exhibit distress in her struggle with the sweater and* MELANIE *turns to help her.*
   Cut to:)

(73. *Interior. Kitchen. Day.*
   Sizzle! MARGARET *breaks an egg into a frying pan full of bacon, sausages, black pudding, mushrooms, tomatoes, fried bread.*
   FINN, *dazzling clean,* MELANIE *in trousers, her hair loose, and* VICTORIA, *are taking their places round the table where* FRANCIE *already sits.*)

FINN: Dammit, I'm going to sit in his chair. (*Sudden silence. Concern, even fear.*) Don't fret, it can't swallow me up.

(*All the same, he sits down with extreme caution. Then, with more confidence, he sets his hands on the arms of the chair, looking patriarchal.* MARGARET *passes plates heaped with breakfast. All eat hungrily.*)

   I am seized with a great and glorious notion. (*Pause. Inquiring looks.*) Let's make today a holiday. Himself being absent. And the swan destroyed.

(*All stop eating, knives and forks in mid-air in some cases. All but* MELANIE, *who remains composed.*)

MELANIE: (*Calmly.*) He chopped it up.

(*She goes on with her breakfast.*)

FINN: I shifted it out there. On the bonfire. Tonight it will burn.

(*He puts unusual emphasis on the word 'burn'.*)

FRANCIE: (*With admiration.*) You mad bugger.

(FRANCIE, *slow reaction, now throws down his knife and fork and claps* FINN *on the back.*)

   He chopped it up!

(*He chuckles. Then he begins to laugh.* VICTORIA, *seeing him, is quickly overcome with laughter.* FINN *laughs.* MELANIE, *it takes her a little longer time to see the funny side but soon she too laughs.*
   MARGARET *slowly smiles. Then chuckles. Then we hear a musical sound, cymbalon or celesta. It is her laughter. At the sound of her laughter, the men's voices die away.* VICTORIA *stops laughing too; she looks solemn and puzzled.*)

MARGARET: Go and fetch my silver necklace, Victoria.

(VICTORIA, *laughing runs in with the necklace on her head at a rakish angle.*

MARGARET *lifts the necklace from the little girl's head and drops a kiss there. The kitchen window is wide open. With some ceremony,* MARGARET *goes towards it and throws out the silver necklace. It turns over and over, catching the light and shining. It whirls off, into infinity.*

   Cut to:)

(74. Interior. Kitchen. Day.

   Some time later. The bull terrier is lapping Guinness from a saucer.

   FRANCIE *is playing a slow air,* MARGARET *sits in* PHILIP's *chair, wearing Cleopatra's gorgeous robe.*

   The room is a mess, breakfast still uncleared and so is lunch – the remains of fish and chips in newspaper. There are several empty bottles of Guinness.

   VICTORIA, *surrounded by the choicest toys from the shop, is asleep on the rag rug, with her head on the sleepy bull terrier.* FINN *sits in the armchair by the fire.* MELANIE *sits on the floor at his feet. He is playing with her hair.*

   A rocket goes by outside. Whoosh!)

MELANIE: Somebody couldn't wait until dark.

FINN: *(Dreamy.)* H'm?

MELANIE: Nothing ... You shouldn't have given Victoria that Guinness.

FINN: It was only a mouthful!

MELANIE: Do you think we should take her up to bed?

(FINN is galvanised into life.)

FINN: Oh yes, I think we should.

(MELANIE dissolves in giggles. The slow air ends. FINN *leans forward, puts his finger on* MELANIE's *lips to quiet her giggling.)*

   Ssh ...

(FRANCIE and MARGARET are locked in an embrace. MELANIE's *eyes grow huge.* FINN *draws her to her feet.*

   Cut to:)

(75. Interior. Girls' bedroom. Day.

   It is growing dark. FINN *tucks* VICTORIA *into bed. When she stirs, he gives her Edward Bear. She snuggles down again, content.*

   MELANIE *sits down on the edge of the bed, brooding.*

   Cut to:)

(76. Exterior. Square. Dusk.

PHILIP *crosses the square; he looks disapprovingly at the bonfire.*
The swan's head and beak are visible among the sticks and broken chairs but PHILIP *does not see them.*
   Cut to:)

(77. Interior. Girls' bedroom. Dusk.
   FINN *and* MELANIE *sit on the edge of the bed, not touching.)*

MELANIE: I thought she was fondest of you, because you were the youngest.

FINN: Did you now.

MELANIE: Surely she is older?

FINN: What difference does *that* make?

*(*MELANIE *is hugging her arms round herself, as if she's cold. Whoosh! Another rocket flies past the window.*
   Cut to:)

(78. Exterior. Front of shop. Dusk.
   PHILIP *stares in blank disbelief at the 'closed' sign on the door. He fishes in his pocket, produces an enormous key, starts to unlock the door.*
   Cut to:)

(79. Interior. Girls' bedroom. Dusk, as before.)

MELANIE: How long has –

FINN: All the time.

(Whoosh – bang!
   Cut to:)

(80. Interior. Kitchen. Dusk.
   There is no light in the kitchen, except for the glowing embers of the fire. PHILIP *flicks the switch. He registers shock and horror at the mess.*
   Cut to:)

(81. Interior. Girls' room. Dusk.
   MELANIE *cranes forward to look out of the window.)*

MELANIE: All that rain is making it hard for the fire to catch. And I don't see the guy. They haven't put the guy on the bonfire yet.

*(*FINN *approaches her from behind.)*

FINN: *(Sly, yet tender, sexual teasing.)* Shall you take all your clothes off now, and I'll finish off your portrait?

(She dissolves in giggles again, seizes him firmly by the shoulders, thrusts him back on to the bed.)

Careful! Mind the little girl!

(They lie without touching, gazing at one another. They suddenly become serious, even grave, as if deliberating the effects of what they may be about to do.
Cut to:)

(82. Interior. Landing. Dusk.
PHILIP*'s hand lies on the doorknob of the room opposite the kitchen – the master bedroom. It lies for a moment, as if* PHILIP *is unwilling to open the door and see what it might contain: then he turns the doorknob. The door opens.*

A beam of unearthly light falls on PHILIP*'s face, which is a mask of shock and horror. The mask shatters, like glass, as his mouth opens.*
Cut to:)

(83. Interior. Girls' bedroom. Dusk.
At the sound of a shriek from below, FINN *and* MELANIE *start up from the bed. Crash from below. Such a crash the dangling light bulb dances, flowers fall from the plant.* VICTORIA *awakes.*

Then bang, crash. Shriek again. FINN *hugs the sisters. All cower together on the bed.*
Crash.
Cut to:)

(84. Interior. The master bedroom. Night.
The wedding photograph showing the children's parents and PHILIP *falls to the ground from the top of a chest of drawers. Its glass shatters as* PHILIP *lunges across the room at* MARGARET*, who darts away from him out on to the landing.*

MARGARET *is screaming.* PHILIP *tries to follow but* FRANCIE *makes a flying tackle and brings him to the ground.* PHILIP *bellows. His bowler hat falls off and rolls across the floor. He reaches inside his coat and produces a chisel. He twists round and threatens* FRANCIE *with the chisel.*
Cut to:)

(85. Interior. Girls' bedroom. Night.
The door flies open; MARGARET *stands there. Bodice ripped, hair streaming. She brings with her a huge wind that makes the curtains flap, the bedcovers flap, the windows rattle – the room seems about to take flight.*

VICTORIA *scrambles forward, clutches* MARGARET*.)*

VICTORIA: Auntie Margrit, Auntie Margrit . . .

MARGARET: Would I part with you, my treasure?

(She scoops up the little girl. She looks with infinite sorrow at FINN *and* MELANIE.)

FINN: Kiss me before you go.

*(*MARGARET *kisses him on the mouth; for the first time, we register she is much taller than he. She kisses him in a very formal and stately way. Her hair billows out round them, concealing him for a moment. Then* MARGARET *kisses* MELANIE. *We are swept up into the red storm of her hair and let down again. The wind increases in strength. The red storm of hair fills the room.*

MARGARET *and* VICTORIA *vanish. Literally. When the wind dies down, they are no longer there.*

The noise from downstairs continues unabated.

Cut to:)

(86. Interior. Master bedroom. Night.

FRANCIE, *menaced by the chisel, backs away against the bed with its disordered sheets.* PHILIP *is winded and breathing heavily;* FRANCIE, *quicker on his feet, manages to rush past him.* PHILIP *lunges at him and sprawls across the bed.*

Cut to:)

(87. Interior. Kitchen. Night.

There is now a terrible silence. Devastation, smashed crockery. The cuckoo hangs out of the cuckoo clock, mutilated by a knife; they are bleeding. The table is smashed. The chairs are smashed.

The bull terrier has leapt up on to the mantelpiece and, as FINN *and* MELANIE *enter, jumps into the portrait of itself and disappears.*

FINN *and* MELANIE *look round the room and see nobody.*

Cut to:)

(88. Interior. Workroom. Night.

Brandishing the chisel, PHILIP *descends into the workroom, in pursuit of* FRANCIE.

The curtains twitch; FRANCIE *disappears inside the theatre. The puppets, hanging from their hooks stir and tremble.*

PHILIP, *on his way to the theatre, overturns* FINN's *workbench. Toys, paint tins and brushes fall to the floor.*

The puppets rattle even more.)

PHILIP: Francie?

(He strides to the theatre, ignoring the sand crackling under his feet. From inside the theatre comes a mocking phrase of fiddle music. PHILIP *roars.)*

Francie!

(He tears open the curtains. The painted beach is there. The sand and shell are there. But the swan's strings dangle, empty, and below them, is a pile of splinters and feathers.)

(89. Interior. Shop. Night.

The parrot is free of its chain and is flying round the shop squawking: No sale!

The shop is in the throes of change; as FINN *and* MELANIE *slip through, a jack-in-the-box pops up and roars with laughter. Dolls stir and titter. The toys are coming to life.* FINN *and* MELANIE *go out through the door. The bell jangles for the last time. The parrot flies out above their heads.* FINN *calls after the parrot:)*

FINN: I served my time, and so did you.

(Cut to:)

(90. Interior. Workroom. Night.

FRANCIE *sits on the catwalk in the flies, fiddle under his chin, looking down at* PHILIP, *who is stirring the refuse of the swan with his foot. The hatchet lies among a pile of splinters and feathers.*

FRANCIE *plays a mocking, ironic phrase on the fiddle.* PHILIP *looks up at him, and hisses.)*

PHILIP: Who touched my swan?

(FRANCIE plays another mocking ironic phrase. PHILIP lunges for the ladder to the catwalk, trips over the hatchet and thumps on to the stage.

There is a rustling and a clicking in the workroom. Slowly, out of the shadows, come the puppets: they descend from their hooks, 'The Artist', the Coppelia doll, some with faces and clothes, many uncompleted, featureless ones. They move towards the theatre, with a clattering, wooden sound. They start to climb up on to the stage.

PHILIP *looks up at a circle of wooden faces, all of which he has created himself.*

FRANCIE *strikes up a lively air. The puppets begin to clap in time. The ballerina doll hauls* PHILIP *to his feet and pushes and prods him into dancing with her. The puppets continue to clap.*

The ballerina whirls PHILIP *round in a succession of pirouettes. The music goes faster and faster. The surrounding, clapping puppets whirl into a blur.*

Cut to:)

(91. Exterior. Square. Night.

The bonfire in the square garden is now so big it threatens to topple over. Dozens of children mill round it excitedly, engaged in forming a rough circle

*round the fire. Amongst the old sofas and floorboards we catch a brief glimpse of
a white neck and a yellow beak.*

*FINN is kneeling by the fire with a box of matches in his hand. To the
unspoken question of a curious child, he says:)*

FINN: Me brother's fetching the guy.

*(He lights a match, touches a twist of paper. At another part of the bonfire,
MELANIE kneels, too. She strikes her match and touches the bonfire with it; a
little flame ripples up.*

*The children continue to assemble in a circle round the fire, watching it catch
with solemn eyes. FINN and MELANIE retreat until they are together again.
Absent-mindedly they hold hands. They are on tenterhooks with anxiety. The
circle of children eye them with faint suspicion; the children could easily turn
against the two adolescents if they do not keep their promise. FINN and
MELANIE peer anxiously at the shop.*

*Behind them, the shop suddenly lights up with brilliant light and all the
fireworks in the window go off, bursting through the glass. FRANCIE emerges
from the door, carrying a limp puppet, trailing strings. A full size puppet.*

The puppet is the image of UNCLE PHILIP.

*The children see FRANCIE and start to laugh and cheer. Some break away
from the bonfire to take a closer look at FRANCIE's armful, forming a rough and
ready procession behind him as he walks towards the fire.*

*FRANCIE's fiddle case is lodged precariously under his arm; a child takes it and
carries it safely for him.*

Cut to:)

(92. Exterior. Square. Night.

*The children have liberated the toyshop and, as the bonfire dies down,
enthusiastically play with hobby horses, masks and dolls from PHILIP's store.
There is much noise and laughter.*

*FRANCIE stands before the embers, playing the fiddle. His outlines waver; it
could be the effect of the heat of the fire. He goes on playing.*

His outlines waver. He goes on playing. He dissolves.

The fiddle remains, suspended in the air, playing itself.

Cut to: FINN and MELANIE silhouetted against the blazing bonfire.)

MELANIE: I already lost everything once.

FINN: So did I.

MELANIE: But then I had a brother and a sister left.

FINN: So had I.

MELANIE: Everything is gone, now.

FINN: Nothing is left but us.

(As if both gripped in the same instant by the same revelation, they turn urgently to one another. But freeze before they touch, at the moment at which the movie ends.)

Alternative to Puppet Drama Sequence

'Pagan Deity'

(48. Interior. Theatre. Day.

The curtain rises on darkness. The only sound is the insistent beating of a drum. As the lights gradually go up, we make out five figures kneeling as if in prayer, their backs to the audience, their bowed heads turned towards a backdrop which shows a stylised, very craggy mountain.

The figures are veiled in white and grey, shroud-like garments, like penitents.)

(Interior. Above the stage. Day.

FINN, *very stressed, is banging away at a drum with one hand whilst fiddling with the organisation ends of a handful of puppets with the other.* PHILIP *crouches over the special effects corner – there is a sheet of iron, to make thunder, and so on.)*

(Interior. Theatre. Day.

Thunder. Lightning. The mountain cracks open, emitting billows of smoke and flame.

Out of the smoke steps a figure naked but for a loincloth – a man, but a man with the head of a huge white ram with gilded horns, therefore not a man but some kind of pagan deity. On his ram's head he wears a wreath of dry twigs and dead leaves and little bones. His limbs and torso are also gilded. Cymbals sound.)

VICTORIA: *(Voice over.)* Who is the funny gentleman?

MELANIE: *(Voice over.)* Sshhh . . .

(Interior. Theatre. Day.

PHILIP *is crashing the cymbals whilst* FINN, *even more stressed, hurls the drumsticks aside and crouches over the puppets below. He flicks the hair out of his eyes.)*

FINN: *(Muttering.)* Cross fingers, hope for the best . . .

(Interior. Theatre. Day.

The cymbals continue as the ram-headed deity exhibits himself to his worshippers who raise their heads and lift their arms in adoration. The veils fall back from their faces as they do so, all but the veil of the central figure, who remains shrouded. Light flickers on the shining torso and limbs of the ram-headed deity. He steps out of the cleft in the mountain, which closes up neatly – bang! – behind him.

The worshippers on either side of the central figure move to the sides of the stage, two on either side, where they are, in effect, parked, their arms still raised; their faces are ecstatic masks. Meanwhile, the centre figure stretches out full-length on the ground in adoration, covered in her veil.

The ram-headed deity stoops down, takes hold of her hands and lifts her up to her feet. He lifts off the veil (which whisks up and off into the flies). She wears a plain, white shift; she has long, black hair. Then he retreats to the back of the stage where he stands impassively, arms akimbo.

The drum starts beating again. FRANCIE plays a preliminary flourish. The girl faces the audience, centre stage.

FRANCIE begins to play a wild, eerie fiddle tune with Central European cadences to it. The girl dances for the delectation of the ram-headed deity, a fierce, rhythmic, primitive dance, slow, at first, but soon gaining speed and passion, to the music of the fiddle and the drum.

The kneeling spectators sway in time but the ram-headed god stays akimbo, impassive, until the girl's dance reaches its climax; she once more flings herself full-length on the ground before him in an attitude of submissive abandon.

The music ceases but the drum-beat continues, like a heart-beat.

The ram-headed god takes the knife from his side and waves it in the air.

The blade catches the light and flashes.

FRANCIE plays a menacing phrase.)

(Interior. Auditorium. Night.

The light flashes from the blade of the ram-headed deity's knife and reflects off JONATHON's glasses; they flash, too.

VICTORIA whimpers and buries her face in MARGARET's lap. MELANIE stares, appalled but fascinated. It is a moment of eerie tension.

FRANCIE repeats the menacing phrase.)

(Interior. Theatre. Day.

The ram-headed god leans forward, with the knife raised; he raises the knife higher; and higher – he is just about to plunge it into the girl's breast . . . and then the hand holding the knife drops to his side. The drum-beat stops. Silence.

The ram-headed deity bends, raises the girl up, takes her chin in his hands and inspects her face closely. Then, ceremoniously, he removes the wreath of dead twigs from his head and places it on hers.

There is a ravishing sound – a harp or a cymbalon; a chord of beautiful music – and the dead twigs of the wreath are transformed into glowy, glowing leaves and berries and the feathers of birds, as live birds raise their heads and stir among the leaves and berries.

The girl turns slowly round on the spot so that everyone can see. There is a ravished sigh, over; we will never know who sighed.)

(Interior. Auditorium. Night.

VICTORIA *removes her head from* MARGARET's *lap and looks towards the stage; she starts to smile. Close-up of* MELANIE's *face as she slowly begins to smile, too.)*

(Interior. Theatre. Night.

There is a repeat of that ravishing chord of music, and the sound, once more, of cymbals; the mountain opens, again, the ram-headed deity offers the girl his arm and leads her towards the smoking cleft.

FRANCIE *breaks into a stately, processional tune; the worshippers all raise and lower their arms in celebration. They look obviously wooden; yet some kind of wailing chorus seems to come from them.*

The ram-headed deity holds the hand of the girl to assist her as she lifts her foot in order to step into the cleft.

And – he leans too far towards her, perhaps; at any rate, their strings tangle and her foot is suspended in the air – it jiggles, it waggles but it cannot descend into the cleft.

The eerie, lyric mood dissolves. The two puppets jig haplessly up and down as their handlers try to separate their strings, the strings only tangle more and more and the puppets knock against one another, with the dull thud of wood on wood, and then sway apart.

The knock dislodges the girl's magic wreath, which hangs over her brow, now, at a rakish angle; she makes a final attempt to step into the cleft but only succeeds in bringing her foot down on the mountain itself with such wooden force that it crumples up beneath her, revealing how it was only made with pasteboard all the time.

The ram-headed deity attempts to seize her by the waist, as if to thrust her bodily into the cleft; her arms involuntarily fly upward and – oops! Off goes his head! Detaches from his body, swinging from its strings like a monstrous Jack O'Lantern.

The torso of the ram-headed deity slowly collapses to the floor.

FRANCIE, *an inscrutable expression on his face, lowers his fiddle.*

The theatre fills with the cheerful sound of FINN's *laughter.)*

(Interior. Auditorium. Night.

MELANIE *has opened her eyes, unclenched her fists, smiles.*

VICTORIA *removes her head from* MARGARET's *lap.*

Then MELANIE's *smile is replaced by a look of pure horror.*

FINN's *laughter modulates into a scream. He falls down from the flies, seems to fall endlessly, his long red hair drifting after him as if he were falling through water, somersaulting as he falls.*

He lands with a crash, on top of the dismembered puppet and lies there, looking completely dislocated. The only sound is his terrible sobbing attempt to breathe.

FRANCIE *and* MARGARET *both knew that something like this was inevitable one day, but are as if transfixed.*

Except that tears flood soundlessly down MELANIE's *cheeks. The children are very distressed.* VICTORIA *wails.* JONATHON, *jerked into reality, claps his hand to his mouth.* MELANIE *half-rises.*

MARGARET *tries and tries but cannot bend her head down to comfort* VICTORIA *because of the collar. Tears splash on to* VICTORIA's *face.* MELANIE *turns towards them as* FRANCIE *puts his arm round them both.* PHILIP *comes on stage, in dinner jacket and bow tie. He is straightening the bow tie. He looks down at prone* FINN.)

PHILIP: Won't use him to work the puppets again.

(FINN *remains motionless.* PHILIP *looks out at the audience; suddenly he points to* MELANIE.)

I'll use you instead of a puppet, Miss.

(MELANIE *is startled but doesn't appreciate fully the implications of this.* FRANCIE *and* MARGARET *are horrified and distressed.* FINN *is the most horrified of all. He moans loudly. He struggles to sit half-upright, blood trickles from the corner of his mouth. He collapses again.* PHILIP *almost to himself.)*

After all, why shouldn't the girl do something for her keep. God knows she eats enough. She's not too big, she won't be out of scale. *(Out loud; firmly.)* That's settled.

Gun for the Devil

(1. Exterior. Country road. Day.

Late afternoon; a dirt track in barren, rocky, semi-arid country on the Mexican border.

Period: roughly 1870s.

Along the track, dragged by a straining team of mules, comes a cart.

A swarthy man with a moustache, a sombrero and a bandolero across his chest drives the cart, swearing at the mules, lashing them unmercifully with his whip.

A pair of companions, on foot, urge the mules on. They, too, look like bandidos.

They are bandidos.

Lashed on to the cart, swaying dangerously at every jolt, is a huge, roughly triangular object wrapped up in canvas so that it is impossible to tell what it might be.)

(2. Exterior. Country road. Day.

A little way from the road, on a hill, stand the ruins of an unusually large, ancient and imposing church in the Spanish colonial style, surrounded by a small, walled churchyard. Birds fly up from the ruins. Out of the graves comes lolloping a mean, thin, rangy dog.

Dog's point-of-view shot: the cart passes over a particularly deep pothole. The parcelled object sways, lurches and emits a vivid, discordant clang.)

(3. Exterior. Town. Day.

A town like the town in every Western you ever saw, a little bit of everything.

Adobe, clapboard. A single store. Dusty and sleepy under the sun; and very, very run down.

A cock stands on a wall, crowing, as children and barking dogs rush out excitedly to surround the approaching cart.

Men and women come to the doors of their houses, look out, shake their heads, laugh.)

(4. Exterior. Saloon. Day.

At the far end of town is a saloon, a two-storey building in classic old West style, with a porch, swing doors and a balcony at the front of the upper floor.

Above the saloon flies the Stars and Stripes (with the appropriate number of stars for the period).

On the shady verandah, in rocking chairs, sit the saloon's manager, ROXANA and her sister, MARIA.

They are both dark-haired, but greying, plumpish women in their forties.

ROXANA is heavily made up and wears a black satin dress with a lace collar; her hair is elaborately coiled on top of her head.

MARIA is a little younger, fiercer looking.

Although her hair, too, is elegantly coiled, she wears men's pants and boots with spurs that are now cocked up on the verandah rails, as they relax sipping beer.

MARIA sits up with a start.)

MARIA: What's going on?

(The cart, followed now by a procession of children shouting and beating out tattoos on saucepans, excited dogs, the village idiot, a chicken or two, the idle and the curious, comes into view.

The cart jolts again, this time emitting two violent discords.

MARIA vaults over the verandah rail, runs towards the cart excitedly.

ROXANA, amused, calls back into the bar.)

ROXANA: It's here at last.

(5. Interior. Saloon. Day.

A typical Western-style saloon interior, a long, mahogany bar with bottles and mirrors behind it: tables, a spitoon, a piano.

A staircase, leading up to a landing. Above the bar in a place of honour is hung a big, antique gun.

At this hour, the saloon is empty but for a man polishing glasses behind the bar.

He is in shirtsleeves and an apron but his appearance is extraordinarily distinguished, aristocratic, even.

He is tall, even gaunt, with a thin, refined face, a silver goatee beard, longish silver hair and dark, melancholy eyes.

This is the COUNT.

He inspects the glass he has just polished, hesitates, then quickly fills it with whiskey and swallows the whiskey down before going out to the verandah to see what all the fuss is about.

As the COUNT leaves, a door opens on to the upstairs landing and a girl and a young man come out on to it.)

(6. Exterior. Path. Day.

MARIA jumps up on to the driver's seat of the cart, pushing away the driver and seizing the reins herself.

There is a burst of ragged cheering from the crowd.)

(7. Interior. Upstairs landing of saloon. Day.

On the upstairs landing, the young man and the girl, she in her petticoat, they have obviously just got out of bed, kiss passionately, ignoring the commotion outside.

On the soundtrack, faintly at first then louder and louder, piano music by Schumann can be heard.)

(8. Exterior. Saloon. Day.

The three other girls employed by ROXANA, *the girl being kissed by the young man is the fourth, have come out on to the upstairs balcony, laughing and waving as the cart passes by.*

They have been interrupted in the process of dressing for the evening's work, and wear wrappers and slippers.

Their faces are unpainted, their hair either in pins or papers or in braids.
One is black.
One is conspicuously blonde and Anglo-looking.
The other is a local girl.
Schumann continues on the soundtrack throughout all this.)

(9. Exterior. MENDOZA'S *Hacienda. Day*

MENDOZA'S *Hacienda is a crumbling mansion ranged round a central courtyard.*

The rooms of the house all open out on to a covered walk that surrounds the courtyard.

The walls are covered with creepers and a fountain in the middle of the courtyard splashes into a broken bowl, but otherwise, apart from a couple of trees, and a few pots of bright flowers, there is only beaten earth, where chickens scratch and a sow wallows in the mud at the base of the fountain.

One of the rooms opening on to the courtyard is a stable, where a number of horses whicker in their stalls.

Into the courtyard, through the open gates, straining mules now drag the cart and its load, amidst much swearing and cursing, especially from MARIA.

The procession has dropped away.
Schumann continues on soundtrack.)

(10. Interior. TERESA'S *bedroom. Day.*

Close-up a crude woodcut of lovers embracing.

After a moment, we realise it is an illustration in a crude chapbook, one of those books that purport to tell you the meaning of your dreams.

Under the illustration are some words of text in Spanish.

Poring over the book is TERESA, *the only daughter of the brigand,* MENDOZA, *and his wife* MARIA.

She lies on her bed in her unique and private bedroom, a pet white rat trapped in her fist, a box of chocolates beside her.

She is eating chocolates and consulting her dream book.

TERESA *is sixteen, pretty, spoiled, sullen, wilful. She still wears her nightie, white, trimmed with broderie anglaise and blue ribbons.*

TERESA'*s hair is uncombed, her face is unwashed, a tray containing remains of her breakfast, lies disregarded beside her bed and a chicken pecks at the crumbs.*

Her bedroom is a mess. Dolls lie scattered amongst dresses she has tried on and then discarded on the tiled floor.

More clothes spill out of chests of drawers, and out of a cabin trunk she has obviously got bored with unpacking.

Fashion magazines, dream books, shoes, stockings, artificial flowers, those huge Mexican paper ones, are scattered thickly everywhere. Sentimental pictures of kittens etc. are pinned up on the stained plaster walls.

Jewellery, tumbled here and there, both real and artificial. Knick-knacks and gew-gaws.

TERESA'*s father denies her nothing he can steal.*

Her bed, a four-poster, has floating curtains of white gauze.

Cherubs and swags of flowers decorate the bedposts and the frame but some of the cherubs have lost their noses, some of the flowers their petals.

The bed is tawdry junk, too, more loot.

But there she lies on lace pillows.

There is a mirror and a washstand with a bowl, a water jug, soap, a mass of bottles of cologne and perfume.

The shutters are shut tight against the afternoon light but it seeps in round the edges.

A goat slumbers unnoticed in a corner.

TERESA *takes another chocolate, bites, spits it out.)*

TERESA: Shit! Violet cream!

(The rat takes advantage of her momentary lapse of vigilance to escape and TERESA *throws herself across the bed after it, spilling the chocolates; and her mother's voice calls out.)*

MARIA: *(Voice over.)* It's come! Teresa! It's here!

(There is a sudden commotion outside.

TERESA *forgets the rat and darts to the window, throwing it open, blinking in the sudden blast of light.*

Schumann continues on the soundtrack.)

(11. Exterior. Courtyard. Day.

TERESA'*s point-of-view shot:* MENDOZA'*s men are unloading the sheeted object, energetically supervised by* MARIA, *as Schumann continues on the soundtrack.*

MENDOZA *himself, vast paunch, vast sombrero covered with gold thread, beaming a mouthful of gold teeth, emerges from the house, followed by a henchman or two.*

TERESA, *still shrugging on a garish silk kimono, jumps out of the window of her room; she is too excited to be bothered to open the door. She rushes to the sheeted object and begins to claw at the wrapping.*

MENDOZA *restrains her impatience, laughing. He takes a vicious sheath knife from his belt and slits open the sheeting with a grand, theatrical gesture.*

The sheeting falls apart to reveal a gleaming, new grand piano.

As soon as the piano appears, Schumann stops abruptly.

Silence, but for the chickens and the grunting of the sow, and a maa-maa from the goat, who has woken up and peers out of TERESA's *window.*

TERESA *smiles, transfigured.*

She hugs her father, kisses him. She hugs her mother.

Then she goes to the piano, almost hesitant with love, and reaches out to slowly stroke its shiny surfaces. She adores the piano.

She props up the flap. She goes to the keyboard, opens it up. Admires the whiteness of the white notes, the blackness of the black. She traces the word 'Bechstein' with an amorous finger.

The adults smile at her delight.)

TERESA: Fetch me a chair.

(A minion rushes for a kitchen chair.

TERESA, *in her kimono, her hair a mess, chocolate stains on her face, sits in front of the piano and raises her hands as if about to play.*

All the bandits, all the servants, her mother and father watching, pleased and proud.

She brings her hands down and strikes a chord.

It sounds all wrong.

She raises her hands and brings them down again.

It sounds all wrong again, but in a different way. Now she is a little nervous. She picks out five white notes. Then five black notes. At random. She wets the edge of her nightie and wipes a smudge of chocolate off a white note.

The audience watches her with the beginnings of reluctant amusement.

TERESA *retains her dignity with an effort.*

TERESA *closes the piano lid and gets up.*

Making a grand statement to everybody there.)

TERESA: Something's wrong with that piano.

(Then, breaking down, she rushes to her mother and buries her head in her bosom as MENDOZA *roars with laughter.)*

(12. Exterior. Saloon porch. Day.
  MARIA *and* ROXANA *sit in rocking chairs, sipping beer. It is mid-afternoon.)*

MARIA: She wanted it so much she thought she could play it.

*(*ROXANA *mimicking a young girl's voice.)*

ROXANA: All the other girls at the convent have pianos!

(She resumes her own voice.)

  You should never have sent her to that bloody place.

MARIA: Her father wanted her to be a lady.

ROXANA: You mean he thought we couldn't teach her?

(They laugh and sip their beer.
  MARIA *draws on a small cigar.)*

MARIA: What she wants, she must have. Her father spoils her and spoils
  her. Then he has enough. Then – bang! he cracks right down. He'll
  have her married off to that fat bastard Garcia in two shakes.

ROXANA: She'll do all right for money. She'll get some kids, she'll calm
  down. She'll stop being such a little madam.

(13. Interior. Saloon. Day.
  *The girl and the young man we saw embracing on the landing are now dressed
for travel; each carries a valise.*
  They hurry down the staircase, hand in hand.
  The boy pauses in front of the piano and salutes it with mock solemnity.)

PIANO MAN: Fare thee well, thou instrument of torture!

(She stifles a giggle and kisses him lightly on the mouth.
  Hand in hand they slip out the back way.
  The COUNT *sits at a table, glass and bottle before him. He does not notice the
runaways, just as they do not notice him.*
  He tips the bottle into the glass.
  The bottle is empty.
  The COUNT *throws it across the bar, rises and walks with exaggerated care to
the bar to get a fresh one.)*

EVANGELINE: *(Voice over.)* He's been on a drunk for two days, now.

(14. Interior. Front bedroom. Day.
  EVANGELINE, *using a cut-throat razor, soap, shaving brush and etc. neatly
laid out before her on a dressing table, is shaving the nape of the neck of*
MERCEDES.

HANNAH *is playing solitaire at a small table.*

Again, they wear wrappers and no make-up.

The front bedroom betrays its nature; it has a brass bed of an elaborate nature, red velvet and tassels everywhere and a big mirror on the ceiling.

There is a gilt-framed picture of a naked lady and several statues of the same sort of thing, some of them upholding unlit lamps, but, at this hour – mid-afternoon – it has the air of a girls' dorm.

The three girls look what they are – working girls enjoying a well-earned break.)

HANNAH: He's what the French call 'dis-ting-gay'. Even when he can hardly stand, he's 'dis-ting-gay'. He calls you ma'am. A real live Count, running a place like this!

MERCEDES: I've heard stories. He's got a past.

HANNAH: Haven't we all.

MERCEDES: Careful, you'll nick . . .

EVANGELINE: Is that . . .

MERCEDES: Fine . . . what's the time?

EVANGELINE: Train goes in half an hour.

MERCEDES: Em and the piano player running off like that together. What a romance!

HANNAH: The Count must have been irresistible when he was young. Roxana was just a two-bit Mexican whore. That's what I call a romance.

(A train whistles in the distance.)

MERCEDES: Wish I were getting on that train, too.

HANNAH: *(Incurious.)* What's stopping you? Go down to the station. Buy a ticket.

MERCEDES: What's stopping *you*?

(15. Exterior. Station. Day.
It is more of a halt than a regular station.
Far from the town.
Telegraph poles.
A shack.

EM *and the* PIANO MAN *are the only passengers waiting as the train, puffing and hissing, arrives.*

The DRIVER *descends.*

EM *and the* PIANO MAN *prepare to climb into a carriage but the* DRIVER *warns them:*)

DRIVER: Bit of delay. Trouble with the engine. I should wait out here. More pleasant.

(Passengers descend to stretch their legs as EM *and the* PIANO MAN, *anxious to be gone, sigh.*

Among the descending passengers is a thin, pale young man with dark hair, rather long; alone of all of them, he carries a valise.

Therefore the stranger intends to stay in this benighted place.

He is elegant, even dandified, in a black velvet jacket; he looks foreign.

He looks about him, lost, appalled by the vast, barren landscape.

He walks along beside the train, looking for a friendly face.

EM *and the* PIANO MAN *are already laughing and happy again.*

He stops beside them.)

STRANGER: *(Viennese accent.)* Pardon me, sir, madame. Is there work in town for a piano player?

*(*EM *and the* PIANO MAN *look at one another amazed; then they start to laugh with delight and turn to the stranger affirmatively.*)

(16. Interior. Room in MENDOZA's *Hacienda. Day.*

The cool, shaded inner room has a long table covered with glasses, empty bottles, cut limes and plates of half-eaten Mexican food.

MENDOZA *and an even more elaborately gilded and weaponed bandido,* GARCIA, *sit in huge, carved chairs laughing uproariously.*

Around them are sprawled followers of them both, busy celebrating TERESA's *betrothal.*

TERESA *herself does not know anything about the betrothal, yet.*

MENDOZA *staggers to his feet and throws his arms around* GARCIA.

He shouts in a mighty voice:)

MENDOZA: Teresa!

(No answer.

MENDOZA *and* GARCIA *lurch outdoors.*)

(17. Exterior. Courtyard. Day.

A goat sleeps in the shade of the piano, which still stands where we saw it last.

The two men ignore it.

Arm in arm, they stagger down the covered passage, past the pillars covered with jasmine and morning glory.)

MENDOZA: Teresa!

GARCIA: Teresa! Beloved! I am coming!

(18. Interior. TERESA's bedroom. Day.
  TERESA's white rat sits among the dressing table clutter.
  TERESA has dressed herself as far as a chemise and bloomers and is taking her hair out of curl-papers in front of the mirror.
  Half her head bristles with new ringlets, the other half bristles with twists of paper.
  She bristles at the sound of drunken voices outside.)

GARCIA: *(Voice over.)* I am coming!

(The door flies open.
  The two huge men fill up the doorway, spread out their arms towards her.)

MENDOZA: Teresa, this is the man you will marry!

TERESA: Who, him? Why –

(GARCIA lunges forward and TERESA leaps up and wraps herself in the bedcurtains.
  She is furious.)

TERESA: Get out of my bedroom at once!

(The sow noses her way in through the open door, unnoticed.
  GARCIA lunges forward for her again and she grabs hold of his pistol, pulls it out of the holster and threatens him with it.)

  Out!

(GARCIA, impressed, falls back.)

GARCIA: What temperament.

MENDOZA: *(Proud.)* She gets it from me.

(To demonstrate this assertion, MENDOZA pulls out a gun of his own, leans back and starts shooting at the chandeliers – bang! bang! bang! picking off the crystal flowers one by one, to TERESA's initial astonishment, then fury, then curiosity, then respect.
  TERESA lowers GARCIA's pistol and looks at her father with awe.
  Shattered glass tinkles round the room.
  GARCIA takes advantage of her loss of guard to put his arm round her again and she, absent-mindedly but very hard, hits his knuckles with the butt of the gun.
  GARCIA yelps.

He sucks his bruised fist as TERESA *raises the gun — a pistol — and shoots a
flower for herself.*
   The sow, meanwhile, starts foraging under the bed.
   GARCIA, *not to be outdone, looks around for something else to shoot.*
   He spies TERESA's *rat.*
   He snatches the gun back from TERESA. *Bang!*
   The sow shrieks and gallops for the door.
   Silence.
   MENDOZA, TERESA *and* GARCIA *all look at one another.)*

(19. Interior. TERESA's *bedroom. Day.*
   Later.
   The men have gone.
   TERESA *perches on the bed.*
   She extends her left hand in front of her and admires it.
   It is weighed down by an enormous diamond ring on her fourth finger.
   She lifts the lid off the empty chocolate box and peeks inside.
   Coffined there is the corpse of the rat, decorated with a sprig of jasmine.
   She puts the lid back on the chocolate box.
   She looks at her ring again.)

(20. Interior. Saloon. Day.
   The stranger stands in the empty bar, looking round him.
   After a moment, the COUNT *comes out from the back room, gaunt, red-eyed
but shrugging on the threadbare jacket of his once-elegant black suit.*
   He eyes the stranger with a mixture of hostility and curiosity.)

COUNT: Whiskey?

STRANGER: One for yourself?

(The COUNT *nods curtly, pours for them both.*
   The STRANGER *chokes on his first mouthful.)*

(The COUNT *catches an intonation in the* STRANGER's *accent that moves him
but, after a twitch of muscle, he remains impassive.*
   The COUNT *drinks down his own drink in a single gulp.)*

COUNT: You get used to it.

(The STRANGER *pushes away his unfinished glass.)*

STRANGER: I didn't come for a drink, I came for a job.

COUNT: A job?

STRANGER: The job of a piano man.

COUNT: We have a piano man.

STRANGER: He just left on the four o'clock train.

COUNT: He left?

(*EVANGELINE, now dressed ready for the evening's work and almost unrecognisable in a low-cut dress and much rouge, hangs over the landing railing, laughing.*)

EVANGELINE: He left with Em. They ran away.

(*The* COUNT *opens the till and peers inside distractedly.*)

EVANGELINE: (*Contemptuous.*) They didn't take any money. They fell in love.

(*She turns her eyes on the stranger.*)

What's your name?

STRANGER: Johann.

EVANGELINE: Johnny. You ever been in love, Johnny?

(*The* COUNT *slams the till shut.*
   He is so agitated he downs the remainder of Johnny's drink.)

COUNT: I'll fetch my wife. She sees to everything.

(*He disappears into the back room.*
   EVANGELINE *comes a few steps down the staircase.*
   The other girls come on to the landing, peering down curiously at the STRANGER.
   EVANGELINE, *fluttering her eyelids in a parodically obvious manner.*)

EVANGELINE: What wind blew you here, Johnny?

JOHNNY: I came on the four o'clock train.

MERCEDES: Where did you get that dreamy accent, Johnny?

(*He looks up at the girls, smiling.*
   EVANGELINE *creeps a little further down the staircase; the others move along the landing with a rustle of skirts.*
   They are all frilled and plumed and clad in fishnet stockings.)

HANNAH: Play us a tune, piano man!

(*He goes over to the piano and caresses the keys briefly.*
   He makes a face; the piano is cranky and out-of-tune.
   But he sits down and starts to play — beautifully — a Strauss waltz.
   The girls creep further and further down the stairs, attracted by the music.

The girls run downstairs and cluster round him.)

(21. Exterior. Outside saloon. Day.

TERESA *arrives on horseback, hastily dressed in men's pants, her stiff ringlets tied back with a piece of ribbon.*

She tethers her horse to the verandah rail and cocks her head to the delicious sound of music coming out of the saloon.)

(22. Interior. Saloon. Day.

The COUNT *returns from the back room followed by* ROXANA, *looking every inch the madam – rouged, curled, low-cut and flouncy, ready for the evening.*

The COUNT *listens for a moment, smiles a smile of rare beauty and turns to* ROXANA.

He bows and clicks his heels.)

COUNT: May I have the pleasure?

(She blushes; she is pleasantly flustered.

She smiles back at him.

Suddenly she is very, very pretty.

The girls nudge each other as the COUNT *and* ROXANA *take the floor.*

ROXANA *and the* COUNT *waltz beautifully, the gaunt old man and the middle-aged madam.*

They waltz like young lovers, fluent, graceful and touching.

After a moment, EVANGELINE *nudges* MERCEDES *and looks at her inquiringly; hand in hand they sweep on to the floor and join in the dance,* EVANGELINE *leading.*

HANNAH *comes down the rest of the stairs and stands by the piano.)*

(23. Interior. Saloon. Day

TERESA's *point-of-view shot from the doorway.*

The saloon is full of music and dancing.

HANNAH *sees* TERESA *peering in through the door.*

She comes forward, holding out her arms.)

HANNAH: Teresa! Come and dance with me!

(With a faint suggestion of double entendre.*)*

I bet you used to dance with girls at that convent!

*(*TERESA *allows* HANNAH *to melt into her arms, she automatically takes the lead.*

Now there are three pairs of dancers, circling the room in fine style – a bravura waltz sequence.

At the end of the dance, HANNAH *and* TERESA *collapse on chairs, laughing and panting and applauding.*

MENDOZA *kicks open the saloon door.*
He is very angry.
He stalks over to where TERESA *has collapsed on the knee of* HANNAH.
He raises his whip and brings it down on TERESA's *cheek.)*

ROXANA: Stop that!

(ROXANA *rushes forward and grabs at the whip but* MENDOZA *pushes her away.)*

MENDOZA: Home at once. Don't dare to come here again. What would your fiancé think?

(TERESA *holds her hand to the red weal on her face.)*

TERESA: I only came to show Auntie my engagement ring.

(TERESA *extends her hand for the admiration of all.)*

ROXANA: Teresa, give your old auntie a big kiss!

(*They cluster, cooing.*
TERESA *kisses* ROXANA, *shrugging off* MENDOZA *as he tries to pull her away.)*

MENDOZA: An engaged girl visiting in a brothel! Nuzzling up to whores!

ROXANA: Mind what you say —

(MENDOZA *sends* TERESA *halfway across the room with a humiliating kick to the backside.*
She is furious, her eyes spit fire, but she can do nothing.
She pointedly addresses ROXANA.)

TERESA: Goodnight, Auntie dear. (*Turning to the* COUNT.) Goodnight, dear uncle.

(*The* COUNT *comes to attention, clicks his heels and kisses her hand, in spite of* MENDOZA's *furious ill-temper.*
JOHNNY *has been watching all this with amusement; for the first time,* TERESA *gets a proper look at him.*
She stares shamelessly.
Her eyes widen, then narrow.
He returns her stare.)

MENDOZA: Home!

(*He seizes* TERESA's *shoulders and marches her to the door.*
He removes a pistol from its holster and twirls it.

TERESA *drags her eyes off* JOHNNY *and stamps out.*
After a moment, MENDOZA *puts away his gun and glances at* MERCEDES.)

(*To* MERCEDES.) I'll buy you a drink.

(*Everybody gets up and shakes themselves, the night's work has begun.*)

(*24. Interior. Saloon. Night.*
  Under the old gun on the wall, the COUNT *pours drinks for a motley collection of bandits, campesinas and passers-by.*
  The girls sit on various knees.
  HANNAH *on* GARCIA's.
  JOHNNY, *at the piano, plays ragtime crisply and succinctly.*)

BANDIT: Give us some real music.

(JOHNNY *is uncomprehending.*)

  Give us some real music, I say!

MARIA: This is an American whorehouse, we play American music.

BANDIT: He's not American.

ROXANA: He's not Mexican, either.

BANDIT: I want some real music!

(JOHNNY *stops playing ragtime and suddenly, dramatically launches into the first bars of a piano transcription of Bach's Toccata and Fugue in D Minor.*
  Consternation in the bar.)

(*25. Interior. Saloon. Night.*
  Peace at last, amidst much disorder.
  ROXANA *assists one last bandit to the door and throws him out.*
  HANNAH *assists* GARCIA *up the stairs, with much weary giggling as he slips and slides and grabs her bum.*
  The COUNT *enjoys a nightcap as he washes the glasses.*
  JOHNNY *closes the piano lid, yawns.*
  The door bangs behind HANNAH *and* GARCIA *as they disappear into the front bedroom.*
  The COUNT *dries a glass, fills it, brings it to* JOHNNY, *puts it on top of the piano.*)

JOHNNY: I'd rather have coffee.

ROXANA: (*Amused.*) Coffee!

(*She goes into the back room.*

The COUNT *– waste not, want not – drinks the whiskey he has poured for*
JOHNNY.*)*

COUNT: *(In German.)* Is it possible that you studied at the conservatoire
in Vienna?

JOHNNY: *(Also in German.)* I did.

*(*ROXANA *returns with the coffee in time to hear this exchange.*
She slams the mug down on the piano.)

ROXANA: No German in this place! Only English. No German spoken,
no Spanish spoken. This is a good American whorehouse.

*(*JOHNNY *gives her a slow, warm, dark smile.)*

JOHNNY: I'm sorry.

ROXANA: *(Softens.)* Wanna see your room?

(26. Interior. JOHNNY'*s room. Night.*
The room is a cupboard with a bed and a table in it, next to the bar.
Nothing else – all very sparse.
ROXANA *sets* JOHNNY'*s valise down on the table, next to a lighted candle in*
a tin stick.
JOHNNY *looks around.)*

ROXANA: God knows what brought you to this place. But you're the
best piano player I ever heard. Only, keep the long-hair stuff until
after hours, right?

*(*JOHNNY *smiles again and nods.*
She lingers a moment.
JOHNNY *is of an age to be this childless woman's son.*
Yet something is troubling ROXANA.
She looks at his slender elegant frame, his dark eyes.
She opens her mouth to speak.
Closes it, without having spoken.
Departs.
JOHNNY *takes from his valise a photograph in a silver frame, somewhat*
faded.
The photograph represents a beautiful woman in costume – the costume is
obviously that of an operatic heroine.
JOHNNY *abruptly kisses the face of the woman in the photograph, then places*
it carefully on the table where he can see it from the bed.)

JOHNNY: *(In German.)* I've seen him, Mama. On my very first day.
Now it's only a matter of time.

(27. Exterior. Back porch. Day.

A washing line is strung down the length of the back porch.

On it, in a small wind, dance a row of exotically frilled undergarments, garters and high-kicking black stockings.

EVANGELINE *feels them to see if they are dry, then unpegs them into a wicker basket she carries on her arm.*

She wears her cotton wrapper and no make-up, her hair in braids.

As she clears the washing line, we see JOHNNY.

EVANGELINE *speaks as if she is continuing a conversation they are in the middle of.)*

EVANGELINE: . . . and they say he met her in a circus. He used to shoot the clothes off her. That was their act. They called him the Demon Marksman. They say . . . *(Lowers her voice.)* . . . that he killed somebody in the Old Country. That was why he had to leave.

(She throws him an interrogative look, she wonders if he knows anything, since he is from the Old Country too.)

JOHNNY: Lots of people have killed somebody. What about Mendoza?

EVANGELINE: That's his profession. He's a bandit. But the Count . . .

JOHNNY: How do you hear all these stories?

(EVANGELINE has filled her basket of washing by now.

EVANGELINE *comes and perches near* JOHNNY, *on the porch steps.)*

EVANGELINE: I hear things.

JOHNNY: Tell me another story about the Count.

EVANGELINE: I heard . . . that he shot at a man and killed a woman.

JOHNNY: Not Roxana?

(EVANGELINE not aware he is teasing.)

EVANGELINE: Oh, no, long before Roxana. Roxana saved him. Roxana keeps him alive. *(Pause.)* What's your story, Johnny?

JOHNNY: I'm looking for somebody.

EVANGELINE: For a man or for a woman?

(JOHNNY smiling his dark smile, leans over and kisses her on the mouth.)

JOHNNY: For a man.

(He jumps from the rail and goes into the bar.

EVANGELINE *stares after him, wiping her mouth, furious.)*

(28. Exterior. Hacienda. Night.

TERESA, *in her nightie, flowers in her hair, strays out of the house, carrying a candlestick.*

She sets the candlestick on the piano, sits in front of it, brings her finger down on middle C. She hits the note repeatedly. Then she tries a scale, manages to get through the scale of C. Then she hits C again.

A window flies open.)

MARIA: *(Voice over.)* For God's sake, Teresa!

(29. Interior. Hacienda kitchen. Day.

A plucked chicken lies on the kitchen table.

MARIA *and her daughter are alone.*

MARIA *inserts her hand up the chicken's back passage and rips out its guts.*

TERESA, *once again in pants and frilly ethnic blouse, watches.*

The sow lurches in the door.)

TERESA: I want piano lessons.

(MARIA throws a handful of chicken guts on to the floor.

The sow eats them.

She takes another chicken. She guts that.)

MARIA: Ask your husband to give you piano lessons.

(MARIA throws more guts to the sow.

She takes yet another chicken.)

TERESA: He's a pig.

MARIA: He's a rich pig.

TERESA: Why did you send me to the convent if you were going to marry me to a pig? I could have learned how to be a pig here.

(She grunts energetically at the sow.)

MARIA: Rich pigs like nice ladies.

TERESA: Garcia killed my rat.

MARIA: You provoked him.

(TERESA makes a sulky face.

She lifts up her hand to console herself by admiring her ring; by now it is a familiar gesture.)

TERESA: He says I'll have a grandfather clock.

MARIA: What more could a girl want?

TERESA: Someone who doesn't wear spurs to bed.

(MARIA *is done with gutting chickens.*
  She takes up a cleaver and whacks each dressed chicken into four.
  Thwack. Thwack. She does this as she continues to talk to TERESA.)

MARIA: Where will you find one like that?

TERESA: Aunt Roxana found one.

(MARIA *raises her cleaver. Thwack.*)

MARIA: She found one on her back. Your father wouldn't let you find a
  husband that way.

(TERESA *ranges round the kitchen, restless, dissatisfied.*)

TERESA: She might give me some hints.

MARIA: You mustn't go to Roxana's.

TERESA: I *love* Aunt Roxana!

(MARIA *sighs.*)

  You go there. If you let me go to Roxana's, her piano man could teach
  me.

MARIA: Not the piano again!

(*30. Interior. Saloon. Day.*
  The saloon is empty but for JOHNNY, *who is inspecting with intense curiosity
  the gun hanging over the bar.*
  He climbs on to the bar itself and takes the rifle down from the wall.
  It is heavy and clumsy.
  He handles it with difficulty.
  The COUNT *comes in.*)

COUNT: What are you doing? Give it to me.

(JOHNNY *reluctantly hands it over.*
  The COUNT *is very angry.*)

  It's mine. I brought it with me from Europe. It's all I have left.
  Nobody touches this gun but me. It hasn't been fired for twenty
  years.

(*He cradles the gun like a baby.*
  JOHNNY *watches, cat-like.*)

JOHNNY: Is it true what I've heard?

COUNT: *(Instantly suspicious.)* Heard what?

JOHNNY: There's an old story in Austria about a gun that fires bullets that never miss.

(The COUNT lays his gun down carefully, pours himself a drink.)

COUNT: Surely nobody believes that.

JOHNNY: The snag is, you have to make a pact with the devil, first.

COUNT: In the Old Country, people believe rubbish like that. But this is the new world. This is America.

JOHNNY: Do you think you can leave the devil behind so easily? In Vienna, in the cafés, they still talk about the gentleman who fled the country after a duel. They called it a shooting accident.

(The COUNT pours another drink.
JOHNNY wanders back to his piano, leans on the back of the chair.
For a moment, the COUNT thinks he has been let off the hook.)

JOHNNY: What brought a man like you to this place? Only whores and murderers live here. Wouldn't a man who'd sold his soul feel safest among the damned?

COUNT: Is it to that we owe the pleasure of your company?

(JOHNNY laughs.
The tension genuinely slackens.)

JOHNNY: They still gossip about that extraordinary marksman. Everyone thought his powers were supernatural.

COUNT: They say the devil taught Paganini the fiddle because no human being could have played so well.

(JOHNNY extends his pianist's hands.)

JOHNNY: But I don't need music lessons!

(31. Interior. ROXANA's bedroom. Night.
A votive light burns before an Infant of Prague.
ROXANA sleeps.
Fumbling, the COUNT undresses.
Thud! of a shoe on the floor.
ROXANA wakes.
In the background, faintly, the sound of Liszt's 'Mephisto Waltz'.
He tumbles on to the bed.
She takes him in her arms.)

ROXANA: Old man, why are you crying?

(*32. Interior. Front bedroom. Day.*
  EVANGELINE *is taking a bath in a tin tub.*
  MERCEDES *scrubs her back.*)

MERCEDES: Same build, same shaped hands . . . they've a definite look of each other.

EVANGELINE: Johnny's just the right age. And he said he came here looking for a man.

MERCEDES: All this way to claim his father!

EVANGELINE: Blackmail him, more like. Towels!

(*She rises, dripping, from the tub as* MERCEDES *holds out a towel.*)

(*33. Interior. Hacienda courtyard. Night.*
  GARCIA *and* MENDOZA *loll in hammocks, drinking tequila.*
  The goats sleep.
  The piano shines silver in the moonlight.)

GARCIA: It's a lovely accomplishment for a lady. You come home after a hard day, she fixes you a drink, she plays you a little music . . .

(MENDOZA *stares at him astonished.*
  Then he carefully sets down his glass.)

MENDOZA: Maria!

(*She appears at the kitchen door, a bloody knife in her hand. She has been killing something for tomorrow's dinner.*)

Go down to Roxana's tomorrow and tell her piano man to come here and give Teresa lessons.

(*34. Interior. Saloon. Day.*
  JOHNNY *stares impassively at* MARIA. *He is concealing intense excitement.*)

JOHNNY: Has she any talent?

MARIA: She can play *one note* very well.

(*He pretends to think about it.*
  Suddenly he stretches out his hand; MARIA *grasps it.*)

JOHNNY: Why not?

(*35. Interior. Saloon. Day.*

JOHNNY, *alone again, is smiling – no, grinning – with uncontrollable pleasure.*

He hugs himself. He spins round and round and round.

He laughs aloud.)

(36. Exterior. Outside saloon. Day.

ROXANA *appears on the upper verandah, watching, with a sad expression, as the* COUNT *and* JOHNNY *disappear off down the road together, apparently absorbed in an intense conversation we can't hear.)*

(37. Exterior. Gulch. Day.

JOHNNY *and the* COUNT *have ended up the valley formed by the dried-up bed of a creek.*

There is a dead tree, rocks. The skull of a cow with curly horns – all very menacing.

JOHNNY *is aiming a pistol clumsily at the skull of the cow.*

He fires.

The shot goes wildly astray.

He curses in German.)

COUNT: Speak English. We've left the old country behind. This is a new world, full of hope.

(JOHNNY looks round the barren gulley.)

JOHNNY: More like the end of hope. Only the vultures look optimistic.

COUNT: The landscape of this country is more ancient than we are. Strange gods live here. I shall never make friends with them.

(COUNT conversational: as if passing the time of day.)

COUNT: Sometimes I think I am already dead and this is hell.

(JOHNNY looks at him sharply, but the COUNT does not seem aware he has said anything out of the ordinary.)

JOHNNY: Is it true Roxana brought you here?

COUNT: All the stories are true. No. None of the stories are true. I was sick. She cared for me. We had no money. Her sister married the bandit and asked the bandit to give Roxana the saloon. We live on the good will of the bandit.

JOHNNY: Did you ever hear of Frederika von Arnim?

(The COUNT is suddenly animated.)

COUNT: The singer? Yes, yes! Her 'Norma'! Her –

JOHNNY: She was offered a great deal of money to sing in San Francisco. I was only a child, ten years old. She left me in Vienna. She told me what presents she would bring me, wonderful American toys – and every time she reached a new place she sent me a postcard. She sang in San Francisco, and then Los Angeles, and then she was offered a *very* great deal of money to sing South of the border.

(*38. Interior. Train. Day.*
Interior of a lavish stateroom, all red plush and gilding.
The beautiful lady of JOHNNY's *photograph, wearing a wonderful pair of diamond earrings, sits at a small table drinking coffee and writing a postcard as rocky border scenery glides by the windows.*
Close-up postcard. Her pen writes: 'Darling Johnny . . .' Then splashes ink wildly across the card as the train comes to a sudden halt. She, too, is thrown across the stateroom.
The chandelier above her clangs and clatters. Everything smashes.
There is the sound of gun-fire and drunken laughter.
The door of the stateroom bursts open. Here comes MENDOZA.)

(*39. Interior. Stateroom. Day.*
MENDOZA *pins the opera-singer against the wall, his knife against her throat. He is forcing her to sing.*
Tears streaming down her face, she sings the first bars of the countess's aria from Act II of The Marriage of Figaro.)

MENDOZA: Not that shit! Give us some real music.

(*He lunges at her with the knife.*
She screams.)

(*40. Interior. Stateroom. Day.*
Now she lies on the carpet, on the stateroom floor.
MENDOZA *kneels above her.*)

JOHNNY'S MOTHER: I am a mother. I have a little son.

MENDOZA: I am a father, I have a baby daughter.

(*He rips open her dress.*)

(*41. Exterior. Trainwreck. Day.*
The cowed passengers, those who have not been shot, huddled in the carriages as the bandidos loot the train.
They have found the wicker baskets of stage costumes that travel with JOHNNY'S MOTHER *and are breaking them open, donning their contents — crowns, robes, fake jewellery, wigs, hats — amid shrieks of laughter.*

Very loud screams.

JOHNNY'S MOTHER *has crawled to the door of her stateroom and leans out, holding her dress together. She screams and screams and screams.*
A shot, from inside the stateroom.
Her head falls forward. She is silent.
MENDOZA *leans out of the stateroom and wrenches off her diamond earrings.)*

(42. Exterior. Gulch. Day.)

COUNT: So you are an avenging angel, Johann. I should have recognised you sooner.

JOHNNY: I will seduce that eager young virgin over her piano lessons and then I will shoot her father without mercy, just as he shot my mother, in front of his daughter's eyes, so that she'll witness it every night in her dreams as long as she lives, just as I do.

COUNT: I hope you can handle a woman better than you can handle a gun or you won't get very far.

JOHNNY: Don't make fun of me.

COUNT: Do you believe in visiting the sins of the fathers upon –

JOHNNY: *(Interrupting.)* Why should his daughter be happy when her son is not? Ever since the letter from –

(Here he chokes on the banality of it.)

– the railroad company, I've been composing a tragedy for the entire Mendoza family, all the time I was growing up in Vienna, where I heard of a gentleman who once made a pact with the devil that ensured no bullet he ever fired would miss the mark . . .

COUNT: Oh!

(JOHNNY is at once solicitous, and quickly puts his arms round him, supporting him.)

JOHNNY: What's wrong?

COUNT: You can take my sin away. The Prince of Darkness is a gentleman; he always keeps his promises, even if they call him by a different name over here.

JOHNNY: I must have Mendoza's blood.

COUNT: Then you belong to the devil already.

(43. Interior. TERESA's *bedroom. Day.*

TERESA *in her pretty dress, hair pinned up and decorated with flowers, is on her knees rummaging in her trunk for something.*
She finds it: it is a little leather box.
She flicks it open and smiles to see what is inside – but we don't see what it is.)

(44. Exterior. Hacienda courtyard. Day.
Interested horses peer over the stable door as a minion drags a rocking chair out into the courtyard.
An enormous pink sunshade has been propped up over the piano, so those who sit on the piano stool are in the shade.
JOHNNY, *carrying a music case, looks bemusedly on as* MARIA *supervises the placement of the rocking chair.*
She is carrying a shotgun.
She plumps down in the rocking chair, shotgun over her knees.)

MARIA: I will chaperone you.

(TERESA emerges from her room.)

TERESA: *(Pert.)* The horses could do it just as well.

MARIA: Horses can't shoot.

(MARIA settles down in the rocking chair.
She has a pail of water in which several bottles of beer cool beside her.
It is the bewitching hour of early evening.
The horses snuffle and gently snort.
TERESA, *acting shy, poses prettily beside the piano; she is somewhat perturbed, however, by the intensity of* JOHNNY's *look.)*

JOHNNY: What attractive earrings.

(TERESA is wearing the diamond earrings MENDOZA *wrenched from the ears of* JOHNNY'S MOTHER.)*

TERESA: My father gave them to me. Do you really like them?

JOHNNY: They remind me – yes. I like them.

(He pulls himself together.)

Please sit down, fräulein, and we'll begin.

(45. Exterior. Hacienda courtyard. Night.
MARIA *opens another bottle of beer.*
TERESA's *head is bent over the piano,* JOHNNY's *head is bent over hers.*
They have progressed to the scale of G.)

(46. Interior. ROXANA's *bedroom. Night.*
   The COUNT *is rummaging through a trunk.*
   He takes out an old book, opens it, lays it on the bed.
   He studies a diagram.
   He slams the book shut.
   He takes a skull, a sealed jar of ancient design, and a mandrake root out of the trunk.
   ROXANA, *outside, tries the door and finds it locked.*
   She rattles the handle.)

ROXANA: *(Outside.)* What are you up to?

(The COUNT *lets her in – he takes her in his arms and buries his face in her bosom.)*

COUNT: He's willing.

ROXANA: To take away the burden?

*(*COUNT *nods.)*

   (Whispering.) Does he know what it means?

*(*COUNT *nods.)*

   Is he your son?

COUNT: No, Roxana.

*(*ROXANA *bursts out sobbing with relief.*
   She kisses his face again and again.)

   Not my son but the angel of death.

(She draws away and looks at him with haunted eyes.)

COUNT: Mendoza invoked him.

ROXANA: How much will it cost?

COUNT: It's a very high price. Roxana, how much do you love an old man?

ROXANA: Very much.

*(*ROXANA *stares at him.)*

COUNT: Do you love this poor old man more than anybody?

(She gasps and bites her lip.
   She lowers her face.
   Tears are streaming down her cheeks.)

ROXANA: I believe I do.

(They embrace.
Then he goes on delving in his occult treasures.
ROXANA *helps him.)*

ROXANA: But nothing must happen to little Teresa.

COUNT: I can't make any promises.

ROXANA: No harm at all.

COUNT: Remember before you met me, the men, the beds. Do you love me best?

*(*ROXANA *is startled by the viciousness in his voice.*
She says without emotion:)

ROXANA: I love you best.

(47. Exterior. Hacienda courtyard. Day.
JOHNNY *and* TERESA *are at the piano;* MARIA, *eyes closed, rocks in her chair.)*

JOHNNY: No, not like that – like this.

(He stands behind TERESA, *showing her where to put her hands on the keyboard.*
His long white hands cover her little brown paws, with the bitten fingernails.
MARIA *brushes away a hovering fly.*
JOHNNY *and* TERESA *play a phrase of an exercise by Czerny.*
TERESA *deliberately presses her head backwards, against* JOHNNY's *shoulder.*
JOHNNY *looks down, amused.)*

Again.

*(*JOHNNY *takes her hands firmly and makes her play.*
The phrase is interrupted by a ripping snore.
TERESA *giggles.*
They turn to look at MARIA, *asleep in the sun with her mouth open.*
Then TERESA *twists her head round and they kiss.*
Clumsily.
She gets up and kneels on the piano stool so they can kiss more easily.
She is so eager that JOHNNY *is at first taken aback.*
TERESA *starts to unfasten* JOHNNY's *shirt.)*

TERESA: Where shall we go?

(Things are going too quickly for JOHNNY.
He catches hold of her hands, to keep her off him.
JOHNNY *glances at* MARIA, *checks the rooms leading off the courtyard.*
No: nobody has spotted them.
But MARIA *stirs in her sleep.*
JOHNNY *is visibly uneasy.)*

JOHNNY: *(Fierce whisper.)* Not here, unless you want me shot.

TERESA: Haven't you got your own room at Roxana's?

JOHNNY: It's right next to the bar. And Roxana would strangle me with her bare hands.

TERESA: If you can wait until night time –

JOHNNY: *(Ironic.)* If *I* can wait –

TERESA: I know the perfect place.

*(*MARIA *stirs again, the shotgun falls from her knee to the floor with a clatter and she wakes.)*

(48. Interior. Ruined church. Night.
Absolute darkness. Then a match is struck: JOHNNY *lights a candle, looks round for somewhere to put it, sets it on what used to be the altar. The light illuminates a figure lying stretched on the ground, covered by a shawl. It is* TERESA. *There is nothing flirtatious in her manner, now. She is in deadly earnest. Unsmiling, she sits up, letting the shawl fall. She is naked. Her hair hangs down her back. But, out of coquetry, she wears her diamond earrings.* JOHNNY *kneels beside her.)*

JOHNNY: You're wearing nothing but diamonds.

(She touches an earring with her right hand.)

TERESA: Daddy gave them to me at my first communion. *(Brief pause.)* You must take your clothes off, now.

(49. Interior. Ruined church. Night.
TERESA'*s laughter echoes round and round the church. Many more candles have been lit, candles of all shapes and sizes, so the cavernous interior is full of uneven light.*

TERESA *sprawls on the spread-out shawl, but* JOHNNY *is putting his clothes back on.)*

JOHNNY: Why were you in such a hurry, Teresa?

TERESA: I'm going to be married.

(She thrusts out her hand with the ring on it. He touches her earrings.)

JOHNNY: I only noticed your earrings. Cover yourself up.

(TERESA wraps the shawl round her and stretches, sensuously.)

TERESA: I thought I might never get the chance to make love with a man who took his boots off first, if I didn't grab at you.

(JOHNNY is amused. He catches hold of her hair.)

JOHNNY: Is that all? You just wanted me to teach you a little elementary fingering.

(They look at one another in the candle-light and then kiss again.
TERESA *breaks away first, pulls the shawl over her head and goes off into the shadows, where she can be heard shuffling and kicking among the dead leaves, sullen, again.)*

TERESA: I bet that's all I'll get from Garcia. 'A little elementary fingering.' Garcia!

(Her face puckers with distaste.)

JOHNNY: Is Garcia your intended?

TERESA: He's a pig, but he's a rich pig. My son will be filthy rich but I've got to get married, first.

JOHNNY: Maybe I've given you a son already.

(TERESA involuntarily clutches her stomach.)

You won't be married. I won't let you be married.

(TERESA looks at him suspiciously.)

TERESA: What does it matter to you whether I'm married or not?

JOHNNY: It matters.

(TERESA lets out a yelp of joy and excitement.)

TERESA: Are you in love with me? Will you take me away? Will you take me to Paris? Or Madrid, there was a girl at the convent from Madrid. We could go to see her. And Vienna. Are you going to rescue me?

(Belatedly remembering what she ought to say.)

Darling!

(She covers his face with kisses.
There is a sudden sharp rustle in the dead leaves.

JOHNNY, *alert at once, slaps his hand over* TERESA's *mouth. They wait in tense silence for whoever has just arrived in the church to manifest itself.*

The lean, mean dog we have seen in the graveyard trots into the circle of light cast by the candles. It sits, looking at them, its tongue lolling. JOHNNY *picks up a stone, throws it at the dog. The dog ignores him.*

TERESA *laughs. They take no further notice of the dog and begin to kiss again.)*

(50. Exterior. Saloon back yard. Day.

JOHNNY *has set a number of empty bottles on top of upright sticks and, with his pistol, is attempting to shoot at the bottles. He misses every time; he is a lousy shot.* EVANGELINE, *in wrapper and braids, sits on the back steps, drinking beer, watching him.)*

EVANGELINE: You don't have any luck, Johnny.

JOHNNY: I wouldn't say that.

EVANGELINE: *(Heavy irony.)* Found that man you've been looking for?

JOHNNY: I'm hot on his track.

(The COUNT *appears on the back porch. He looks older, sicker, more haggard.*
EVANGELINE *hushes up at once, takes a long sip of beer but does not budge. She wants to see whatever there is to see happen between these two.)*

COUNT: The moon is in eclipse tonight.

*(*JOHNNY *takes aim at another bottle.)*

JOHNNY: How fascinating.

COUNT: When the moon is in eclipse there is nothing but darkness covering the entire world; only the beasts of darkness are out, seeking whom they may devour.

*(*EVANGELINE *looks anxiously at the* COUNT *as he takes a flat bottle from his pocket and drinks. Clearly he is on another drunk. But* JOHNNY *drops his pistol, a glory in his face.)*

(51. Interior. Front bedroom. Day.
But the blinds are drawn.

EVANGELINE *is still drawing on her eyebrows.* MERCEDES *and* HANNAH *are already prepared for the evening. In the distance, the train whistle blows.)*

MERCEDES: Train's late again.

EVANGELINE: I wish I were on that train. Nothing's felt right, since Johnny came.

MERCEDES: Just because he doesn't even notice you're there.

HANNAH: He's got his eye on finer things, he's aimin' for Miss Teresa.

EVANGELINE: . . . titless virgin . . .

HANNAH: She's ready for it. She's ready for anything.

EVANGELINE: He'll get his ass shot off if he tries it with her.

MERCEDES: She'll be married to Garcia soon as the wedding dress is ready.

HANNAH: She won't get much joy from Garcia. I should know.

MERCEDES: They're going to marry her in the old church, get a priest in from town.

ROXANA: (*Voice over.*) Girls! Company!

(*The girls stop giggling, look at one another with a sigh, gather themselves together for work.*)

MENDOZA: (*Voice over.*) Beautiful Miss Evangeline, condescend to descend the staircase!

(EVANGELINE *groans.*)

(*52. Interior.* ROXANA's *bedroom. Night.*
  The COUNT *unwraps an object from a bundle of blood-stained linen.*
  It is a severed hand.
  In the background, music, noise, laughter, singing from the bar.)

(*53. Interior. Saloon. Night.*
  The bar at the end of the evening; all is swept up, tidied away. Only a frilly garter left floating in a pool of spilled beer.
  JOHNNY *is alone, moving smoothly around turning down the lamps. The* COUNT *appears from the back room. He is white-faced and looks unwell.*)

JOHNNY: Roxana –

COUNT: Sound asleep. Are you –

JOHNNY: More than ever.

COUNT: Just one thing. Teresa.

JOHNNY: (*Bristling.*) What about Teresa?

COUNT: Revenge can cost too much.

JOHNNY: Not for me.

COUNT: Don't visit the sins of the father upon the child.

JOHNNY: If Teresa gives me back my mother's earrings, I'll take her to Vienna.

(The door closes behind them.)

(54. Exterior. Gulch. Night.

Darkness, except for a few vague gleams which we soon make out to be the torsos of JOHNNY and the COUNT, each stripped to the waist, kneeling close together as the COUNT marks out a pentacle.

We do not see what he is using to make the marks; only, that the lines he draws are vaguely phosphorescent, so in a moment the two men kneel within the centre of a five-pointed star of glowing, greenish light.

Point-of-view shot: JOHNNY and the COUNT. All that is visible outside the glowing pentacle are the shapes of the ears of prickly pear and a sky of absolute darkness.

JOHNNY shivers. The COUNT puts an arm around him. The COUNT begins to recite something in a very low voice, so low the words cannot be made out.

A rushing sound, faint at first, then louder and louder. A wind has risen up and grows every moment stronger.)

(55. Interior. ROXANA's room. Night.

ROXANA, fully dressed, lies on her bed sound asleep. Her shutters rattle as the wind beats against them.

On the dressing table, propped upright, is a macabre candlestick – the severed hand which we saw the COUNT unpack a little while ago. The fingertips have each been lit; each burns with a slow, greenish flame. (This is the sorcerer's 'Hand of Glory', guaranteed to make the inhabitants of the place where it is lit sleep the sleep of the dead.)

The wind rattles against the shutters with greater and greater fury until at last they burst open, to bang and crash against the walls outside.

Night things – huge dead leaves, bats, night bird's feathers – blow into the room. Still ROXANA sleeps.)

(56. Interior. Front bedroom. Night.

The wind rips through and through the room, making the carpet billow, raising the sheets off the bed – we cannot make out the identity of the figures sleeping there – blowing loose face powder left in an uncapped box into a dust storm.)

(57. Interior. TERESA's room. Night.

TERESA sleeps, until the wind bursts her shutters open and then shatters the glass in her tall window with a great, musical crash that makes her sit bolt upright, at once fully awake.

She screams, as the curtains on her bed whip about.)

(58. Interior. Gulch. Night.

JOHNNY *screams. The* COUNT *claps his hand over* JOHNNY's *mouth. Their two figures are almost hidden by whirling plumes of dust. Entering the pentacle, we see, from their point-of-view shot, the dust form and coalesce into vague shapes of shaman's masks. There is no sound at all but that of the terrible wind.*

Bizarre deities of all kinds coalesce and dissolve like a series of hallucinations.

The figures and the dust storm blot out the COUNT *and* JOHNNY.)

(59. Exterior. Gulch. Night.

The moon is out once again, the stars are shining; all calm, all clear. A brilliant night. There is a pentacle marked out in the dust, but it no longer glows.

The COUNT *and* JOHNNY *lie in the pentacle as if dead. The lean, mean dog sits outside the pentacle, watching them.*

JOHNNY *is the first to rouse. He shakes the* COUNT *awake and feeds him a drink from the flat bottle in his trouser pocket.*

There is as much urgency as tenderness in his ministrations. The COUNT *drinks and coughs.)*

JOHNNY: Where's the gun?

COUNT: He's come. These were only his messengers. He's waiting at home.

*(*JOHNNY *helps the* COUNT *to his feet. They step carefully out of the pentacle. The dog pads after them.)*

(60. Exterior. Outside saloon. Night.

A Navajo, hair in braids, turquoise necklace, slouch hat, sits in ROXANA's *rocking chair, boots propped on the verandah rail, rocking in the moonlight. A gun is propped beside him. He clicks his fingers.*

The lean, mean dog runs to him.

The COUNT *assisted by* JOHNNY, *is nearly home. He is pale and shaking. He greets the visitor with elaborate courtesy that costs him much effort.)*

COUNT: My dear sir! Is it really you, after all these years? How very pleasant to see you again.

*(*JOHNNY *has not realised the identity of this newcomer until this moment. He interrupts the* COUNT, *unimpressed:)*

JOHNNY: Got the gun?

(The Navajo reaches for the gun propped against the railing and casually tosses it to him.)

COUNT: Payment on account.

(He tips his hat, rises, steps from the verandah. He mounts his pony, then casts the COUNT *a look of, almost, affection.)*

INDIAN: You'll sleep well.

COUNT: How soon?

INDIAN: *(Almost with pity.)* Soon enough, but not as soon as you'd like.

(He rides off, the dog at his heels. In the immense stillness of the night, his hoofbeats can be heard for a long time.

The COUNT *sinks into the rocking chair he has just vacated.*

JOHNNY, *meanwhile, examines the gun.*

It is a straightforward Winchester repeater and it is brand new. The devil could have bought it yesterday. It looks perfectly normal. JOHNNY's *disappointment is obvious.*

A rooster – an early bird – comes out from the back yard behind the house and starts pecking in the road.)

JOHNNY: What's so special about it? I could have picked one up just like this in the store.

(The rooster flaps up on to the post at the end of the porch and spreads its wings, preparatory to crowing.)

COUNT: You never need reload it and the bullets will never miss their target.

JOHNNY: Is that true?

COUNT: I know.

(Wonderingly, JOHNNY *takes hold of the gun and raises it. Idly, he aims at the rooster and presses the trigger.*

The rooster tumbles off its perch in a shower of feathers. JOHNNY *laughs aloud in delight but the* COUNT *speaks sadly through his laughter.)*

COUNT: Don't waste the bullets. They're not cheap.

(Johnny is silenced.)

Besides, one of them belongs to him. You will take aim, you will pull the trigger – but the bullet will go where *he* wants.

JOHNNY: Is that what happened to you?

(The COUNT *nods slowly.)*

COUNT: I shot at a man but killed his wife. She was my only sister.

JOHNNY: Which one is his bullet?

COUNT: You never know that. You only find out afterwards.

(61. Interior. JOHNNY's room. Day.

JOHNNY has shut the shutters so all is dark. A candle is lit in front of the photograph of his mother. He lays the new gun down in front of the photograph, for her to see.)

JOHNNY: One by one, Mother. Mendoza and all his companions.

(The photograph does not move or speak. It remains so much shiny paper.)

(62. Interior. TERESA's bedroom. Day.

TERESA's mirror reflects a bride, in a white lace mantilla.

TERESA turns away from the mirror, looking sour. She aims a kick at the seamstress who kneels at her feet. MARIA lies on the unmade bed with her boots cocked on the coverlet, smoking a small cigar.)

MARIA: Temper, temper!

TERESA: I don't want to get married!

MARIA: You won't wheedle your father out of this one.

(TERESA wrenches her skirts out of the seamstress's hands and runs out into the courtyard. MARIA calls after her.)

It won't be too bad! You can always come home and practise the piano whenever you want!

(63. Exterior. Courtyard. Day.

TERESA sits down at the piano, and plays a series of crashing chords.)

(64. Interior. Church. Night.

TERESA and JOHNNY lie in post-coital silence, by the light of a candle lantern. TERESA lies on her stomach, her face pressed into her arms. Her shoulders start to heave. JOHNNY, in spite of himself, touches her shoulder with a certain tenderness.)

TERESA: Take me away. I don't want to marry Garcia.

(She sits up, pulling her shawl round her.)

I don't want to be stuck out here all my life. Do you know who I really admire? Aunt Roxana. She got away, and she worked for a living, and she chose her own man.

JOHNNY: You know what she worked at, of course.

TERESA: It's not much different to being married to Garcia.

JOHNNY: Being married to Garcia is better paid. And she ended up back here, after all that.

TERESA: Take me away! Like the last piano man did Em. Take me to El Paso and then desert me, I don't care, I'll have seen a bit of life besides this pigsty and the stinking convent.

JOHNNY: I've important things to do before I go away, Teresa. If you still want to go with me afterwards –

(*He gives her a veiled look. How is she to know he plans to kill her father? She stares right back. Then suddenly she flings herself on him, pushing him back down on to the rustling dry leaves.*)

(*65. Interior. Saloon. Night*

Close-up a vast, hairy belly on which the tattoo of a Mexican señorita undulates. Vast amounts of laughter accompany this spectacle.

The belly belongs to GARCIA. *It is exposed during the traditional party thrown by the bridegroom the night before the wedding.* JOHNNY's *piano has been supplemented by a Mariachi band.* ROXANA's *girls are supplemented by a posse of freelances brought in for the occasion.* GARCIA, *shirtless, in a feathered hat borrowed from one of the girls, is dancing a vulgar parody of a Mexican dance.* MENDOZA *himself is his dancing partner.*

The COUNT, *behind the bar, pours himself a shot of whiskey and downs it.* EVANGELINE *and* HANNAH *stand at the foot of the stairs, permitting themselves to look supercilious.*)

EVANGELINE: Does Teresa know about that tattoo?

HANNAH: She'll get a diamond ring for looking at it, which is more than I ever got.

(JOHNNY, *unnoticed, quits the piano and approaches the bar, carrying with him his mug of coffee. He raises it to the* COUNT *in mock salute.*)

COUNT: I could almost ask you . . .

(JOHNNY *smiles, shakes his head and whistles a few bars of Chopin's* Funeral March.)

At least remember, 'the prince of darkness is a gentleman'. Spare Teresa the sight of the murder.

JOHNNY: She's got temperament. She'll do well in Paris, Rome, Vienna . . .

(*66. Exterior. Hacienda. Courtyard. Day.*

The sun blazes down on an open carriage lavishly bedecked with ribbons and flowers.

MENDOZA, *looking hungover under a sombrero positively dripping with gold thread, holds the reins, waiting for his daughter.*

Here comes the bride.

But she doesn't look her best, sullen and nervous in her wedding dress although her earrings and engagement ring blaze. She throws her bouquet into the carriage and jumps in after. Her mother appears, smoothing down an unaccustomed silk dress. Boots appear beneath the hem as she climbs into the carriage beside TERESA.

MENDOZA *cracks the whip and the carriage rolls out of the courtyard. His entourage, all dressed up, too, follow on horseback, cracking their whips and hallooing.)*

(67. Interior. JOHNNY's *room. Day.*

JOHNNY *kisses the photograph of his mother and sets it down again.*

It is time. He picks up the rifle. He crosses himself. He closes the door behind him softly, as though someone in the room were sleeping.)

(68. Interior. Church. Day.

Except for the lack of a roof, you would not recognise it as the ruined church for a huge altarpiece is propped in place behind an altar covered with a lavishly embroidered cloth and various pieces of splendid ecclesiastical plate. There are pews in place, too. And everywhere masses and masses of flowers.

A priest stands in front of the altar, waiting. In front of the priest stands GARCIA, *ready and waiting, but looking as hungover as* MENDOZA.

The pews are filled with bandits and their respectably mantilla'd women.

The men all bristle with weapons and ammunition belts but all their heads are uncovered, as befits a church.

ROXANA's *three girls, very neatly and inconspicuously dressed, hatted and gloved, looking lovely and respectable, sit reticently at the back of the church.*

But ROXANA *and the* COUNT *are absent.)*

(69. Interior. ROXANA's *bedroom. Day.*

The COUNT *lies in bed, very ill.* ROXANA *bends over him anxiously, one arm in her jacket, her hat already on.)*

COUNT: Stay here with me, Roxana.

ROXANA: I *must* go, old man. I promised her. Are you sure you can't drag yourself out of bed to see your only niece get married?

(The COUNT *coughs hideously.)*

COUNT: I'm dying, Roxana.

*(*ROXANA, *torn, puts her hand to his forehead and is reassured.)*

ROXANA: Hang on for just another couple of hours, old man. I promise I'll be back in time for your deathbed.

(ROXANA *slips her other arm into her jacket.*
The COUNT *buries his face in the pillow.*)

(*70. Exterior. Town. Day.*

MENDOZA *drives his sulky daughter to her wedding. The wedding procession takes the same route away from the hacienda as did the cart that brought the piano into the hacienda.*

In front of them, on the road, blocking their way, trots an Indian on a pony. Behind him lollops a familiar, lean, mean dog. MENDOZA *whips up his horses and trots forward.*

The Indian gets off the path. Impassive, he watches the wedding procession pass.)

(*71. Interior. Church. Day.*

GARCIA, *standing in front of the priest, produces a pocket watch from his breast and consults it. She is late. The congregation stirs and settles itself again.*

EVANGELINE *brushes away a fly that is bothering her as* ROXANA, *flustered and untidy, slips into the pew beside her.*)

(*72. Exterior. Church. Day.*

TERESA *ignores her father's hand and jumps down from the carriage. She is darkly furious. No sign of* JOHNNY! *She looks round, eyes flashing. Nothing.*

Her mother kisses her cheek but TERESA *is too agitated, too mean, to respond.*

Her father extends his arm. TERESA *reluctantly accepts it. She gives one last backward look. Nothing for it, now.*)

(*73. Interior. Church. Day.*

Holy organ music. TERESA's *diamond earrings flash as she processes with her father down the aisle to arrive beside her bridegroom. She gives him a swift glance of furious dislike.*)

PRIEST: Dearly beloved –

(*The priest falters.*
Priest's point-of-view shot: JOHNNY, *outlined against the sunshine, streaming in through the open church door, a black figure brandishing a gun.*)

JOHNNY: Mendoza! Do you remember how you came by your daughter's diamond earrings?

(MENDOZA *looks round, open-mouthed.*
JOHNNY *shoots* MENDOZA *directly between the eyes.*)

(*74. Exterior. Train. Day.*
A scream; JOHNNY'S MOTHER *appears at the open door of the train.*

A shot. She falls. But the scream continues.)

(75. Interior. Church. Day.

The scream continues. It is MARIA. *She has been sitting next to* ROXANA. *Now she rushes out of the pew with a knife in her hand.*

JOHNNY *shoots* MARIA.

TERESA *stands immobile, looking down at her father's body.*

The scream continues, although the knife drops from MARIA's *hand and she falls backwards into* EVANGELINE's *arms. Her spurs clatter on the stone floor.*

JOHNNY *shoots* GARCIA, *who falls. Then he shoots the priest.*

A hail of bullets bounce uselessly round JOHNNY *but none touch him. He turns and vanishes, just as* TERESA *wakes from her trance.*

It is TERESA *screaming.*

Waking from her trance, she runs down the aisle. The scream is cut off in mid-flight.)

(76. Exterior. Church. Day.

TERESA *and* ROXANA *hug, weeping, outside the church. Then, hand in hand, they run down the path away from the church towards the town and the saloon.)*

(77. Exterior. Town. Day.

TERESA *and* ROXANA *run, panting, through the town. It is like a parody of the arrival of the piano; people look out of their windows, children run a little distance with them, chickens crow.)*

(78. Exterior. Outside Saloon. Day.

The COUNT, *cadaverous, looking as if near death, stands on the upstairs balcony – or, rather, has propped himself against the wall – carrying the ancient gun that used to hang on the wall of the bar.*

Slowly, shakily, he raises it.

TERESA *and* ROXANA *come into shot, hugging one another, panting, on the porch.*

TERESA *and* ROXANA *come into shot.* TERESA *looks up and sees the* COUNT *and his raised weapon. Her eyes widen with horror.*

The COUNT *is aiming at* JOHNNY, *standing some distance away on a knoll.*

JOHNNY *catches sight of the* COUNT, *and deliberately shoots him.*

But it is the devil's bullet.

TERESA *falls, without making a sound.*

A huge silence.

ROXANA *kneels by the dead girl and uselessly speaks to her.)*

ROXANA: Teresa! Teresa!

*(*JOHNNY *approaches soundlessly and looks down at* TERESA.)*

JOHNNY: It was the bullet. It was the devil's bullet.

ROXANA: I don't understand. He –

(Jerk of the head towards the balcony, where the COUNT is slumped.)

– understands.

JOHNNY: I meant to take her away, afterwards. Once I'd got the earrings back, I'd have taken her to Vienna.

ROXANA: Take her earrings. She doesn't need them.

(She slips one earring from TERESA's ear and offers it to JOHNNY. She offers it again, forcefully, thrusting it at him. He backs away, a look of horror on his face. He drops the gun, turns and runs just as ROXANA's girls arrive on the scene and console ROXANA.

They are followed by other surviving members of the congregation, white, shocked, silent, accusing.

The COUNT, on the upper balcony, leans over the railing; he is very shaky, now.)

COUNT: Roxana!

(She does not look up.)

Roxana! Do you love me best!

(Still she doesn't look.)

(79. Exterior. Edge of desert. Day.

A region of white, fantastic rocks, arid soil and burning sun. It is almost noon. JOHNNY, riding an exhausted horse, shades his eyes to look ahead.

JOHNNY's point-of-view shot: a few white buildings in the distance.)

(80. Exterior. Indian village. Day.

An adobe village. JOHNNY rides in; but the village seems deserted. No smoke from the chimneys, not a sign of life. He dismounts in the deserted square and draws water from a pump. He splashes his face. A ragged, filthy boy emerges from a derelict house.)

SMALL BOY: The smallpox came. All dead. Come see.

(JOHNNY follows him. He opens a door.

JOHNNY looks inside.)

(81. Interior. Adobe house. Day.

JOHNNY's point-of-view shot: flies buzz on an unburied corpse in a murky interior.)

(82. Exterior. Village. Day.

JOHNNY *slams the door and leans against the wall, retching.*

The boy is gone.

A neighing. The horse, possibly refreshed by a rest, is trotting off by itself, down the street, off and away.)

JOHNNY: Come back!

(But the horse shakes its ears and breaks into a canter.

JOHNNY *walks down the dead street. All that moves is a familiar, lean, mean dog, who has been sleeping in a patch of shade. Now it wakes and follows* JOHNNY *at a discreet distance.*

At the end of the village, gazing across the acres of desert before JOHNNY, *a figure wrapped in a poncho is propped against the wall of a house – a figure so still, so silent that at first it seems like another corpse. A hat is pulled down over its face.*

JOHNNY *appears.*

The figure tips up its hat, rises, smiles. It is the Indian.)

INDIAN: I was waiting for you. We have some unfinished business.

FADE OUT

The Christchurch Murder

(Exterior. Victoria Park. Day.

Birdsong, unnaturally loud, in an intense silence punctuated by the rhythmic blows of an axe on wood.

A grey, blustery day in the lovely wilds of Victoria Park in the Cashmere Hills on the outskirts of the city of Christchurch, New Zealand.

A tin sign for Kia-Ora orange squash swings outside a little rustic-style tea room. The door stands ajar. Trees grow all round. A path leads uphill, through the trees, to the left. In front of the tea room, a metalled road.

The over-loud birdsong, the thwack of an axe, the forlorn look of the place, all produce an intense sense of disquiet.)

(Interior. Tea room. Day.

Close-up a white plate holding a half-eaten scone smeared with raspberry jam, a dirty knife, on a marble-topped, crumb-scattered table.

There is a tea-cup, half-full of cold tea, on the table, too. Two glasses containing dregs of orange squash and squashed straws. A puddle of spilt milk. A plate of the cakes of the country – lambingtons, iced fancies. The chairs are pushed untidily back.

The room is painted dirty white. On the walls, a calendar for 1953, an advertisement for ice-cream, a faded newspaper clipping of a photograph of the young queen in coronation robes. A pay telephone stands beside the half-open door. In the wall, opposite, another door: toilets.

Birdsong, axe-blows continue.

The proprietor of the tea room, MRS GRAHAM, middle-aged, cleans the table, grubby apron, carpet slippers, stacks cups, glasses, plates, balances the plate of cakes as well, and returns to the counter, where glass bells cover cakes, scones, curling sandwiches. Her slippers go slip, slap, on the lino.

She puts the used tea things down and tips the nibbled scone into a bucket of waste – crusts, potato peelings, apple cores – under the sink behind the counter.

Branches of shrubs knock against the window over the sink. Through the window, among the trees, a huge, wild-looking man in a plaid shirt, with a big beard, raises an axe.)

(Exterior. Victoria Park. Day.

The camera takes in a sweeping panorama – mountains, wide, green plain, the city of Christchurch at the foot of the hillside down which, in the distance, two girls come running.

NERISSA LOCKE*'s long, blonde hair blows out romantically in the wind; she is fifteen, strikingly good-looking in a fine-boned, English way. The other,* LENA BALL, *fourteen, is smaller, darker. Although elsewhere in the film Lena walks with a pronounced limp, here she does not limp. Both move with fluid grace, unhindered by their maroon gymslips (of the old-fashioned kind, pleated from a high yoke, sashed) and their school blazers.*

The girls throw back their heads and laugh but we cannot hear them. They look wild, ecstatic, beautiful, free as they run down the hill, towards the camera.)

(Interior. Tea room. Day.

MRS GRAHAM *tips the dirty crockery into the chipped enamel bowl in the Belfast sink and turns on the tap. Splash.*

Outside, the axe continues.)

(Exterior. Victoria Park. Day.

A section of the path in a high, lonely place. Vast view of the surrounding hills.

On the path lies a set of dentures.

Just off the path, there is a bush.

From behind the bush protrudes a leg.

A leg in a lisle stocking and a sensible shoe.

Just the one leg.

Then, as if the roots of the bush began to bleed, blood starts, first, to seep, then to drip, then to pour out from beneath the bush, forming channels and runnels that finally come together in such a way that they flood the frame.)

(Exterior. Victoria Park. Day.

The two girls catch sight of the roof of the tea room. They halt, breathless, changing before our eyes from two free spirits into ordinary schoolgirls.

Ordinary . . . until we realise their maroon gymslips are covered with fresh blood, which from a distance, did not show up on their dark-red uniforms.

They turn towards one another. They reach out their blood-stained hands to one another. Hand in hand, they walk decorously on.)

NERISSA: It's for the best. It's for us.

*(*LENA *sees the blood on her friend's hand, then on her own; an expression of consternation crosses her face. She looks baffled, pained.* NERISSA *hugs* LENA.)

(Interior. Tea room. Day.

MRS GRAHAM, *washing up concluded, hangs the drying-up cloth on its hook, shuffles out to replace the chairs tidily at the table.*

MRS GRAHAM's *point-of-view shot – somewhat foreshortened, so that they look huge,* NERISSA *and* LENA *stand in the doorway, drenched in blood.*
MRS GRAHAM *cries out, knocks over a chair, backs away.*
LENA *pushes her hair back from her face. Her hand leaves a red mark on her forehead.*)

LENA: *(Toneless; as if repeating a lesson.)* My mother's had a fall, she hurt her head. We couldn't make her get up.

MRS GRAHAM: Come on in.

(NERISSA's *arm round* LENA's *shoulders, the girls come into the tea room.* MRS GRAHAM *goes to the door, shouts:* Ollie!)

(*The sound of the axe stops.* OLLIE *comes to the tea-room door, carrying a hatchet. He disposes of it by sticking it into a log.*)

MRS GRAHAM: Mrs Ball's had a bit of an accident. Just pop up the hill and –

LENA: *(Agitated.)* She cracked her head wide open. She's dead. I'm sure of it. Send for an ambulance.

OLLIE: Sounds as if you need a hearse.

MRS GRAHAM: *(Shocked reproof.)* Ollie . . .

NERISSA: *(Awesomely composed; patrician tones: marked British accent.)* Please call the University. Ask my father to come and take us home.

(MRS GRAHAM *pointedly addresses* LENA.)

MRS GRAHAM: Want me to ring *your* daddy, Lena?

(LENA *has been studying her bloody hands. She looks shrunken, chilled.*)

LENA: I want to wash my hands.

(*Interior. Washroom. Day.*
A bleak, concrete washroom – a sink, a single tap, a square of cracked mirror, a roller towel. The blood turns the water pink as the girls wash.
LENA *catches sight of her face in the mirror, the red mark on her forehead.*)

LENA: Got a hanky?

(NERISSA *produces a lace-trimmed one. She dips the corner of the handkerchief in the wash basin and wipes off the red mark.*)

LENA: Let me –

NERISSA: See? All gone.

(Interior. Tea room. Day.

The girls sit at the table from which MRS GRAHAM *cleared the plates, warming their hands on cups of tea.* MRS GRAHAM *is using the telephone.*

She hangs up and comes across to the girls, fiddling with her apron out of embarrassment and nerves.)

NERISSA: Is my daddy coming?

MRS GRAHAM: *(Embarrassed.)* Not the professor, the professor isn't it. Not the professor, *(Slight hesitation.)* the other gentleman. Lena, shall I phone your dad now?

*(*LENA*'s face is now quite white. She tries to speak but her teeth are chattering too much.* MRS GRAHAM *snatches the tea-cup before it falls from her shaking hand.)*

NERISSA: *(Wise.)* Shock, you know.

(Outside, the bell of an ambulance.)

(Exterior. Outside tea room. Day.

The ambulance, ringing its bell, and the police car have arrived at the same time. There is a mild panic. Two uniformed ambulancemen jump out of the one, two detectives out of the other as OLLIE *comes down the path at a stumbling run.)*

FIRST DETECTIVE: What does she look like?

OLLIE: Strewth!

(Interior. Tea room. Day.

NERISSA *keeps a protective arm round Lena. The ambulancemen and one detective talk to* OLLIE. *The other detective listens to* MRS GRAHAM, *eyeing the girls thoughtfully as she talks.)*

MRS GRAHAM: Well, Mrs Ball – you know, Ball the fishmonger, anyway, Mrs Ball, *this* one's *(Gesturing towards* LENA.*)* mother – this is Lena Ball, known her since she was so high, but the other one's the professor's daughter, Rock or Locke or something like that. Forgotten what else they call her . . . anyway, they all came and had tea – well, Mrs Ball had tea, the girls had squash, didn't fancy anything to eat, Mrs Ball didn't finish her scone, but they were happy and laughing and then they said they were going off for a walk and I said, 'Oh, isn't it a bit chilly', but Mrs Ball said she'd promised the girls so –

(Then she finds she can scarcely speak, her mouth has gone quite dry.)

FIRST DETECTIVE: *(To the girls: gently.)* Do you feel up to taking us back there?

NERISSA: *(Peremptory: putting him in his place.)* No.

(Exterior. Outside tea room. Day.

DOUGGIE QUINN *attempts to park his suave convertible, with its teak dashboard and red-leather upholstery, beside the police car.* QUINN *matches his car perfectly – moustache, tweeds, flat cap, upper-class British accent and, on this occasion, a very bad temper. He crashes the gears, manoeuvres the car, gives the police car a glancing blow, meanwhile muttering under his breath:)*

QUINN: Damn, blast, damn . . .

(The ambulancemen, the detectives and OLLIE *troop out of the tea room. The ambulancemen fetch a stretcher from the ambulance. One detective pauses as* QUINN *gets out of the car.)*

FIRST DETECTIVE: The Ball girl's in shock. Got a rug?

QUINN: *(Grand.)* In the trunk. Get it yourself.

(He slams his door and goes into the tea room, leaving the detective to collect the rug. The others start off up the path.)

(Interior. Convertible. Day.

The car whizzes along the long, straight road that leads from the Cashmere Hills into Christchurch. LENA, *wrapped in a tartan travelling rug, stares blankly out of the window in the back seat.* NERISSA *squashed beside her, is high with nerves, excitement, anti-climax.)*

NERISSA: She fell and she said: oh! and rolled a little way and, would you believe it, her denture fell out –

*(*QUINN *watches her minutely in the driving mirror.)*

QUINN: Stow it, Nerissa.

NERISSA: She hit her head, you see, that was what dislodged the denture –

QUINN: *Stow it!*

(She stops short, halted by the violence of his tone. He goes on, grim:)

QUINN: Two hundred years ago, they'd have burned you both for witches.

(She sticks her tongue out at him, making a grotesque face, knowing he can see her in the mirror. LENA *lolls sideways; she has lost consciousness.)*

(Exterior. Entering Christchurch. Day.

The car passes a terrace of canopied, red-brick shops; crosses the railway tracks; passes the rooftop plaster Kiwi – advertising Kiwi bacon – that tells us for sure what country we are in.)

(Interior. Ball family fish shop. Day.

An old-fashioned fish shop, decorated tiles, sawdust on the floor, a marble slab, a glass cashier's booth, inside the booth an upright telephone and a black cat sitting washing itself beside the cash register.

LEN BALL, LENA's father, a big, soft, fair, unassuming man, in white apron and straw boater, fillets a large fish.

The telephone rings inside the cashier's booth. MR BALL puts down his knife, wipes his hands on his apron, goes to answer. The cat rubs against his hand; automatically he strokes its head.)

MR BALL: *(Into the receiver.)* What?

(He doesn't understand, can't believe his ears. Automatically he goes on stroking the cat; it purrs loudly.)

What's that?

(Exterior. Outside LOCKE family house. Day.

Dusk is approaching. The LOCKE family house, a huge, wooden, colonial structure with a big verandah and lots of gingerbread, looms out of its lush garden like the witch's house in 'Hansel and Gretel'. QUINN's car screeches to a halt. He blasts on the horn.

NERISSA leaps out, full of energy, and dashes up the steps as her mother, MARY LOCKE opens the door.

MARY LOCKE is a cool, elegant woman making the most of her last years of youth. Her blonde hair is done up in a smooth French pleat, her fingernails are impeccable, seams straight, heels high. NERISSA has inherited her mother's looks but there is no love lost between them.

QUINN lifts LENA out of the back of the car. Rolled up in the rug, she is unconscious.)

MARY: *(Recoiling.)* Nerissa, you're covered with –

(QUINN, carrying LENA, pushes past MARY and NERISSA into the hall.)

QUINN: This one's passed out.

(He kicks the front door shut behind him. The glass in the upper panels rattles.)

(Interior. Hall of LOCKE house. Day.

A mirror. A telephone table beneath it. NERISSA dances down the hall.)

NERISSA: White stuff came out along with the red stuff. What a mess!

QUINN: *(To* MARY, *under his breath.)* The Ball woman copped it.

MARY: What!

QUINN: Could have been you, Mary.

*(*QUINN *reaches round his rug-wrapped parcel to open the sitting-room door. He leaves a red smudge on the white paint. Officer-class tone of command: indeed, he is an ex-officer.)*

Wipe that off.

*(*MARY *shocked and speechless fumbles in the sleeve of her jumper for a tissue.)*

Nerissa, come here.

(Interior. LOCKE *sitting room. Night.*

A band-box pretty room with Regency stripe wallpaper, Redouté rose prints, careful arrangements of flowers. An expensive room. A copy of the latest Vogue *has just arrived, seamail, and lies on the coffee table.*

QUINN *dumps* LENA *on the sofa, goes to draw the chintz curtains.* NERISSA, *now a little subdued, creeps towards her friend.* MARY *looks with distaste at the soiled tissue and drops it in an ashtray before she takes a cigarette from the silver box on top of the drinks cabinet, lights it with the table lighter. She and* QUINN *have been waiting for something terrible to happen; now it has. She is almost relieved.)*

QUINN: *(To* NERISSA.*)* Strip off.

*(*NERISSA's *jaw drops.)*

MARY: *(Removing a shred of tobacco from her tongue.)* Do as he says.

(After a quick, deep drag, she starts to strip LENA. NERISSA *turns her back on* QUINN — *her movements are jerky, speedy. She,* QUINN *and* MARY *are now all in a heightened state of nerves.*

In her vest and knickers, NERISSA *looks very young and vulnerable.* QUINN *gathers the girls' discarded clothing into the rug in which he wrapped* LENA.*)*

NERISSA: *(Reluctant; nevertheless, she understands what he is doing.)* Wait.

(She slips off her white anklesocks and gives them to him. There is blood on the socks.)

MARY: Bed. Scoot.

(Interior. LOCKE *family wash-house. Night.*

A sink, a twin-tub washing machine, drying racks hanging from the ceiling, an ironing board — all the equipment of a domestic laundry. QUINN *pokes the contents of his bundle into the washing machine. He pauses, panting. He examines the rug in which he'd wrapped* LENA, *rolls it into a ball, stows it under the sink.*)

QUINN: *(To himself.)* Garden incinerator for *that* little number.

(He pours soap flakes into the washing machine.)

QUINN: Murderous little bitches . . .

(Interior. LOCKE *family kitchen. Night.*
An empty milk saucepan stands on the stove of the big old-fashioned kitchen. MARY *crumbles tablets into two mugs of hot chocolate.* QUINN *comes into the kitchen, holding blood-stained hands away from him. He turns on the taps in the kitchen sink, washes his hands.)*

MARY: *(Indicating the mugs of chocolate.)* Sleeping tablets. Anything to get Rissa to pipe down. 'White stuff came out along with the red stuff.' Christ.

QUINN: Where's Colin?

MARY: Sherry. With the Bishop.

(They laugh despairingly, mirthlessly at the incongruity of it. MARY *spoons sugar into the mugs. Suddenly she lets go of the spoon.)*

We should never have let Nerissa go on that damn trip. 'One last time. Please, Mummy!' Christ!
    I was talking to Lena's mother just last week.
    She was a thoroughly decent woman, the poor cow.
    Oh, *Christ.*
    That other little hussy led her on, didn't she, Douggie? Didn't she? DIDN'T SHE?

(Interior. Hospital. Night.
In the cubicle, a sheeted figure lies on a bed. MR BALL, *clumsy with surprise, holding his hat gauchely in front of him with both hands, approaches the bed.)*

MR BALL: *(Hesitant.)* Mum?

(A nurse pulls back the sheet.
    Close-up MR BALL. *We see the condition of the ruined head from* MR BALL's *reaction to it.*
    He shakes his head, as if shaking away flies.)

Mum!

*(*JEAN BALL, *his elder daughter, comes up behind him and takes his arm. He*

turns to her blindly. She hugs him. MR BALL *weeps, perhaps for the first time in his life, heavy, painful tears.* JEAN *weeps, too.)*

(Interior. NERISSA'*s room. Night.*

NERISSA'*s room is lush. This neglected child's parents assuage their guilt by lavishing material things upon her. A dressing table laden with toilet waters and talcum powders – specifically teenage, 'period' products, Helena Rubinstein's 'Apple Blossom', Elizabeth Arden's 'Blue Grass' – boasts a heart-shaped mirror and tulle skirts. A white wardrobe bulges with smart clothes. Fluffy rugs, pretty floral wallpaper, curtains to match. Her own record player, a stack of seventy-eights. Books in a low, white case –* Enid Blyton, Angela Brazil, Little Women, *the* Brontës, Barbara Cartland, Lorna Doone, Keats, Shelley, *masses of film annuals, stacks of glossy film magazines – all suggesting wide, avid, undirected reading.*

Signed glossies of movie stars cover the walls. A plant-stand in front of a picture of James Mason holds a candle, lit and burning, a jamjar full of wildflowers. There is a big travel poster for Los Angeles. A constellation of pictures of Orson Welles as Harry Lime in The Third Man, *cut out of newspapers and magazines, is pinned round the head of the oversize bed.*

In spite of the pretty things it contains, the general feeling in the room isn't quite right – as if the idea of 'a young girl's room' had been taken to parodic excess. It is like a Fifties movie set.

Under a pink satin eiderdown, NERISSA *sits up in bed with a mug of hot chocolate on the night-table beside her, painting her fingernails – Revlon 'Love That Pink'.*

In the hollow of the eiderdown between her raised knees there is a rustling pile of banknotes, a shifting, clinking mound of coins.

Travel brochures litter the eiderdown.

LENA *lies in bed beside* NERISSA, *staring vacantly into space. Her untouched mug of chocolate gathers skin on the floor beside the bed.*

The sleeping tablets have had no effect on NERISSA. *She spreads out her left hand like a starfish, to dry the nails, and leans back, admiring the effect.)*

NERISSA: Nothing can part us, now. We are bound together for ever.

*(*LENA *does not move or make a sound.)*

(Exterior. Outside LOCKE *house. Day.*

Early morning. The police car we have seen before glides to a halt in front of the house.

A curtain moves at an upstairs window.

NERISSA *peers out.)*

(Interior. NERISSA'*s room. Day.*

NERISSA, *in quilted satin dressing gown and fluffy mules, bounces excitedly to the bed where* LENA *is uneasily sleeping.* NERISSA *shakes* LENA.)

NERISSA: They're here! We must stick to the script, whatever happens!

(LENA *shudders and stirs. Voices downstairs, in the hall.*)

Wake up!

(*Slowly, painfully,* LENA *prises her eyes open.*)

LENA: What's the matter? Mum? Mum –

(*Aghast, she wakes to the reality of the day.*)

(*Interior.* LENA *and* JEAN's *bedroom. Day.*
  LENA *wakes to the reality of the day.*)

MRS BALL: Don't want to be late, first day back.

(*Her mother stands by her bed, hanging a freshly ironed blouse over the back of the chair on which the red Girls' Grammar gymslip lies ready.* MRS BALL *is plain, rather plump, sad faced, enveloped in a pinafore.*
  JEAN's *bed is already empty; her nightdress lies on the pillow. The room is modestly, almost meanly, furnished. All is painfully clean. By Lena's bed, a pile of film annuals.*
  LENA, *half-asleep, thrusts her legs out of bed. She wears flannelette pyjamas. She squints at her mother accusingly.*)

LENA: (*As if it is her mother's fault she cannot.*) I was dreaming I could dance.

(*Exterior. Outside* BALL *house. Day.*
  A fine spring morning. The BALLS' *house is modest – one storey, tin roof, verandah. A bike is propped against the verandah rail.*
  JEAN BALL, *eighteen, crisp and neat, dark dress, white collar, clatters down the steps on her way to work. She calls back:*)

JEAN: 'Bye, Mum!

(LENA *follows her, slowly. She bumps the bike down the two steps to the road. She wears gymslip and blazer and the round felt hat that is the most hated part of the school uniform, held on under her chin by gnawed elastic. A brown canvas satchel on her back. Her limp is very pronounced.*
  Her mother comes out on to the porch and waves, with a faint, sad smile, as Lena pedals off. Lena coldly raises her hand in salute in return.)

(*Exterior. Christchurch. Day.*

As soon as LENA is out of sight of the house, she takes off her hat and slings it across the handlebars of her bike.

She rides through the town on her way to school, offering a capsule tour of Christchurch.

She enters a busy street, passing her father's shop. The door is wide open. Just before she reaches it, her father (no more than a vague figure in white) opens the door and empties a pail of ice and water into the street.

The water flies through the air, separating out into shining drops, crystals of ice and a hail of tiny silver fish.

LENA rides through a puddle, crunching ice and dying fish beneath her wheels.

She passes shops, a department store; then rides through Cathedral Square, with its grey stone cathedral, bus stops, tram stops, cinemas, its big Rover showroom with a window full of gleaming cars.

She slows down to savour the billboards of the cinemas, the posters, the glossy stills. A wide variety of movies are showing that week, including Pandora and the Flying Dutchman.

She passes the Art-Deco-style milk bar, the only teen meeting place in town. Inside the milk bar, a yawning girl in pink-gingham pedal-pushers wipes down the tables. This girl could almost be a different species from the Grammar School girls.

LENA crosses the river, with its willow-lined banks. She is nearing school; she puts her hat back on and speeds up. Everywhere uniformed girls now converge on the school on foot, by bike. MISS JOHNSON, the English teacher, chubby, busy, hurries along with her big leather briefcase.)

(Exterior. Outside gate of Christchurch Girls' Grammar. Day.

The school, Victorian Gothic, surrounded by asphalted yards marked out for netball and tennis; these courts are sectioned off with wire mesh.

The playground is already full of uniformed girls, playing hopscotch, playing tag, gossiping. More pour in through the wrought-iron gates as LENA rides up to them.

CAPTAIN QUINN's glamorous convertible screeches to a halt, forcing LENA on to the pavement, off her bike. She glares at the car and its occupants.

LENA's point-of-view shot: the car door opens. NERISSA climbs out gracefully. She wears her new uniform with an air; no satchel, but a grown-up briefcase of polished hide. She carries her hat in her hand as if it were an elegant accessory.

She bends down to speak to the man in the driving seat.)

(Interior. QUINN's car. Day.

The engine is running. QUINN, sullen, hand on the handbrake, anxious to be off, glares at NERISSA's pretty ironic smile. Reluctantly, he puts a half-crown piece in her outstretched palm.

Her fingers close over it.

Her smile widens into a grin.)

(Exterior. Outside school gates. Day.

Girls stare after the car. The crowd parts automatically to let NERISSA, *a swan among geese, through.)*

SCHOOLGIRL: *(Envious.)* Was that your father?

NERISSA: *(Crisp; contemptuous.)* No. Just a man we're thinking of buying a car from.

(Interior. Cloakroom. Day.

Long rows of coat-racks. Lockers where street shoes are kept during the day. Girls mill round, hanging up coats and hats, sitting to unfasten sturdy, laced Oxfords and change into soft, strapped Mary Janes.

NERISSA *sits, composedly changing her shoes. In the murk of the cloakroom, her hair and wonderful 'English' complexion shine.*

MISS JOHNSON *rushes up to her, beaming.)*

MISS JOHNSON: Nerissa Locke, isn't it. Welcome to the Girls' Grammar.

(The girls near by stir and murmur; what is the fuss about? NERISSA *gives* MISS JOHNSON *a small, tight smile and bends forward to fasten her shoe.* MISS JOHNSON*'s look of approval turns to mild anxiety as* NERISSA*'s hair swings across her face.)*

MISS JOHNSON: I say. Your hair, dear.

NERISSA: What's wrong with my hair?

MISS JOHNSON: We usually wear long hair in plaits.

NERISSA: *I* don't.

*(*LENA, *eyes on* NERISSA, *hangs up her coat, brushing against the girl next to her as she does so.)*

LENA: Ooops . . . sorry.

(The other girl, chatting animatedly to a friend, ignores LENA. LENA *is hurt.)*

(Interior. School chapel. Day.

Morning prayers. Light filters through stained glass; a Bible is open on a lectern. The school motto: Semper fidelis.

The girls stand in rows singing: 'To Be a Pilgrim'. A piano accompanies. All hold hymn books. A shaft of light falls on NERISSA *through one of the high windows.* LENA *stands behind her, watching light play on* NERISSA*'s hair.*

The hymn ends.)

HEADMISTRESS: Let us pray.

(*The girls incline their heads. As they do so,* LENA *reaches out and touches* NERISSA*'s hair.*

NERISSA *jumps as though a charge of electricity has passed from* LENA *to her. She turns; their eyes meet.*)

HEADMISTRESS: (*Intoning.*) Dearly beloved . . .

(*Interior. Classroom. Day.*

Chalked on the blackboard: JOHN KEATS, 1795–1821. *The girls sit, with varying degrees of attention, over open books. It is* NERISSA*'s turn to read aloud.*)

NERISSA: I saw pale kings, and princes too,
    Pale warriors, death-pale were they all,
Who cried: 'La Belle Dame sans merci
    Hath thee in thrall!'

I saw their starv'd lips in the gloam
    With horrid warning gapéd wide,
And I awoke, and found me here,
    On the cold hill side.

And this is why I sojourn here
    Alone and palely loitering,
Though the sedge is wither'd from the lake,
    And no birds sing.

(*She recites beautifully.* LENA *gazes at* NERISSA *as if bewitched.*

When NERISSA *finishes the poem, she catches* LENA*'s eye again, and almost falters, has to fumble for her chair and sit down suddenly;* LENA*'s gaze is of burning intensity.*)

MISS JOHNSON: That was lovely, Nerissa. And so it should be! Girls, Nerissa's father is the new professor of English Literature at the university. She has poetry as her heritage.
And she arrived here from England only just this last month so it's up to us to make her feel at home.

(*Exterior. School grounds. Day.*

Break time. Netball practice. The rest of the girls run, shout, play games, talk secrets, according to age.

NERISSA *idly watches the netball practice through the wire netting fence. The other girls make no attempt to approach her – she is far too intimidating.* LENA *stumps past* NERISSA *on the opposite side of the wire netting.* NERISSA *watches her, curiously. Then* LENA *stumps back.* NERISSA *watches her with even more attention. Sure she has captured the other girl's attention, LENA returns one more time. This time, she stops.)*

LENA: You've got a funny name.

NERISSA: Shakespeare. *The Merchant of Venice.*

LENA: If you could teach me to talk like you, I'd give you anything you want.

NERISSA: I make a lot of demands on my friends. Not many people are strong enough.

LENA: I'm tough. I can take it.

(Both girls now begin to walk along the wire-netting fence towards the point where they will meet.)

You've got hair like a filmstar. Like Deborah Kerr, but with more sensuality.

NERISSA: I don't know. What about *From Here to Eternity*?

LENA: I sat the programme round, then sat it round again.

(They arrive at the end of the wire-netting fence. They stop. They look at one another.)

NERISSA: Don't you think Hollywood must be wonderful?

(Interior. LENA and JEAN's bedroom. Night.

JEAN, in a rayon slip, sits at the modest dressing table, putting her hair in curlers. She is vague and dreamy. LENA, in her flannelette pyjamas, sits up in bed. Her satchel, spilling books, lies on the floor. An exercise book is open on the bed; LENA is peeking inside her pencil case, lovingly as if the pencil case contained something very precious.

Close-up inside the pencil case, a freshly cut lock of blonde hair.)

LENA: There's a new girl at school.

(She closes the pencil case.)

She's got naturally curly, long blonde hair. Not like yours.

JEAN: *(Tolerant, even amused. She is used to Lena's ways.)* Lucky little thing.

LENA: Her father's a professor at the university. She's got a lovely voice. She's going to give me elocution lessons.

(JEAN is too kind to laugh but she raises her eyebrows.)

(Exterior. Outside LOCKE *home. Night.*

Under the stars of the Southern hemisphere, the LOCKES' *new home blazes with light streaming from uncurtained windows.*

Figures can be seen moving backwards and forwards inside.)

(Interior. COLIN LOCKE's *study. Night.*

Bookcases, empty as yet, line the walls. A huge desk. No family photographs on it, only a framed, signed photograph of F. R. Leavis. A silver tray with a decanter and glasses on top of a glass-fronted cabinet.

Tea chests containing books half-fill the room. COLIN LOCKE *is unpacking and arranging his library. Piles of books already stand on the desk, chairs, floor.*

COLIN LOCKE, *a tall, thin, balding man in his late thirties, has come to Christchurch solely as a career move.*

QUINN *pokes his head round the door.)*

QUINN: Care to join us for a nightcap, old chap?

*(*LOCKE, *without looking up, gestures to his decanter.)*

Then I'll go and take care of Mary, shall I?

*(*LOCKE *opens a book and consults it.)*

COLIN: *(Seemingly unaware of innuendo.)* You do that small thing.

(Interior. Sitting room. Night.

The sitting room is still under wraps. MARY LOCKE *is hanging one of her Redouté rose prints. The windows reflect the room. The sofa is covered with a dust sheet; tea chests, everywhere. On top of one tea chest, a bottle of gin, tonic, glasses.*

QUINN *creeps up behind* MARY *and plucks at her buttons – she wears her high-necked cardigan back to front, Barbara Goalen-style.)*

MARY: Now, now, Douggie.

(Interior. NERISSA's *room. Night.*

NERISSA's *room is also not yet unpacked but she is taking time off to indulge in her favourite pastime, dressing up. She wears one of her mother's straight black skirts and a cherry-red cardigan buttoned down the back – exactly what her mother is wearing. Her hair is done up in a French pleat. She leans towards the mirror, applying her mother's lipstick. ('Rubies in the Snow':) She steps back.*

She looks exactly like her mother.

She glances over her shoulder to see if her seams are straight.

Then she deliberately inserts one hand inside her cardigan, reaching up from below, and palpates her left breast. She addresses herself in the mirror.)

NERISSA: *(Imitating her mother's clipped tones to perfection.)* Christ, Douggie, not in front of the kid.

(Interior. Cinema. Day.

On the screen, the credits of Pandora and the Flying Dutchman, *directed by Albert Lewin, 1951. James Mason, Ava Gardner.*

Towards the back of the packed cinema, NERISSA *and* LENA *loll against one another, rapt.* NERISSA *wears attractive Saturday clothes – a pleated skirt, a sweater – but* LENA *has on a skimpy cotton frock, a hand-me-down from* JEAN, *and her school blazer because she doesn't have another jacket.*

They become aware of rustling and giggling in the row behind. Both glance over their shoulders.

LENA *recognises the snoggers; they are her sister,* JEAN, *and* JEAN's *boyfriend,* STAN. *She cowers.)*

NERISSA: *(Icy, furious.)* Some of us came here to watch the picture!

*(*STAN *and* JEAN, *amazed, laugh but desist.)*

(Interior. Cinema. Day.

On screen: the twined bodies of the two fated lovers are dragged out of the sea in the nets of fishermen, two lovers united in death and eternity.)

(Exterior. Countryside. Day.

The girls cycle down a country road.)

NERISSA: Do you believe that love is stronger than death? Mad love?

LENA: It depends who loves, it depends who dies.

NERISSA: I say, that's frightfully good.

LENA: I could worship that man. His quality of velvet menace . . .

NERISSA: Let's make a little shrine in my room and light candles to him.

(Beat.)

That was your sister, wasn't it.

LENA: *(Reluctant.)* Yes. With Stan. He works in the same office. I wouldn't die for Stan. Funny what some people will settle for.
I want . . . so much. *(She repeats, insistent; we realise she is insatiable.)* I want *so much!*

NERISSA: I'll tell you how we get our start in the movies. We go to the Masons' home and offer to babysit for Portland.

LENA: How do we find the house?

NERISSA: Send for one of those maps of Hollywood that show you where the stars live. There's a box number in *Photoplay.*

LENA: Once ensconced in his house, we use our contacts to infiltrate the film industry. (*Sincere.*) You'll soon get a job modelling or acting, something like that. You're quite pretty enough.

(NERISSA *accepts this as no more than her due.*)

NERISSA: What about you?

LENA: I'll direct. Direct, write, produce. You'll be my star.

(*Exhilarated, they freewheel wildly down a slope, gathering speed frighteningly quickly, fearless, shrieking ecstatically.*)

(*Interior.* LOCKE *kitchen. Day.*

A pair of beautiful hands, with red varnished nails, are preparing an elaborate tea tray – white linen cloth, sprig of jasmine in a posy vase, Royal Doulton china, napkins, rolled cucumber sandwiches, a saucer of lemon slices.

All we see of MARY LOCKE *as she prepares the tea tray are her hands, but we hear the click of her high heels on the tiled floor.*

The beautiful hands pick up the tray.)

(*Interior.* LOCKE *house. Day.*

The tray goes down the passage to PROFESSOR LOCKE's *study. His door stands slightly ajar.*

Close-up a bare foot in a smart, high-heeled sandal kicks the door open.

The tray is borne aloft into the study. MARY *breaks into song.*)

MARY: 'Tea for two and two for tea,
          Me for you and you for me – '

(*Interior.* LOCKE *study. Day.*

COLIN LOCKE *sits behind his desk, surrounded by books and papers. He is reading the journal,* Scrutiny. *He looks up as* MARY *comes in, smiling appreciatively.*

COLIN's *point-of-view shot:* MARY *is naked, but for her sandals, a string of pearls, and a frilly apron.*)

COLIN: Have you ever thought of taking up naturism?

(MARY *bursts into furious tears. She slams the tray down on the desk. Tea spills out of the spout of the pot on to the traycloth.*)

MARY: Never say I didn't try!

(*Exterior. Cathedral Square. Night.*

LENA *and* NERISSA *part affectionately and bike off their separate ways.*

NERISSA *wings through the dark, smiling, joyous.*)

(*Interior.* LOCKE *sitting room. Night.*

MARY *hasn't turned the light on. She has slipped into a silk kimono. She takes a cigarette from the silver box, lights it at the table lighter, opens up the radiogram, sets down the arm on a record.*

The voice of Edith Piaf singing 'No Regrets' fills the darkened room.

MARY *paces, listens, cries.*

The sound of the front door slamming is heard above the music.

MARY *hastily dries her eyes.)*

MARY: Douggie? Is that you?

(NERISSA *opens the sitting-room door, turns on the light switch.*

MARY *blinks away the last of her tears.)*

NERISSA: *(Shouting to make herself heard.)* What are you doing, sitting in the dark?

MARY: *(Also shouting.)* Why shouldn't I if I want to?

(The record ends, leaving them staring at one another, wondering why they are shouting.)

NERISSA: *(Normal voice.)* Can I bring my friend home next Saturday?

MARY: Friend? What friend. You don't make friends. You're famous for it. Every time they kick you out of another school, they always make the point: 'she finds it difficult to find friends who meet her high standards.'

NERISSA: *(Defiant.)* Lena Ball.

MARY: Lena Ball.

NERISSA: Her father runs that fish shop.

MARY: What fish shop?

NERISSA: Where you got the crayfish.

MARY: What, that big, fat man? Is his daughter at the Girls' Grammar?

NERISSA: She's nice.

MARY: Christ. What an egalitarian place New Zealand is.

(Exterior. Cathedral Square. Day.

Sunday morning. Brilliant sunshine. Church bells. The good folk of Christchurch gather to attend matins. COLIN *and* MARY LOCKE, *in elegant suits, hats, arrive in front of the Cathedral, accompanied by their lovely daughter, also in suit and hat.*

A white van chugs through the square. It has: L.W. BALL, FRESH FISH, *written on the side.*

NERISSA *lingers behind her parents to watch it carry off her new-found friend as dignified elders greet* COLIN *and* MARY.)

(Interior. Cabin of BALL *delivery van. Day.*

LENA *peers out of the window, gazing after the disappearing figure of* NERISSA.

She, JEAN, MR *and* MRS BALL *and a big picnic basket are crammed into the cabin.* MR BALL, *in Sunday suit and hat – the clothes he will wear to visit his wife's body in hospital – drives.* MRS BALL, *in cloth coat and felt hat, the clothes she will wear to be murdered, sits beside him. He pats her thigh. She gives him a small, secret smile. Radiant with anticipation she looks quite lovely.*

LENA, *school blazer hunched over hand-me-down dress, is sullen.)*

(Exterior. Outside nursing home. Day.

BOBBS, *the youngest* BALL *child, a Down's Syndrome eight-year-old, lives in a handsome, colonial building surrounded by well-cared-for gardens. There is no sense of a madhouse or a prison; all is comfort and kindness.*

The whole sequence of the Sunday visit to BOBBS *is done in warm, glowing colours.*

A small boy appears on the nursing-home steps. He dashes down into the arms of MRS BALL *as she runs forward to meet him. She picks him up, hugs him. He beams. He is very lovable. His father picks him up and swings him round.* JEAN *comes up to kiss him, smiling.* LENA *stays in the cabin, miserably.)*

MR BALL: Come on, Bobbs! Picnic!

(A kind-faced nurse appears at the nursing-home door to wave them off.

LENA's *point-of-view shot: she watches from the cabin as the family party dawdle back to the van. The party is quite complete without her.)*

(Exterior. Victoria Park. Day.

LENA *sits, arms round her knees, among the debris of the picnic, watching the others attempt an improvised game of rounders.*

BOBBS, *chasing a ball, toddles up to* LENA. *She looks at him apprehensively. He puts his arms round her neck.)*

LENA: Go away. I can't play rounders with you. I've got a bad leg.

(He hugs her. Reluctantly, she cuddles him back. Then kisses his cheek, she can't resist.)

MRS BALL: Bobbs! Your turn!

(He rushes back to his mother at once. LENA, *upset, looks longingly after the little boy and the game she can't play.)*

(Exterior. Seashore. Day.

Sunset. The water shines brilliantly. The white van drives along a deserted road by the shore. MRS BALL, *with* BOBBS *on her lap, occupies the seat with the view.)*

(Interior. Cabin of delivery van. Day.

MRS BALL *points out the seabirds to* BOBBS.)

MRS BALL: Look, lovie, see the birdies!

(Black swans swim on the shining water.)

Oh, Bobbs, look!

*(*LENA, *squashed under the empty picnic basket, huddles in her blazer, miserable, left out.)*

(Exterior. Outside nursing home. Day.

MR *and* MRS BALL *stand at the top of the steps,* MR BALL *with the blissfully sleeping* BOBBS *in his arms.*

He is in the process of handing the child back to the nurse. MRS BALL *kisses* BOBBS's *cheek.)*

MR BALL: See you next week, Sister.

(She takes the sleeping child warmly, then looks at the BALLS *in distress, genuinely upset at having to mention money.)*

NURSE: Oh, Mr Ball, next week . . . d'you think you could have a word with the almoner? I hate to mention it, but there's the question of one or two little extras.

MR BALL: Certainly, Sister. Of course, Sister.

(Interior. Cabin. Day.

The van drives back along the road to Christchurch. Now MRS BALL *sits next to* MR BALL. LENA *has got her book out – her school textbook copy of Keats's poems – and is darkly reading.* MR BALL *drives with his hand on his wife's knee.* JEAN *sleeps.)*

MR BALL: Good day, Mother?

MRS BALL: Lovely.

(Interior. BALL *living room. Night.*

A faded old three-piece suite in uncut moquette; a bookcase with some of

LENA's *schoolbooks, some knitting pattern books, a few paperback novelettes, a pile of Reader's Digests, a film annual. A table, chairs. A sideboard.*

On the sideboard, photographs of JEAN *and* LENA, *as children, and one, in a silver frame, of* MRS BALL *with* BOBBY *as a baby on her knee. It is impossible to tell from the photograph that* BOBBY *is a Down's Syndrome child.*

There is no wedding photograph.

Through the open door, in the back kitchen, MRS BALL *is filling a kettle for tea.)*

MRS BALL: Lena, get out the cups.

*(*LENA *opens the sideboard, gets out a stack of cups and saucers. She takes them to the table. Then, deliberately, she picks up a tea-cup and hurls it to the ground. It smashes.*

MRS BALL *appears in the doorway, distressed.)*

MRS BALL: Stop that.

*(*LENA *picks up another cup.)*

MRS BALL: Put that down and sweep up.

(As if doing her mother a great favour, LENA *puts the cup down again. She turns back to the sideboard and picks up the photograph of* MRS BALL *and* BOBBY.

She gives her mother a bright, artificial smile.

She raises the photograph above her head as if she were about to smash that, too.)

MRS BALL: Lena!

*(*JEAN *comes in from the passage, at a run. She treats* LENA *warily, as one would a wild animal, approaching her from behind.)*

JEAN: Calm down, Lena. Be a good girl.

(She catches LENA *off her guard, snatches away the photograph, gives it to her mother.*

LENA *covers her face with her hands, bursts into tears, rushes from the room.)*

(Interior. MR *and* MRS BALL's *bedroom. Night.*

Old-fashioned bed (brass?). On the mantelpiece, another framed photograph of BOBBY, *this time taken by a professional photographer of the High Street kind.* MR *and* MRS BALL *lie in the light from a street lamp that seeps in through the drawn blind.*

MRS BALL *cries quietly.*

MR BALL, *in striped pyjamas, tries to take her into his arms.*

She pushes him away, sadly.)

MRS BALL: It makes my heart turn over.

MR BALL: She's not a happy girl, Mother.

MRS BALL: I wish I could make her happy.

(Exterior. Netball court. Day.
Girls in maroon knickers play netball in the background, supervised by MISS
FERGUSON. LENA *and* NERISSA *lounge beside the wire netting, fully dressed.)*

NERISSA: I'm glad you told me about him, Lena. You mustn't be ashamed.

LENA: He's the Monster of Glamis. He's the dark secret of the Ball family.
Mum must have done something dreadful to be saddled with him.

*(*NERISSA *watches the athletic girls on the pitch leap and run.)*

NERISSA: How did you get your limp?

LENA: *(Gruff.)* Polio.

NERISSA: *(Genuine sympathy.)* Oh, poor thing.

LENA: I was in hospital a year. I was six. I was in an iron lung, at first. They thought I'd never walk again.

(She has never considered the drama of it before, not until NERISSA *says:)*

NERISSA: You might have spent the rest of your life in a wheelchair!

LENA: I learned to walk again. It was a struggle. At least it gets me off all that. *(She makes a face and gestures at the netball pitch.)*

NERISSA: I'm excused games because of TB.

LENA: What Keats died of.

NERISSA: I got better then but I might still die of it. I have to have a check-up every six months. I'm always scared my lungs will flare up and I'll have to go back to a sanatorium again.

LENA: My family never came. I lay and watched a patch of sunlight. Little patch. It moved along the wall. I was all alone. For a year.

NERISSA: They sent me to Switzerland. I was the youngest person in the sanatorium, I was ten. Switzerland was much too far away for them to come and visit, so *they* never came.

LENA: We've got rotten parents. They don't deserve lovely, clever daughters like us.

NERISSA: *(Only half-joking.)* I make them pay.
I say, *Strangers on a Train* at the Roxy, this week.

(Interior. LOCKE kitchen. Day.
Unsupervised, the girls raid the larder for their tea.)

LENA: I liked the bit where you saw the murder reflected in her sunglasses. That was original. I wish I'd thought of that.

NERISSA: Hot chocolate, not boring old tea. Cut some bread, for toast.

(She emerges from the larder clutching a white jar.)

This is good on toast. 'Gentleman's Relish'. It's Quinn the Thing's favourite, he's stocked the larder with it, enough for years, although he *says* he's looking for a place of his own.

LENA: *(Lightly.)* Roger the lodger.

NERISSA: Daddy came out by himself, first of all, to check things were all right, then Mummy and me were shipped out later, with the furniture. There was Quinn, at the Captain's table, on his way to sell Rovers. Ex-RAF, you know. Officer class.

LENA: What did the band play?

(NERISSA puts bread under the grill to toast; she holds out her arms to LENA.)

NERISSA: Slow fox trot.

(NERISSA hums a tune. They dance round and round the kitchen table, like Fred and Ginger, first a little clumsily then with more and more brio. LENA's limp does not manifest itself.)

LENA: *(As they dance.)* Shipboard romance. The time, the opportunity, the moonlight on the afterdeck. White dinner jackets. Her silk dress slithers to the ground.

(NERISSA bends backwards, LENA supports her in a striking pose borrowed from a musical.)

(Interior. NERISSA's bedroom. Night.
The tray, stacked with dirty dishes, is stowed away under the bed. The curtains are drawn, candles lit, throwing eerie shadows. Candles on the dressing-table illuminate the mirror, from which LENA's face looks back at herself, astonished.

NERISSA has just given her a facial. Made up, LENA looks much older, even more secret, even more of a witch – but a desperately sexy witch.)

LENA: It *does* make a difference.

(NERISSA twitches away the towel with which she has swathed LENA *while she made her up.)*

NERISSA: You should see my mother without her face on. She looks all washed out. She won't let *me* wear make-up until I'm sixteen, mean pig. *(Imitating her mother's voice.)* 'If you want to go round looking like a tart . . .'

(Interior. NERISSA*'s room. Night.*
    The candle wax is dripping down the sides of the candles.
    The girls are finishing off their shrine to James Mason. The plant-stand is in place in front of the photograph. NERISSA *puts a handful of garden flowers, arranged in a jamjar, reverently down on the plant-stand.*
    LENA *lights the fresh candle standing ready.*
    First NERISSA, *then* LENA *kiss the photograph. Both are now heavily made up. Each leaves a neat, lipstick kiss on the surface of the photograph.*
    They kneel, they close their eyes. They are playing a game, playing roles, but their discontent gives the game a bitter edge.)

LENA: What are you praying for?

NERISSA: *(Fierce.)* To wake up tomorrow and *be* Deborah Kerr, instead of just looking like her.
    I would be less bored in Hollywood.

LENA: Let's go, then.

NERISSA: Have you got a passport?

LENA: How do I get one?

NERISSA: You need your birth certificate, I think.

(Interior. NERISSA*'s bedroom. Night.*
    The candles are burning low; melted wax has collected at their bottoms. LENA *stands in the middle of the floor with her hands clasped behind her back.)*

LENA: Oh, what can ail thee, knight at arms –

NERISSA: Round vowels, Miss Ball! Round O's! O! O! O!

*(*LENA *throws a pillow at* NERISSA. *She parodies the sound.)*

LENA: O! O! O!

*(*NERISSA *joins in.)*

NERISSA: O! O! O!

(Emitting a stream of these high, round, 'O's, the girls prance round the room

*like gigantic birds. The candles do strange things with their dancing shadows.
They don't sound human; they sound fantastic, ominous, as if emitting stylised
cries of distress.)*

(Interior. LOCKE *hall. Night.*
  The girls stand at the front door; outside, a horn beeps.)

LENA: *(Perfect English accent.)* Thanks so much.

NERISSA: Pleasure! Don't forget. Passport.

(The horn beeps again; LENA *opens the front door and calls:)*

LENA: Coming, Dad!

(Interior. Cabin of BALL *van. Night.*
  They drive across the river, towards home.)

MR BALL: Where had her parents gone, that you got your own tea.

LENA: *(Purposely vague.)* They've bought a little summer place out at
Fort Levy, they'd gone to get it into shape.
Nerissa says I can go and stay with her out there.

MR BALL: You'd better get that stuff off your face before your mother
sees you.

(Interior. BALL *bedroom. Day.*
  LENA *crouches in front of the chest of drawers, rapidly going through its
contents.*
  *She brings out an old shoebox full of papers from the bottom drawer of the
chest. She spills the shoebox's contents on the bed, hastily riffles through it. She
picks out several documents all pinned together, inspects them.*
  *She finds what she is looking for – her birth certificate – and gives a big sigh of
satisfaction. She removes it from the other birth certificates, gives it a quick look.*
  Then looks again, scrutinises it more closely.
  *The birth certificate gives her mother's name as 'Jones'. And specifies that she
is unmarried. The father's name is there, all right –* LEONARD WILLIAM BALL.
But the birth certificate shows that LENA's *parents never married.*
  LENA *looks at the other birth certificates.*
  *Then folds them up, pins them back together, stuffs everything back in the
shoebox.*
  Her face is filled with curiosity and satisfaction.
  *She puts her own birth certificate in her gymslip pocket, puts the shoebox back
in the chest of drawers, makes sure everything is as she found it.*
  As she kneels in front of the chest of drawers, MRS BALL *opens the bedroom
door.)*

MRS BALL: Lena! What are you up to!

(LENA *brazens it out.*)

LENA: I was looking for my birth certificate.
I found it, Mum. It makes very interesting reading.

(MRS BALL *sits down heavily on the bed.*)

MRS BALL: Jean knows. I was going to tell you when you were a bit older. We never did anything wrong.

LENA: All the same, I'm a bastard as well as a cripple.

(MRS BALL *flinches at the word, 'bastard'.*)

MRS BALL: Your father got married when he was overseas in the forces, when he was Jean's age. She's a Catholic, she won't divorce. She's on the other side of the world. What difference does it make?

LENA: Every time I do anything official – apply for a passport, something like that – everybody will know what my mother did. That she –

(MRS BALL *draws in her breath sharply and cuffs* LENA *round the ear before she can finish.*
LENA *can't believe it. She touches her ear, looks aghast at her mother and rushes past her out of the room.*
After a moment, MRS BALL, *breathing heavily, terribly upset goes after her.*)

(*Interior.* BALL *home. Day.*
The sound of the toilet flushing comes from the bathroom. MRS BALL *pauses, listens, goes on into the living room.*

(*Interior. Living room. Day.*
MRS BALL *leans on the table, trying to recover herself.*
LENA *appears in the living-room doorway, white faced, accusing, tragic.*)

LENA: Mum, I'm bleeding. You made me bleed when you hit me. It's all your fault.

(*Interior. Hairdressing salon. Day.*
Close-up the ramping plaster Elizabeth Arden 'Blue Grass' horse, presiding over the salon.
The place is packed. Every pink plastic seat occupied by a client ensconced beneath a hooded drier. MARY LOCKE, *swathed in lilac towels, smokes whilst a girl in a lilac overall piles up her hair in a sculptural coiffure.*)

HAIRDRESSER: Lucky we could fit you in, Mrs Locke. The afternoon of the Armed Services Ball is our busiest time.

MARY: Any chance of a manicure?

(Interior. NERISSA's room. Day.
LENA and NERISSA sit on the floor, in Saturday clothes.)

NERISSA: Didn't she ever tell you? I've had mine for ages. Now you can have babies.

LENA: *(Making a face.)* Ugh.

NERISSA: There's this rubber thing. If you don't want babies, you put it up inside you.

LENA: How horrible.

NERISSA: Mummy's got one.

(Interior. MARY LOCKE's bedroom. Day.
A pretty room in the same style as the sitting room. Crystal bottles on the dressing table. A sense of class.
The wardrobe swings open to reveal a classic early Fifties ball dress in ivory satin and chiffon, swishing on a hanger. High-heeled, silver sandals stand ready, flimsy stockings, suspender belt.
NERISSA and LENA tiptoe in. LENA shakes the ball-dress skirt so that it dances.)

NERISSA: She loves to dance. When she's going to a party, she comes in to say goodnight in her party frock. The skirts go, swish. She smells lovely. She bends down to kiss me. Her earrings brush my cheek.

LENA: *(Envious.)* My mother never goes out in the evenings, at all. She keeps herself to herself.

(She opens the top drawer of the dressing table and tosses a foamy pile of lingerie into the air.)

You'd never catch her in tarts' knickers, even if she *has* dropped three bastards.

(NERISSA extracts a plastic case from beneath the lingerie.)

NERISSA: Nobody told Miss Jones about this little contraption.

(She opens the case and picks out, between thumb and fingertip, her mother's diaphragm. She blows off a cloud of the cornstarch with which it is dusted.)

LENA: However do you get it all inside you!

NERISSA: I don't know.

(She bends the diaphragm into a bow and releases it with a twang. It flies across the room. They rummage in the dressing-table drawer.

NERISSA strips off her skirt and jumper, pulls on one of MARY's black lace slips.)

LENA: *(Appreciative.)* Very tarty.

NERISSA: Let's dress up.

(They ransack the drawers and wardrobe with increasing excitement, riffling through blouses, sweaters, suspender belts, bras, hats. NERISSA chooses a taffeta skirt with an off-the-shoulder blouse, pulled well down, mesh stockings, high-heeled sandals. LENA puts on a tight, black, polo-neck sweater and the straight black skirt we have seen MARY wearing. LENA looks at herself doubtfully in the mirror.)

NERISSA: Come here.

(She wields a big pair of scissors. She seizes hold of LENA's skirt and snips the right seam as far as the thigh.)

LENA: Won't your mother be angry?

(She extends her leg, watching herself in the mirror.)

NERISSA: She wouldn't dare.

(She throws LENA a black beret from the wardrobe. LENA tries it on at an existential angle.

She really does look like the conventional image of a tart.)

NERISSA: *(Singing.)* 'Underneath the lamplight, by the city square . . .'

LENA AND NERISSA: *(In triumphant unison.)* 'My own Lili Marlene, my own Lili Marlene.'

(Interior. LOCKE kitchen. Day.

QUINN, fresh home from the Rover showroom, comes into the kitchen to find the girls are getting their tea. They are still in fancy dress, and have made up their faces, too. He carries a leather chauffeur's cap.)

QUINN: Isn't that one of Mary's skirts, Lena?

NERISSA: Not now.

QUINN: Mind you don't go out like that. Somebody might get the wrong idea.

NERISSA: *(Pert; contemptuously defiant.)* What idea might *that* be?

QUINN: God, you're a spoiled brat, Nerissa. If you were my daughter . . .

(Arms akimbo, full of impudence and irony, low-neck blouse, sexy, challenging, she faces him.)

NERISSA: Well, I'm not.

(LENA picks up the tea tray, nervously.)

LENA: Let's go up, Deborah . . .

(He watches them leave the room, sexually irritated by them, then he tries on the leather chauffeur's cap, looking at the effect in the mirror over the sink. He tilts it rakishly.)

(Interior. LOCKE hall. Night.

LENA and NERISSA watch through the banisters of the upstairs landing as COLIN helps MARY into a fur wrap.

LENA and NERISSA's point-of-view shot: the beautiful couple — MARY, superbly elegant and icily beautiful in the ball dress, turns like a model to show off her best points. COLIN is smart in evening dress.

The girls stare, hungry and wistful.

The doorbell rings. COLIN opens the door. QUINN, sporting the chauffeur's cap, salutes.)

QUINN: The motor is at your disposal, sir, madame.

MARY: *(Laughter.)* Douggie, you clown!

(Laughing, they go out, slamming the door, leaving a silence.)

NERISSA: She never did.

LENA: Never did what?

NERISSA: Never came to kiss me goodnight. No rustling taffeta. No 'Jolie Madame'. I was making it all up.

(She leaps to her feet, strides off in the direction of MARY's room, nearly hysterical.)

I'm going to rip that rubber thing to pieces —

(LENA follows her, calmer. NERISSA's outburst is interrupted by a fit of coughing. She catches hold of LENA, hugs her tight.)

Oh, God, I'm not well. I'm so glad you're staying the night.

(LENA holds her, soothes her.)

(Interior. QUINN's *car. Night.*

MARY *and* COLIN *sit like royalty in the back. Christchurch glides by.)*

MARY: Like riding through Toy Town.

*(*QUINN *adjusts the driving mirror to catch* MARY's *eye.)*

QUINN: The pumpkin will pick you up prompt at midnight, Cinders.

MARY: Lovely, Douggie. What a treat! My very own chauffeur!

(She stretches luxuriously, smiles – all for his benefit.)

COLIN: 'Fraid I'll have to stay on well after that, myself. Duty calls, you
know.

MARY: *(In a Larry the Lamb voice.)*
Oh, Mr Mayor, sir!

COLIN: *(Tetchy.)* You're perfectly at liberty to plead a headache and piss
off whenever you please. Just don't make a scene, that's all.

(Interior. LOCKE *upper landing. Night.*

LENA, *in pyjamas, comes out of the bathroom. She hugs the wall as she hears
voices and sees pale shapes outside the glass panels on the front door.*

LENA's *point-of-view shot: the front door opens;* MARY *and* QUINN *come
into the lighted hall. He pulls off her wrap. He takes off the chauffeur's cap and
throws it on to the hall stand.)*

QUINN: How did you enjoy dancing with the Lord Mayor of
Christchurch without any knickers on, you naughty little thing.

*(He presses her up against the wall, fumbling with his trousers. She is limp and
faint with desire.*

LENA, *expressionless, pads away. After a few seconds, she returns with
NERISSA, in her dressing gown. NERISSA looks pale and ill.*

They watch through the banisters, intent as QUINN *and* MARY *have sex
against the wall downstairs.)*

(Interior. NERISSA's *bedroom. Day.*

A nightdress flops into a suitcase, open on NERISSA's *bed. The suitcase is
covered with luggage labels from exotic places. It already contains underclothes,
books, film-star magazines.*

LENA *is helping* NERISSA *pack.* NERISSA *looks ill, fretful, not smart, almost
plain. She wears her Sunday tweed skirt, a clean blouse.* LENA *touches
NERISSA's luggage labels lovingly.)*

LENA: What a shame I can't get a passport, yet. Stupid bureaucracy. Or I

could have whisked you off out of their clutches somewhere warm
and nursed you back to health.

(NERISSA *gives the James Mason shrine a regretful look. Its flowers are dead,
its candle burned out.*)

NERISSA: I'll just have to abandon the shrine.

(*Sound of vehicle on gravel outside.*)

MARY: (*From below.*) Nerissa! The car's here!

NERISSA: Pass my jacket.

(LENA *solicitously helps her on with it.*)

MARY: (*From below.*) We haven't got all day, you know!

NERISSA: Kiss me goodbye.

(*Shyly,* LENA *kisses* NERISSA*'s cheek.* NERISSA *is shy, too.*)

(*Exterior.* LOCKE *house. Day.*
    LENA*'s bike is propped on the front porch.* QUINN *waits, in the convertible.*)

NERISSA: (*Balking.*) Why isn't my daddy taking me to the sanatorium?

MARY: You know very well Colin can't drive. It's very kind of Douggie
    to give up an afternoon's work to take us.

(NERISSA*'s face crumples.*)

    Oh, don't be theatrical, Nerissa. It's only for three months or so.
    Then you'll be fit as a fiddle.

(*She stows* NERISSA*'s suitcase away in the boot. Then, touched by remorse, she
takes* NERISSA*'s hand.*)

    The sooner we get there, the sooner you'll start to get better.

(NERISSA *clutches hold of* MARY*'s hand, grateful.*)

NERISSA: (*To* LENA.) Write to me. Write lots.

LENA: (*With a sob.*) Get well soon.

(NERISSA *climbs into the back of the car.* MARY *closes the door and gets in
beside* QUINN. *They drive off.* LENA *waves, once. She doesn't cry again. Her
face sets hard.
    After the sound of the car dies away, the sound of New Zealand birdsong is
unusually loud.*)

(*Interior.* MARY LOCKE*'s bedroom. Day.*

The curtains are drawn, but the sun shines through. MARY, *in a negligée, opens the plastic case that contains her diaphragm.*
The rubber has been ripped to pieces.)

(Interior. COLIN LOCKE's *study. Day.*
MARY, *eyes ablaze, confronting* COLIN *across his crowded desk.)*

MARY: I'll send her grapes and face–cream and buns and choccies and all the damn' copies of *Photoplay* her film-besotted little brain can absorb but I positively and absolutely refuse to go and visit her. Not after what *she's* done.
Why don't *you* go?

COLIN: Why should I go? She isn't my daughter.

MARY: That's not true!

COLIN: *(Surprisingly gentle.)* Don't let's argue again. The point is, we'll never know.

MARY: Nothing ever went right because of her.

COLIN: *(Again, surprisingly gentle.)* At least protect my career. You owe me that.

MARY: My cash greased the wheels of your bloody career.

COLIN: Guilt is a wonderful thing.

(They catch one another's eye and laugh reluctantly. They have been together a very long time. MARY *comes round to his side of the desk, sits on the arm of his chair.)*

MARY: Colin . . . I'm sorry it didn't work out, here, Colin. We should never have come.

COLIN: *(Cool.)* It wasn't working in Aberystwyth, either, Mary.

(Chilled off, MARY *retreats to the other side of the desk. She reverts to her familiar, brittle tone.)*

MARY: No doubt the Nerissa problem will resolve itself in time. Thank God she's found a little film fan to be friends with.
I say, perhaps Lena and her mum might find it in their hearts to visit Nerissa.

COLIN: *(Already immersed in papers.)* That's a thought.

(Exterior. Road. Day.
The white van passes the Kiwi bacon sign.)

(Interior. Sanatorium. Day.

Everything white. NERISSA *lies in a white bed. Books, movie magazines on her locker. Instead of photographs of mother and father, a picture of James Mason in a frame.* MRS BALL, *in her Sunday clothes, sits by the bed,* LENA *beside her.*

MRS BALL *presents* NERISSA *with a bulky newspaper package.*

NERISSA *unwraps the package to reveal a glass jar of whitebait. It is such an unexpected present she begins to laugh. The laughter provokes a fit of coughing.*

As she coughs, agitating the bed, the jar of fish falls to the ground, breaking, scattering fish, liquid and broken glass.

MRS BALL *seizes* LENA*'s hand and drags her away as a nurse comes flying to pull the curtains round* NERISSA*'s bed.)*

(Interior. Sanatorium. Day.

Outside the ward door, LENA *throws herself to the floor.)*

LENA: If you don't let me stay with her, I'll scream and scream and scream –

(The nurse comes out of the ward, carrying a tin basin containing fragments of glass and fish.)

NURSE: *(To* MRS BALL.*)* Well meant, I'm sure.

*(*LENA *hastily gets to her feet.)*

NURSE: She's over it, now. Go back in, if you like.

(She goes on down the passage, her rubber soles squeaking.)

LENA: *(Softly; with menace.)* If you don't let me stay, I'll tell them all you're nothing but Dad's prostitute.

*(*MRS BALL*'s face looks shocked, grieved, stoic.)*

(Interior. Sanatorium. Day.

LENA *has pushed her chair as close as she can get to* NERISSA, *in her white bed. Glasses of milk stand disregarded on the locker.* LENA *removes pile after pile of foreign mail from the interior of the locker.*

She shakes out on to the bed an array of steamship brochures – Auckland–San Francisco; Wellington–Los Angeles; and so on.)

LENA: How shall we raise the fares?

NERISSA: *(Vicious.)* On our backs.

LENA: 'The bed and the beautiful.' You're on your back in here but *you* can't do it.

NERISSA: *You* must. Until I get better.
    Just go out and . . . do it.
    You've got the perfect clothes.

LENA: How much should I ask for?

NERISSA: *(Fretful.)* Oh, I don't know. There's so much we don't know!

LENA: What about my leg?

NERISSA: Nobody will notice, in the dark.
    Our mothers do it with men they're not married to. Both of them.
    We're just following an old family tradition.

(They laugh; a passing nurse looks at them benignly, pleased that the visitor is cheering up poor NERISSA.)

    You can always pretend it's James Mason.
    Do it and write me a long account. It's terrific experience, for a writer.
    I dare you.

(Exterior. Cathedral Square. Night.
    LENA, *transformed, weaves her way among the movie posters in the deserted Square, in the costume she and* NERISSA *invented in* MARY's *bedroom. Her limp has modified to a sexy hobble. She does not look grotesque but genuinely vicious, feral, desperate. She is not nervous. She slips in and out of the shadows as if at home in them.*
    QUINN's *convertible enters the Square. She spots it at once.* QUINN *drives slowly, not quite kerb-crawling.*
    After a moment, LENA *steps boldly forward, flaunting her outrageous get-up.*
    QUINN *sees her. He slows down. They exchange a long look. She smiles and licks her lips, a gesture she has obviously copied from the movies.*
    QUINN *accelerates away.)*

(Exterior. Riverbank. Night.
    A MAN, *unshaven, in work clothes, pushes* LENA *under the willows. Icy moonlight.*
    The willows become agitated. There is the sound of the MAN's *harsh breathing, a whimper from* LENA, *the gurgle of the river. Then a sharp intake of breath – he has hurt her.*
    The MAN *parts the branches of the willows and comes out, fastening his trousers.)*

MAN: You should have told me it was your first time.

(LENA follows, holding her skirt together at the side.)

LENA: Aren't you going to give me any money?

(The man bolts down the road. LENA is left holding out her hand beseechingly.)

(Interior. BALLS' bedroom. Night.
  MR *and* MRS BALL *sleep. There comes a thunderous sound of running water.* MRS BALL *jerks awake;* MR BALL *stirs, murmurs, sleeps on.* MRS BALL *sits up, sleepily thrusting her feet into carpet slippers.)*

(Interior. BALL bathroom. Night.
  Chipped enamel bath, geyser. Dentures in glass.
  LENA *is running herself a hot bath. She pulls off her clothes, tests the water with her elbow. There is dried blood on her legs, and a few bruises.*
  A little knock at the door.)

MRS BALL: *(Softly; over.)* Lena? What are you doing!

(LENA bolts the door. She plunges into the bath. Another knock.)

MRS BALL: *(Over.)* Lena!

(LENA looks at the door with hatred. The door shakes. LENA plunges into the tub and obsessively scrubs herself as her mother rattles the door handle and knocks repeatedly.)

(Exterior. Cathedral Square. Day.
  LENA, *in school uniform, posts a bulky envelope into a post box.*
  She looks around, at a loose end. The milk bar is doing brisk business; the Square is full of shoppers, homeward-bound schoolchildren. She looks very little, very lonely. In the Rover showroom, QUINN *is talking to a rich client.*
  She wanders past the cinemas.
  She sees the posters and stills for The Third Man.
  As she goes towards the box office to buy her ticket, the zither music from the film starts playing.)

(Interior. Sanatorium. Day.
  NERISSA *sits up in bed, looking pink and well.* LENA *sits beside her.)*

LENA: I've fallen in love.

NERISSA: *(Mock horror.)* It won't affect business, will it?

LENA: Better than James Mason, Deborah. A man called ... Harry Lime.

(A DOCTOR *in a white coat, stethoscope round his neck, clipboard in his hand, approaches them.)*

DOCTOR: Nerissa, dear, some very good news –

(Exterior. Outside LOCKE *house. Day.*

The two girls sit in the back of the convertible, pleased, almost overcome with the occasion. MARY *hands* QUINN *a clinking carrier bag – gin, and bottles of tonic. He stows it away in the boot, where other bags are already stowed.*

COLIN *comes out on the porch, looking like an absent-minded don.)*

COLIN: Good of you to give the girls their treat, Quinn.

*(*MARY *smiles at* COLIN, *gives him a quick peck on the cheek.)*

MARY: Us and our little chaperones.

(Exterior. Coast road. Day.

The convertible swoops down the beautiful road beside the sea where MRS BALL *showed* BOBBY *the black swans. The top of the convertible is down.* MARY*'s hair is covered by a silk scarf, she wears dark glasses.* NERISSA *wears dark glasses, too.)*

(Exterior. LOCKES' *seaside house. Day.*

MARY *and* QUINN *sit on the porch of a simple, creeper-covered wooden house with a tin roof, directly on the rocky shore. They sip gin and tonic; bottles and a sliced lemon lie on a table between them. There is the sound of seabirds. It is a ravishingly beautiful bay with only one or two cottages, a couple of farms visible.*

MARY, *in floral print, high heels, is immaculate – and stunningly out of place. Her dark glasses are now perched on top of her head.*

She smokes elegantly, compulsively.)

QUINN: Next stop, South Pole.

MARY: Bizarre.

QUINN: End of the world.

MARY: I can't tell you how alien all this seems. Even the ocean isn't interested in us. I don't think it could be bothered to drown me, if I fell in.
Christ. I hate this ocean.

QUINN: You're urban to your pretty little fingertips, aren't you, Mary. Bond Street. Rue de la Paix. You're missing the bright lights.

MARY: I can tell you one thing – I like it out here in the sticks a whole lot better than back in that damn' town, with Colin bobbing and curtseying and currying favour with all the respectable citizens of Toy Town.

QUINN: Mary . . . my firm wants me to transfer. To South Africa.

Jo'burg. Ever been to Jo'burg? Imagine Paris, minus the frogs. Soaked in sunshine. Wonderful nightclubs, wonderful bands ... cheap staff, plenty of it, you'll never have to wash your own stockings again, Mary.

(She turns to him as if a miracle had occurred; as she does so, she knocks over her gin and tonic.)

(Exterior. Port Levy graveyard. Day.

LENA *and* NERISSA *linger in the little country graveyard in the lee of a tiny, wooden church, looking at the stones.* LENA *motions to a stone with her foot.)*

LENA: Here's a girl who killed her mother.
   Childbirth. See?

NERISSA: Is that all. I thought you meant with an axe. Such as we might have to try, one day, if they get too much on top of us.

(Exterior. Port Levy. Day.

They wander out of the graveyard and go down the unpaved, rutted lane towards the sea.)

NERISSA: I wish there was nobody alive in the whole world but us.

LENA: Happy?

(NERISSA nods.)

(Exterior. Seashore. Day.

The waves, very clear, very pure, wash in on the pebbles. Tender, evening light. Seabirds hover and cry. The girls are quite alone.

Their sandals lie discarded on the shore. They paddle in the surf, hand in hand. A sense of lyrical joy.

Close-up LENA, *smiling.)*

LENA: Malibu Beach must be just like this. Can you swim?

NERISSA: I learned in Bermuda.
   Let's swim out to sea, let's swim to that yacht.

NERISSA: Lena! It's ... the Dutchman's yacht!

LENA: No, it's Harry Lime's yacht. Wait until you meet him. Let's swim out to the yacht, let's swim from here to eternity, Deborah.

NERISSA: No costume.

LENA: No spectators.

(She pulls her dress up over her head but keeps on her vest and knickers. She tosses the dress back on to the beach and plunges out towards the setting sun.
NERISSA *impulsively follows suit.*

They splash one another, duck, dip, swim; they are riotously happy, deliriously so.)

(Exterior. Porch. Day.

In front of a spectacular sunset, MARY *mops up spilled drink.* QUINN *sets down two fizzing, fresh glasses and sits heavily in his basket chair again.)*

MARY: The Nerissa problem.

QUINN: She needs a firm hand.

MARY: *(Ambiguous.)* Your hand?

QUINN: Ship her off to a halfway-decent boarding school in Jo'burg, where she can mix with her own kind.

MARY: Schools have been a problem in the past, Douggie.

(They are rudely interrupted. LENA *and* NERISSA, *in soaking underwear, arrive tumultuously from the beach in an exalted condition.*

They are mad with happiness.

They launch themselves on the two adults, LENA *on* QUINN, NERISSA *on* MARY, *in an ambiguously playful way – part boisterous rough-housing, part the beginnings of genuine violence. The glasses go flying.* MARY *is flung to the floor.)*

(Exterior. Christchurch. Day.

The convertible, top down, comes to a halt, its progress impeded by a flock of sheep.

Enormous baaing.

Inside the car sit MARY *and* QUINN – MARY *gloved, hatted, on her way to pay a call.* MARY *irritated, leans out of the window, shooing the sheep.*

QUINN *blasts the horn. The sheep mill about.*

In a shop window, a poster advertising the Christchurch Annual Show.)

(Exterior. Outside BALL *home. Day.*

The convertible has come to a halt. QUINN *leans across to open* MARY*'s door.)*

QUINN: Tell Mrs Ball to give her daughter a good thrashing with a wet fish.

*(*MARY *gives him a wan smile.)*

(Interior. Cinema. Day.

LENA *and* NERISSA, *in school uniform, lean against one another in the cavernous depths of the almost deserted weekday afternoon cinema. Zither music.*

On the big screen, the scene in The Third Man *on top of the Big Wheel in the Prater Gardens. Orson Welles and Joseph Cotten sit together, looking down at the crowds below. Orson Welles asks if Joseph Cotten would even notice if one of those little ants stopped moving.)*

(Interior. BALL *living room. Day.*

A stream of mahogany-brown tea pours into a cup on the BALLS' *dining table.*
MRS BALL *pushes the cup and saucer over to* MARY, *indicates the sugar bowl.*
MARY *strips off her gloves, folds back the little veil on her hat.)*

MARY: We need to talk about our children.
Mind if I smoke?

(MRS BALL *reaches up to the mantelshelf and brings down a tropical shell of great beauty for* MARY *to use as an ashtray.)*

MRS BALL: Nothing ever made her happy, not even the breast.

(Interior. BALL *living room. Day.*

MARY *taps long ash off her cigarette into the shell. The two women sit at the table, empty tea-cups before them. They are not exchanging confidences, exactly – one speaks about herself for a while and, when she stops, the other speaks about* herself. *All the same, a sense of deep intimacy is building up between them, in spite of their differences.)*

MRS BALL: Then there was Bobbs. It was a high forceps delivery. I had a haemorrhage.
I never could summon up much enthusiasm for you-know-what after that.
But, Bobbs! He's such a joy. I think they love you more.

MARY: Pretty bad time with Nerissa, myself. The nurse stuffed a hanky in my mouth. 'Bite on that or you'll wake the whole bloody nursing home,' she said, the cow, may she rot in hell.
'Here's your daughter, isn't she adorable.' I could hardly bear to look at her, she looked so like her father. Fighter pilot. One of the Few. One of the ones that didn't come back.
Colin fought the war on his arse; bravo, Colin! Always look after Number One.

MRS BALL: Jean was old enough to understand about Bobbs but Lena never did. All she knew was, she wasn't our baby any more.

MARY: 'Have no care, For Johnny Head-in-Air . . .'

(Tears run down, blurring her mascara.)

MRS BALL: When Lena got sick, they wouldn't let us visit. Hospital policy. They thought she'd never walk again but she's only got the tiniest limp, now, hasn't she? *(Insistent.) Hasn't she?*

MARY: *(Shocked by* MRS BALL's *violent tones.)* Yes, of course. Nobody would notice.

MRS BALL: When she came home after all that, she couldn't do a thing for herself. The two of them, helpless. But one of them would never . . .

So.

It was a wrench.

I won't say what it costs. Nothing would be too much. They take such care.

It broke my heart.

MARY: Of course, the hell of it is, she might be Colin's kid, after all. He wouldn't give up his blasted conjugal rights, would he. If only I could be sure . . .

(She dries her eyes, pulls herself together.)

(Exterior. Cathedral Square. Day.
NERISSA *and* LENA *come out of the cinema.)*

NERISSA: Let's stay and see it round again!

LENA: We've got to get home, remember. We're on a tight rein, since you spilled Quinn's gin.

NERISSA: I really liked Harry Lime. I did. I liked his sense of innate superiority. He makes sense. *(Low urgent.)* How's the running away fund?

LENA: Static.

NERISSA: Let's get back to work in earnest. I'll get to grips with Quinn. You –

*(*LENA *gives a mysterious smile and puts her finger to her lips. They go off towards the river, singing the Harry Lime theme together.)*

(Interior. BALL *living room. Day.*
The shell is almost filled with ash.)

MARY: They were laughing and shouting like mad things. I was afraid for them. Nerissa, just out of the sanatorium . . . I know it sounds silly but I was even afraid for Douggie and me.

MRS BALL: If she broke anything, I'll pay.

MARY: No. She didn't.

(Beat.)

Does she?

MRS BALL: Sometimes.

MARY: Nerissa manipulates. And rips things up.

MRS BALL: Sometimes I think Lena could make the cups jump off the table of their own accord.
When she met your girl, she started brushing her hair without me telling her to. She started cleaning her nails. It was a relief.

MARY: When she met your girl, she started to glow. Somebody thought she was wonderful. Somebody saw things the same way.

MRS BALL: I blame myself. If we'd been decently married, Bobby would have been a normal, healthy boy. Lena would never have got sick. I don't blame Len. He's only a man. I should have been strong.

MARY: *(Violent.)* I blame God.

(Exterior. Christchurch. Day.
LENA *and* NERISSA's *point-of-view shot: a truck filled with lowing cattle wobbles along the street.)*

LENA: Here's your chance to see Hicktown in carnival mood. It's the Annual Show.

NERISSA: Is there a carousel, as well as animals?

LENA: There's even a Ferris Wheel.

(Exterior. LOCKE house. Day.
Whistling, the mailman puts letters in the LOCKE mailbox.)

(Interior. LOCKE kitchen. Day.
COLIN *enters as* MARY, *frilly apron, rubber gloves, air of mild distaste, is washing up. He carries an opened letter. He looks like the cat that has got the cream.)*

COLIN: *(Immense self-satisfaction.)* Guess what. It paid off.

(MARY holding out her rubber-gloved hands so as not to make him wet, hugs him.)

MARY: Oh, darling, well done!

COLIN: Cambridge at last.
So.
When I go back in September, you can make your way discreetly to Jo'burg and no bones broken, right?

MARY: I must phone Douggie at the showrooms.

(She strips off her rubber gloves.)

COLIN: *(Genuine, if cool, concern.)* Sure he's the one, Mary? Really, truly sure?

MARY: He knows how to handle me, Colin.
And remember, he's prepared to take on Nerissa, too.
Poor Nerissa! She won't know what's hit her!

(They smile at each other companionably.)

COLIN: I say, it isn't too early for a drink, to celebrate, is it?

(Something in his smile makes MARY, on her way to the telephone in the hall, pause; this is not a man who gives up his conjugal rights easily, after all. She looks wary, nervous.)

(Exterior. Showgrounds. Night.
A prize-winning cow, sleek, black and white, doe-eyed, a rosette pinned to its halter, in a pen. LENA and NERISSA, in school uniform, inspect it.)

LENA: Kim Novak.

NERISSA: Joan Crawford. Kim Novak's a Guernsey. I told them I was at choir practice.

LENA: I just walked out. I'm not speaking to her. It's Mum's fault. She telephoned school. God knows what she said.

NERISSA: *(Mimicking a teacher.)* 'We think it's best to separate you two for a little while.'

(They walked over crushed grass, dangling their hats by the elastic. NERISSA digs in her blazer pocket, produces a lipstick, hands it to LENA.)

LENA: 'Cherries à la Mode'. Lovely.

(She applies it. Then NERISSA applies it. They walk past pens of livestock;

past a revivalist's tent, where a band plays outside, a woman beats a tambourine. LENA *puts on a flaunting, sexy walk for the woman's outraged benefit.)*

(They come to a booth with extraordinary pictures painted on the shuttered sides – a freak show. As yet, no customers, although a seedy man touts a roll of tickets.)

FREAK SHOW PROPRIETOR: Come on, girls, give yourselves a treat. Come and see the bearded lady, come and see the two-headed calf. Take a look at the alligator boy – you'd never believe it unless you saw it.

(Interior. Freak Show. Night.

An elderly woman sits in a rocking chair, knitting at a grey, shapeless garment. The interior of the tent is in darkness but for a bulb over her head. She sports a neat Van Dyke moustache and imperial.

We make out two shapes in the surrounding dark – LENA *and* NERISSA. *There is no sense of anybody else in the tent.)*

NERISSA: *(Whisper.)* It's false.

*(*LENA *leans forward and tugs at the woman's beard. Tears well out of her eyes and run down her cheeks but she doesn't move or speak. She goes on knitting.)*

LENA: *(Genuinely contrite.)* Sorry!

(Another light goes on. It lights up a two-headed calf lying on a heap of straw, as if asleep.

First one of the heads bleats, then the other. As they stare, clutching at one another's hands, a voice calls urgently:)

ALLIGATOR BOY: *(Voice over.)* Touch me! Touch me!

(The other lights go off; a third goes on. A boy swims in a glass tank. He raises an arm to show them the scales.)

ALLIGATOR BOY: Put in your hand and touch me.

(He rolls over on his back.)

ALLIGATOR BOY: *(Suggestive, obscene.)* Touch me here.

LENA: Go on. I dare you.

(Nervous, reluctant, disgusted, NERISSA *extends her hand towards the glass tank.)*

(Exterior. Showground. Night.

An enormous Ferris Wheel, brightly illuminated, goes round against the night sky. All is gaudy light and blaring music from rides and sideshows, vendors of toffee apples, drinks.

LENA *and* NERISSA, *shrieking with laughter, rush through the crowds that now fill the showground. There is a big carousel, with a blaring steam organ and ornately carved horses; as* LENA *and* NERISSA *pass it,* STAN *and* JEAN *come riding by on the same horse, looking disgustingly normal.*

The girls come to a stop; their laughter dries up.)

LENA: I'm glad we saw them, though. Because that's what we are. Freaks. Not like other people. Freaks.

NERISSA: But they were ugly.

LENA: You can be a beautiful freak. We are. We're beautiful freaks.

(Interior. LOCKE *house. Night.*

The hallway is in darkness, although a light burns on the upstairs landing. NERISSA *tiptoes towards her mother's bedroom, carrying the lipstick she has borrowed.*

She opens the bedroom door.)

(Interior. MARY's *bedroom. Night.*

NERISSA's *point-of-view shot:* MARY *and* QUINN, *unclothed, in bed together, frozen in mid-giggle at the sight of* NERISSA; *each holds a glass. An opened bottle of Australian champagne on the night-table. An empty bottle rolls on the floor.*

NERISSA, *cool as a cucumber, goes to the dressing table and puts down the lipstick.)*

NERISSA: I need some new shoes. Fifty pounds would cover it.

QUINN: *(Barking laugh.)* Game's up!

MARY: *(Refills her glass and holds it out to* NERISSA.*)* Come and sit down, darling, and have some champagne.
Douggie is going to be your stepfather.

(Dumbfounded, NERISSA *stares.* QUINN *grins spitefully.)*

QUINN: We're getting out of this damn' backwater pretty sharpish, I can tell you. We'll find a boarding school with locked wards to cope with you, young lady.

*(*NERISSA *looks bereft.* MARY *relents.)*

MARY: You'll come to us in the holidays. We'll have a big house, with servants, and a swimming pool. Wonderful sunshine! You'll like it. I promise. *(Unexpectedly wistful.)* You might even condescend to smile, from time to time.

NERISSA: *(Wild hope.)* You're not taking me to California, are you?

MARY: Whatever made you think of California? We're off to South Africa. Much nicer!

NERISSA: But Lena and I are going to Hollywood! We've been saving up for ages!

MARY: Hollywood?

(She and QUINN laugh, startled, not unkindly amused. NERISSA can't bear that. She becomes hysterically angry.)

NERISSA: You can't stop me! We'll let nothing stand in our way, do you hear? Nothing!

(She rushes to the dressing table, seizes a lipstick and makes huge, slashing marks criss-cross on the mirror, cancelling out the image it reflects — MARY and QUINN, in bed, thunderstruck — with violent, bloody strokes.)

(Interior. BALL living room. Night.

Light filters into the room from a street lamp outside. Lena, in pyjamas, crouches by the telephone, whispering.)

LENA: I don't believe it.
    Oh, God.
    Tell me it isn't true.
    Yes. All right. It's never too late for that.

(Exterior. Cathedral Square. Night.

The Square is deserted. A paper blows by in the gutter. The milkbar is locked up. Iron grilles on the cinema entrances. LENA, in black beret and split skirt, looks round the square. Heavily made up, she looks feral and a little mad.

Nothing doing in the Square.

She cuts down an alley. Her heels go clip-clop, irregularly — her limp is evident.

Other footsteps, in counterpoint, echo the irregular clip-clop of her heels.

She slows down, deliberately.)

(Exterior. Riverbank. Night.

LENA ducks under the weeping willow and turns to face her pursuer. His face is hidden by shadows. He is much bigger than she is.

Silence, except for the sound of the river.

Ceremoniously he opens his shirt.

LENA *gasps.*

His torso is wonderfully carved and ornamented – elaborately, beautifully tattooed.

The branches shift; moonlight floods his face. It, too, is elaborately tattooed – a beautiful face, beautifully decorated, although not according to our standards of beauty.

LENA*'s face, with the beginnings of joy in it; for once, life is living up to her expectations.)*

(Interior. BALL *kitchen. Day.*

The room is filled with steam; the steam comes from a boiler on the gas ring – washing day. MRS BALL*, hair in scarf, throws clothes into the boiler from a clothes basket and stirs them round with a wooden paddle.*

She picks up a pair of white cotton knickers. She pauses, scrutinises them carefully. She does not drop them in the boiler.

Knickers in one hand, paddle in the other, she rushes out of the kitchen.)

(Interior. JEAN*'s and* LENA*'s bedroom. Day.*

JEAN*, dressed, scours face powder out of a gilt compact on to her face in front of the mirror.* LENA*, still in pyjamas, sits on the side of the bed, dragging a comb through her hair. There are still crumbs of mascara on* LENA*'s lashes, stains of lipstick on her mouth.)*

MRS BALL: What are you up to?

*(*LENA *screams as* MRS BALL *seizes her and belabours her with the paddle.* LENA *covers her head with her arms.)*

JEAN: Hold on, Mum –

*(*MRS BALL*, breathless, lets her arm fall.* LENA *peers out from between her fingers.)*

LENA: *(Hiss.)* I'll kill you for that.

MRS BALL: Sneaking out at night –

LENA: I'll leave home, I'm going to Hollywood.

*(*JEAN *can't help it, she guffaws.)*

MRS BALL: *(Weary.)* News to me.

LENA: Nerissa's going to be a big star. I'm going to write scripts for her.
    Write, produce, direct. I'm going to Hollywood with Nerissa.
        She cares more about me than any of you do.

(She dives under the covers. The covers heave. She is crying. JEAN *and* MRS BALL *step forward.* JEAN *gives her a warning look.* MRS BALL *takes a deep breath.)*

MRS BALL: I'm sorry I hit you, Lena. I only hit you because I was upset. I don't want you to get into trouble, Lena.

JEAN: (*Under her breath.*) One good thing, she won't get into *that* kind of trouble with Nerissa Locke.

(MRS BALL *is shocked.*)

(*Interior.* BALL *kitchen. Day.*
    MRS BALL *throws the offending garment into the boiler.* LENA, *ready for school, comes into the kitchen, red-eyed.*)

MRS BALL: (*Conciliatory.*) You'd better get some breakfast.

(LENA *takes the bull by the horns.*)

LENA: Mum. I've got thirty pounds saved up.

(MRS BALL *registers surprise.*)

Give me the rest of the fare. I could be happy in Hollywood, with Nerissa.

(MRS BALL *breaks down.*)

MRS BALL: Stop it! Stop it! Stop it!

(*Interior. School toilets. Day.*
    A row of cubicles, a row of sinks. Deserted. LENA *comes in, looks round, turns on tap in sink. A cubicle door opens,* NERISSA *comes out. They hug each other eagerly.*)

LENA: It's Mum's fault they won't let us sit together. She telephoned school. She hates me. She beat me with the washing paddle. She won't give me a penny and it's urgent, now. We've *got* to run away, before they whisk you off to South Africa.

NERISSA: They want to send me to a convent to get rid of me. They can get rid of me by giving us the fares.

LENA: My mother, she's the real problem. She'd lock me up before she'd·let me go. She's standing in the way of our happiness.

(*Their eyes meet; they exchange the same, transfigured look that they did when they first saw one another at prayers in the school chapel.* NERISSA *speaks, very slowly.*)

NERISSA: It has to *look* like an accident.

LENA: There's a place we take Bobbs, for picnics. It's the perfect place for . . . an accident. It's way up in the hills.

NERISSA: So high up that people look like ants.

LENA: Think of it this way, that we've got to write the script for the perfect murder, and then we've got to stick to it.
And then we'll be free.

(Exterior. BALL back yard. Day.
MRS BALL removes dry washing from the line and stows it in a basket. LENA, in blazer, throws her satchel on the grass and approaches her mother from behind. She kisses her under the ear.)

LENA: Sorry, Mum.

MRS BALL: I should hope so.

LENA: I was just upset about Nerissa going to South Africa. I *shall* miss her but, after all, it isn't the end of the world.

MRS BALL: Then what's all the silly talk about Hollywood?

LENA: Just a girl's dream.

(She helps her mother unpeg the clothes.)

Mum . . . Friday's a half-holiday. As a special treat, because she *has* been such a good friend, could you take us up to the Cashmere Hills?

(Interior. BALL bedroom. Night.
MR and MRS BALL lie in bed together, sedate, dignified, terribly married.)

MRS BALL: So I said yes. What else could I say?

MR BALL: Thank God she's stopped acting up.

MRS BALL: She said, let's show Nerissa our special place, where we take Bobby. I suppose that girl *has* been a good influence, in the long run.

(But her face is unbearably sad.)

MR BALL: *(Very gentle.)* What's wrong, lovie?

MRS BALL: *(Like a child.)* What did I do wrong, Dad?

(Exterior. Cathedral Square. Day.
In Sunday clothes, sensible shoes, MRS BALL walks through the Square past the cinemas. LENA, in school uniform, minus hat, holds her arm.
QUINN comes to the door of the Rover showroom and follows them thoughtfully with his eyes, until he sees NERISSA, also in school uniform minus hat, running forward excitedly to meet them. The tram arrives, blocking his view.
QUINN, looking thoughtful and troubled, turns away from the door.)

(Exterior. Tram stop. Day.
    The girls stand back courteously to allow MRS BALL *to climb into the tram.)*

NERISSA: *(Under her breath.)* Have you got it?

*(*LENA *pats her bulging pocket.)*

(Interior. Tram. Day.
    The rocking, swaying tram crosses the railway tracks, passes the Kiwi bacon sign. The girls sit together, MRS BALL *in the seat in front of them, her back to them.*
    NERISSA *leans over towards* LENA *as* LENA *opens her pocket to show* NERISSA *the murder weapon as slyly as if it were a dirty picture.)*

(Exterior. Outside tea room. Day.
    The girls come out of the tea room, followed by MRS BALL, *as* OLLIE *passes, with his axe on his shoulder. The sight of him sends the girls into fits of giggles; they are in a state of great, barely suppressed excitement.* MRS BALL *calls back into the tea room:)*

MRS BALL: Thanks!

(It is cold and grey. She shivers as she inspects the afternoon, pulls her coat tight.
    The sound of axe blows begins.
    Birdsong, very loud.
    The girls – both girls – dance ahead up the path, as if released from a spell. MRS BALL *follows more slowly, walking as if her feet hurt, in spite of her sensible shoes.*
    A heavy middle-aged, sad-faced woman walking towards her own death.
    She has a great deal of dignity, as she grits her teeth and follows the mad girls.)

(Exterior. Victoria Park. Day.
    MRS BALL *is nearing the picnic spot. We can hear the eerie laughter of the girls but not see them.*
    The camera pauses to watch MRS BALL *walk sturdily into the distance.*
    In the distance, we see her fall.
    She falls as if it were inevitable she should fall.)

(Exterior. Victoria Park. Day.
    She falls heavily on her face – the girls have tripped her up.
    The girls leap out from behind the bush where they have hidden themselves and kick her into the bushes that will conceal her body. She cries out, in accusation and sorrow:)

MRS BALL: Lena!

(Her face is badly grazed, her hat has fallen off. She raises herself up on her arms, looks round, dazed.)

LENA: *(In supplication, in terror.)* I can't stop now!

(She brings the murder weapon out of her pocket; it is a brick wrapped up in one of her mother's own lisle stockings.

  Close-up MRS BALL's *face, stoical, accepting, resigned, even forgiving.)*

MRS BALL: *(Softly, as to an injured child.)* Lena . . .

(Freeze on her face.)

STAGE PLAY

Lulu

Lulu

ACT ONE

(Empty room in a large house. Attic, maybe.

Shuttered, broken light shafts. Art treasures stacked in piles. Neglected. Dust. Tarnished mirrors. Stepladder. Chandelier. Sofa.

Sound of feet on stairs. Door opens. Silhouette.

SCHOEN *moves into room, looking, searching. Sounds of . . . what? Laughter, voices, quarrels, all ghostly, 'in the air'. Running feet; music; glass smashing; applause.*

He pulls off dust covers – dust in the air. He finds – stumbles upon – The Picture.

The music resolves, still heady, dizzy. Voices more clearly heard.)

SCHWARTZ: *(Voice off.)* Is she a friend of yours?

SCHOEN: *(Abrupt, but to himself apparently.)* Never.

(He steps back, admiring the portrait. Lights brighten.)

Lovely!

SCHWARTZ: *(Voice off.)* Are you sure you don't know her?

SCHOEN: Of course not.

(The sounds [voices, etc.] are fading under the music, which is itself thinning . . .)

SCHWARTZ: *(Entering.)* Not quite finished.

SCHOEN: How did you –

(SCHWARTZ, rapt, doesn't hear. He appears not to notice SCHOEN.)

SCHWARTZ: She always brings her husband with her. I ply my brush; he bends my ear . . .

SCHOEN: How did you meet her?

SCHWARTZ: One fine day, on the studio door: knock, knock, who's there? Why, a belly! A belly on legs, and not a belly in its first youth, either. Would I, asks the belly nicely, be so kind as to make a portrait of the belly's beloved wife? You know me, brush for hire. Wheel her on. Mrs Belly, Mrs Bum, Mrs Geriatric Belly-Bum – all the same to me. Next morning, with a shy pride, really rather touching, he ushers in the most luscious bit of jail bait that ever brought a gleam to these jaded eyes.

(SCHOEN *stiffens.* SCHWARTZ *doesn't notice.*)

Up pipes Belly: 'Kindly show my wife to the changing rooms.' *That* threw me – thank God, nothing incriminating in the bedroom. The old man protects the door with his body. Out she pops in two ticks, dressed up in this crazy pierrot costume.

(*He shakes his head in remembered wonder, gazing at the bedroom door as if he expected it to fly open and reveal* LULU *this very minute.* SCHOEN *stares in the same direction, as if in a trance.*)

SCHOEN: And her husband stood guard?

SCHWARTZ: My little heart went pit-a-pat, I can tell you. 'How do you want me?' she says. God, that giggle of hers! I thought Belly would bust a gut but it's only her little joke. *So* lovely. *So* sexy. Just take a look at that costume.

(*He goes out through the door that leads to his bedroom.* SCHOEN *addresses the portrait of* LULU, *puffing out cigar smoke.*)

SCHOEN: Of course, you *are* extremely attractive. And don't you know it!

(SCHWARTZ *returns, carrying the pierrot costume tenderly in his arms, as if it were a bride he was carrying across the threshold.*
   The music we heard earlier . . . fairground quality . . . a puppet dance . . . mechanical, ghostly.
   SCHWARTZ *holds the costume up and shakes it; for a moment the costume lives a brief, dancing life of its own.* SCHOEN *sighs. There is a powerful sense of fetishism about the men's reactions to the pierrot costume.*)

SCHWARTZ: It's all-in-one.

SCHOEN: How on earth does she get into it?

(*They are almost breathless when they think of* LULU, *half-naked, clambering into this garment.*)

SCHWARTZ: (*Exhalation of breath.*) I can't think!

(SCHOEN *takes hold of one leg and spreads it out.*)

SCHOEN: Huge!

(*The costume 'dances' between them. The music accelerates.*)

SCHWARTZ: She rolls the left one up –

(SCHOEN *glances at the portrait.*)

SCHOEN: As far as the knee.

(*The men laugh. Excited. Private.*)

SCHWARTZ: It's not what she does, it's the way that she does it.

(SCHWARTZ *drops the game all at once. He bundles up the pierrot suit, crushes it under his arm. The music ceases abruptly.*)

(*Bleak.*) God, she's a tease.

SCHOEN: How dare you!

(*He is about to slap* SCHWARTZ's *face – or does so.* SCHWARTZ *retreats. Sounds of a woman's laughter.*)

SCHOEN: Dear God!

(*The door flies open. Here are* DR GOLL *and his wife,* LULU.
LULU, *a tiny, plump, fluffy, big-eyed blonde, sports lavish furs, very high heels and a chic little hat, all of which she wears with a delightful wit, as if she saw the funny side of her own attractiveness. Her manner is exuberant; at first sight she seems the perfect, frivolous, high-spirited society beauty, her exuberance given pathos by a certain child-like vulnerability. That is her special quality for these sophisticated gentlemen: the piquant charm of a child play-acting the seductress. She is seventeen years old. Like all those who make a living out of pleasing others, she is well aware of her precarious position in the world. She knows her role, the charming child (who, when she is naughty, can be punished 'for her own good'). She plays it, charmingly. Underneath, she is tragic, driven, doomed.*)

GOLL: Fancy meeting you here, old chap!

SCHOEN: (*Kissing* LULU's *hand.*) Madame Goll.

GOLL: What brings you here?

SCHOEN: My fiancée is having her portrait painted.

(LULU *dances downstage to the discarded portrait propped on the table leg, kneels to look at it, first hitching up her skirt, revealing a good deal of silk stocking.*)

GOLL: Where have you got her tucked her away?

SCHOEN: She prefers to sit after lunch.

GOLL: Such a secret he's kept it!

(LULU *gets up.*)

LULU: Does she look as . . . charmingly serious as this all the time?

SCHOEN: (*Frosty reproof.*) She only recently left convent school.

(GOLL *comes to inspect the portrait, head cocked. He and* LULU *are smiling wickedly.*)

GOLL: I would have said, 'Not your usual type, old boy.' (*He laughs.*)

LULU: It's terribly naughty of you to keep her waiting. How long? Two years?

SCHOEN: We'll announce the engagement the week after next.

(GOLL *dismisses all this briskly, and turns to* LULU.)

GOLL: No time to waste, Little Nell!

(*He claps his hands.*)

LULU: I must say, I thought sitting for my portrait would be more fun.

(SCHWARTZ *looks up, affronted. Meanwhile,* LULU *has manoeuvred herself in front of* SCHOEN *in such a way that he is forced to help her off with her furs. He cannot resist burying his face in them as he does so.*
   LULU *wheels away from him sharply. Abruptly, as if disgusted,* SCHOEN *tosses the furs to* SCHWARTZ, *who is hovering in front of the bedroom door.*)

SCHWARTZ: If the young lady would . . .

(*He opens the door for her and closes it behind her, hangs her furs on the hatstand.*)

GOLL: Now, tell us all about that delicious wee morsel who was slipping back into her things last time we came?

SCHWARTZ: The lady in question granted me just one sitting out of the goodness of her heart. I met her on a St Cecilia Society outing.

(*The two older men raise their eyebrows, turn to one another, chuckle.*)

GOLL: I don't understand these arty types.

SCHOEN: I envy him his moral superiority. He starves for his art, d'you see. That puts him on a different moral plane, evidently.

(They laugh.)

SCHOEN: Why don't you give him some financial backing. Might be a big saving, in the long run – think of it, you could slip into the studio any time you fancied, see what's going on. Or coming off!

(He nudges GOLL; they roar with mirth. LULU emerges from the bedroom at last in her pierrot costume, with her hair fluffed out in curls. She looks extravagantly sexy in the white satin slip but in a perversely childish way, like a little girl decked out for a fancy-dress party in too precocious a costume. The men stop laughing.)

LULU: How do I look?

(GOLL parks his cigar in his mouth and gives her a little round of applause. SCHOEN is silent. She approaches him with a dancing step.)

LULU: Do I look nice?

SCHOEN: I can't imagine a lovelier –

LULU: How nice?

SCHOEN: I don't suppose you even begin to understand the effect you have on men.

LULU: *(Vulgar.)* Wanna bet?

(LULU turns to her husband and throws her arms round his neck. GOLL pats her bum, looking smug.)

GOLL: Your bra straps . . .

(He tucks in a flimsy silk string.)

LULU: *(Monroe-esque.)* I'd like to leave it off altogether. It's terribly constricting.

(He slaps her bum, again. She clambers on to the podium.)

GOLL: *(Settling down on the sofa.)* Let me enjoy the scenery.

(LULU rolls up her left trouser leg as far as the knee.
Music – 'in the air' at first. Then, as the men behave increasingly like uninhibited voyeurs, it becomes coarser, more insistent.)

LULU: *(To SCHWARTZ.)* Sufficient?

(SCHOEN joins GOLL on the sofa, but does not sit, merely rests one leg on it in a debonair fashion. LULU cocks her head, assesses SCHWARTZ's expression, rolls up her left trouser leg as far as mid-thigh.)

That better?

GOLL: *(To* SCHOEN.*)* Move your head so . . . That's the best angle.

LULU: All my angles are best angles!

SCHWARTZ: *(To* LULU, *businesslike.)* More right knee, please.

SCHOEN: *(Carving a voluptuous shape out of the air.)* You must . . . undulate, permit her to undulate on to the canvas.

*(*SCHWARTZ *ostentatiously ignores this advice.)*

SCHWARTZ: The light's good today. That's something.

GOLL: I say, man, you're clutching away at that brush like –

(An improper simile springs to his mind, he smiles with secret pleasure.)

like a schoolboy his –

*(*SCHOEN *abruptly guffaws.)*

Fling her on to the canvas, man!

SCHWARTZ: Yes, Dr Goll.

SCHOEN: Think of her as a still life. As a basket of fruit. As a bouquet of wonderful flowers.

SCHWARTZ: Yes, Mr Schoen. *(To* LULU.*)* Lift up your chin a bit.

*(*LULU *obeys.)*

LULU: I'd like to part my lips, if you think that looks all right.

(She does so. It looks all right.)

SCHOEN: *(To* SCHWARTZ.*)* But you! You are neuter. You must stay cold as ice. You'll lose all the art if you let in any feeling.

SCHWARTZ: Yes, Mr Schoen.

GOLL: D'you see, art must imitate nature in such a way that it stimulates the intellect.

LULU: If I wet my lips . . .

(She runs her tongue along her lips, a very sexy performance. The performance is directed at SCHWARTZ.*)*

SCHWARTZ: *(A courting speech.)* Make sunshine for me. Smile.

(LULU gives him a real smile. Maybe flash of camera magnesium. Music abruptly stops too.)

GOLL: *(To LULU.)* You must pretend our Leonardo here doesn't exist.

LULU: *(Outrageous.)* He can't do anything but paint, anyway!

(They love that. They chortle. The doorbell rings.)

LULU: Door.

SCHWARTZ: Excuse me.

(He goes out of the double doors.)

GOLL: *(To LULU.)* Try to smile less.

SCHOEN: Don't waste your *best* on him.

(ALVA SCHOEN, SCHOEN's twenty-year-old son, pushes past SCHWARTZ into the studio. ALVA has the assurance of inherited wealth.)

ALVA: Good morning, Father.

LULU: Why, it's little Alva!

ALVA: I wish you were still in show business. I'd so love you to dance in my new revue!

(LULU gives a little shake of herself in polite acknowledgement.)

SCHOEN: What brings you here?

GOLL: Perhaps he's 'commissioned' something on the side . . .

ALVA: *(To SCHOEN.)* I want you to come to the dress rehearsal. Come and see the little Corticelli girl. She's the young Buddha. She dances as if she'd just risen from the Ganges.

GOLL: Risen from the Ganges, eh?

ALVA: Come with us. Now. At once.

GOLL: No. Not possible.

ALVA: There's absolutely the most spectacular chorus number.

GOLL: Risen from the Ganges? Where's the young Buddha in Act Three?

ALVA: Come and see!

GOLL: *(After a second's hesitation.)* No.

ALVA: We can go on to the usual place afterwards. If you think the young lady looks peaky, you could arrange a private consultation, Dr Goll.

GOLL: Don't tease.

ALVA: There are tame monkeys and two Brahmins and lots and lots of little girls –

(ALVA has teased too near the bone. GOLL's good humour evaporates. He snaps.)

GOLL: Don't mention little girls!

(Silence . . . LULU laughs, teasing. Again, silence.)

Can't spare a moment from this sitting, d'you see. By the time I got back, this dauber would have wrecked the whole thing.

SCHOEN: Come, now, I'm sure he can manage perfectly well by himself for five little minutes.

GOLL: Next time.

ALVA: The daughters of Nirvana are quivering with anticipation.

GOLL: Daub, daub, splatter . . .

SCHOEN: They'll never forgive us if we arrive without you.

(GOLL abruptly changes his mind.)

GOLL: Fine, five minutes. I'll just take five minutes off.

(He peers at the portrait, then at LULU.)

Her hair looks like an implant. Terrible. Keep your mind on the job, Raphael.

ALVA: Hurry!

GOLL: *(To LULU.)* I'll be off. Five minutes. No more. I promise.

SCHOEN: I've a cab waiting downstairs.

(They rush off, laughing, like schoolboys released from lessons. LULU ostentatiously rearranges her rolled-up trouser leg but SCHWARTZ, huddled over the easel, is too resentful and preoccupied to notice.)

SCHWARTZ: Bastards. They make you eat shit. As if a bellyfull of shit was better than a bellyfull of nothing. Funny thing, it is. It is. And don't they know it. Bastards. Could you bear to lift up your right hand, d'you think?

(LULU *does so, a faint smile on her lips.*)

SCHWARTZ: You must think I'm pathetic.

LULU: He'll be back in a jiffy . . . Watch your step.

SCHWARTZ: I can't do anything except paint. You said so yourself.

(*He paints on.*)

LULU: I don't believe it.

SCHWARTZ: Don't you ever get lonely, all by yourself in that great big apartment, while your husband's out giving his professional opinion of other women's private parts?

LULU: (*Composedly.*) We've got a housekeeper.

SCHWARTZ: Good company, huh?

LULU: She dresses me.

SCHWARTZ: Ball gowns.

LULU: (*Derisive.*) Not likely! Dance costumes! (*She hums a tune.*) Hungarian dancing. Spanish – olé! Skirt-dance.

SCHWARTZ: Who gives you your dancing lessons?

LULU: Himself.

SCHWARTZ: What?

LULU: He strikes up on the fiddle. He hits my legs with the bow.

SCHWARTZ: Scenes from the home life of an eminent gynaecologist. God. Tell me what you wear for your lessons.

LULU: Décolleté top, of course – décolleté to a degree. Close-fitting. Well, snug. Well. Second skin sort of thing. And there's a green skirt, layered frills, outer layer bright green but paler and paler as you get further in until you reach the pair of white lace –

SCHWARTZ: Keep your knickers out of it!

(*He looks as if he is about to lay down his brush.*)

LULU: Keep your mind on the job!

(*She wriggles.*)

SCHWARTZ: Are you perfectly comfortable?

(She wriggles again.)

LULU: Perfectly. Why? Aren't you?

(She reaches round her back. SCHWARTZ *watches, startled, as she withdraws, via one of the wide arms of the pierrot costume, a flimsy lace brassière. She takes a deep breath, dangling the garment in the air.)*

LULU: Let it all hang out!

(She giggles and throws the bra in a corner. He hurls his brush to the floor.)

SCHWARTZ: Your husband can't leave you alone for a minute, can he.

LULU: *(With a touch of real bitterness, if* SCHWARTZ *could hear it.)* My husband does what he wants.

(He lays his hand on her thigh. She pushes it away.)

LULU: Paws off! I'm not up for grabs.

SCHWARTZ: *(Retreating.)* Just teasing –

LULU: Oh, no you weren't. The devil makes work for idle hands.

SCHWARTZ: Naughty girls deserve a smack –

*(*LULU *shrieks merrily and leaps off the throne as he lunges. Music: heady, mocking, elusive.)*

LULU: Can't catch me!

(She dives behind the sofa. SCHWARTZ *throws himself headlong, seizes hold of her wide trouser leg.)*

SCHWARTZ: Gotcha!

*(*LULU *gives a little shake and slips out of the costume. Underneath she wears exquisite cami-knickers. She throws the pierrot costume over his head and climbs the stepladder.)*

LULU: I'm going to climb right out of this studio.

*(*SCHWARTZ *fights free of the pierrot costume and throws it on the floor.)*

SCHWARTZ: Bad, bad, bad –

LULU: I'm climbing right up to the sky and I'm going to pick off all the stars to stick in my hair . . .

(Music at crescendo. SCHWARTZ *seizes hold of the ladder and shakes it.* LULU

screams, jumps down and pushes SCHWARTZ *on to the floor. She escapes; she stands by the little table breathing heavily.)*

LULU: I told you. *Hands off.*

(She squints assessingly at the portrait of SCHOEN's *fiancée. She reaches out and prods it with her toe.* SCHWARTZ, *panting, gets up.)*

SCHWARTZ: Let's stop this, let's be friends.

(He puts his arm around her from behind and tries to kiss her. She picks up his portrait of SCHOEN's *fiancée and breaks it over his head. She has been longing to destroy the portrait ever since she saw it.*
Music stops.
All the laughter drains out of the situation as soon as she does so.)

LULU: *(Unsmiling.)* I told you. Hands off. I *told* you.

*(*SCHWARTZ *stands like a fool, the painting sticking out like a ruff around his neck.)*

SCHWARTZ: Oh God. Dear God.

(He pulls the ruined painting off his head with as much dignity as he can muster, props it against the ottoman, looks at it.)

There goes ten weeks' work.

*(*LULU, *deceived by his apparent calm, comes up to look, too.)*

LULU: *(Unnecessarily.)* Look what a big hole you've made.

(He emits a high-pitched scream. He lunges at her; he intends to rape her. LULU *flings herself dramatically on to the sofa, instantly prone.* SCHWARTZ *halts, at sea. Then, a moment of decision – he goes and bolts the studio door.* LULU *sits up when his back is turned, peering anxiously to see what he is doing; as soon as he turns round, she flops down again. He sits beside her on the sofa and takes her hand. She opens her eyes.)*

My husband. He –

SCHWARTZ: *(Interrupting.)* What are you feeling?

LULU: Out of my depth.

SCHWARTZ: *(Ghastly serious, as if confessing to a crime.)* Oh, Jesus, I think I've fallen for you.

LULU: I fell in love with a student. Once upon a time.

SCHWARTZ: Nell.

LULU: He had twenty-four scars. From duelling. Twenty-four.

SCHWARTZ: Little Nell, I think I've really fallen for you.

LULU: I'm not really called Nell. I –

(He kisses her, clumsily, as if it pained him.)

   I'm called Lulu.

SCHWARTZ: No. Eva.

LULU: Eva.

SCHWARTZ: Eva.

(She understands: she smiles; then yawns.)

LULU: Got the right time, Adam?

(He takes out a pocket watch.)

SCHWARTZ: Ten thirty.

(LULU takes the watch from his hand and idly opens and closes the back.)

LULU: It's ten thirty-five, in actual fact. Not half past. Just think. You
   lost us five whole minutes.

SCHWARTZ: *(Urgent.)* Kiss me.

*(She takes hold of his chin, squints at him, gives him a quick peck on the cheek,
turns away.)*

LULU: You ought to give up smoking. It's like kissing an ashtray.

SCHWARTZ: Try to understand. Try to be kind.

*(Things are getting out of hand; she's nervous. She throws his watch up in the
air and catches it, avoiding his eye.)*

SCHWARTZ: What do you really feel?

LULU: What do *you* really feel?

SCHWARTZ: You hide your feelings.

LULU: *(Genuinely astonished.)* Who? Me? I've no need.

(SCHWARTZ gets up. He looks dazed.)

SCHWARTZ: My God, what am I doing?

(LULU is gripped by a sudden, real, terrible fear. She pushes him violently away from her.)

LULU: Don't kill me!

(She leaps from the sofa and crouches down behind it, hiding. SCHWARTZ shakes his head, sadly.)

SCHWARTZ: You've never been in love, have you.

(LULU's face comes up cautiously over the back of the sofa.)

LULU: *(From the depths of unguessable experience.)* It's you're the one who's never been in love.

(He turns to her with a look of wild surprise on his face. This tender moment is brutally interrupted by a shrilling peal on the doorbell. The door handle jerks convulsively.)

GOLL: *(Offstage.)* Open this door!

(LULU screams and ducks down behind the sofa again.)

GOLL: *(Beating the door with his fists.)* Open this door at once!

(SCHWARTZ looks at LULU cowering out of sight, then starts off towards the door. She leaps out and makes almost a rugby tackle at him, grasping his knees, preventing his moving.)

LULU: He'll beat me to death.

(SCHWARTZ looks down at her, disgusted, furious.)

SCHWARTZ: Stop that. Get dressed.

(The door caves in. GOLL, red-faced, frothing at the mouth, charges in like a bull and halts, taking in the spectacle of LULU in her underwear clutching SCHWARTZ's knees.)

GOLL: Swine

(He falls in a fit. He threshes; he twitches; he lies still. There is a silence. LULU slowly detaches herself from SCHWARTZ's legs and stands up.)

LULU: I think you'd better tidy up a bit.

(SCHWARTZ bends over GOLL, as LULU backs off.)

SCHWARTZ: Dr Goll?

(No response.)

SCHWARTZ: I think he's hurt his head. (*Suddenly brisk.*) Let's get him up on the sofa.

(LULU *retreats towards the door.*)

LULU: I don't want to touch him.

(SCHWARTZ *tries to raise him.*)

SCHWARTZ: Come on, Dr Goll.

LULU: He's past hearing.

SCHWARTZ: Come and help me.

LULU: He's too heavy. Even with both of us, he'll be far too heavy.

(SCHWARTZ *gets up.*)

SCHWARTZ: He needs a doctor.

LULU: He's just so terribly heavy, you see.

(SCHWARTZ *picks up his hat from the hatstand. He goes out hurriedly.*)

LULU: (*Her elocution lessons-acquired accent evaporates.*) Okay. Point taken. You can get up now.

(*Pause.*)

(*In a piercing voice.*) Daddee!

(*Nothing doing.*)

(*Music – a slow, weird, eerie parody of the earlier 'chase'. She starts to walk round the stage, making a huge detour in order to avoid the corpse, heading for the discarded pierrot costume. She gives the corpse a sideways glance.*)

Watching my feet, are you? How'm I doing? Want to hit my legs, Daddy?

(*She walks with exaggerated care now, a dancer's walk, arching her insteps, keeping one eye on the corpse all the time, just in case.*)

He's scrutinising every step.

(*She is now virtually dancing. She makes a little arabesque in order to lean over him and pluck up the pierrot costume. She peers down at him. She retreats on tiptoe. Returns for another look. Then she shimmies for him; then she twirls; then she performs a high kick. Nothing doing.*)

Oh, come on. Wakey wakey.

(She extends one elegant foot and prods him with her toe; then she edges away chastened, clutching the pierrot costume to her for comfort.
  Music stops.)

He's dead all right, this time. Bring down the curtain, the show's over. He's dropped me right in it. Gawd, whatever will I do?

(Clutching the pierrot costume, she addresses him, full of sadness.)

Nobody to say a prayer for you. What a way to go.

(She wanders downstage, still clutching the pierrot costume; almost as an afterthought, she slips it back on. SCHWARTZ returns.)

SCHWARTZ: So. He's still out.

LULU: I think he means it, this time.

SCHWARTZ: Can't you show a bit of compassion?

LULU: Compassion? He liked me to show a bit of leg.

(Ostentatiously, she rolls up the left trouser leg of the pierrot costume, as if for the corpse's pleasure. SCHWARTZ raises his eyebrows, kneels, feels for GOLL's pulse. He speaks reassuringly to the corpse.)

SCHWARTZ: The doctor will be here very soon.

LULU: Don't bother with an ambulance, just call a hearse.

SCHWARTZ: Don't let's give up so easily.

LULU: *He's* given up.

SCHWARTZ: At least go and change out of those clothes.

(LULU smiles at him — seductive, or is it derision?)

What's stopping you?

(Very deliberately, she steps out of the pierrot costume; then equally deliberately, rolls down the strap of her cami-knickers over her bare shoulder.
  Music — very quiet, echo of the 'male' voyeurism earlier.
  SCHWARTZ stares, aghast, but can't keep himself from reaching out to touch. Then he recoils violently, as if her skin contained a charge of static. Now LULU herself backs away from him, towards the sofa, still provocatively extending the lingerie string, and SCHWARTZ, as if taking part in a dance, unable to prevent himself, follows her. She sits on the sofa. SCHWARTZ kneels at her feet. She puts her arms round his neck and rests her cheek on the top of his head.)

LULU: Please . . .

SCHWARTZ: *(Lost.)* Yes?

(LULU catches sight of the corpse, lying there glassy-eyed and accusing.)

LULU: He's watching us . . .

(SCHWARTZ springs up and away, as if stung.)

SCHWARTZ: You disgust me.

LULU: *(Breathless.)* I'm disgusting? What about you? It takes two to be really disgusting!

(SCHWARTZ drops all hypocritical pretence; he stares at her, genuinely fascinated by her lack of affect.)

SCHWARTZ: Don't you feel anything?

LULU: I'm numb with shock. It'll wear off. Then I'll suffer. He's staring at me.

SCHWARTZ: He's staring at me, too.

LULU: Coward!

(SCHWARTZ takes out his handkerchief and wraps up his hand with great care; when it is well and truly covered, he bends down and closes GOLL's eyes.)

  Scared?

(SCHWARTZ turns on her in fury.)

SCHWARTZ: No!

(LULU is upset by the violence of his reaction. Her tone is almost conciliatory.)

LULU: I was only teasing. I'm going to be an extremely wealthy widow, of course.

(SCHWARTZ stares at her, scarcely believing his ears. He laughs, gently.)

SCHWARTZ: They gave you a refrigerator instead of a heart.

(LULU ignores him.)

(They catch one another's eyes; they glare suspiciously. SCHWARTZ rushes over to her and clutches her hand.)

SCHWARTZ: Look at me!

LULU: What's biting you.

(He forces her to her knees.)

SCHWARTZ: Look at me!

LULU: Know what I see when I look deep into your eyes? I see me. Me in a bloody silly clown suit.

(*He pushes her away. She goes sprawling but collects herself with aplomb and heads for the bedroom.*)

LULU: I really must change.

(SCHWARTZ *catches her shoulder and pulls her round to face him.*)

SCHWARTZ: Who are you? What are you?

LULU: (*Struggling, scared.*) Stop it!

SCHWARTZ: Can't you tell the truth?

(LULU *realises these questions are not going to be about her paternity or her origins; she calms, answers in a normal voice.*)

LULU: I don't know.

SCHWARTZ: Do you believe in God?

LULU: I don't know.

SCHWARTZ: Is there anything that you'd swear by, swear to tell the truth by? Like your mother's grave. Would you swear by your mother's grave?

LULU: I don't know. Let go. You're hurting.

SCHWARTZ: Do you believe in anything?

LULU: I don't know.

SCHWARTZ: Have you got a soul?

LULU: I don't know.

SCHWARTZ: Have you ever been in love?

LULU: I don't know.

(SCHWARTZ *raises his eyes to heaven.*)

SCHWARTZ: She really doesn't know.

(LULU, *impassive, now coldly furious, repeats her part of the litany without expression.*)

LULU: I don't know. Just what is it, exactly, that you want to know?

(SCHWARTZ *is furious.*)

SCHWARTZ: Get dressed! Now!

(*She shrugs and goes off into the bedroom, banging the door behind her.* SCHWARTZ *edges towards the corpse.*)

SCHWARTZ: Tell you what, let's trade places. You can have her back again. I'm not strong enough. I haven't sufficient faith, and I've lived off servility too long. I'm terrified of being happy. Isn't it a scream. (*He screams.*) I never touched her. Honest. Wake up!

(*He kneels and, very tenderly, ties his handkerchief round* GOLL's *chin, to keep his mouth shut. Then, finding himself kneeling, he starts to pray.*)

Please God, let me be happy. Make me strong enough, make me free enough, to be happy. Not for my sake, God, but for *her* sake.

(LULU *comes out of the bedroom, fully dressed but in stockinged feet, so she looks unexpectedly tiny. She carries her shoes in her left hand and holds her dress together under her left arm. She raises her left arm, dropping her shoes with a clatter;* SCHWARTZ *looks round. He and the audience can see the gaping seam at the side of her dress.*)

LULU: (*Small, rather pitiful voice.*) Could you do up the hooks and eyes for me? My hand's shaking too much.

ACT TWO

(The bare white space of the studio is now spanned by a gallery that terminates right, in a staircase that comes down to the stage. The gallery and staircase are transparent – airy structures of perspex and chrome. The double doors stay where they are, but the wall with the extra door in it is now on the left. A few objects have turned the studio into an awesomely stylish living room. The table has been transformed into a structure of slate and steel; on it stand a decanter and glasses. An elegant small black desk – the colour scheme of the room is black and white – stands to the right of the central doors, at the back of the stage. The sofa has been bleached and covered in a fabric of broad black and white stripes. In front of the sofa is a zebra-skin rug. LULU's portrait stands on an easel. LULU herself, in a crisp white broderie anglaise negligée, lies on the sofa, leafing through the Tatler. Her face is already perfectly made up, her hair is tied up with a big white chiffon bow on top. She has the air of a model adopting a pose, although there is, as yet, nobody there to see.)

HENRIETTE: Here's ze mail, madame. There's ze 'at to take back to ze millinaire's, this morning, madame – will that be all?

LULU: That's fine . . .

(HENRIETTE minces out; LULU follows her thoughtfully with her eyes. She picks up a letter, opens it, skims.)

SCHWARTZ: *(Offstage.)* I've shifted that Spanish dancer. Fifty thousand marks.

LULU: Who says?

SCHWARTZ: *(Offstage.)* Sedelmeier in Paris. That's the third picture gone since we got married. Can it last, I ask myself.

LULU: 'Senior Executive Officer von Zalnikov has the honour to announce the engagement of his daughter, Charlotte Marie Adelaide, to Dr Ludwig Schoen.'

SCHWARTZ: *(Offstage.)* High time. He's been 'unofficially' engaged for longer than we've been legally married.

(LULU tucks the card away in her décolletage. SCHWARTZ enters.)

I've been asked to show in the International Exhibition in Petersburg. Can't think what to paint.

LULU: What about a nice young lady?

SCHWARTZ: You'll have to sit for me, again.

LULU: Aren't there any other nice young ladies who would do?

SCHWARTZ: I can't get it right with anyone but you.

LULU: *(Double entendre.)* Can I do it lying down?

SCHWARTZ: Do it any way you like.

(Silence. They both look at each other.)

Every time I look at you, it's like the first time. Such a show. Such a shock of pleasure.

LULU: *(Playfully seductive.)* Tiger!

(He comes back to her, fondles her hair.)

SCHWARTZ: I'm not used to pleasure. I keep thinking, it'll make me blind . . .

(LULU caresses his hand, then draws it inside the opening of her negligée. He hesitates, looks at the door.)

LULU: All work and no play makes Jack . . .

(SCHWARTZ now makes no attempt to disengage his hand.)

SCHWARTZ: I wish . . . I just wish . . .

(The doorbell rings.)

SCHWARTZ: Damn!

LULU: Nobody at home!

SCHWARTZ: Maybe it's the man from the gallery.

LULU: I don't care if it's King Kong.

SCHWARTZ: I'll only be a minute.

(He leaves LULU, a mite disgruntled, on the sofa. She takes out SCHOEN's engagement announcement, looks at it again and tears it across. She stows the pieces away under the cushions as SCHWARTZ returns.)

SCHWARTZ: Some beggar outside, says he's a war veteran – you deal with him, I've no change.

(His sexy mood has evaporated. He does not notice LULU gives a great beam of pleasure at his piece of information.)

SCHWARTZ: *(Brisk.)* I'd better get on with it.

(He disappears into the studio as one of the double doors opens and SCHIGOLCH pokes his head around the door, grinning.

LULU rushes towards him, kisses him, drags him in, leads him to the sofa and settles him down.

He is an elderly, puckish, dilapidated figure, small of stature, shabby genteel of manner, distinctly reminiscent of a Beckett tramp, comic, vicious, criminal.)

SCHIGOLCH: I'd imagined someone rather more suave. With more of an air, you understand. Whereas your new husband gives the impression he's not quite sure what to do with his hands. He seemed startled to see me.

LULU: However could you bring yourself to beg from him?

SCHIGOLCH: My darling one, I dragged myself all the way across town this morning with the intention of touching you for a loan, not him.

LULU: How much?

SCHIGOLCH: Two hundred, if you've got the cash handy. Or three. Some of my clients have evaporated.

(LULU goes to the little black desk and rummages there, extracting a roll of notes. She peels some off, hands them to him, he pockets them without counting.)

SCHIGOLCH: Apart from that, I'd a great desire to sneak a peek at Lulu's little nest.

(LULU makes an expansive gesture.)

LULU: Help yourself.

SCHIGOLCH: Breathtaking. Reminds me of my own place, of course. Well, my dear, you've come a long way.

LULU: Better than pounding the pavements.

SCHIGOLCH: And yourself?

LULU: Good . . . ish.

SCHIGOLCH: Let's just hope it lasts.

LULU: *(Affectionate.)* Miserable sod. *(Indicates bottle on table.)* Fancy something?

SCHIGOLCH: What's on offer?

(He rummages through the bottles.)

Not a real drinker, then.

LULU: Not yet. Drink has a different effect on different people, you know.

SCHIGOLCH: Does he beat you?

LULU: He just nods off. I half-thought you'd dropped off your perch.

SCHIGOLCH: The sun has set but still I cannot sleep.

(Music – a quality of 'memory-loss', a threatening melancholia.)

SCHIGOLCH: This is what I always wanted for you, Lulu. You were cut out for all this. The lush life.

LULU: When I remember . . . *(She makes a grimace and shivers.)* Ugh!

SCHIGOLCH: How do you pass the time? The occasional French lesson?

LULU: I lie in. I sleep late. *(She starts to stretch.)*

SCHIGOLCH: Just like a real lady. Perfect. But what else?

LULU: When I wake up, I s-t-r-e-t-c-h until something cracks.

SCHIGOLCH: And after you've cracked?

(Pause. They stare. Music stops.)

LULU: Mind your own business.

SCHIGOLCH: You *are* my business. I may not be long for this world but could I rest easy in my bed of clay if I knew my Lulu wasn't making the most of herself? Never!

(He looks at his empty glass and pours himself another drink.)

LULU: *(Sulky.)* Huh.

SCHIGOLCH: You want jam on it.

LULU: You don't know what you're talking about, you old bugger.

SCHIGOLCH: Don't tell me you spare a pang for the spanking wanker and his compulsory high kicks.

LULU: *(Resentful, stretching out one leg and contemplating it.)* My dancing days are over.

SCHIGOLCH: His, too. Come, now. Is my treasure troubled in her mind? She can speak freely.

Didn't I have faith in you when you were nothing but two enormous eyes?

What are you, now?

(LULU *draws her legs up under her, mimes being a cat.*)

LULU: Miaow!

(SCHIGOLCH *strokes her hair.*)

SCHIGOLCH: And very nice, too. My little stray has found a good home and I can pass on in peace. (*Sniffs beneath own armpit.*) Just as well. I'm rotting, already.

LULU: Every day, I anoint myself with oil. Then I dust myself with powder. I'm good enough to eat.

SCHIGOLCH: Haute cuisine for worms.

(LULU, *cuddled in his arms, affectionately pinches his cheek.*)

LULU: The worms that eat *you* won't get fat.

SCHIGOLCH: (*Spiteful.*) And I suppose you think you're better off, with your fine young body. I suppose you think your admirers are going to pickle your beautiful corpse and put it in a glass box and worship it. Well, they won't. They'll keep on telling you how lovely you are until you go out of fashion. Then they'll toss you out with the garbage.

(*They draw apart.*
There is a pause.)

LULU: (*Icy.*) Finished?

SCHIGOLCH: I'll find my own way out.

(*They stand up, looking angrily at one another. They laugh, embrace, kiss each other on the cheek. The doorbell shrills. They hear* SCHOEN *coming, so* SCHIGOLCH *slips the bottle back on the table on the way out (back door).*

LULU *turns back to the double doors, through which* SCHOEN *enters. She flings herself at him. He pushes her off, looking round.*)

LULU: Relax. Walter's working.

SCHOEN: I want to talk to you. In earnest.

LULU: (*Suggestive.*) You didn't want to *talk* to me yesterday.

SCHOEN: That was yesterday. You must stop coming to see me.

(LULU *picks up the bottle from the table and taps it invitingly.*)

LULU: Drinkies?

(*Then she notes the post-*SCHIGOLCH *level of liquid in the bottle and frowns.*)

SCHOEN: Thank you, no. 'Drinkies'. God. Have I made myself clear?

(LULU *shakes her head.*)

Very well. On your own head be it. You have the choice. Either you behave like a respectable married woman, or –

LULU: Or?

SCHOEN: I shall have to speak to your husband.

(LULU *calls out at once.*)

LULU: Walter!

(SCHOEN *clutches her arm and hushes her.*)

SCHOEN: Have you gone crazy?

(LULU *smiles beatifically. She has called his bluff.*)

LULU: Aha!

(*She returns to the sofa and sits down composedly in a pretty attitude of attention, cocking one leg over the other in a modestly provocative way.* SCHOEN *is thoroughly exasperated.*)

SCHOEN: You don't seem to be able to get into your thick skull what I'm trying to do for you.

LULU: Why are you scared of me? You've got what you always wanted.

SCHOEN: Stop that! I haven't tied the knot yet, remember. Lulu, I *want* this marriage and I want it to function *as* a marriage.

LULU: We can meet whenever you've got an hour free.

SCHOEN: We can meet whenever you're with your husband.

LULU: (*Self-assured.*) You don't really mean that.

SCHOEN: Your husband will know what I mean. He happens to be my friend.

LULU: He's my friend, too.

SCHOEN: God, he's a baby. Otherwise he'd have guessed.

LULU: I wish he would! Make him jump out of his pram.

(She leaps up and begins pacing round the room. Her suppressed boredom and resentment come flooding out.)

I'm his muse and his inspiration and all that crap but he never notices a blind thing about me. He's got eyes but he keeps them tight shut.

SCHOEN: Once he starts to look around –

LULU: You do it . . . open his eyes for him. I'm bored. I'm starting to let myself go . . . look at me, lounging around in my dressing gown until all hours.
    Would you believe, he says he never in all his life felt the need to go with women. Until now, of course.

SCHOEN: He's been painting naked ladies ever since he was fourteen, surely.

LULU: Come off it, he's scared stiff. *(She laughs briefly and mirthlessly.)* He isn't scared of me, I'll say that for him.

SCHOEN: Lots of girls would love to have a homebody like that for a husband.

LULU: Come off it. Go on. Corrupt him. You know how. I feel such a fool, stuck up on my bloody pedestal.

SCHOEN: I thought artists were hot-blooded, passionate, unconventional. Isn't he supposed to be an artist?

LULU: *(Briefly mimics the pose of* SCHWARTZ's *portrait.)* I made him into an artist.

SCHOEN: *(Reflective.)* And I made him famous, of course.

LULU: He hasn't the faintest idea who I am or what I am. If he knew, he'd tie a stone round my neck and drop me in the sea.

(She falls silent, wistful. There is a moment's silence. SCHOEN *collects himself. He starts for the door but cannot resist turning back for one last word.)*

SCHOEN: Lulu, I've married you off not once but twice. You live in luxury. Your husband's a great painter. What more do you want? Time to settle down, Lulu. Love him. Between us – kaput. All over. The end.

(He collects his hat and heads for the door. Music: dangerous, tense.)

LULU: *(With considerable dignity.)* Remember, when I tried to steal your watch? I was hungry, you got me a sandwich. I was cold. You tucked me up in your jacket. 'Long past your bedtime, girly,' you said, and brought me home. Anybody else would have called the police. Then you sent me away to school and taught me how to be a – a – a – *(Voice breaks on a sob.)* a lady. If there's anybody in the world I belong to, body and soul, then it's you. I don't know what would have become of me if it hadn't been for you.

SCHOEN: I thought a healthy young man of your own age would keep you busy.

LULU: I've been a dancer and I've been a model and I'm quite happy to earn my living like that. But I draw the line at love on demand.

SCHOEN: I've sacrificed enough already because of my liaison with you. I *need* this marriage. And what's the point of your ideal husband if people see you waltzing in and out of my house all the time like a bitch on heat.

LULU: You think a wedding-ring gives you the right to despise me! Oh, isn't she going to get on your nerves! She doesn't know anything, that one. Butter isn't the only thing that wouldn't melt in her mouth.

SCHOEN: I can do anything I want with that girl. Anything.

LULU: If you think I'm jealous of that little kid, you've got another think coming.

SCHOEN: That 'little kid' isn't quite a year younger than you.

(They glare at one another, standing at opposite ends of the sofa. Then SCHOEN *abruptly changes tack.)*

Mignon, Mignon, set me free. *(He is begging.)*

*(*SCHWARTZ *comes in from his studio.)*

SCHWARTZ: What's going on?

(The moment is gone. LULU *snaps.)*

LULU: *(To* SCHOEN.*)* Tell him. Go on.

*(*SCHWARTZ *looks from one to the other, sensing the tension between them.)*

SCHWARTZ: Whatever is the matter with both of you?

LULU: Nothing to do with you.

SCHOEN: Shut up.

(LULU bursts into furious tears.)

LULU: Bastard!

(She runs out. SCHWARTZ clatters back down the stairs. He is angry.)

SCHWARTZ: Getting your jollies, are you, making her cry?

SCHOEN: Sit down.

SCHWARTZ: I beg your pardon!

SCHOEN: *Sit down.*

(SCHWARTZ reluctantly sits on the edge of the sofa. He is furious – furious because his work has been interrupted, furious because his patron has made his wife cry, furious because of what he sensed between SCHOEN and LULU when he came into the room.

SCHOEN *paces the floor, searching for words.)*

SCHWARTZ: *(Peremptory.)* Well?

SCHOEN: You married into a lot of money – half a million, to be precise.

SCHWARTZ: So have I pissed it against the wall?

SCHOEN: Not yet.

SCHWARTZ: Would you be kind enough to reveal to me the significance of this extraordinary scene.

SCHOEN: You married half a million.

SCHWARTZ: Sue me.

SCHOEN: You've got yourself a name, now. You can have anything you want.

SCHWARTZ: What are you getting at?

SCHOEN: The past six months have been unadulterated bliss for you. Everybody envies you your wife. She, on the other hand, she deserves a husband she can respect.

(SCHWARTZ looks at him blankly. Then he looks at his paint-stained hands.)

SCHWARTZ: *(Bitter.)* She doesn't respect me. Tell me more.

(SCHOEN drops his vagueness and adopts a man-of-the-world air.)

SCHOEN: Just . . . keep an eye on her.

SCHWARTZ: *(Instantly suspicious.)* What?

SCHOEN: *(Snaps.)* We're not children, for God's sake!

SCHWARTZ: What has she been up to?

SCHOEN: *(Sighs.)* You married half a million.

(SCHWARTZ seizes SCHOEN by the throat. SCHOEN fights him off, forces him to sit down on the sofa.)

SCHOEN: No. No. This is a serious business.

SCHWARTZ: What's she up to?

SCHOEN: You just tot up all you owe that girl. Then balance it against your own sins of omission.

SCHWARTZ: *(Coming to the point at once.)* Who's the man?

SCHOEN: Why? Do you want to fight a duel?

SCHWARTZ: How long has it been going on?

SCHOEN: I didn't come to cause a scandal.

SCHWARTZ: *(Shaking his head.)* You've got it wrong . . . You don't understand her.

SCHOEN: You've got to face the truth . . . *(A silence.)* When I first met her . . .

SCHWARTZ: When was that?

SCHOEN: When she was twelve.

SCHWARTZ: *(Bewildered.)* She never told me.

SCHOEN: She used to sell flowers outside the Alhambra Café. Barefoot, in rags. Every night, from midnight on, she'd pick her way among the tables, offering little bunches of violets to the gentlemen. Violets. *(Chuckles.)*

SCHWARTZ: *(Voice pale with astonishment.)* She never said.

SCHOEN: I'm only telling you now so that you understand it's not a question of innate depravity. Far from it.

SCHWARTZ: She told me her aunt looked after her when she was little.

SCHOEN: There's a very wonderful woman I know, runs a very special little private school – she smoothed off the rough edges, taught her her manners, what to order, what to wear and so forth. God, she blossomed! If you've failed to bring out the best in her, you've only yourself to blame.

(SCHWARTZ *buries his head in his hands.*)

SCHWARTZ: Oh, God.

SCHOEN: *(Hearty.)* No 'Oh Gods' please. You've been perfectly happy for six months. Nothing can spoil that. Don't think of yourself as a loser – you just won half a million, didn't you!

SCHWARTZ: She told me she'd never . . . never . . .

SCHOEN: *(Laughs heartily.)* Good heavens, man, apart from anything else, there was Goll!

(*He rests his hand companionably on* SCHWARTZ'*s shoulder for a moment. He feels absolutely in control, now, and richly generous, in much the mood of a man making a speech at the wedding of a favourite daughter.*)

Live within the demands she makes on you and you'll be very, very happy.

SCHWARTZ: He made her wear gym slips.

SCHOEN: But he made an honest woman of her! She managed to coax him to the altar, after all . . . (*He feels it is safe to risk a risqué remark.*) . . . well, I daresay you've some idea of her powers of persuasion yourself, by now!

(SCHWARTZ *does not join in his chuckle. He seems quite calm, now, no longer dazed.*)

SCHWARTZ: How did she meet Goll?

SCHOEN: Through me, of course. After my first wife died, after I started to put out the first delicate feelers in the direction of the lady who is now my fiancée . . . *She* tried to ruin it, of course. She'd made up her mind she was going to marry me, would you believe!

(SCHWARTZ *leaves sufficient silence before he speaks to allow* SCHOEN *to register the impropriety of this last remark.*)

SCHWARTZ: And when Goll died? Did she –

SCHOEN: *(Brutal; time to put this young man in his place.)* You married half a million.

(*Pause.*)

SCHWARTZ: I wish I'd starved to death in a garret.

(SCHOEN remembers that SCHWARTZ is a man who 'lives on a higher moral plane'. He will console him by assuring him that corruption is both normal and inevitable.)

SCHOEN: So you think I'm not compromised, myself. Who isn't. Your half-million wedding settlement gave you the right connections. Now you're a famous painter. You haven't the right to judge her. Don't apply middle-class standards to a person of her background.

SCHWARTZ: I don't understand.

SCHOEN: The gutter. Utter degradation. I found her in a state of utter degradation.

SCHWARTZ: Found who?

SCHOEN: Your wife.

SCHWARTZ: Eva?

SCHOEN: I used to call her Mignon.

SCHWARTZ: I thought her name was Nell.

SCHOEN: Goll called her Little Nell.

SCHWARTZ: I always called her Eva.

SCHOEN: I never knew her real name.

SCHWARTZ: *(Absent-minded.)* Do you think *she* knows her real name?

(SCHOEN has done his duty and feels a sense of release. He wants to get back to his office but can't resist one last piece of advice. He never can.)

SCHOEN: Call her what you want but give her what she needs. She was in her seventh heaven with Goll and he wasn't one to pull his punches.

(SCHWARTZ winces.)

SCHWARTZ: She said she'd never responded, you know what I mean, never had a real –

SCHOEN: Pull yourself together.

SCHWARTZ: She swore on her mother's grave.

SCHOEN: Her mother hasn't got a grave.

SCHWARTZ: I don't belong in this world.

(He folds his arms round himself and rocks backwards and forwards. He screams, just as he screamed in his speech over GOLL's corpse in Act One.)

SCHOEN: What's wrong?

SCHWARTZ: Terrible pain!

(SCHOEN *dismisses the pain as, probably, indigestion.*)

SCHOEN: Take care of her. Yes, she belongs to you. But for how long?

(SCHWARTZ *clasps his chest, pointing to his heart.*)

SCHWARTZ: Terrible pain, here.

(SCHOEN *cunningly appeals to his greed.*)

SCHOEN: Think of that half-million! That ought to make the pain go away.

SCHWARTZ: I wish I could cry.

(*He starts up from the sofa, suddenly filled with determination.*)

SCHWARTZ: I must go and have it out with her.

SCHOEN: That's the ticket. Kind but firm.

(SCHWARTZ *disappears through the studio door . . . It bangs behind him. Alone,* SCHOEN *wipes his brow.*)

SCHOEN: Whew!

(*Then he recalls that* LULU *did not go into the studio.*)

But . . . Lulu went upstairs.

(*Pause.*
   A terrible scream.
   LULU *appears on the gallery.*)

LULU: Oh, Gawd.

(SCHOEN *goes to the studio door and raps briskly.*)

SCHOEN: Open this door.

(*Silence. He knocks again. Silence. He tries the handle. The door is locked from inside.*
   LULU *comes slowly downstairs.*)

LULU: (*She doesn't believe it herself.*) He'll have a good cry. Then he'll feel better.

(SCHOEN *tries the door handle again.*)

SCHOEN: Is there an axe in the kitchen?

(LULU stares at him, bewildered. There comes a reverberating groan. She is instantly serious. She heads for the door.)

SCHOEN: Where are you off to?

LULU: Doctor.

SCHOEN: Oh no, you don't. Not with me here.

(She understands everything perfectly. If a doctor finds SCHOEN here, his reputation will be lost.)

LULU: *(Spitting out each word.)* Serves you right.

(They snarl. The doorbell rings, loud and long. LULU makes a move to answer.)

SCHOEN: Stay where you are.

(The doorbell rings again, twice, agitatedly. SCHOEN gestures impatiently and goes out through the double doors to answer it himself. While he is out, LULU creeps up to the studio door, kneels, listens. SCHOEN returns with ALVA. ALVA is very excited.)

ALVA: There's been a revolution in Paris.

SCHOEN: There happen to be other things to think about.

(LULU sits on the floor, legs sticking out in front of her like a child, so forlorn that even in the midst of his excitement, ALVA notices.)

ALVA: You look down in the mouth.

(A choking noise, SCHWARTZ's death rattle, comes from the studio. All three are transfixed.)

LULU: *(With dignity.)* God have mercy on you.

(SCHOEN rattles the studio door handle.)

SCHOEN: Where's that axe?

LULU: The axe? Oh, the axe.

(She wanders off, disorientated. SCHOEN pulls himself together with a visible effort. This is a characteristic trick of his, perhaps learned from a character-training manual.)

SCHOEN: So. There's been a revolution in Paris.

ALVA: There's chaos at the paper. The phone lines are jammed. No one knows what to write.

(*The doorbell rings,* SCHOEN *breaks down. He rushes at the studio door, beating it with his fists.*)

SCHOEN: Walter! Walter!

ALVA: Shall I break the door down?

SCHOEN: He's the one who had all the fun, and now we've got to clean up his messes.

(LULU *comes back, cradling an axe in her arms as if it were a baby.*)

LULU: The maid is home.

SCHOEN: Then shut the door, for heaven's sake.

ALVA: Give me that thing.

(*He wedges the blade of the axe between the doorpost and the lock.*)

SCHOEN: Press harder.

ALVA: It's coming.

(*He smashes the door down. The door jumps out of its lock. He drops the axe and staggers back.*)

LULU: (*To* SCHOEN.) After you.

(SCHOEN *turns away abruptly.*)

LULU: (*Taunting.*) Give you a funny feeling, huh?

(SCHOEN *stiffens. He marches sternly into the studio.* ALVA *collapses on to the sofa, sprawling full length. Suddenly* LULU *breaks. She throws herself at* ALVA's *feet, grasping his knees.*)

LULU: Take me away.

ALVA: Where?

LULU: Anywhere. Just as long as I'm not on my own.

SCHOEN: (*Reappearing.*) The bloody, bloody fool. I'm done for.

ALVA: He must have suddenly realised what he'd taken on.

SCHOEN: Where did he keep his papers?

LULU: In the desk.

(SCHOEN rummages.)

SCHOEN: Where in the damn desk?

(LULU pushes him aside, pulls out a drawer and dumps its contents on the floor.)

LULU: See? All present and correct. Don't be scared. No dark secrets. Not our Walter.

(SCHOEN goes down on his knees, sifting through the papers.)

SCHOEN: I might as well go into a monastery. Now.

(LULU stirs the papers with her foot. She unearths the wad of banknotes from which she paid SCHIGOLCH.)

LULU: Write him a lovely obituary. Call him the Leonardo de nos jours.

(She licks her fingers and starts counting the banknotes.)

SCHOEN: What's the point.

(He gestures towards the studio door.)

There lies my engagement. R.I.P.

ALVA: *(In exactly the same tones that LULU had used.)* Serve you right.

SCHOEN: Go ahead! Shout it from the rooftops!

ALVA: If you'd only done the decent thing by this girl *(Indicates Lulu.)* when Mother died!

SCHOEN: Meanwhile, my engagement is bleeding to death.

(LULU stows the banknotes in her handbag.)

LULU: I'm clearing off now. If anyone cares.

SCHOEN: The *Late News* will be on the streets in half an hour. I daren't go out. I'll be lynched.

ALVA: You'll just have to go away for a while.

SCHOEN: What? And let the tongues wag?

(LULU, on her way to the door, has stopped short at the sofa. She stares at it, as under a sudden spell. She reaches out to touch it.)

LULU: Just think. Only ten minutes ago *he* was lying on this sofa.

SCHOEN: After all I've done for him. And the stupid bastard ruins my life.

(LULU *gives him a stricken look and collapses on the sofa.*)

ALVA: Hypocrite.

LULU: (*Weary.*) Cut it out, Alva. We're all in this together.

ALVA: Too true.

(*He goes over to the sofa and sits on the arm.*)

SCHOEN: What do you propose to tell the police?

(ALVA *and* LULU *look at one another and shrug. They look very brother and sister-ish, perched on the sofa together.*)

LULU: Nothing.

ALVA: He wanted to be at one with his destiny.

LULU: He always had a morbid streak.

(*They start to giggle.*)

SCHOEN: (*Irony.*) He was a man whose dreams had all come true.

LULU: (*Even more irony.*) But he paid a high price for them.

(LULU *and* ALVA *sigh in unison and stare at* SCHOEN, *in unison;* SCHOEN *flares up at* ALVA.)

SCHOEN: Don't think I don't know what you're getting at! You're the one who wouldn't stand for the idea of brothers and sisters. You've only yourself to blame.

(*They continue to look at him in disbelief.*)

ALVA: You don't understand human nature.

LULU: There's still time for a little 'late news' all your very own.

(*She swiftly sketches a pregnant belly on herself with a gesture of her hand.*)

SCHOEN: (*Exploding.*) That fool didn't think twice about the consequences.

(*He takes a deep breath and regains his presence of mind. He addresses* ALVA *calmly.*)

A revolution in Paris, you said.

ALVA: Pandemonium at the news desk.

SCHOEN: Not many column inches to spare for a run-of-the-mill suicide, then. I own the paper. I decide what's news.

(*The pair on the sofa gaze at him coldly.*)

I wish the police would come.

(*The doorbell rings.*)

ACT THREE

(Music coming through from the onstage chorus numbers.
LULU*'s dressing room.*

Red curtains hang down to the stage from the gallery, creating a smaller, more intimate space. The only door visible in this crimson enclave is the one on the left, also painted red. On it is hung a huge gold star. The portrait of LULU *hangs centre back. Light bulbs ring its frame. Where the black desk stood stands a dressing table laden with make-up, its mirror also ringed by light bulbs. Beside it, right, a screen, and a bentwood hatstand from which hang a variety of stage costumes on clothes hangers. The small table, minus a cloth, now boasts an ice-bucket containing a bottle of champagne and glasses; it stands downstage, on the left. The sofa, covered with a zebra-skin throw, stands downstage right.*

Sound of humming from behind the screen; LULU *is singing to herself. Pop!*
ALVA *in dinner-jacket and white tie uncorks the champagne.)*

ALVA: They went wild. Never seen anything like it.

LULU: *(From behind the screen.)* Not too much for me. Is he going to come tonight?

ALVA: D'you mean my father?

LULU: Who else.

(SCHOEN bustles in without knocking.)

ALVA: Talk of the devil!

(LULU looks over the top of the screen.)

LULU: *(Reproachful.)* You write all about me in the papers but do you come and see for yourself? Do you hell!

(SCHOEN drops a kiss on top of her head.)

SCHOEN: *(Hearty.)* At it day and night, my dear! Hard at it. All for your sake. See how well the publicity campaign worked, the theatre's packed. By the way, keep downstage more.

LULU: I've got to get used to the lights.

ALVA: She does what we've rehearsed.

SCHOEN: Then rehearse it again! *(To LULU.)* What's the next number?

LULU: Flower girl.

SCHOEN: *(To ALVA.)* Tights?

ALVA: Long dress.

SCHOEN: Is that meant to be symbolism?

ALVA: *(Frosty.)* Don't you ever look at a dancer's feet?

SCHOEN: What counts is where the audience looks.

ALVA: *(Still frosty.)* The punters would appear to be perfectly satisfied.

SCHOEN: So they should be. I've spent the last six months telling them she's the hottest thing in Europe. She shifted the French revolution off the front page. Power of the press, eh?

(He drops his gloves on the table, having reduced LULU's and his son's success to ashes. He consumes a glass of champagne.)

SCHOEN: *(Elaborately casual.)* Has the prince dropped in?

ALVA: Nobody's dropped in.

LULU: A prince? What prince? Are you fixing me up with yet another chinless wonder?

SCHOEN: *(Ignoring her.)* Shall I see you later?

ALVA: Are you with someone?

SCHOEN: I can get rid of them. Usual place?

ALVA: Twelve-ish?

SCHOEN: Right.

(He picks up his gloves, goes out. He leaves a pause behind him.)

ALVA: He was in a rotten mood. Don't let him upset you. Save yourself for the last act.

(LULU comes out from behind the screen dressed in a long Grecian-style white dress with flowers in her hair. She carries a basket of violets, which she puts down on the table when she picks up her champagne glass.)

After all, I keep the climax for the last act. Everything else is foreplay.

LULU: You reveal me little by little.

(Glass in hand, she slowly extends one leg to reveal the way her long white dress is slit all the way up one side.)

LULU: Flower girl. Gawd. If I'd tried to sell flowers in front of the Alhambra Café in this get-up, they'd have run me in.

ALVA: You were a babe-in-arms.

LULU: Do you remember what I looked like? That first time? When I tiptoed into your room, that time, when we were both kids?

ALVA: Dark blue dress. Black velvet collar. Eyes like saucers.

LULU: I was looking for somewhere to hide.

ALVA: My poor mother. She'd been sick in bed for two years.

LULU: You were playing with your toy theatre. You said, did I want to play, too.

ALVA: Our toy theatre.

LULU: I can still see you, pushing the little figures backwards and forwards.

ALVA: I went to pieces when I found out about you and my father.

LULU: You clammed up on me. Froze. Couldn't get a word out of you.

ALVA: Oh God – I worshipped you. When Mother died, I stamped off to my father then and there and ordered him to marry you or I'd challenge him to a duel. Just imagine. I was seventeen years old.

LULU: He told me.

ALVA: Now I'm older, I feel sorry for him.

LULU: Is that fiancée of his still *intacta*?

ALVA: She really loves him, you know.

(LULU *abruptly shoves her glass towards* ALVA; *he tops it up.*)

ALVA: You drink too much.

LULU: I've got to make him see me when I dance. *Really* see me. I'm only really me when I dance. Not that he cares. He only put me on the stage in the first place so that I'd get off with a sugar daddy and out of his hair.

ALVA: Do you know, I've always wanted to write a play for you.

LULU: Why don't you write plays that are a bit more like life?

ALVA: Nobody would believe them.

LULU: I'm a much better actress in real life, better than anyone ever is on a stage.

ALVA: I like to see the punters mad with rapture.

LULU: I'd like to see myself mad with rapture.

ALVA: You always look like that when you dance.

LULU: Don't think I don't know what I'm doing. Each and every one of those suckers down there thinks he's the only one I'm dancing for, the one who'll drive me mad with rapture.

ALVA: How do you know that?

LULU: A feeling . . . a shiver up my spine.

(A shrill bell rings to call her on stage.)

ALVA: (Lightly.) You are extraordinary . . .

LULU: Where's my shawl . . . (Reminds herself.) Stay downstage, stay downstage . . .

(ALVA affectionately wraps her in her shawl, gives her a peck on the cheek. She raises a radiant face.)

LULU: Wish me luck. I want him to go mad with rapture, too.

(ALVA sends her on her way with a slap on the backside.)

Ouch!

(She disappears through the door. ALVA looks after her, fondly. The dressing-room door opens. PRINCE ESCERNY enters – tall, thin, evening dress, monocle, heavily suntanned, nervous, desiccated, mad.)

ESCERNY: (Hungarian accent.) She didn't really move me profoundly until the middle of Act Three.

(Renewed baying offstage.)

ALVA: (Absently.) Yeah . . . She really gets her teeth into this number.

ESCERNY: I had the rare pleasure of meeting the artiste once at Mr Schoen's house; when I visited him to discuss the publication of the journal of my travels around Lake Tanganyika.

(ALVA looks up and recognises ESCERNY. He rises, shakes hands.)

ALVA: My father was very impressed by your work.

ESCERNY: She doesn't seem to see the audience. She seems to be aware of her own body and nothing else. When she dances she is celebrating her own body. Worshipping it.

(*Renewed cheers and applause of the audience.*)

ALVA: Here she comes.

(*He opens the door for flushed, breathless* LULU. *She throws her shawl over the screen.*)

LULU: I did three curtain calls. (*To* ESCERNY.) Is Mr Schoen in your box?

ESCERNY: No.

LULU: (*Crestfallen.*) He must have buggered off somewhere.

ESCERNY: He's in the last stalls box on the left.

LULU: He's ashamed of me.

ALVA: (*Conciliatory.*) He was late, he couldn't get a decent seat.

LULU: (*To* ALVA.) Go and ask him if he liked me better, that time.

ALVA: I'll send him up.

ESCERNY: He clapped.

(LULU *whips round, all attention.*)

LULU: Sure?

ALVA: (*Sympathetic.*) Take a rest, now.

(*He goes out.* LULU *looks at* ESCERNY *with a mixture of interest and derision; she is aware that* SCHOEN *has offered her for sale to him.*)

LULU: Mr Schoen send you up?

(ESCERNY *nods and smiles. She nods back, grim.*)

LULU: I must change. Where did you say he was sitting?

ESCERNY: In the left stalls box furthest from the stage.

(LULU *nods, then begins to count off on her fingers.*)

LULU: Five more to go . . . dancing girl, ballerina, Queen of the Night, Ariel, Lascaris . . .

(*She gives* ESCERNY *a dazzling smile and retires behind her screen.* ESCERNY *paces up and down, hands behind back.*)

ESCERNY: Have I completely misunderstood you? Or am I right about the way you smile when the crowd finally loses its head? Something, almost, of pain in that smile, as if the baying of the crowd grates harshly after the ecstasy of the dance. Something, almost, of agony in that smile. And then I wonder whether, in your heart, you don't find it pure torment, when you degrade your art by dancing for the pleasure of the filthy-minded rabble.

(LULU's head appears above the screen for a moment, startled. ESCERNY doesn't notice her. She watches him pace, then hastily ducks down again as he turns and begins to pace back towards her.)

Your smile. When I see your sad, radiant smile, I ask myself: might she be glad, one day, to abandon the hysterical glare of the limelight?

(LULU, unseen, throws her white dress over the screen.)

That marvellous smile suggests a woman whose . . . pride . . . might be potent enough to permit her to respect a man who . . . gave himself to her . . . absolutely.

(LULU, unseen, throws a pair of white stockings over the screen. Then she emerges from behind the screen in a black leather corset with high black boots. ESCERNY gives a grunt of surprise and satisfaction. LULU is still lacing up her corset at the back.)

I wouldn't think of keeping you from dancing. Except, instead of the sweaty mob, the stench of beer and tobacco, the animal roaring, there would be a small, select audience. Very select. Very small. One. Audience of one connoisseur.

(LULU goes to the dressing table, leans forward and examines her face in a calm, objective, professional way.)

ESCERNY: Picture it. A garden, by moonlight. The rippling of the lake . . . You could dance for me, there. At night.

(LULU goes on staring at her face.)

I need, you understand, to relax. When I go off to Africa, to explore, I can never relax for a moment. The discipline . . . iron discipline.

(LULU turns at the word 'discipline', biting her fingernail.)

One has to force oneself to be a real man all the time. So, when I come home, I let myself go. I don't give orders any more, I like to take them. I like to submit. It's a perfectly natural reaction.

(LULU thrusts out her booted foot. ESCERNY kneels and kisses it. He sighs.)

What is the question of the age? I'll tell you – it's 'What does a woman want?'

(*He stretches out until he is flat on his back. He takes her booted foot and places it on his forehead.*)

Can a woman imagine more happiness than to have a man utterly in her power?

(LULU *poses as dominatrix for a moment. Then she bursts out laughing and kicks him, not hard, so that he rolls away from her.*)

LULU: You must be joking.

(*She turns back to the dressing table, takes a brush and brushes powder over her face.*
ESCERNY *gets to his feet, dusting himself off, not displeased with the way things are going.*
LULU *gives him a quizzical stare. He is edging closer and closer to her.*)

ESCERNY: It might make a man happy even if you weren't faithful to him. It might even make him happier . . . than to be loved.

LULU: If you think that, you've never been loved at all.

(*She presents him with her back.* ESCERNY *goes back to pacing up and down while* LULU *struggles with the corset. She gets the knot free at last and inhales deeply.*)

LULU: That's better!

(*The bell rings. She takes the costume for the skirt-dance from the hatstand.*)

Cheers. I'm on.

(ESCERNY *rises, clicks his heels, kisses her hand.*)

ESCERNY: May I stay a little longer? I should like to be alone, now.

(LULU *raises her eyebrows.*)

LULU: As long as you don't mess about with my clothes or anything.

(*She takes her shawl and goes out.* ESCERNY *goes to the dressing table, picks up the brush with which she has powdered herself and lightly dusts his own face. He inspects himself absently in the mirror. He puts the brush down.*)

ESCERNY: She is too perfect to be real.

(*Applause, off, as* LULU *greets her audience.* ALVA *comes in, letting in a burst of applause with him, whistles, etc.*)

ALVA: They can't get enough.

ESCERNY: Is she coming back?

ALVA: She'll change in the wings.

(Music: then gasps; the music stops. The bell rings, and continues to ring; now it sounds like an alarm. Shouts. Confusion.)

ALVA: Oh God, what's going on? Come on!

(They rush out, leaving the door open. The bell stops.

LULU, *in a white ballet skirt covered by her shawl, comes in and closes the door behind her. She is trembling; she looks deeply upset. She lies down on the sofa and arranges the shawl over her so that she cannot be seen.* ALVA *returns. He stops still when he sees her.)*

ALVA: Do you feel faint?

LULU: *(Without moving.)* Shut that door.

ALVA: Go back on stage, at least.

LULU: Did you see him?

ALVA: See who?

*(*LULU *sits up.)*

LULU: With his fiancée!

ALVA: *(Furious.)* What?

*(*SCHOEN *bursts through the open door, slamming it behind him. He wears evening dress, white silk scarf, etc. He is white with rage.* ALVA *turns on him.)*

ALVA: You could have spared her that.

SCHOEN: What the hell's got into her? *(To* LULU.*)* How could you do this to me?

(He bolts the door. Then he advances on LULU *menacingly.)*

You're billed to dance and dance you will.

LULU: *(Her voice is flat with despair.)* You want me to dance for your fiancée.

SCHOEN: You can't say who you want to watch you dance and who you don't. You've signed a contract. You're paid your money –

LULU: *(Flash of spirit.)* That's none of your business.

SCHOEN: *(Ignoring her.)* You'll dance for whoever buys a ticket and I'll sit in my box with whoever I please.

ALVA: I wish to God you'd stayed in your damn' box.

(There is a furious knocking on the door from outside.)

That's the stage manager. *(Calls.)* Just a minute! *(To LULU.)* Do you really want me to cancel the performance?

SCHOEN: Get down on stage.

LULU: Give me five minutes. Put on the next number. Nobody's going to notice whether I go on now or in five minutes.

ALVA: Do you mean five minutes?

LULU: The bloody show must go bloody on.

(The hammering on the door starts up again.)

ALVA: Coming!

(He flies off, banging the door shut behind him, relieved.)

LULU: Now I know where I stand. Now I know what you really think of me. So you want me to dance in front of your fiancée – kick my legs up and let her watch. Thanks.

SCHOEN: *(Sneer.)* Considering where you've sprung from, it's a wonder they still let you exhibit yourself in front of decent people.

LULU: *(Irony.)* Of course, decent people just don't know what to do with themselves when I flash my bum, do they.

SCHOEN: On the contrary. Your shamelessness is your greatest asset. And what a triumph you've just had! I could scarcely keep a decent girl from walking straight out of the theatre when you came on! But you won't be a great star until you've lost that last shred of self-respect that still keeps you just this side of obscenity.

LULU: I don't care what people think about me. I've never pretended to be better than I am.

SCHOEN: *(Righteous indignation.)* So that's your true self, is it, flaunting itself out there on stage!

LULU: You know what you said just now about me losing 'my last shred of self-respect' . . . Well, I don't think I ever had any. Not self-respect *as such*.

SCHOEN: Don't play games.

(LULU *draws her knees up under her chin; she looks like an orphan child, wistful, apologetic, sad.*)

LULU: What ever would have become of me if you hadn't saved me?

SCHOEN: Do you really think you're saved?

(LULU *abandons her child-like pose and laughs with a wild, wistful voluptuousness. She shows, for the first time, a touch of the tiger. She would do anything so as not to lose* SCHOEN.)

LULU: No, thank God . . . ! And I'm ever so, ever so happy.

(*She throws her arms round him mockingly, clinging to his neck. He forces her off violently.*)

SCHOEN: Right. Now dance!

LULU: Oh, I'll dance, all right. I'll dance my dance, my way, no matter who watches.

SCHOEN: On you go.

LULU: Let me pull myself together. They'll ring when they want me.

(SCHOEN'*s self-righteousness is fading. The past is rising up between them.*)

SCHOEN: I sacrificed so much for you. And look at you now.

LULU: (*Pert.*) Perhaps you over-estimated the benefit of your influence.

SCHOEN: Spare me your wit.

(*Pause of one heart-beat.*)

LULU: The prince dropped in.

SCHOEN: What if he did?

LULU: I'm off to Africa with him.

SCHOEN: Africa?

LULU: Why not? I thought you only put me on the boards so that some moneybags would sweep me off them again.

SCHOEN: But not to Africa.

LULU: Then why didn't you let me faint in peace, turn your back, walk away?

SCHOEN: I need to make you see what you are. I need to make you see at whom you shouldn't look.

LULU: Whatever happened to your will power? You've been engaged for three years. Why don't you marry her? Why do you always put the blame on me? *You* told me to marry Goll. *You* told me to marry that painter. You, you can invent governments and unmake prime ministers. You turned me into a famous dancer. You can do anything. Go ahead. Get married. It's easy. What's stopping you?

SCHOEN: *(Furious.)* I suppose you think you're stopping me!

LULU: *(Triumphant.)* Now you're angry! I can't tell you how happy it makes me to see you so angry. It makes me proud to see the depths you'll sink to, and you want to pull me down with you, pull me down as low as a man can pull a woman, because you think that then you won't possibly be able to love the thing you've made of me. But you're hurting yourself much more than you're hurting me. You know you can't keep control of yourself – leave me alone! For your precious fiancée's sake! Before you have a change of heart. Now. Go.

SCHOEN: I'm not scared of you any more.

LULU: Scared of me? You ought to be scared of yourself. I don't need you. Go away. *Please.* And don't blame me, this time. You think that all I have to do is faint and your future promptly expires, do you? Huh! Or maybe you still believe, underneath it all, that I'm a tart with a twenty-four-carat heart who'll kiss you goodbye dutifully when you say, time's up, baby. Well, I'm not. And I won't.

SCHOEN: Don't tell me what I think. You've sent two men to their graves, already. Take your prince and finish him off, too. Just keep away from me.

LULU: *(Irony.)* I'll take care to lock my bedroom door.

SCHOEN: *(Temper flaring up again.)* As God is my witness, I hate you, I hate you, I hate you.

LULU: That's because of my working–class origins.

SCHOEN: It's because you're depraved.

LULU: Oh, wonderful! I am depraved and I am to blame! There. Now you're absolved. You can go on thinking of yourself as a paragon of moral virtue, always and ever upright! *(Vicious double entendre here.)* Otherwise how could you marry that poor ignorant girl!

SCHOEN: *(Equanimity gone.)* You're asking for a thrashing!

LULU: *(Quick as a flash.)* Yes, please! Who do you have to fuck to get a decent thrashing round here!

SCHOEN: Shut up!

LULU: Just go ahead, marry her. Bless you, my children. And I can watch the poor, miserable baby dancing herself to death instead of her watching me.

SCHOEN: *(Raising his hand.)* God forgive me.

LULU: *(Mocking.)* Oooh, he's going to hit me!

(He slaps her face. She drops to her knees and clasps his thighs in a parody of ecstatic submission.)

More! More!

(But she can scarcely contain her laughter. SCHOEN *drops his aggressive pose and shakes his head from side to side, dazed.*

He pushes LULU *aside, after a few moments – she sprawls on the floor, weak with laughter – and staggers to the door. He stops short, with his hand on the doorknob.)*

SCHOEN: I can't let the poor girl see me like this.

*(*LULU *calms down and sits up.)*

LULU: You are a man without a conscience. You dominate half the world. You are utterly ruthless. You're quite prepared, in cold blood, to wreck this innocent girl's life. You can do exactly what you please but you know just as well as I do that –

*(*SCHOEN *lurches to the sofa and collapses, head in hands.* LULU *continues triumphantly:)*

– that you are too weak to leave me.

(Pause.
   SCHOEN*'s shoulders heave.)*

LULU: This is going down a real treat, I can tell you. Balm to my battered ego.

*(*SCHOEN *sobs.)*

Gawd! Look at you! One minute you're about to beat me to a pulp, next minute you've turned into a . . . a ravening wimp.

SCHOEN: I can't go to her like this.

LULU: You can't stay here like this, either. Out!

(SCHOEN turns to her, utterly vanquished.)

SCHOEN: What shall I do, Mignon?

(LULU rummages about among the pots and jars on the dressing table. She produces a little account book, flicks through it until she finds an empty page. She picks out an eyebrow pencil. SCHOEN realises what she is up to.)

SCHOEN: No.

(LULU brings him the open accounts book and the pencil and kneels beside him.)

LULU: *(Dictating.)* 'My dear young lady . . .'

(SCHOEN pushes away the accounts book.)

SCHOEN: I can't.

LULU: *(Remorseless.)* 'My dear young lady . . .'

SCHOEN: You're dictating my death sentence. You know that?

LULU: Go on!

(He writes.)

'My' *(Relishing the word.)* 'conscience will not permit me to link your fate with my own. I assure you that I am not worthy of your heart.'

(SCHOEN turns imploringly to her.)

Get on with it! 'I write this at the side of the woman who has me in her power.' *(She is almost overcome by giggling as she dictates this.)* 'Forget me. Signed, Ludwig Schoen.'

SCHOEN: Oh, God!

LULU: *(Serious.)* Oh, no. You mustn't 'Oh, God' her. Sign it. 'Ludwig Schoen. P.S. Do not try to save me.'

(SCHOEN finishes writing, drops pencil and account book on the floor and slithers off the sofa to collapse at her feet. She fondles his head. She looks pleased and pretty and very innocent and fresh in her white ballet dress.

There is a knock on the door; the FIANCÉE *bursts in, followed by* ALVA. *The* FIANCÉE *takes one look and turns away.* LULU *gives* ALVA *a great beam of laughing triumph; she's pulled it off at last! She's finally got the only man she ever loved to promise to marry her.)*

ACT FOUR

(The SCHOEN *residence.*

Dumbshow of the house being redecorated. Candles are lit. LULU*'s portrait, this time in a flamboyant gilt frame, goes up on the wall. Thunderous organ music; footmen, maids, scamper round. A lavish fringed cloth – maybe a cashmere shawl – is thrown over the sofa. There is a nude statue – Venus. The* COUNTESS GESCHWITZ, *in gents natty suiting, fedora in hand, is saying goodbye to* SCHOEN – *impeccable in business suit – and* LULU, *in some form of extremely glamorous at-home wear.* LULU *looks wonderfully tended, exquisite hair, exquisite make-up.*

An impression of stifling wealth.)

GESCHWITZ: So we shall look forward to seeing you at the Women's Arts Ball!

LULU: Me, but not my husband.

GESCHWITZ: Never . . . ! It's a 'women's only' event, after all!

(A look of disgust crosses SCHOEN*'s features.)*

Just for once, *you* can wear the trousers. Promise!

LULU: *(Peals of laughter.)* White tie and tails! I promise!

*(*GESCHWITZ, *fully aware of* SCHOEN*'s disgust, kisses* LULU*'s hand, clicks her heels and exits in ironic manner.)*

SCHOEN: What does that . . . woman want?

LULU: *(Renewed peals of laughter.)* I'm sure *I* don't know! Darling, do try to get away after lunch, if you can. We could drive in the park together. *(Wistful.)* I'd love that.

SCHOEN: *(Mean.)* You know I'm not free today. I must be at the Stock Exchange to look after my investments.

(He turns to leave.)

LULU: What about me! Aren't *I* one of your investments?

(She pursues him from the stage.)

Aren't I? Aren't I?

(As soon as the stage is empty, GESCHWITZ *sneaks back in, on tiptoe, looking round herself furtively.)*

(From the gallery above comes a tremendous thump, followed by a shriek of mirth. GESCHWITZ *claps her hand to her mouth in surprise and slips behind the screen.* SCHIGOLCH, *somewhat the worse for wear, appears at the top of the stairs. He shouts to somebody behind him.)*

SCHIGOLCH: I suppose the wee lad's got no heart for this, seeing as how he brought it up in the lavatory.

RODRIGO: *(Off.)* Just a spot of bother with his little legs.

*(*SCHIGOLCH *negotiates the stairs in the manner of an early Chaplin drunk sketch.)*

SCHIGOLCH: What silly sod went and polished the stairs?

(He slithers down the last few stairs and collapses in a ragged heap on the floor, muttering and expostulating, as RODRIGO QUAST, *a circus strong man, in shabby evening dress, appears aloft, bearing a fifteen-year-old schoolboy,* HUGENBACH, *in his arms.* RODRIGO *proceeds down the stairs with his limp burden.* SCHIGOLCH *heaves himself upright.)*

SCHIGOLCH: Toss him lightly to the ceiling and catch him by his feet. That'll wake him up.

HUGENBACH: *(Kicking out.)* They'll kick me out of school if I don't behave.

*(*RODRIGO *lays him down on the sofa.)*

RODRIGO: You may go to a posh school, but you've not got what *I'd* call an education. *This* is where you get 'educated'.

*(*SCHIGOLCH *gestures largely round the room.)*

SCHIGOLCH: *(As if an announcement.)* 'Here, in this gracious apartment, amidst splendour and luxury, many men have learned the most important lessons of their lives.' Let me administer a wee droppie that'll put hairs on your chest.

*(*SCHIGOLCH *hands him the flask top, filled with liquor.*
HUGENBACH *drinks, splutters, coughs, holds out the flask top for a refill.)*

RODRIGO: Don't give him too much or he won't be able to perform, and we'll get it in the neck.

SCHIGOLCH: Do either of you gentlemen smoke, by any chance?

(HUGENBACH *produces a gold cigar case and snaps it open.*)

HUGENBACH: Genuine Havanas.

RODRIGO: Courtesy of Daddy in the Police Department, eh?

HUGENBACH: I wrote her a poem, yesterday.

RODRIGO: You wrote her a what?

SCHIGOLCH: You wrote her a what? What did he write her?

HUGENBACH: A poem.

RODRIGO: (*To* SCHIGOLCH.) A poem.

SCHIGOLCH: He promised me a fiver if I fixed him up an assignation, and he writes her a poem?

HUGENBACH: Who actually lives here?

RODRIGO: We do.

SCHIGOLCH: That is . . . every day the Stock Exchange is in session. Cheers!

(SCHIGOLCH *raises his flask to* HUGENBACH *and drinks.*)

HUGENBACH: Should I read it out to her, first?

SCHIGOLCH: What is he talking about?

RODRIGO: His poem. He wants to keep her waiting. Literary foreplay.

SCHIGOLCH: (*To* HUGENBACH.) Just run off and . . . play by yourself.

RODRIGO: (*Roaring with laughter.*) Why don't you both run off and play with yourselves?

(*He seizes the flask top from* HUGENBACH's *hand;* SCHIGOLCH *fills it.*)

Cheers!

(*He drinks.* SCHIGOLCH *drinks from his flask, to keep him company.*)

SCHIGOLCH: Cheers! Well, all I can say is, he will just have to do until something better turns up.

(LULU *comes in in a flurry of perfume; she wears an elegant ball dress, deeply décolleté, with flowers at her bosom. She kisses* SCHIGOLCH, *then* RODRIGO, *in a film-star manner.*)

LULU: Oh, how lovely, darlings!

(HUGENBACH struggles to his feet. LULU casts him back into the depths of the sofa and perches on its arm.)

Well, well, dear boy, you've found yourself some nice friends.

(HUGENBACH, overwhelmed, reaches out and touches her corsage.)

Do you like my orchids? Don't they smell good?

(She thrusts her bosom into HUGENBACH's face. With a moan, he falls back.)

SCHIGOLCH: I suppose I'd better stick something in *my* bosom.

(He rummages through the vase of flowers, casting those he rejects to the ground.)

LULU: *(To HUGENBACH.)* Do you dance?

RODRIGO: Dance? He can't even stand up.

LULU: You don't tango standing up.

(She drags HUGENBACH to his feet and during the ensuing dialogue, dances a vivid tango with him – herself leading – in the background. HUGENBACH follows her lead as if hypnotised; he probably would fall over if she were not holding him up.

SCHIGOLCH *trashes the entire vase of flowers. They lie scattered on the ground around him. He fingers one last lily. This he inserts in his buttonhole and squares up smartly, like a bridegroom at the altar.)*

SCHIGOLCH: Originally, you know, *I* intended to marry her.

RODRIGO: *(Incredulous.)* You mean you intended to marry her?

SCHIGOLCH: At one point, weren't *you* intending to marry her?

RODRIGO: Yes, of course.

SCHIGOLCH: Who hasn't intended to marry her?

RODRIGO: So she isn't your daughter?

SCHIGOLCH: It never occurred to her.

HUGENBACH: *(Panting.)* Then who is her father?

SCHIGOLCH: What's he talking about?

RODRIGO: Her father.

SCHIGOLCH: She did without.

LULU: *(In a dramatic tango pose.)* What did I do without?

ALL THREE: A father!

LULU: Virgin birth, that's me. *(To* HUGENBACH.*)* How do you get on with *your* father?

RODRIGO: I personally get on very well with his cigars.

SCHIGOLCH: *(To* LULU.*)* All secure?

*(*LULU *takes a key out of her bosom and dangles it in front of* SCHIGOLCH's *nose.)*

SCHIGOLCH: *(Lewd.)* You should have left it in the hole.

LULU: Whatever for?

SCHIGOLCH: So your husband can't open it from the outside.

RODRIGO: Isn't he at the Stock Exchange, and in his hands the fate of millions?

*(*LULU *lets go of* HUGENBACH, *who slithers to the floor.* LULU *throws the key lightly from hand to hand.)*

LULU: Possibly, today, he might wish to indulge his paranoia.

RODRIGO: Then, if he should return, I shall toss him lightly to the ceiling.

*(*FERDINAND, *young, clumsy, blushing, raw-boned in a footman's uniform, comes in through the double doors.)*

FERDINAND: Mr Schoen.

(Consternation. RODRIGO *jumps up, is about to hide behind the screen, but withdraws aghast at what he finds there. He snatches the paisley shawl off the back of the sofa and scuttles downstage left; he throws the shawl over the statue and hides behind it.*

SCHIGOLCH *swallows the key and makes for the staircase.*

HUGENBACH *slides off the sofa and rolls under the table.*

LULU *gathers up the fallen flowers and poses like a model beside the table with the flowers in her arm, on the point of arranging them.)*

LULU: Tell him he may enter.

*(*FERDINAND *goes out.* HUGENBACH *lifts the hem of the tablecloth and looks out. He whispers hoarsely.)*

HUGENBACH: I hope he's just forgotten his hat. Then we can be alone.

(LULU *pokes him with her toe. He disappears.* FERDINAND *ushers* ALVA *in. He is in evening dress.* LULU *makes an exclamation of pleasure.*)

LULU: Alva!

ALVA: They're going to hold the matinee by lamplight apparently. I've –

(*He catches sight of* SCHIGOLCH *laboriously dragging himself upstairs.*)

ALVA: Dear God, what's that?

LULU: Old friend of your father's.

ALVA: Never set eyes on him!

LULU: Old soldiers, you know. Former batman. Down on his luck.

ALVA: Is father . . .

LULU: He left for the Exchange. Shall we have a spot of lunch? It doesn't start until two.

(ALVA *can't take his eyes off the scarecrow figure of* SCHIGOLCH *as it disappears along the gallery.*

LULU *thrusts the flowers back into the vase, retaining one rose with which she tickles* ALVA's *ear, gaining his attention.*)

LULU: Do I look nice?

ALVA: Need you ask?

LULU: When I looked in the mirror, I envied your father.

ALVA: Why? (*Touch of irony.*) Because you make him so happy?

(FERDINAND *enters right, wheeling a trolley, doing his best. He lays the table for two. He sets out an ice bucket with champagne, and a plate of hors d'oeuvres. His expression is sour. He throws a bitter glare at* ALVA *and goes back to his hiding-place.*

ALVA *unpops the champagne and pours. He and* LULU *seat themselves at either end of the table.* LULU *unfolds her napkin. She gives* ALVA *a pleased smile.*)

LULU: There. Isn't this nice. You and me. Just like when we were kids. Brother and sister.

ALVA: I don't feel particularly brotherly.

(*He reaches for her hand. The table jumps up and down.*)

   Jesus!

(He bends down with the intention of looking under the table. LULU *grabs his hand.)*

LULU: My fault! I'm . . . trembling.

ALVA: Really?

(He looks at her hand, grasping his, and lays it gently on the table without letting go.)

ALVA: If we hadn't grown up together –

LULU: *(Hastily.)* – Like brother and sister. That's why we're so close, Alva.

ALVA: Have you ever heard about repression? Do you know what it is?

*(*LULU *pats her hair with her free hand. She has* not *heard about repression; nor felt the need for it.)*

Repression and idealisation. You deny your desire, you tell yourself it doesn't exist, you transform its object into something untouchable. But lately it's all begun to fall apart, I can't deny my feeling any more, I –

(The tablecloth quivers convulsively. All the others in hiding-places put out their heads for an instant.)

ALVA: I say, whatever is –

LULU: I'm convulsed with emotion.

(She lowers her head; her shoulders shake.)

ALVA: You were like my soiled madonna, and I thought that if I venerated you enough, all the mire of the street would fall away. I couldn't even think of, of defiling you.

LULU: How different to your dear father.

*(*FERDINAND *reappears and makes with the trolley; he takes away the untouched hors d'oeuvres and puts down a roast chicken with a shaking hand.)*

ALVA: *(To* FERDINAND.*)* Are you sickening for something?

LULU: *(To* ALVA.*)* Leave him alone.

FERDINAND: I'm not trained to wait at table. I'm supposed to be the chauffeur.

*(*SCHOEN *appears behind drapes.)*

SCHOEN: My own son –

(RODRIGO *sees* SCHOEN *and ducks back behind.*)

Everywhere I look . . .

(LULU *has now seen* SCHOEN, *too.*)

LULU: (*With a big effort.*) What do you mean, 'Lately everything's been falling apart'?

(ALVA *takes her hand. And does not let it go. Slowly, hesitantly, looking to her for approval, he raises her hand to his lips.*)

ALVA: Will you look at this hand?

LULU: What's wrong with it?

ALVA: Nothing. That's the problem.

LULU: I can't help that.

(RODRIGO *lifts the edge of the shawl and peers out.* GESCHWITZ *peeps from behind the screen.*)

SCHOEN: Another one!

(*As* LULU *looks on apprehensively;* ALVA *rises, comes round the table, stands behind her, runs his hands up her bare arms and caresses her shoulders. His manner is tentative, pleading.*)

ALVA: Mignon . . .

LULU: Oh, God!

(*She breaks away from his embrace, knocking over her gilt chair. She flees for the sofa and throws herself down. She is genuinely distressed.*)

Don't! Whatever you do, don't! Let's go to the theatre, now, before anything terrible happens.

(ALVA *goes after her, throws himself at her feet.*)

ALVA: (*Abandoning restraint.*) Where you're concerned, I've got no pride, I've got no decency –

LULU: D'you think I'm depraved, too?

ALVA: No, I don't. I think you're an angel. Kill me, if you want. Go on. Destroy me.

(SCHOEN *rips down the curtain so that he stands in full view of the actors below. Then, with great dignity, he comes downstairs, holding a revolver.*

ALVA, *stunned, gets up.*
SCHOEN *takes* ALVA *by the shoulders.)*

SCHOEN: Alva?

*(*ALVA *gets to his feet, moving like a sleepwalker.)*

There's been a revolution in Paris.

ALVA: So. There's been a revolution in Paris.

SCHOEN: They're all over the place at the paper. The phone lines are jammed. No one knows what to write.

ALVA: I'd better go to Paris and see for myself, hadn't I.

*(*SCHOEN *leads* ALVA *out.* RODRIGO *bursts out from behind the statue and dives for the table, lifting up the tablecloth.)*

HUGENBACH: Full up!

*(*RODRIGO *flings himself down behind the couch as* SCHOEN *returns.* SCHOEN *locks the door and nudges the shawl which hid* RODRIGO *with his revolver.)*

SCHOEN: Where has *he* got to?

LULU: *(Desperate courage.)* Slipped out for a breather.

SCHOEN: Jumped off the balcony, did he?

LULU: Well. He *is* an acrobat.

SCHOEN: See how deep you've dragged me into your own filth!

LULU: *(Heroically pert.)* Should have brought me up better, then, shouldn't you.

SCHOEN: I am rich in choices, I have three . . . Either I can drown in your corruption with you. Or I can hang myself. Or . . . I can murder you.

(He points the revolver at LULU. *She straightens up.)*

LULU: Shut up and kill me, if that's what you want.

(But that is just what makes SCHOEN *put up his gun, saying that – as, of course, she knew it would, or, at least, was sufficiently sure it would to make it worth a try. As the scene progresses, we realise it is a version of one that has been played between them again and again, each time coming more perilously close to real violence; but, until this time, it has always remained a game. In this game,* LULU *is cast as the dominatrix, and truly believes that she is so; that she can, if*

necessary, stop the game. In fact, SCHOEN, *relishing the role of victim, is really calling all the shots because it is his game, he invented it and he foots the bill.)*

SCHOEN: I gave you everything and asked for nothing in return except the respect any decent servant gives his master.

LULU: *(Bristling.)* So you think of a wife as just another servant, do you?

SCHOEN: *(Ignoring her.)* And now you've run out of credit.

LULU: Not likely. My account's still in the red, thanks very much.

(She smooths out an imaginary crease in her dress. It is time to call a halt to this round of the game.)

LULU: How do you like my new dress?

SCHOEN: Get out! Or I shall go mad and kill my son.

*(*LULU *is truly horrified. He has moved into a new league. She backs away.)*

I try and I try but I can't shake you off. You are a sickness of my soul. I want so badly to be cured of you, Mignon.

(He thrusts the revolver at her, presses it into her hand, curls her fingers round the handle, points it at her breast.)

Don't be scared of it. Think how easily you can cure me. If you love me, make me well.

*(*LULU *collapses on the sofa, clutching the revolver. She turns it over and over in her hands.)*

LULU: Somehow, I don't think it'll go off, you know.

SCHOEN: Do you remember how I saved your life? Well, this is how to say, 'Thank you'.

*(*LULU *is regaining her self-possession minute by minute.)*

LULU: You're very sure of yourself.

SCHOEN: I'm not scared of a prostitute.

*(*LULU *experimentally fires a round into the ceiling, to make sure.* RODRIGO *leaps up from behind the sofa and flies up the staircase.* SCHOEN *spins round.)*

SCHOEN: Who was that?

LULU: Just a touch of your paranoia again, darling.

SCHOEN: Exactly how many men have you stowed away here?

(He snatches the revolver from her.)

Let me help you entertain your guests.

(He quests round the room, pulling down curtains, pictures, smashing things, etc. He thrusts the screen aside and drags out GESCHWITZ.*)*

GESCHWITZ: You're hurting!

*(*SCHOEN *gets her arm up behind her back. He hisses between his teeth.)*

SCHOEN: Do stay to dinner, Countess!

(He drags her into the room on the left, shuts her in and turns the key in the lock. Then he sits heavily down beside LULU *on the sofa and shows her the revolver as if it were a dirty picture, or his prick.)*

SCHOEN: Look at me. Look me in the eye. Do you expect me to let my chauffeur fuck my wife in my own house? God knows, I pay him enough already. Look at me!

(With a superhuman effort, LULU *gets up off the sofa. The game is getting seriously out of hand; she makes a last effort to bring things back to normal.)*

LULU: Speaking of the chauffeur, let's drive to the opera.

(He thrusts her back down on the sofa and straddles her.)

SCHOEN: Who's in the driving-seat now?

(He mimes intercourse, briefly. Then, panting, he turns the revolver in LULU's *hand against her own breast, again.)*

This is a mercy killing. You're going to put me out of my misery. Aren't you. *Aren't you.* This is the happiest night of my life. Pull the trigger.

(Pause of one heart-beat.)

LULU: *(Voice of sweet reason.)* You could always get a divorce.

SCHOEN: After you've driven me to the brink of suicide. Divorce you? Let somebody else have you? You are part of me. Give *me* the revolver.

LULU: *(Whisper.)* Please.

SCHOEN: I'll spare you the bother of killing yourself.

*(*LULU *tears herself away from him and drags herself up to her full height.)*

LULU: I'm not worth any the less just because people have killed themselves on my account. You betrayed your best friends with me. Now you're married to me. You could hardly betray yourself with yourself, could you? I never, ever wanted to be different from the way people wanted me, and nobody ever wanted to see me differently from the way I am. Why do you want me to kill myself because of that?

SCHOEN: Get down.

(LULU looks up, startled.)

SCHOEN: Down on your knees.

(LULU sinks to her knees.)

Pray for strength.

(HUGENBACH knocks over the table and rushes out from beneath it.)

HUGENBACH: Help!

(SCHOEN turns. LULU fires five shots into his back. She continues to pull the trigger after the gun has emptied itself.
SCHOEN stands for a moment, upright, astonished. Then he begins to sway. HUGENBACH catches him as he falls forward, and lowers him on to the sofa. SCHOEN sees HUGENBACH for the first time.)

SCHOEN: Good God. Children's hour.

(LULU drops the gun and bends over the sofa, noisily hysterical with grief and shock.)

SCHOEN: Get out of my sight. Where's Alva?

LULU: I love you. I've always loved you.

SCHOEN: *(In a perverse way he is thoroughly enjoying this.)* Prostitute. Murderess. Isn't Alva coming? Water.

(LULU distractedly fills a champagne glass. ALVA appears above.)

ALVA: What's happened?

LULU: I shot him.

HUGENBACH: It was an accident.

(ALVA rushes down the stairs and tries to lift SCHOEN.)

ALVA: We must get you to bed.

SCHOEN: Don't touch me. I'm parched.

(LULU offers him the glass of champagne.)

Typical.

(He gulps.) Don't let her get away with it, Alva. It's your turn next.

ALVA: *(To HUGENBACH.)* Help me get him to bed.

SCHOEN: No. Please. No. Murderess. More champagne.

ALVA: He'll be more comfortable in bed.

(He and HUGENBACH get SCHOEN on his feet and lead him to the door, left.
LULU stays near the table, holding the glass; absent-mindedly, she drinks
from it. ALVA finds the bedroom door is locked and turns the key.
GESCHWITZ falls out of the room.
SCHOEN clicks his heels, stands to attention – the force of conventional
politeness is as strong in him as that. Then he topples full length, with a crash.)

LULU: The worst is over.

(She puts down her glass, crosses to the body, kneels and closes its eyes. Then
she stands up and looks this way and that; she is about to make a run for it.
ALVA shoots out an arm.)

ALVA: You just stay put.

GESCHWITZ: *(To LULU, in a voice rich and ringing with relief.)* I thought he
was going to kill you.

LULU: *(To ALVA; calm at first, but with increasing hysteria.)* Don't turn me
over to the police. I'll do anything you want, Alva, only don't turn
me over to the police. I'm still young. I'll always be good to you,
Alva. Don't turn me over to the police. Alva! Look at me!

(Knocking at the door.)

ALVA: Too late. Here they are.

(He goes to open the double doors.)

HUGENBACH: *(Disconsolate.)* I'll be expelled from school.

ACT FIVE

(The same as Act Four, but the room has been dismantled. White sheets hang down from the gallery and from the banister of the staircase. All the furniture is covered in dustsheets, including the sofa. LULU's *portrait is conspicuous by its absence.* ALVA, RODRIGO, *bulging out of a footman's uniform, and* GESCHWITZ, *in a voluminous black travelling cape, pace round the set like caged animals.)*

RODRIGO: He gets off on keeping us waiting.

GESCHWITZ: *(Tetchy.)* Oh, do be quiet.

RODRIGO: I like that! How can I keep quiet? I'm hyper to a fault; I'm in overdrive. It's all got on top of me. And here's another thing, my good fellow – how come a year in the nick plus three weeks in intensive care have done such wonders for her complexion?

GESCHWITZ: *(Abstracted.)* She's lovelier than I've ever seen her.

RODRIGO: God forbid I base my future career on your eye for the girls.

ALVA: Over and over again, I ask myself – what right did I have to write that play about her?

(The other two give him a cold glance. All continue their pacing. ALVA *slaps his fist into his palm, an affirmative gesture inherited from his father.)*

But that's the curse that's crippling writers today! *Literariness!* When what we need to make an art that speaks to the masses is sheer, stark, brutal realism! Christ, I'm through with Art. I'm going to throw in my lot with real people, not desiccated intellectuals, but with people who live vital, real, instinctual lives . . . I did that in the last play. She's the *realest* woman I know. She's been in prison for a year now, and I put her in my play. And isn't it ironic, I couldn't find a producer anywhere. When my father was alive, they came flocking. Not any more. The play went on at some fringe theatre venue.

*(*ALVA *comes to a halt in the middle of the stage and grasps the hands of* GESCHWITZ. *She stares through him while he addresses what is obviously a set speech to her.* RODRIGO *continues to pace.)*

Countess von Geschwitz, I know that woman shot my own father dead in this very room and society has exacted a terrible price from her for it, but, in the very deepest sense, how could anyone with a heart and compassion hold Lulu responsible for a crime committed in the grip of folie à deux? I don't know whether or not you *will* succeed in rescuing her. But I can't find enough words to express how much I admire your devotion to her, your self-sacrifice, your disregard for your own life. I don't think any man has ever risked so much for a woman. I don't know how you stand for money, but I do know that bribing jailers isn't cheap. Can I offer you a loan – say, twenty thousand marks? Cash?

(The doorbell rings three times.)

GESCHWITZ: *(Relieved.)* That'll be the old man.

(ALVA lets him in.)

SCHIGOLCH: Dark as the grave in here! Why did you board up the windows? Such lovely sunshine outside. Well. I'm bushed. I hope Paris will prove less of a strain.

RODRIGO: Booked us in anywhere tomorrow night?

SCHIGOLCH: Trust me.

ALVA: Countess, there are ten thousand marks in this briefcase.

GESCHWITZ: Thank you. No.

ALVA: Please.

GESCHWITZ: *(To SCHIGOLCH, impatient.)* Let's be off.

SCHIGOLCH: You needn't be in such a hurry. We're five minutes' walk from the prison. I can whisk her back in a trice.

ALVA: Oh. Are you bringing her here?

SCHIGOLCH: Are you scared?

ALVA: Scared! Me! What! Here, leave by the other door. It's safer.

(They go off up the stairs.)

RODRIGO: Why ever did you offer that cow money?

ALVA: Mind your own business.

RODRIGO: What about me? I had to corrupt a great many sisters in the prison infirmary, you know. To say nothing of bribing the doctors, the lawyers, the probation officers . . . those swine cost enough to fund a presidential campaign.

ALVA: The Countess paid you back every penny. She also pays you a salary of five hundred marks a month. Can this love for the afflicted prisoner be quite as pure and disinterested as he claims, I ask myself. I've learned to admire the Countess a lot. You, no. You may be a 'material witness' to my father's murder, but that doesn't make us blood brothers. If the Countess hadn't taken you on, you'd be drunk in the gutter by now.

RODRIGO: And what would have become of you if you hadn't sold that rag of your father's for two million marks! You'd have got off with some boss-eyed little chorine, ended up a stable boy in the circus. What great work is it that you've finally put your name to? A blood-and-thunder melodrama with starring roles for my fiancée's legs, that got put on in a room over a pub when no decent theatre would take it!

(Footsteps and voices outside. RODRIGO *strikes an attitude.)*

RODRIGO: Hark! Do I hear the voice of my beloved?

ALVA: They can't be back already. Hide.

*(*RODRIGO *slips behind the sheeted statue. He pokes his head out.)*

RODRIGO: To think I hid in this very spot a year ago today!

(He heaves a sentimental sigh and withdraws. ALVA *opens the double doors.* HUGENBACH, *dishevelled, comes in.)*

ALVA: I know you, you're –

HUGENBACH: Alfred Hugenbach. I ran away from reform school this morning. I need your help. I've got a plan.

ALVA: What are you talking about?

HUGENBACH: Are we alone?

ALVA: Yes. What plan?

HUGENBACH: I've worked it out down to the last detail. If I had any money, I wouldn't have come to you.

ALVA: Would you kindly tell me what you're talking about?

HUGENBACH: Do you need to ask? *She* must mean a lot to you, from what you said in court. You were the best of the defence witnesses.

ALVA: No, you were. You said my father tried to make her shoot herself.

HUGENBACH: Yes. He did. But nobody believed me.

ALVA: Where are you living?

HUGENBACH: With this prostitute. She's family, in a way. She's got a child by my father.

ALVA: Who *is* your father?

HUGENBACH: Chief of police. That's how I know the prison so well. In the first courtyard, there's an iron ladder that goes up to the roof. You can only get into the attic from the skylight, there's no other way. The attics are full of old floorboards and woodshavings and rubbish. I'll make a big bonfire up there.

ALVA: You'll burn to death.

HUGENBACH: Of course I will, if nobody rescues me. I need some cash to get into the first courtyard. It's not a bribe, exactly, but the warder needs a loan so he can send his kids off on holiday this summer.

ALVA: How did you escape from reform school?

HUGENBACH: I jumped out of the window.

(RODRIGO *steps out of his hiding-place.*)

RODRIGO: Would the gentlemen prefer coffee in the music room or on the verandah?

HUGENBACH: Where did you spring from? From the same place! (*With rising hysteria.*) He's hiding in the same place as last year!

ALVA: I've taken him on the staff. He's very reliable.

HUGENBACH: I'm an idiot for coming here.

RODRIGO: Oh yes, we've met before. Now, why don't you just bugger off home to your step-mother. If I ever catch sight of you again, I'll kick your head in.

ALVA: Shut up.

HUGENBACH: I'm an idiot.

RODRIGO: Besides, she's been dead for three weeks.

(*Pause of one heart-beat.*)

HUGENBACH: It's not true.

RODRIGO: Listen to this.

(He unfolds a newspaper clipping from his wallet and hands it to HUGENBACH.)

HUGENBACH: *(Reading aloud.)* 'The murderess of Mr Schoen has been mysteriously struck down by cholera . . .' But it doesn't say she's dead!

RODRIGO: Not in so many words, no. You'll find her grave in the back left-hand corner, behind the rubbish tip. There's some little crosses without names on. She's under the first one. Hang up your wreath and piss off back to borstal.

HUGENBACH: It's not true.

ALVA: Oh yes, it is. Now I must ask you to go. Doctor's orders. No visitors.

HUGENBACH: I'd have done anything to make her happy. There's nothing left worth living for, now.

RODRIGO: And if you summon up the cheek to pester me, or my esteemed colleague here, or my distinguished friend Mr Schigolch, ever again, I'll shop you to the coppers for premeditated arson. You could do with three years in the slammer to teach you into what you shouldn't stick your little fingers. Sod off.

HUGENBACH: I'm such an idiot.

(RODRIGO picks up HUGENBACH bodily and throws him out of the double doors. He closes the doors behind him.)

RODRIGO: I'm surprised you didn't hand over your wallet, too.

ALVA: *(Abstracted.)* That boy's little finger is worth all of your obese and repulsive body.

RODRIGO: If my fiancée is going to end up as a limited company you can leave me out. What I want is, to turn her into a really stunning acrobat. I'll really put myself out for that. I'll work my nuts off. But that means it's me who says what young men can come calling and what not.

ALVA: That boy has something rare in this day and age . . . God knows if you can call it gallantry. But don't you remember how he shouted at the judge, 'How do you think you might have turned out yourself if you'd had to sell flowers barefoot round the cafés when you were only ten?'

RODRIGO: I'd have smashed his face in. Thank God for borstal, to teach the young respect for the Law. I've ordered a two-inch thick hippopotamus-hide whip specially for her. Kisses or the lash, it's all the same for women. They want attention, see. Doesn't matter what kind. Give 'em a good going over now and then, good for the complexion, good for the soul. She's still only just twenty years old. Buried three husbands, already. God knows how many lovers. High time she settled down. The snag is, a man needs the seven deadly sins tattooed on his forehead before she'll give him a second look. Pure evil, that's what gets her juices working, know what I mean.

ALVA: No moral fibre. That's my problem. And a chronic deficiency of heart. Not like that boy. That boy!

(*The sound of dragging footsteps along the gallery.* SCHIGOLCH *appears at the head of the stairs,* LULU *on his arm. She is wrapped in the* COUNTESS'*s black wrap, looks haggard and drawn. She leans heavily on* SCHIGOLCH'*s arm as they come downstairs.*)

SCHIGOLCH: Don't forget we're bound for Paris, tonight.

(RODRIGO *gapes at* LULU.)

RODRIGO: Oh, God.

LULU: (*To* SCHIGOLCH.) Slow down a bit.

RODRIGO: How did you have the nerve to break out of the nick with a face like that on you?

SCHIGOLCH: Pipe down.

RODRIGO: I'll fetch the police. I'll report you. This is the living skeleton who's going to take the Folies Bergère by storm! Fat chance!

SCHIGOLCH: Don't insult the lady.

RODRIGO: What a pair of con artists! I'm off to the Law.

SCHIGOLCH: Don't forget there's a price on her head! Hurry!

(RODRIGO *storms out through the double doors, slamming them.* LULU *sits down on the sofa, heavily.*)

LULU: He won't, of course.

SCHIGOLCH: Good riddance. Now I must go and book the sleepers.

LULU: (*Stretching until something goes c-r-a-c-k.*) Oh, freedom! Oh, God!

SCHIGOLCH: I'll be back in half-an-hour. We'll have a big celebration at the station restaurant. (*Kisses her fingertips.*) Champagne!

(He exits through the double doors. LULU *looks round, luxuriating in the room.)*

LULU: Good to be home! *(She notices a lack; she sits up sharply.)* Here, where's my portrait?

*(*ALVA *fills the glasses.)*

ALVA: I hid it in my room.

LULU: Go and get it, there's a dear. Let me have a look at myself.

(She takes her glass gratefully and drinks.)

I'd sweep out my cell in the morning and sneak a look at my face in the tin dustpan. It's a terrible thing, not being able to see your own face.

ALVA: You need to rest.

LULU: I've been resting a whole year.

*(*ALVA *goes to fetch the picture.* LULU *smiles into her glass.)*

LULU: He's got it bad.

(She takes a reflective sip.)

If only . . . I hadn't shot his father in the back.

*(*ALVA *comes back from the room on the left, carrying the portrait. He props it up against the small table. They inspect it.)*

ALVA: I turned your face to the wall.

LULU: Didn't you ever give it a once-over, for old times' sake?

ALVA: *(Stiff.)* I was too tied up, selling off the newspaper. Countess Geschwitz wanted to take care of the picture but she was scared in case the police searched her apartment.

LULU: Now she's finding out how the other half live, courtesy of the women's prison.

ALVA: How did she pull it off?

LULU: She spent hours practising doing herself up to look like me. She paid me a visit half an hour ago. We swapped clothes. She's still there. Except she's not the Countess Geschwitz, any more, she's the little tart that shot the press baron.

(She gives ALVA *a veiled look. He doesn't notice. He is contemplating the portrait.)*

ALVA: You haven't changed.

LULU: I'm a bit haggard. Prison really gets on your nerves.

ALVA: You looked wretched when you got here.

LULU: I wanted to scare off the Jumping Jack. What have you been up to all this time?

ALVA: I wrote a play about you. It had a cult success.

*(*LULU *gives a ripple of laughter. She stares deep into her glass, to hide the smile.*
ALVA *looks at her directly.)*

With you, it's a straightforward existential decision: either I write plays about you, or I make love to you.

(Pause.)

LULU: When I was in prison, night after night I'd have the same dream. It kept on coming back. I dreamed I'd fallen into the clutches of a sex murderer.

(She shrugs, laughs.)

*(*ALVA *is startled.*
Pause.)*

Give me a kiss.

(She puts her glass on the floor and opens her arms.
ALVA *comes and kneels beside her on the sofa.)*

ALVA: When I look into your eyes, I see my own face as if it were reflected in troubled water.

LULU: Kiss.

(She puts her arms round his neck. They kiss.)

ALVA: Your lips have lost weight.

*(*LULU *giggles, sits him down on the sofa, and sits herself on his knee.)*

LULU: What's the matter? Is it my aroma? We did have a bath in prison, you know, once a month. Regular as clockwork. Nice cool water. As soon as we hit the water, the wardresses went through our pockets.

(ALVA *strokes her hair.*)

Or are you really scared you won't be able to write any more poems
about me if –

ALVA: Don't know. Not sure.

(LULU *kicks off one of her shoes. She kicks off the other one as* ALVA *puts his
finger on her mouth.*)

ALVA: Don't think of anything else. Be grateful for this moment.

LULU: (*A kind of satanic flirtatiousness; does she want to find out if he is the
fatal lover of her dreams?*) Hush. Remember. I killed your father.

ALVA: That doesn't stop me loving you.

LULU: Lean back.

(*She plants a chaste kiss on his forehead.*)

ALVA: Oh, Granny, what big eyes you have . . . big, black eyes. They
haven't changed a bit. Still the eyes of that little girl, opening the door
of my room, shyly, silently . . . and then you saw the toy theatre and
your eyes lit up like penny candles. If I didn't know you by your eyes,
I'd think you were a real *femme fatale*.

LULU: (*Honest, sad.*) I only wish I *was* a real femme fatale. I've made a
bit of a botch of it so far.

(*Pause.* LULU *rests her head against his shoulder.*)

ALVA: Is it wrong for brother and sister to do it, Lulu?

(*He presses her backwards on the sofa.*)

LULU: (*Faint.*) Somebody might come in.

(*He holds back the two wings of the black cape; underneath she wears an
institutional white shift.*)

ALVA: Let them.

LULU: Come to Paris with me.

ALVA: Isn't the old man going with you?

LULU: He's probably buggered off.

(*She lies back on the sofa, drawing* ALVA's *head to her breast. Then she is
seized by a dreadful thought and sits upright all at once.*)

ALVA *hurt, resentful, moves away from her. Her voice is raucous with terror.)*

Alva . . . isn't this the very same sofa where your father bled to death?

*(*ALVA *pushes her back again, pressing his hand over her mouth. With the other hand, he pulls off his necktie and unfastens his shirt.)*

ALVA: *(Almost menacingly.)* Hush.

ACT SIX

(Paris. A fabulous white and gilt salon. The gallery has disappeared. There is a pair of doors in both the right and the left-hand walls: between the right-hand pair of doors, a rococo console table with marble top, laden with ice-buckets, champagne, glasses; above it, the portrait of LULU, in yet another exotic frame – white and silver, this time. The double doors are open, to reveal a gaming table. Centre, the sofa, this time upholstered in white satin. A huge, gilt and crystal chandelier. A lively group moves around the salon, chattering.

RODRIGO, ALVA *and* GESCHWITZ, *plus* LULU *herself, are present. All, except* LULU, *wear tuxedos. The other men wear lounge suits –* PUNTSCHU, *the shady banker;* HEILMANN, *the journalist; and the* MARQUIS CASTI-PIANI, *police spy, existential pimp and* LULU's *current lover, therefore a man with the mark of Cain on his brow. A group of women of fairly easy virtue –* MADELINE DE MARELLE, BIANETTA GAZIL, LUDMILLA STEINHERZ. MADELINE *has brought her twelve-year-old daughter,* KADEGA, *with her. All the women are dressed up to the nines, but none more so than* LULU.

She is in white satin and diamonds, a hugely plunging neckline, long white gloves. Her hair is swept up and topped by a small white plume like the one circus horses wear – her whole outfit is a child's idea of glamour. BOB, *fourteen years old, snappy footman's uniform, passes through with a tray of champagne. The party take glasses and go through into the gaming room; as they depart,* CASTI-PIANI *takes* LULU's *arm, detaining her.* GESCHWITZ, *seeing this, lingers agonisedly as* BOB *closes the double doors on the others.* CASTI-PIANI *notices* GESCHWITZ, *lingering agonisedly. His mask drops.)*

CASTI-PIANI: Scram!

(She departs for the gaming room, hurt, proud, closing the door emphatically behind her; she is too well-bred to slam it.)

LULU: *(Businesslike.)* How much?

CASTI-PIANI: Money isn't enough any more.

LULU: If you want me to go with you, you needn't threaten me.

CASTI-PIANI: That's not the point. I've told you again and again – you're not my type. I didn't take your money because I loved you, I said I loved you so I could get your money. I'd much rather screw Bianetta than you. Any time. You're like a Chinese meal, my darling – a hundred tiny dishes, a hundred different exquisite little taste sensations, then half an hour later you're starving again. And even by

Parisian standards, you've been doing it too long. You're jaded. You'd ruin a boy's nervous system. All this makes you superbly well qualified for the position I've picked out for you.

LULU: I didn't ask you to find me a job.

CASTI-PIANI: I told you I used to run an employment agency.

LULU: You told me you were a police spy.

CASTI-PIANI: Yes, but you can't live on a hundred and fifty marks a month, not in Paris. My colleagues all live off women, so I thought – moonlight a little, I've got the contacts . . . I've helped all sorts of young women to find themselves enjoyable and stimulating work. They thank me for it. You'll thank me.

LULU: I'm not cut out for that sort of thing.

CASTI-PIANI: That's not the point. This is the point: the price on the head of Mr Schoen's killer is a thousand marks. All I have to do to get my hands on it is to whistle to the gendarme on the corner. On the other hand, Mr Oikonomopoulos in Cairo has offered me twelve hundred marks for you. That's two hundred more. Besides, I'd rather see you settled down than rotting in a prison.

LULU: I'd never settle down in a brothel. I might have done it when I was fifteen, I suppose . . . When I thought I was never, ever going to be happy, ever again. So I indulged myself, I gave myself a little present, I treated myself to a revolver. It was night, it was snowing, I didn't even bother to slip my shoes on, I picked up that revolver, bolted out, ran to the park. I was going to shoot myself. I was laid up in hospital for three months, after that, and I didn't set eyes on a man all that time.

That's when he started coming to see me. My man. As soon as I closed my eyes, there he was, night after night, walking through my dreams, stalking me, looking for me. Only me. The man for me. Ever since then, even at night, even in the pitch dark, I can tell from a hundred yards if he is the one. If I act against that instinct, I feel foul and filthy and soiled, and it takes weeks before I can stand my own company again. It's as if I've betrayed myself. And now you think I'm prepared to sleep with all and sundry, all in a day's work, do you?

CASTI-PIANI: All and sundry don't patronise the Oikonomopoulos establishment.

(LULU *raises her eyes to the ceiling.*)

All I had to guarantee was that you spoke French. You've got a gift for languages, you'll soon pick up a working knowledge of English. You'll live in a lavish apartment with a view of the El-Ashar Mosque, walk on Persian carpets, dress in Paris frocks, drink as much champagne as your clients can afford, and you'll be your own mistress, to a certain extent. Come on, come on . . . you don't have to put your heart into it. The last thing Oikonomopoulos wants working for him is a woman of passion.

LULU: Is this Egyptian gent really willing to stump up twelve hundred marks for a woman he's never set eyes on?

CASTI-PIANI: I sent him the pictures you gave me.

LULU: *(Toneless.)* You sent him the pictures I gave you.

CASTI-PIANI: His need was greater than mine. He'll probably hang the one of you as Eve over the front door to drum up custom. And there's another thing to take into account – you'll be safe. It isn't the easiest thing in the world to extradite a whore from an Egyptian brothel.

LULU: You're asking me to swap one prison for another.

CASTI-PIANI: Then permit me to whistle up the gendarmerie.

LULU: There's still thirty thousand marks left from the sale of the newspaper.

CASTI-PIANI: Your dumb little scribbler friend put it all in Jungfrau Railway shares. I don't touch shares. Think. You could be in Marseilles tomorrow morning. The Mediterranean crossing takes five days. You're closer to prison in Paris than you are anywhere. I can't think how you've lived here for a year without being spotted. Or shopped. But your indiscriminate appetite for male flesh means that one of my colleagues in the force will strike lucky any day now. Then you cease to be any concern of mine. The bars will clang down on you once again. Make up your mind. The night train leaves for Marseilles at half past midnight. If you haven't come to your senses by eleven, I'll call the police. Otherwise, I'll pop you in a cab and take you straight to the Gare de Lyon.

LULU: What's your game? I mean, really?

CASTI-PIANI: I want to save your skin.

LULU: I'll go to America with you. I'll go to China. But I won't sell myself. I can't sell the only thing I've ever owned. You can have every single thing we've got left.

CASTI-PIANI: Please believe me. You have nothing I want. If we don't leave this house tonight, you and your bizarre entourage will be heading back for Germany tomorrow, under escort. And don't think shopping you would be the worst thing I've ever done in my life, either.

(He goes into the gaming room as ALVA *comes out, flushed and excited.)*

ALVA: Geschwitz is just about to lose her shirt. Puntschu has promised me another ten Jungfrau shares. Even La Steinhertz has made her cautious little profit. Come on!

(Then he remembers something. For all his excitement, it makes him sad.)

Oh. By the way. That boy. Hugenbach. Remember? He killed himself.

LULU: But he was tucked up safe and sound in the Reformatory.

ALVA: He hung himself. With a sheet. It was in the Berlin paper.

(A great cry goes up in the gaming room. ALVA *dashes back as* GESCHWITZ *comes out.* LULU *brushes past her, blindly.* GESCHWITZ, *heartstruck, clutches her arm.)*

GESCHWITZ: Why can't you bear to be alone with me?

LULU: Because I'd rather be alone by myself.

GESCHWITZ: You've made me terribly unhappy. The least you could do is be polite.

LULU: I treat you just like I do any other woman. Why don't you do likewise?

GESCHWITZ: Have you forgotten why I stayed in prison and you went free?

LULU: God, when I think of the things I promised you, I could throw up.

GESCHWITZ: Do you mean you never meant it?

LULU: Never meant what – about being in love with you? So what!

GESCHWITZ: I feel sorry for you. I feel so sorry for you. When I think of that creature you've got yourself tangled up with –

LULU: What are you talking about?

GESCHWITZ: That evil little pimp, Casti–Piani.

LULU: *(Lashing out.)* You're not fit to speak his name! You're not really a human being. You're not a man, you're not a woman. Go and make Bianetta an offer. She'll take you on, if you name the right price.

(*The double doors are now flung open and the guests all troop into the salon.* LULU *is even more annoyed.*)

LULU: What's going on!

PUNTSCHU: Pause for refreshments!

(*He slips his hand into* MADELINE'*s décolletage. She laughs merrily.*)

MADELINE: Everybody's on a winning streak.

BIANETTA: Even the bank has won.

CASTI-PIANI: Then we needn't go easy on the bubbly.

ALVA: I have this absolutely foolproof system at cards. Marquis, can I interest you in my system?

(ALVA *opens a door, right. The guests go through to supper.* RODRIGO *holds* LULU *back.*)

RODRIGO: Have you considered my proposition?

LULU: Go ahead and report me to the police. I haven't got twenty thousand francs left.

RODRIGO: Don't lie to me, you cow. You've got twice as much as that, *he* told me so just now.

LULU: Blackmail him, then. He does what he likes with his money.

RODRIGO: Thanks very much. It'd take three weeks before it sunk in I was putting the screws on. Meanwhile, my fiancée writes: tout est fini.

LULU: Oh, God. Engaged, again.

RODRIGO: I suppose you think I should have asked your permission! I ran into her, if you must know, in the toilets at the Folie Bergère, the night yours truly got booed off.

(LULU *chuckles derisively.*)

She presided in state. You wouldn't think what a woman in her position can salt away in twenty years. The concierge of the convenience. Tomorrow I shall go to the town hall and slip a ring on her finger. At last . . . a woman who loves me for myself.

LULU: Go with my blessing.

RODRIGO: I'd rather go with your twenty thousand marks. I told her I'd got it under the bed.

LULU: And you claim she loves you for yourself!

RODRIGO: Celestine loves me for my mind, not for my body. Unlike you. She's gone beyond all that. She's seen it all.

(Pause of one heart-beat.)

Do I get my cash by tomorrow evening or not?

LULU: Chance would be a fine thing.

RODRIGO: Why don't you give poor old Alva a tumble, just for once. He's pining for it. He'd stump up the necessary at the twang of a bedspring. Why are you saving it for Casti-bloody-Piani?

LULU: Shall I ask the Marquis to see you out?

RODRIGO: Comme vous voulez, ma chérie. If I haven't got the cash by tomorrow evening, I'll turn you in. Au revoir.

(HEILMANN comes back into the salon.)

LULU: If you're looking for Madeline, she isn't here.

HEILMANN: I'm looking for something else.

RODRIGO: Second door on the right.

LULU: Did your fiancée teach you to say that?

(HEILMANN opens the second door on the right and bumps into PUNTSCHU, the banker, adjusting his dress.)

HEILMANN: Excuse me.

PUNTSCHU: Madeline is waiting for you, Heilmann.

HEILMANN: I won't be a moment.

(He rushes into the room PUNTSCHU has just left. LULU goes back into the gaming room; RODRIGO follows her. PUNTSCHU unfastens his tie.)

PUNTSCHU: Phew, things are hotting up in there.

(BOB brings in a telegram on a silver salver.)

BOB: For Monsieur Puntschu.

PUNTSCHU: *(Reads.)* 'Shares in the Jungfrau Railway have gone through the floor.' H'm. *(Reaches into his pocket for a coin and tips* BOB.) And what might you be called, young man?

BOB: They call me Bob, for short.

PUNTSCHU: Were you born in Paris?

BOB: Yes, sir.

PUNTSCHU: How old are you?

(KADEGA comes in.)

KADEGA: Where's Mummy?

PUNTSCHU: My, what a pretty little lady.

KADEGA: I've looked for Mummy everywhere.

PUNTSCHU: Be patient. Mummy will come back soon.

(Looking at BOB.)

Knee breeches, too. Oh, God! I'm coming over all peculiar.

(He goes off through a door.)

KADEGA: *(To BOB.)* Have *you* seen my mummy?

BOB: Perhaps she went through there.

KADEGA: What's so interesting in there?

BOB: Come and see.

KADEGA: What are you talking about?

BOB: Having a bit of fun.

KADEGA: All right.

(MADELINE storms in from the door through which HEILMANN left.)

MADELINE: There she is! Aren't you ashamed, you wicked boy?

KADEGA: Oh, Mummy! I was just looking for you!

MADELINE: Looking for me, were you? Who told you to come and look for me? And what are you doing with this oaf?

(BOB sneaks off as MADELINE takes her daughter by the shoulders and shakes her. As the other guests emerge from the supper room, KADEGA bursts into tears.)

MADELINE: No snivelling, if you please, miss!

(Smack on the leg. KADEGA cries with redoubled fury.)

PUNTSCHU: Tears, idle tears!

MADELINE: Just nerves. Take no notice.

PUNTSCHU: Don't be hard on her. It's the difficult age.

GESCHWITZ: Can we get back to the game?

(They return to the gaming room. BOB comes in and whispers to LULU; she nods and remains on stage. BOB lets in SCHIGOLCH, through a side door.)

SCHIGOLCH: *(Glancing at BOB.)* Where did you find him?

LULU: At the circus.

SCHIGOLCH: He's a bit broad in the beam.

LULU: Don't you love it!

SCHIGOLCH: How much do you pay him?

LULU: Ask him yourself.

SCHIGOLCH: My French isn't good enough.

LULU: *(To BOB.)* Close the doors.

(BOB leaves them via the double doors, having gone round closing all the doors.)

SCHIGOLCH: I'm in urgent need of five hundred francs. I've taken an apartment for my girlfriend.

LULU: What? You've found yourself a girlfriend?

SCHIGOLCH: She assures me she was very pretty when she was a young woman.

LULU: Does she need the money badly?

SCHIGOLCH: She'd like to settle down.

(LULU collapses on the sofa with a sob.)

LULU: Oh, God!

SCHIGOLCH: *(Tetchy.)* Now what?

LULU: Everything's gone wrong.

SCHIGOLCH: *(Tender.)* You've been overdoing it, my dear. You should lie down for a bit.

(LULU begins to cry. He sits down beside her on the sofa and cradles her in his arms.)

Go on, have a good cry. That's right. Get it out of your system. You used to cry like that fifteen years ago. I've never heard anybody bawl the way you did. And you didn't have ostrich feathers in your hair, then, nor silk stockings, nor high-heeled shoes. You didn't have shoes at all.

LULU: Take me home with you. Tonight. We'll find a cab downstairs.

SCHIGOLCH: Of course you can come home with me. What's wrong?

LULU: He's going to turn me in.

SCHIGOLCH: Who is?

LULU: The Jumping Jack.

SCHIGOLCH: I'll deal with him.

LULU: Thanks.

(She cuddles up content.)

SCHIGOLCH: Get him to come to my place and he's a goner. Think of my little room, with its splendid view of the river, several floors up. But he won't come of his own accord.

LULU: What's the address?

SCHIGOLCH: 25, Quai de la Gare.

LULU: I'll make sure he gets there. I'll send him over with the loony Countess. Hurry.

SCHIGOLCH: I'll roll out the carpet.

LULU: Tomorrow morning, bring me his gold earrings.

SCHIGOLCH: I never noticed his gold earrings.

LULU: Cut them off before you chuck him out of the window.

SCHIGOLCH: And what will happen after that, my dear?

LULU: I'll hand you over five hundred francs.

SCHIGOLCH: What an old meanie you are! Haven't you anything else on offer?

LULU: Name your price.

SCHIGOLCH: We've almost reached the tenth anniversary of our divorce. Perhaps a little remembrance of things past . . .

LULU: (*Bursts out laughing.*) Is that all! Any time you like, you naughty old man! But what about your girlfriend?

SCHIGOLCH: She'll never see sixty years again. She'll never see her teeth again.

(LULU *gives him a peck on the cheek.*)

LULU: Promise?

SCHIGOLCH: I've always kept my word to you.

LULU: Swear.

(SCHIGOLCH *lays his hand on her thigh.*)

SCHIGOLCH: I'll see to him tonight. By all I hold dear.

LULU: 'By all I hold dear'. (*Big sigh.*)

(SCHIGOLCH *continues to caress her thigh.*)

I feel calmer already.

SCHIGOLCH: I don't.

(*She takes away his hand affectionately.*)

LULU: Not now. They'll be at your place in half an hour. Take a cab.

SCHIGOLCH: I'm halfway home already.

(*They get to their feet.* LULU, *suddenly distraught, clutches at her thigh.*)

LULU: Oh, God. My garter. It's come undone. It's bad luck. You know that?

SCHIGOLCH: Keep still.

(*She rests her leg on the sofa;* SCHIGOLCH *skins back her skirt and fastens her garter.*)

LULU: It's an omen. Spilled salt. Crossed knives. This is worse.

SCHIGOLCH: (*Genuine affection.*) Not for you, my lucky one. I'll see to that.

(LULU sees him out through one of the right-hand doors. While she is gone, CASTI-PIANI punches RODRIGO onstage through one of the left-hand doors.)

CASTI-PIANI: What did you tell that woman?

RODRIGO: *(Panting.)* Go fuck yourself!

CASTI-PIANI: Out with it! You tried to get her to go with you!

RODRIGO: That's a lie.

CASTI-PIANI: She told me so herself. You threatened to turn her in if she wouldn't. I ought to shoot you.

RODRIGO: I don't need to threaten her to get her to go to bed with me.

(Breathing heavily, they stare at one another.)

CASTI-PIANI: Thanks. That's all I needed to know.

(He dashes out of a right-hand door.)

RODRIGO: I should have chucked him up to the ceiling and let him stick there.

(LULU comes back.)

LULU: And where have you been?

RODRIGO: *(Straightening his tie.)* Now he knows what happens when a man tangles with Rodrigo Quast.

LULU: Who knows?

RODRIGO: Your dear, sweet Casti-Piani. Why on earth did you tell him I tried to seduce you?

LULU: Didn't you ask me to sell myself to my dead husband's son for twenty thousand francs?

RODRIGO: It's your duty to give that poor boy a bit of fun. You shot his father dead in front of his very eyes, didn't you. As for Casti-Piani, he'll think twice before he crosses my path again. I'll tie Turk's head knots in his guts.

LULU: Countess Geschwitz will lend me twenty thousand francs if you put her out of her misery. She's desperate for you. She'll jump into the Seine if you go on playing hard to get.

RODRIGO: What's she waiting for?

LULU: Your body.

RODRIGO: Tell her to jump, then.

LULU: Just take her off with you tonight, and I'll deposit twenty thousand for you at the post office in the Avenue de l'Opéra tomorrow.

RODRIGO: And what if I don't?

LULU: Turn me in. Alva and I are skint.

RODRIGO: Shit.

LULU: She loves you very, very much.

RODRIGO: Who would have thought she'd fancy a bit of rough?

LULU: She's pure as the driven snow, withal.

RODRIGO: If there *is* a God, he'll damn you for your sense of humour, apart from all the other things.

LULU: She's waiting. What shall I tell her?

RODRIGO: Tell her it just came off in me 'and.

LULU: Fine.

(*She turns towards the doors to the gaming room.*)

RODRIGO: Hang on! Are you absolutely positive about the twenty thousand francs?

LULU: Ask her yourself!

RODRIGO: Tell her it's on. I'll wait upstairs. I must go and order a ton of caviare to keep my strength up.

(*He goes into the supper room.* LULU *opens the double doors and beckons* GESCHWITZ *out of the gaming room.*)

LULU: Darling. Save me.

GESCHWITZ: What do I do?

LULU: Take Jumping Jack to the Quai de la Gare.

GESCHWITZ: Then what?

LULU: He says, if you won't sleep with him tonight, he'll shop me to the police in the morning.

(GESCHWITZ *turns to* LULU, *horror on her face.*)

GESCHWITZ: You know I can't do that.

LULU: Then just say 'no' very firmly once you get there and he'll have to accept it, won't he. Oh, God! Why did he have to fall for you?

GESCHWITZ: If I turn him down, he'll beat me up. I know all about that. Is this another of your trials of love?

LULU: Your loss if he turns me in.

GESCHWITZ: I don't understand how I can save your life by going through this ordeal. It's the worst thing that could happen to me.

LULU: (Sly.) Perhaps . . . he'll put you right, know what I mean?

GESCHWITZ: (Deeply reproachful.) Oh, Lulu . . . Lulu . . . I've lost my faith . . . I'm so unhappy. My life lurches between misery and despair.

LULU: Don't torture yourself. I don't know, I . . . Oh, God! *Men*. Sometimes . . .

(She lays her hand in its white glove on GESCHWITZ's sleeve. GESCHWITZ stares at the glove, mesmerised.)

GESCHWITZ: Sometimes.

LULU: Sometimes I remember what you promised me, and the way you kept your promises. No man has ever kept a promise he made to me. And then I remember . . . that I didn't keep any of my promises to you, either . . . and I remember some of the other things that we did, that I try not to remember, and yet – all the same, I *do* remember.

GESCHWITZ: (Radiant.) Yes . . .

LULU: (In a rush, as if coming to a sudden decision.) If you can hold off the Jumping Jack until tomorrow, I'm yours. His vanity is at stake. Plead with him. Ask him to take mercy on you.

GESCHWITZ: It's always tomorrow.

LULU: Tomorrow. I'll be waiting for you. I won't open my eyes until you get here. I won't look at the chambermaid, I won't let in the hairdresser. You. The first thing I see tomorrow, when I open my eyes. You.

GESCHWITZ: (Heroic.) Send for him.

LULU: 25, Quai de la Gare. It's a small hotel. They're expecting you.

GESCHWITZ: 25, Quai de la Gare. Let's get it over with.

LULU: Come out, Rodrigo.

(RODRIGO *comes out of the supper room, eating caviare from a tin with a soup spoon.* BOB *follows, carrying a salver with a bowl of ice on it.*)

GESCHWITZ: (*To* RODRIGO, *poker-face.*) I adore you. I long for you. Be kind.

(RODRIGO *swallows the last mouthful of caviare noisily, thrusts can and spoon back into the bowl of ice on the salver and offers* GESCHWITZ *his arm.*)

RODRIGO: Off to the slaughterhouse!

LULU: Good night, darlings, and good luck.

(*She sees them out tenderly. As soon as the door closes behind them, she grabs* BOB's *arm.*)

Quick! Come with me. Get your clothes off –

(*She draws him into the supper room as the gamblers come out of the gaming room.* HEILMANN *is thrusting a piece of paper at* PUNTSCHU. *The atmosphere is ugly.*)

HEILMANN: You *must* take it, sir!

PUNTSCHU: It won't do, old chap. It just won't do.

HEILMANN: So you won't let me get my own back, you bastard!

BIANETTA: These Prussians!

MADELINE: What's going on?

LUDMILLA: He's taken his money.

HEILMANN: And then the prick quits.

PUNTSCHU: Me? Leave a game? No, no, no! But the gentleman must put down hard cash. He can try to sell me that rubbish during office hours, if he wants, but I'm not in my office now.

HEILMANN: These aren't rubbish – they're shares in the Jungfrau Railway. You sold them to me yourself.

PUNTSCHU: But when one gambles amongst gentlemen, old chap, one needs hard cash.

KADEGA: What is he talking about, Mummy?

MADELINE: I really don't know.

HEILMANN: Bloodsucker!

PUNTSCHU: Be reasonable, old chap. Your shares are worthless. The Jungfrau Railway just crashed. *(The small joke pleases him; he smiles.)* Crash, bang, wallop. All over. Finito! Phut! A cable arrived with the news half an hour ago.

ALVA: That's it. We're all done for.

PUNTSCHU: What about me? I've lost my entire fortune.

MADELINE: Eighteen years on my back gone down the drain!

(She faints.)

KADEGA: Mummy! Wake up! She's dead!

(PUNTSCHU and BIANETTA leave hastily, hand in hand. HEILMANN tears up his shares and scatters them around. LUDMILLA approaches him.)

LUDMILLA: Don't cry over spilt milk. Drop a note to a certain address in Berlin. You can make up all the cash you've lost.

HEILMANN: You strangely interest me.

LUDMILLA: Let's go and have a bite of supper. We can put together a nice little report between the two of us before they clear the tables for breakfast.

HEILMANN: Don't you ever sleep?

LUDMILLA: Why waste the night?

(They slip out. Meanwhile, ALVA is bending solicitously over MADELINE.)

ALVA: Hands like ice. Still breathing, though. God, she's a fine figure of a woman . . . If I unfasten her corsets, she can breathe better . . .

(As he fumbles with MADELINE's breasts, LULU comes in in BOB's livery.)

LULU: Is there any cash left?

ALVA: Why the fancy dress?

LULU: The police will be here in two minutes flat. We've been dropped right in it. Stay, if you want.

ALVA: Oh, God!

(They grab hands and run out together, suddenly like brother and sister again.)

KADEGA: Wake up, Mummy. They've all gone away.

MADELINE: *(Coming to.)* My youth and golden days, all gone. Such is life.

KADEGA: I'll earn our living, now. I don't want to go back to that bloody convent.

MADELINE: Darling, you don't know what you're talking about.

KADEGA: Mummy, take me with you to the music-hall.

MADELINE: What, you in your baby clothes?

KADEGA: Don't I look pretty in my school uniform?

MADELINE: So be it. God forgive me. We'll go to the Olympia first thing tomorrow.

(KADEGA *hugs and kisses her, pleased. A voice outside, stentorian, interrupts.*)

GENDARME: Open in the name of the law!

(*Two* GENDARMES *burst in, followed at a more leisurely pace by* CASTI-PIANI. *One* GENDARME *seizes* MADELINE's *arm, the other seizes* KADEGA's.)

GENDARME: You're under arrest!

SECOND GENDARME: You, too.

(MADELINE *and* KADEGA *start to protest.*)

CASTI-PIANI: No, no, officers! Neither of these ladies!

(*He looks around with amusement.*)

It seems the bird has flown.

ACT SEVEN

(The studio of the first act, with its slanting roof and its skylight; but – the walls are streaked with grime and possibly worse, there are long tears in what turns out to have been wallpaper, the glass in the skylight is cracked and the rain that clatters upon it drips through into a chipped enamel bowl strategically placed underneath. The little table, bare of a cover, sadly splintered, keeling over where one leg has broken, holds a brown bottle and a spluttering paraffin lamp. The sofa is still upholstered in white, as it was in the preceding act, but is now indescribably filthy and has been slit lengthwise with a knife.

ALVA *lies on the sofa, wrapped in a travelling rug. The leather strap used to fasten the rug when it is not in use hangs from a nail in the back wall, beside the double doors.*

Against the left wall, SCHIGOLCH *relaxes stretched out on a scabby mattress. Rain beats against the skylight.)*

SCHIGOLCH: Hark at the rain. Sounds like applause.

ALVA: It's her first night with the public. They're giving her a big hand.

(They laugh.

LULU *comes in through the door in the right wall, wearing a soiled cotton dress, a man's jacket from an ancient suit over her shoulders, in grubby white anklesocks, shoeless. Her hair has grown, grown out of curl, is no longer particularly blonde, hangs lankly round her neck. Her face is grubby. She has a defeated, exhausted look. She bends, picks the bowl of water up off the floor, puts it on the table, shifting the bottle to make room.)*

SCHIGOLCH: That's right, have a good wash before you go out.

ALVA: Cleanliness is the jewellery of the poor.

LULU: I wish you two would leave me alone.

(She washes her hands, looks round for a towel, sees none and listlessly shakes off the water drops.)

ALVA: I dreamed we were having dinner at Maxim's. Just you and me. And the champagne was running over the tablecloth and dripping down the sides.

SCHIGOLCH: You'll never guess what I dreamed of last night. Christmas pudding! Yes. A phantom Christmas pudding bobbed before my dreaming eyes, for ever delicious, for ever indigestible, for ever out of reach.

LULU: I wish one or the other of you would give me a bit of support.

ALVA: Don't forget to put your shoes on.

SCHIGOLCH: A journey of a thousand miles begins with one little step, as the Chinese sage says. Best foot forward! God, she's such a moaner. Always was. You should have heard her twenty years ago. She needs a good stoking up. After she's been at it a week, wild horses won't be able to keep her off it.

ALVA: The basin's overflowing already.

LULU: Where shall I empty it?

ALVA: Out the skylight.

(*She puts the lamp and bottle on the floor, drags the table to a spot beneath the skylight, climbs up, opens the skylight, tips out the water. She performs all these tasks with ceremonious and elaborate sarcasm; the two men, prone, watch. She breathes in the fresh air.*)

LULU: The rain's stopping.

SCHIGOLCH: You've wasted the rush-hour.

(*She stands, arms akimbo, on the table, surveying the squalid room and its occupants.*)

LULU: I wish I were dead.

ALVA: (*Vicious, with enthusiasm.*) Me, too. Don't go out, tonight. Stay put, we'll all starve together.

(*LULU leaps from the table with a violent grace that reminds us she was once a dancer; she stands over ALVA, furious.*)

LULU: You've never brought home so much as one single penny in all your pampered and over-privileged life, you idle sod. Why don't you go out and peddle your arsehole, give me a rest.

ALVA: I wouldn't send a dog out on a night like this.

LULU: But you're quite happy to send *me* out, aren't you.

ALVA: I won't touch your filthy money.

SCHIGOLCH: She fed an entire family from what she earned on her back when she was fifteen. And now she'd rather see us croak than go out and give herself a good time.

LULU: I wouldn't have to keep out of the lights if you hadn't sold off my clothes.

ALVA: You can't say I didn't try. I tried too damn hard. Night and day, day and night, I didn't think of anything else, only the system. Always the system. The foolproof system. Might just as well have flushed the cash straight down the toilet. Nothing left. Not a whisker. Life is a gamble but God rigs it.

SCHIGOLCH: Why don't you slip on your shoes and take a little stroll? I know in my water I won't get much older in this attic. I've lived long enough, God knows, and no regrets. I do believe at midnight I might totter out for a whisky at the Cosmopolitan Club. Only yesterday, the barmaid told me that if I played my cards right there was a distinct possibility she might succumb to my charms.

LULU: I can't stand much more of this.

SCHIGOLCH: Kindly leave the room as you would wish to find it.

(With an irritated sigh, LULU pulls the table back centre stage and puts the lamp back in place. She picks up the bottle and drinks from it. SCHIGOLCH is seriously displeased.)

SCHIGOLCH: That's right! Now the punters can smell you a mile off!

LULU: Don't worry, I won't drink it all.

(She takes another swig. ALVA stirs and speaks with sudden forcefulness.)

ALVA: No. I won't permit my wife to walk the streets.

LULU: (Derisive.) Peter, Peter, pumpkin eater,
                    Had a wife but couldn't keep her . . .

ALVA: (Whining.) It's not my fault, if I can't keep you, is it? You laid me up, didn't you?

LULU: What?

ALVA: Who dragged me into this shit? Who made me my own father's murderer?

LULU: So you got your finger out sufficiently, for once, and put it on the trigger! Huh! When I see you stretched out there on the sofa like a . . . a . . . a fucking catatonic, not doing nothing except whine, I wonder why I did anything so plain bloody stupid as killing your father!

(She storms off into her room, right hand door.)

ALVA: She gave me what she got from Casti-Piani.

SCHIGOLCH: There's a touch of the devil in her, but she's still young. If she suffers enough, she's bound to ascend to heaven in the last act.

ALVA: She was born out of her time. Old Russia, that would have suited her. The Scarlet Empress. That's her down to the ground.

(LULU comes back, wearing plimsolls with the backs trodden down.)

LULU: State of that staircase, I'll probably take a nose-dive. Christ, it's cold! 'Good-time girl'. Gawd. How pathetic.

SCHIGOLCH: You'll feel better once you've scored.

LULU: I don't care. Couldn't give a monkey's. *(She drinks.)* That warms me up, a bit. To hell with it all.

(She goes out through the double doors, slamming them.)

SCHIGOLCH: As soon as we hear the footsteps on the stair, we must tuck ourselves away in our little hidey hole.

ALVA: Oh God, what a waste. When I remember what she was like when she was a child . . . I grew up with her, really. We were like brother and sister.

SCHIGOLCH: I think, I hope, I pray she'll outlast me.

ALVA: My mother was still alive. I came across her quite by accident, she was putting her clothes back on. Dr Goll was on his way to our house, to give her a once-over. It was the day my very first poem was published. Turned out her hairdresser had read it, of all things. 'Drive your hounds over the mountains, they will come back to you, dust on their paws . . .'

SCHIGOLCH: *(Ironic.)* Lovely. Lovely.

ALVA: Then there was that ball at the Spanish Embassy. She was wearing a pink net frock with only a satin slip underneath. Dr Goll seemed to have a feeling he wouldn't last much longer, he asked me to dance with her, to make sure she behaved herself. My father couldn't take his eyes off us. She had eyes only for him, only for him. All the time we were waltzing. They never took their eyes off each other. Then she shot him. It's incredible, really.

SCHIGOLCH: I don't think she's going to have any luck tonight, you know.

ALVA: *(Peevish.)* Is it any wonder, the way she's let herself go. She was just a little girl, in those days. That lush woman's body, and inside there was this bright-eyed joyous, fun-loving five-year-old.

(This is a little young even for SCHIGOLCH. *He raises his eyebrows.* ALVA *doesn't notice.)*

Of course, she was only three years younger than me, then. God, it seems like half a lifetime ago! She gave herself such airs, such a woman of the world, but she had to get me to explain the plot of 'Tristan and Isolde' to her. She really knew how to listen. It's the most seductive thing in the world, when a woman knows how to listen . . .

My funny little sister, she carried on like a giddy schoolgirl even when she married the good doctor. And then, her next role, a muse of that unhappy, suicidal, half-crazed painter. Then the artist's widow turns into my father's wife. I took my father's wife to be my mistress. So be it. We think we have choices, we think we make choices, but it's all beyond our control.

SCHIGOLCH: Let's hope she doesn't exercise *her* right to choose at this juncture and drag some penniless tramp back here because she likes the cut of his jib.

ALVA: When I kissed her for the first time, she was wearing her wedding dress. I think she sometimes thought of me when she was in bed with my father. It didn't happen often, mind. She took what she needed from the chauffeur, the bootboy, men she met on the street. But, on those rare and fated occasions when she made love to my father, I think it must have been *my* soul she saw deep in his eyes.

(SCHIGOLCH has been listening to this with visibly rising nausea. Now he hears something else; he sits up, cupping his ear with his hand.)

SCHIGOLCH: Footsteps . . .

(ALVA throws back the rug.)

ALVA: No. I'll throw the bastard downstairs.

SCHIGOLCH: Into the cubby-hole with you. How can she go about her business if we're taking up all the room?

ALVA: What if he wants . . . something obscene?

SCHIGOLCH: So what. He's only human, like the rest of us.

ALVA: At least leave the door ajar.

SCHIGOLCH: Whatever for?

ALVA: Then we can hear what they're doing.

(SCHIGOLCH pushes ALVA towards the door, left.)

SCHIGOLCH: Just keep your trap shut.

(He closes the door firmly behind them. LULU opens one of the centre doors and comes in with MR HOPKINS, a big man with a clean-shaven face and a suspiciously friendly smile. He wears a tweed cap and a tweed deerstalker: he carries a dripping umbrella. He opens the umbrella and props it up to dry. He takes off his cape and lays it neatly on the sofa.)

LULU: My little room is over there. This way. I'm afraid it isn't very cosy.

(MR HOPKINS puts his fingers to his lips.)

What do you mean by that?

(MR HOPKINS puts his hand over her mouth.)

I don't understand.

(MR HOPKINS closes her mouth with his fingers. She shakes herself free.)

Don't worry, nobody can hear.

(MR HOPK:NS puts his forefinger to his lips, shakes his head, points to LULU, opens his mouth as if to speak, points to himself and then to the doors.)

My God, what a madman.

(The door left opens a crack. ALVA and SCHIGOLCH peer through.)

SCHIGOLCH: He's barmy.

ALVA: She only brought him back to make us feel rotten.

LULU: *(To HOPKINS.)* Will you give me some money?

(MR HOPKINS holds her mouth shut and gives her a ten-shilling note. She looks at it, holds it up to the light. He looks at her questioningly. She shrugs and puts it in her jacket pocket.)

LULU: That'll do, I suppose.

(He holds her mouth shut and takes two half-crowns out of his pocket, gives them to her. LULU pockets them.)

You're a real gent.

(She takes the lamp from the flower-stand and leads him into her room. ALVA and SCHIGOLCH creep out from the cubby-hole on all fours.)

ALVA: We can't hear anything from here.

SCHIGOLCH: Haven't you heard it often enough already?

ALVA: I'm going to listen at the keyhole.

(He kneels. SCHIGOLCH *quickly searches the pockets of* MR HOPKINS*'s cape. He finds nothing but a pair of gloves. He sneers. Then he pulls out a book, inspects the title, chuckles, reads aloud.)*

SCHIGOLCH: Listen to this. 'Instructions for those who are, and those who want to be, servants of Christ, with a preface by the Rev. W. Hay.' Just what we need!

*(*ALVA *gets up.)*

ALVA: The good Lord left him in the lurch this time.

SCHIGOLCH: London's useless, you know. The English are useless. The whole place is going to the dogs. That man in bed with Lulu isn't even wearing a tie!

ALVA: Let's get back in the broom cupboard. Perhaps he'll give her another little present when he says goodbye.

SCHIGOLCH: She went and picked up the first man that came along, the soppy trollop. Never a thought for us. *(Vicious.)* I hope she gives him something to remember her by.

(They hastily disappear as LULU *opens the right-hand door and enters, lamp in hand, followed by* MR HOPKINS*, buttoning himself.)*

LULU: Will you come and see me again, dearie?

*(*MR HOPKINS *holds her mouth shut.* LULU *shrugs. She helps him on with his cape; he grins at her horribly, a grin which is his friendly smile carried to excess. She throws her arms round his neck but he pushes her away and kisses her hand. He leaves.)*

LULU: *(Toneless.)* Christ. That one really got on my tits.

*(*ALVA *and* SCHIGOLCH *emerge.)*

ALVA: How much?

LULU: Fifteen bob. Take it. I'm going back down.

SCHIGOLCH: Fifteen whole shillings! What a spree we'll have!

ALVA: Sh! He's coming back.

(They all listen intently.)

LULU: That's not his footsteps.

SCHIGOLCH: Perhaps he recommended us to a friend.

(GESCHWITZ *lets herself in through the double doors, carrying a rolled-up canvas. There is absolute silence. All three stare at her with a complete lack of expression. She is used to them; she shakes the rain off herself.*)

GESCHWITZ: If it's bad timing, I'll go away again. But I haven't spoken to a living soul for ten days. I didn't get the money. My brother wouldn't even answer my letters.

SCHIGOLCH: And now you want to move in with us, do you?

LULU: I'd better get back to my beat.

GESCHWITZ: Where are you going, dressed like that? Don't worry, I didn't come empty-handed. A junk dealer in Leicester Square offered me a pound for it but I couldn't bear to part with it. You can sell it if you want.

(*She unrolls the canvas. It is* SCHWARTZ's *portrait.* LULU *bursts into furious tears.*)

LULU: Throw it out of the window!

(*She snatches the canvas from* GESCHWITZ's *hands but* ALVA *wrestles it from her.*)

ALVA: Oh no, you don't. Let me look.

(*He unrolls it, holds it out at arm's length.*)

ALVA: H'm.

(*He thrusts it at* SCHIGOLCH, *who holds it up against his chest so that they can all see it.* LULU *stops crying and dries her eyes.*)

ALVA: When I look at that face, all our catastrophes seem inexorable. Now I know why I am ruined. There's danger oozing out of every pore of her. She's like a pirate ship; she's come to wreck the bourgeoisie with the terrible weapon of her sex.

(LULU *blows her nose noisily.*)

LULU: Pack it in.

SCHIGOLCH: We must hang it up. Our clients *will* be impressed.

ALVA: Let me. I know how.

(He pulls four nails out of the wall, takes off his left boot and nails the picture up on the wall, beside the right-hand door, using his boot as a hammer.)

SCHIGOLCH: *(To* GESCHWITZ.*)* How did you get hold of it?

GESCHWITZ: I crept back to the flat and cut it out of the frame after you all ran away.

SCHIGOLCH: It's going to give the room such an air. Like a real salon.

(ALVA *pulls* LULU *over to the portrait by the arm. He compares them.)*

ALVA: You still have those same huge, innocent eyes, in spite of everything. But that miraculous bloom on the skin, the glow, the freshness, the radiance you seemed to carry inside you – and your throat, that used to be so lovely – what happened to your throat –

SCHIGOLCH: Gone to the knacker's yard. All the same, she can point to that picture and say: I used to be very beautiful, you know. And people will say, Yes. You certainly were. Nobody could ever say that about me.

ALVA: High summer for a woman is when she's ripe to destroy a man. That's the way of it. When you're living with a woman, day in day out, you don't notice how her looks are going.

SCHIGOLCH: Oh, come on now! Down there on the corner, provided she keeps the light behind her, I'd pit her against the competition any day! Besides, the midnight punter isn't on the lookout for a pretty face. His aspirations are more spiritual. He wants a girl who looks as though she won't pick his pocket.

LULU: *(Weary.)* I'd better go and see if you're right.

ALVA: Oh no, you're not. Not while I live and breathe.

GESCHWITZ: Where are you going?

ALVA: To pick up a man.

GESCHWITZ: Lulu!

ALVA: She's done it once already, tonight.

GESCHWITZ: I'll go with you.

SCHIGOLCH: Find your own pitch, then.

GESCHWITZ: I'll protect you. Look – *(She fumbles in her bag and produces a gun.)* – I've got a revolver.

LULU: I'm going to kill myself. This minute. I can't stand this any longer.

(*She dashes out through the double doors.* GESCHWITZ *importunately pursues.*)

GESCHWITZ: Let me come with you!

SCHIGOLCH: Here's a turn-up. The return of the horse-faced Countess.

(ALVA *throws himself on the sofa.*)

ALVA: I don't want to live much longer.

SCHIGOLCH: I should have grabbed her by the hind leg and tethered her to the bedpost. She'll scare off trade.

ALVA: She cast me down upon my bed of sickness and then she thrust a crown of thorns upon my brow.

SCHIGOLCH: All the same, the Countess has got guts.

ALVA: This is the moment of truth. This attic is the bullring. She is the toreador. I am the wounded bull. Release me. Release me from this torment.

SCHIGOLCH: Let's face it. If the old trouper hadn't lured the Jumping Jack to my room, he'd still be on our backs.

ALVA: Death. Infinitely seductive. Infinitely inaccessible.

SCHIGOLCH: Let's have a little light on the subject, old chap. Turn up the lamp.

ALVA: Oh God, what a mess I've made of my life!

SCHIGOLCH: Oh God, what a mess this rain has made of my overcoat!

ALVA: You want to know the best joke of all? I did it on purpose! I knew what I was doing. I was absolutely self-aware. I went right ahead, in full possession of all my faculties, and squandered the splendid promise of my youth.

SCHIGOLCH: The lamp's running out, that's what's the matter. By the time she gets back, it'll be dark as the womb in here. Not half so snug, alas.

ALVA: I set out deliberately to court the life of physical experience. 'Le dérèglement de tous les sens.' I thought that was how you got to be a great poet – you plunged into the gutter. God, what a fool I've been!

I've martyrised my sensibility for my art, and I haven't written one word since my father died.

SCHIGOLCH: I hope those two girls split up. Nobody with any sense takes on two girls.

ALVA: Of course they'll split up.

SCHIGOLCH: Here they come, now. We'd better slip away.

ALVA: I'm staying put. Shift myself for the sake of fifteen lousy bob just when I've got comfy? No thanks!

SCHIGOLCH: (With a note of genuine reproof.) If there was a trace of decency left within you, you'd know when it was time for a gentleman to make his excuses and leave.

(He goes off through the left-hand door with vestigial dignity. ALVA grunts and pulls the rug up over his head, concealing himself.

LULU opens the door, accompanied by a young black man in far too elegant clothes.)

LULU: Come on.

KUNGU-POTI: Those stairs were very dark.

LULU: It's a bit brighter in here.

KUNGU-POTI: Is this your boudoir?

LULU: Right in one.

KUNGU-POTI: It's cold.

(LULU hands him the brown bottle.)

LULU: Want something to warm you up? Don't know where the glass has got to.

KUNGU-POTI: I don't care.

(He drinks.)

LULU: You're terribly handsome.

KUNGU-POTI: My father is the Sultan of Uahube. I will inherit a kingdom twice the size of England. I have six wives in London, three English and three French. But happily for you, sometimes . . . I like to slum it.

LULU: How much will you pay me?

KUNGU-POTI: One pound.

LULU: In advance.

KUNGU-POTI: Never.

LULU: All right. Give it to me after but show it to me now.

KUNGU-POTI: No. *(He grabs her.)* Come on.

LULU: Let go!

KUNGU-POTI: Where's the bed?

(He thrusts her back towards the sofa.

ALVA throws back the rug and seizes hold of KUNGU-POTI. There is a brief struggle, which ends when KUNGU-POTI produces a cosh from his pocket and hits ALVA over the head.

ALVA falls with a groan.

KUNGU-POTI drops the cosh and runs out.

LULU trips over ALVA's body as she runs after him, but she does not stop.)

LULU: Wait!

(SCHIGOLCH creeps out of the left-hand door.)

SCHIGOLCH: Alva? Alva . . .

(He kneels beside the prone form and gingerly touches his head.)

Who'd have thought the young man had so much blood in him . . . We must hide you away, my dear, or you'll give the clients the willies. Shift!

(He drags ALVA's corpse into LULU's bedroom and returns. He tries to turn up the lamp, with no success.)

I must be off, or there won't be any Christmas pudding left at the Cosmopolitan Club. God knows when the girls will be back.

(He turns and addresses the portrait.)

SCHIGOLCH: Oh, my dear, my darling, my baby, my Lulu, you don't know the score. You never did. How could you? You can't make a living out of love because love is your life.

(GESCHWITZ comes in.)

If you're planning to stay overnight with us, Countess, perhaps you'd be kind enough to see that nothing gets stolen.

GESCHWITZ: It's very dark in here.

SCHIGOLCH: It will get darker. Young Mr Schoen has already turned in for the night.

GESCHWITZ: She told me to come on ahead.

SCHIGOLCH: Quite so. Would you direct . . . any inquiries for me to the Cosmopolitan Club?

(*He shambles out through the double doors, closing them behind him gently, almost reverently.* GESCHWITZ *sits on the sofa.*)

GESCHWITZ: I've got to see every single thing she does. I mustn't flinch. I've got to find out what she's really like. But she doesn't even know what she's really like, herself. Nobody does. If they did, they couldn't bear it. They tell lies all the time but they don't know when they're lying and when they're telling the truth, and they never stay the same from one minute to another, either. You never know where you are. Here she is, my lover. There she goes, a perfect stranger. Everything flies apart.

Only little children are pure.

But not for long.

One good thing, you can't be unhappy when you're hungry. Then all you can think of is filling your belly. But as soon as we're fed, oh! what won't we do for the sake of happiness! Oh God, and whenever did love make *me* happy!

Perhaps I ought to drown myself. She wouldn't cry over me. I'm just another of the poor fools she uses and abuses when the need arises. She's despised me from the day we met.

I could always cut my throat.

Night after night, after night, after night, I dream about Her. Just as she bends down to kiss me, I wake up.

I'm a lost soul. A lost soul.

(*She casts around the room; her eyes fix on the rug strap, hanging on the wall from its nail.*)

GESCHWITZ: An execution. A hanging.

(*She takes the strap from the wall and examines it. Then she climbs up on the sofa. She buckles the buckle end of the strap round her neck. Then, standing on tiptoe, she fixes the other end of the strap to the handle of the skylight, above, with a clumsy knot. She stands for a moment, strung up. Then she jumps. The knot undoes itself.*

GESCHWITZ *falls heavily to the floor. She bursts into tears.*)

(*Floods of tears.*) Oh God . . . Am I meant to drag myself on for years . . .

(She crawls towards the portrait of LULU *and beseeches it.)*

I love you. Pity me. Pity me. Pity me.

*(*LULU *opens the double doors and comes in with* JACK THE RIPPER, *a dishevelled man with red-rimmed eyes and – yes – the mark of Cain upon him.* GESCHWITZ *throws herself across the room and clutches* LULU's *legs.)*

JACK: Who's she?

LULU: That's my mad sister. Take no notice. *(To* GESCHWITZ.*)* Get down. *(To* JACK.*)* Don't let her put you off.

JACK: She isn't your sister, she's your girlfriend. *(Patting* GESCHWITZ's *head.)* Poor little doggie.

*(*GESCHWITZ *crawls off to* SCHIGOLCH's *mattress and lies there, sobbing.)*

Do you know what you're doing.?

LULU: 'Course I do.

JACK: You're not English.

LULU: I'm German.

JACK: Where did you get such a lovely mouth?

LULU: *(Spark of the old, seductive* LULU.*)* My mother gave it to me when I was born.

JACK: How much? I don't have money to burn.

LULU: Want to stay the night?

JACK: Can't. Married.

LULU: Say you missed the last tram.

JACK: How much?

LULU: A pound.

JACK: Good night.

LULU: Don't go!

JACK: Why do you want me to stay the night? So you can go through my pockets once I've dropped off?

LULU: I'm not that kind of girl. Stay. Please.

JACK: How much?

LULU: Ten bob.

JACK: Too much. Just starting out, are you?

LULU: First time tonight. Stay with me. I'm lonely.

JACK: Have you got a kid?

LULU: No. *(Flash of spirit.)* But I was a very pretty woman once upon a time.

JACK: Anyone live here apart from you two?

LULU: No.

JACK: What about down below?

LULU: Room to let.

JACK: I was watching you for a long time. I liked the way you walked. I thought, a girl with a walk like that has got to have a lovely mouth.

LULU: You certainly like my mouth.

(Beat.)

Why are you staring at me?

(JACK snaps out of it.)

JACK: Down to my last shilling.

LULU: That's all right.

JACK: Give me a tanner back, for the tram.

LULU: Haven't got change.

JACK: Look in your handbag.

(LULU opens out her bag.)

Let's see.

(He grabs a ten-shilling note.)

I'll have that.

(LULU tries to grab it back.)

LULU: I'll change it tomorrow and give you half.

(JACK shakes his head.)

Oh. Oh, all right. Keep it.

(LULU *picks up the lamp and holds it in front of the portrait for a moment,* *drawing Jack's attention to it.*)

JACK: Here, that's never you. I see you've stopped taking care of yourself. We don't need that lamp. There's moonlight.

(*He takes the lamp from her and puts it down in front of the portrait with a* *certain ritualistic emphasis. He takes a last look at the portrait as* LULU *opens* *her door. They go inside.*

GESCHWITZ *gradually stopping crying, sits up, rocking herself to and fro.*)

GESCHWITZ: I won't spend another night with these dreadful people. I'll go back to Germany. My mother will pay for the ticket. I'll go to university. I'll study law. I'll fight for women's rights.

(*A terrible scream rings out.* LULU, *barefoot, in a torn slip, opens her bedroom* *door.*)

LULU: Help!

(GESCHWITZ *pulls the revolver out of her bag, runs to the door, pushes* LULU *behind her, and aims.* LULU, *panicked, clings to* GESCHWITZ's *trousers,* *distracting her.* GESCHWITZ *kicks out at her.*)

GESCHWITZ: Let go, for God's sake!

(JACK, *in shirtsleeves, with bloody hands, slips out through the open door, bent* *double, and plunges a knife into* GESCHWITZ's *stomach. She fires a shot* *uselessly at the ceiling and collapses, whimpering.*

LULU, *on hands and knees, scrambles away, leaving a trail of blood.* JACK *follows, knife raised. She catches hold of the brown bottle, smashes it, lunges at* *him with the broken neck. He kicks her ankles, knocking her down. She screams* *again, once. He picks her up in a ghastly parody of tenderness.*)

JACK: I've never seen a mouth like yours.

LULU: No. Don't. No.

JACK: Yes. Yes. Yes.

(*She goes limp. He carries her into the bedroom as a bridegroom might carry a* *bride.*

LULU *screams, one more time, in a huge, piercing arc.*

Silence.

After a pause, JACK *comes out of the bedroom. He looks around, spots the* *washbasin, washes his hands.*)

JACK: (*As he washes.*) Lots of spirit, that one. Jack certainly knows how to pick 'em. (*Looks round for a towel.*) Not even a towel! These freaks are poor as piss. *(He bends down and dries his hands on* GESCHWITZ's *travelling cape.)* Don't be scared, love, your fort's quite safe with me. It'll be all over in a minute.

(He looks round briefly, perhaps looking for something to steal. Then he goes out of the door, whistling.

There is a pause, during which LULU's *bedroom door creaks open but nothing comes out. Then* GESCHWITZ *manages to drag herself to her knees.)*

GESCHWITZ: Lulu! darling!

(With exquisite pain and effort, she starts dragging herself over the floor in the direction of LULU's *room.)*

Let me look at you one last time . . . I'm here, we're together. We'll be together for ever . . .

(She collapses.)

Oh, damn.

(She dies.)

APPENDIX

PREFACE TO
Come unto These Yellow Sands

For me, writing for radio involves a kind of three-dimensional story-telling. Anyone, anywhere, who sits down to tell a story, from the narrator of fabulous epics in a pre-literate African community to a travelling salesman embarking on an anecdote in a bar, does so without the help of visual aids, and his or her narrative, however complex it might be thematically, will extend through time in, more or less, a straight line, its course determined by the characteristic copulas of the story: 'and then' . . . 'but then . . .' Radio may not offer visual images but its resources blur this linearity, so that a great number of things can happen at the same time. Yet, as with all forms of story-telling that are composed in words, not in visual images, radio always leaves that magical and enigmatic margin, that space of the invisible, which must be filled in by the imagination of the listener.

It is this necessary open-endedness of the medium, the way the listener is invited into the narrative to contribute to it his or her own way of 'seeing' the voices and the sounds, the invisible beings and events, that gives radio story-telling its real third dimension, which is the space that, above all, interests and enchants me.

This is only one way out of many of using radio and none of them is the *right* way; all are possible ways – I'm not proselytising for a pet method! This is, just, the way I like to use radio, not for creating dramas on a theatrical model so much as to create complex, many-layered narratives that play tricks with time. And, also, to explore ideas, although for me, that is the same thing as telling stories since, for me, a narrative is an argument stated in fictional terms.

Tricks with time – and also with place, for radio can move from location to location with effortless speed, using aural hallucinations to invoke sea-coast, a pub, a blasted heath, and can make extraordinary collage and montage effects beyond the means of any film-maker, not just because of the cost of that medium but also because the eye takes longer to register changing images than does the ear.

Even when the theatrical model exists in radio drama, when it is either an adaptation from the stage or bears a strong relation to the stage, it depends for its effects on the very absence of all the visual apparatus that sustains the theatrical illusion. In a radio drama studio, the producer, the actors, the technical staff, create an illusion, literally, out of the air. Although there is a beautiful precision about the means available for the creation of that illusion. If you want to invoke a windy day on radio, you can specify just what kind of wind you want: summer, winter, spring winds, a gale, a breeze, wind in trees, in bushes, over water. Every wind in the world is stored away in the sound archives, somewhere on a disc. The resources are insubstantial but infinite. An Oriental market? Near East or Far East? At dawn, at noon, at dusk? If a Near Eastern market, with or without the muezzin?

The sound effects create their own system of signs for the ear, and language itself, the principal means of sustaining the radio drama illusion, may be richer and more evocative by far than that of real life, can release itself entirely from the conventions of everyday speech, can explore all kinds of rhetorical devices and linguistic tricks in order to do the work of sustaining an imaginary world.

Because of the absence of the visual image, radio drama need not necessarily be confined to the representations of things as they are. Since radio drama, or fiction for radio, or story-telling with radio, or any other use of radio at all other than for pure information-giving or opinion-giving, starts off from a necessary degree of stylisation, it has always attracted and continues to attract, the avant-garde. (Peter Redgrove's contemporary work for radio is scarcely conceivable in any other medium.) It is a medium that writers love.

There is also radio's capacity to render the inner voice, the subjective interpretation of the world . . . It is, *par excellence*, the medium for the depiction of madness; for the exploration of the private worlds of the old, the alienated, the lonely. As a result, plays about the inner lives of the mad, the old and the lonely have become almost Radio Three clichés, along with apocalypses and Kafkaesque existential confrontations of non-communication set in nameless, featureless places. I've been tempted, but always tried to avoid, these themes; although I've certainly done one play about a notable madman, I resisted the temptation to write it solely from his point of view.

Born in 1940, I was a child of the Radio Age – although, then, we still called it 'the wireless' – as present-day children are the children of television. Weaned on the now defunct Children's Hour, one of the most potent memories of my childhood is that of a serial, always repeated around Christmas, made out of John Masefield's fantastic novel, *The Box of Delights*, with its cast-list of piratical rats and time-travelling Renaissance philosophers, its ineffable atmosphere of snow and mystery. In an unselfconscious way, *The Box of Delights* used all the resources of radio to create what we now call 'magic realism' and perhaps that long-ago Children's Hour serial influenced me far more profoundly than I'd like to admit.

But I started writing for radio, myself, because of a sound effect. I made it quite by accident. Sitting in my room, pencil in hand, staring vacantly into space instead of getting on with whatever it was I was supposed to be doing, I ran the pencil idly along the top of the radiator. It made a metallic, almost musical rattle. It was just the noise that a long, pointed fingernail might make if it were run along the bars of a birdcage.

Now, I thought, what kind of person might have such fingernails? Why, a vampire, famed for their long, sharp fingernails (all the better to eviscerate you with!). Now, what kind of vampire would have both long, elegant fingernails and an elegant, gilt birdcage? A lady vampire, perhaps. I alliterated her. A lovely lady vampire. And she must be plucking those twanging, almost musical notes out of her birdcage because, like me, she was bored . . .

Bored, though, with what? With the endless deaths and resurrections she, the sleeping beauty who woke only to eat and then to sleep again, was doomed? A lovely lady vampire; last of her line, perhaps, locked up in her hereditary Transylvanian castle, and the bird in that gilded cage might be, might it not, an image of the lady herself, caged as she was by her hereditary appetites that she found both compulsive and loathsome.

So I laid aside the task I had in hand (now I misremember what it was), and researched vampires, and Transylvania. I invented for the lovely lady vampire, whom Anna Massey later gravely incarnated with such beautiful assurance, a hero out of the *Boys' Own Paper* circa 1914, who would cure and kill her by the innocence of his kiss and then go off to die in a war that was more hideous by far than any of our fearful superstitious imaginings. I never thought of any other medium but radio all the time I was writing the script of the play, *Vampirella*. It *came* to me as radio, with all its images ready formed, in terms of words and sounds.

The script arrived at the BBC on the desk of the producer, Glyn Dearman, with whom I've worked ever since, and whose style, sensitivity and enthusiasm would irradiate dramatised readings of the London telephone directory. It was the happiest possible introduction to radio drama and I was forthwith hooked.

Later on, I took the script of *Vampirella* as the raw material for a short story, *The Lady of the House of Love*. It was interesting to see what would and would not work in terms of prose fiction. It was the discursive element in *Vampirella* that could not be contained in the short story. The narrative line of the short story did not have sufficient space to discuss the nature, real and imagined, of vampirism, nor did it have sufficient imaginative space to accommodate cameo guest appearances by the Scottish cannibal, Sawney Beane, with his bagpipes and his ravenous children, nor the unrepentant Parisian necrophile, Henri Blot. Even Vampirella's father, Count Dracula himself, was forced to bow out of a narrative that had become leaner, more *about* itself, less about its own resonances, and more consistent in tone.

In radio, it is possible to sustain a knife-edge tension between black comedy and bizarre pathos. ('Poor wee thing,' sighs Vampirella's governess over her charge's hideous longings.) This is because the rich textures of radio are capable of stating ambiguities with a dexterity over and above that of the printed word; the human voice itself imparts all manner of subtleties in its intonations. So *The Lady of the House of Love* is a Gothic tale about a reluctant vampire; the radio play, *Vampirella*, is about vampirism as metaphor. The one is neither better nor worse than the other. Only, each is quite different.

Two of the scripts published here, *The Company of Wolves* and *Puss in Boots*, started off as short stories but these aren't adaptations so much as reformulations. As radio, both stories found themselves ending up much closer to specific types of genre – *The Company of Wolves* took on more of the characteristics of the pure horror story, became almost an exercise in genre until, now, it seems to me even a kind of homage to another radio fixture of my childhood, those mini-dramas of terror presented by Valentine Dyall as *The Man in Black*. The transformation of man into wolf is, of course, the work of a moment on radio and no werewolf make-up in the world can equal the werewolf you see in your mind's eye.

But *Puss in Boots* reverted very nearly to the exact form of the *commedia dell'arte* on which I'd modelled the original story in the first place. Puss was always Harlequin all the time, and Tabs was Columbine, while the young lovers, the old miser and the crone were all originally stock types from the early Italian comedy, from which the British popular form of pantomime is derived. That is why the whole thing is set in Bergamo, the town in Northern Italy where *commedia dell'arte* was especially cherished.

Recording *Puss in Boots* was the most fun I've ever had in a radio drama studio and the actors, somewhat breathlessly, concurred, although the production staff, faced with co-ordinating twanging bedsprings, heavy panting and Tchaikovsky's *1812 Overture* (with cannon) could not, at the time, see the funny side.

If *Puss in Boots* is an Old Comedy for radio, it is one that could only have been done in radio, not just because of the copulations, both feline and human, with which the script abounds, but because of the army of rats; and the acrobatics; and . . .

And the presence of the margin of the listener's imagination. Listening to the play when it went out over the air, I forgot I'd seen Andrew Sachs and Frances Jeator, Puss and Tabs respectively, acting in the studio; I heard the sharp, cunning voices of urban cats, unscrupulously charming as only cats who live by their wits can be. As for the pace, the spice, the *brio* of Glyn Dearman's production; well, I'd envisaged, shall we say, a balletic effect, hadn't I. A ballet in words. A ballet for radio?

Well, why not? We'd already done a picture gallery. Working on the fruitful paradox, that radio is the most visual of mediums because you cannot see it, I decided to paint some pictures in radio. Not, I hasten to add, my own pictures, but copies of somebody else's. I cheated a little, because they were not only narrative pictures, i.e. pictures that tell a story, but also pictures that could be construed as telling tales about the man who painted them. Who was a Victorian painter of fairy subjects named Richard Dadd, whose promising career terminated in his early twenties after, during an attack of paranoid schizophrenia, he cut his own father's throat. Dadd never recovered from his madness and spent the rest of his life in insane asylums; encouraged to continue painting, his style changed, although his subject matter unnervingly did not, and he produced the brilliant and disquieting canvases on which his fame rests in the hospital that later became Broadmoor.

Come unto These Yellow Sands, my play about Dadd, isn't precisely story-telling for radio, nor is it art or cultural criticism, although there is a lot of that in the script. The contradiction between the kitsch content and the distorted style of the paintings of Dadd's madness, together with his archetypal crime of parricide, committed under a delusion of madness – committed in a state of not-knowing, in fact – seem to me expressions of the dislocation of the real relations of humankind to itself during Britain's great period of high capitalism and imperialist triumph in the nineteenth century, during Dadd's own long, alienated lifetime. And I don't see how it would have been possible for me to discuss Dadd in the way I wanted in any other medium than radio, with its ability to cross-cut from subjective to objective reality, from the inner, personal voice to the conflicting voices of those bearing witness to the diverse manifestations of that inner voice. From the apparently real to the patently imagined. From a Victorian mad-doctor discussing Dadd's case-notes to Oberon, King of the Fairies, discussing the marginalisation of folklore in the bourgeois period.

So *Come unto These Yellow Sands* isn't a documentary at all, nor, really, a play, but a piece of cultural criticism in the form of a documentary-based fiction in which the listener is invited inside some of Dadd's paintings, inside the 'Come unto These Yellow Sands' of the title and into that eerie masterpiece, 'The Fairy Feller's Master-Stroke', to hear the beings within it – the monsters produced by repression – squeak and gibber and lie and tell the truth.

On and off, I discuss with Glyn Dearman the idea of a play of the same kind about Jackson Pollock that would re-invent Pollock's paintings, and his times, in the same way as we re-invented Dadd's paintings for radio, with the aid, this time, of the BBC Radiophonic Workshop, perhaps. *That* would be a challenge.

Indeed, radio remains a challenging medium, because so much is possible in it. I write for radio by choice, as an extension and an amplification of writing for the printed page; in its most essential sense, even if stripped of all the devices of radio illusion, radio retains the atavistic lure, the atavistic power, of voices in the dark, and the writer who gives the words to those voices retains some of the authority of the most antique tellers of tales.

PRODUCTION NOTES

RADIO PLAYS

Angela Carter's own account of the background to her first four radio plays is given in the Preface to *Come unto These Yellow Sands*, included above as the Appendix.

Vampirella

Vampirella was first broadcast on BBC Radio 3 on 20 July 1976. The cast was as follows:

VAMPIRELLA/ELIZABETH BA'ATHORY	Anna Massey
HERO	Richard O'Callaghan
MRS BEANE	Betty Hardy
DRACULA/SAWNEY BEANE/HENRI BLOT	David March
CLERK OF COURT/GATEKEEPER	David Graham
PEASANT BOY/CHILD	Elizabeth Lindsay

Director: Glyn Dearman

Come unto These Yellow Sands

Come unto These Yellow Sands was written at the end of 1978 and first broadcast on BBC Radio 3 on 28 March 1979. It won the Sony Award for the Best Drama Documentary of that year. The cast was as follows:

RICHARD DADD/LANCS. GOBLIN	Philip Sully
MALE NARRATOR/YORKS. GOBLIN	Philip Voss
FEMALE NARRATOR/FEMALE RUSTIC	Frances Jeater
OBERON	John Westbrook
HENRY HOWARD/DADD SNR	Godfrey Kenton
PUCK/CHANGELING	Andrew Branch
SIR THOMAS PHILLIPS	William Eedle
TITANIA	June Tobin
LANDLADY	Margot Boyd
CRAZY JANE	Sheila Grant
FRITH/WEST COUNTRY GOBLIN/RUSTIC GOBLIN	Peter Baldwin
DOCTOR	Noel Howlett
FAIRY FELLER/SCOTS GOBLIN	Eric Allan
SHOPKEEPER	Harold Kasket

Director: Glyn Dearman

The Company of Wolves

The Company of Wolves was first broadcast on BBC Radio 3 on 1 May 1980. The cast was as follows:

RED RIDING HOOD	Elizabeth Proud
WEREWOLF	Michael Williams
NARRATOR	John Westbrook
GRANNY	Katherine Parr
MOTHER	Eve Karpf
WEREWOLF'S BRIDE	Elizabeth Rider
HUNTER/2ND HUSBAND	Peter Baldwin
LITTLE BOY	Jeremy Booker
LITTLE GIRL	Emma-Kate Davies

Director: Glyn Dearman

Puss in Boots

Puss in Boots was first broadcast on BBC Radio 4 on 20 December 1982. The matter of the multiple-orgasm accompaniment to the *1812 Overture* was referred before transmission to the Controller of Radio 4, Monica Sims, who allowed the scene to stand. The cast was as follows:

PUSS	Andrew Sachs
HERO	Mick Ford
HAG/3RD CITIZEN	Doris Hare
TABS/GIRL	Frances Jeater
PANTALEONE/2ND CITIZEN	Alan Melville
UNDERTAKER/CITIZEN/SMALL TRADESMAN	Stephen Thorne
CITIZEN'S WIFE/WIDOW	Madi Hedd
4TH CITIZEN/GAMBLER/COUGHER	Peter Arne

Director: Glyn Dearman

A Self-Made Man

In early 1981, after directing Ronald Firbank's *Valmouth* for Radio 3, Glyn Dearman suggested Firbank's life as a subject for dramatisation. In a letter to Dearman, Carter described the resulting play as an 'artificial biography':

> The format is a fake radio documentary, plus a fake literary critical seminar; the male narrator and female narrator – I've used a split narrator, again, as in *Come unto These Yellow Sands*, to have a different texture of voices and the male narrator is a *bit* like Daddy, the female a *bit* like Baba.

She also made detailed suggestions for the music:

> For the ragtime sequence, could we have Jelly Roll Morton doing 'Doctor Jazz'? (I've got it on Side Two, Band One of *The King of New Orleans Jazz*, Jelly Roll Morton and his Red Hot Peppers, RCA RD27113, but I guess it will be easily to hand in the library.)

This is the one in which Jelly takes a vocal break: 'Hello, Central, give me Doctor Jazz. He's got what I want I'll say he has . . .' etc. I haven't timed it but it might be possible for *this* to be the bit with which Firbank sings along, in his everso everso Edwhardian.

Most of her suggestions were incorporated in the recording of the play.

Carter completed the script at the end of 1982. The play was recorded in June 1983. (Before broadcast, on BBC Radio 3 on 4 May 1984, six minutes were cut from the recording to fit a 60-minute slot.) The cast was as follows:

FIRBANK	Lewis Fiander
FEMALE NARRATOR	Frances Jeater
MALE NARRATOR	John Westbrook
LORD BERNERS	Timothy Bateson
SIR OSBERT SITWELL	John Webb
OLD FIRBANK/MAITRE D	James Garbutt
NANCY CUNARD	Lisa Goddard
DADDY/CYRIL BEAUMONT	Peter Tuddenham
BABA/YOUNG AMERICAN	Kate Binchy
AUGUSTUS JOHN/VAN VECHTEN/RAISLEY MOORSOM	James Bryce
SEWELL STOKES	Geoffrey Collins
A.C. LANDSBERG/EWAN MORGAN	Clive Panto
PHILIP MOELLER/MAURICE SANDOZ/GRANT RICHARDS/SIEGFRIED SASSOON	Eric Allan
WYNDHAM LEWIS/HANNEN SWAFFER	Kerry Francis
BAUDELAIRE/HAROLD NICOLSON	Brett Usher
VICAR/WAITER/OSCAR WILDE	James Kerry
YOUNG MAN/YOUNG AMERICAN/FORREST REID	Tom Hunsinger
ENGLISH/CONTINENTAL WAITER/DUNCAN GRANT	Michael Spice

Director: Glyn Dearman

LIBRETTO

Orlando: or, The Enigma of the Sexes

The idea for an operatic version of Virginia Woolf's novel *Orlando* (1928) was conceived in 1976 by John Cox, then Director of Productions at Glyndebourne. In 1979 Michael Berkeley agreed to compose the music and suggested Carter as librettist. She wrote a rough outline, followed by two drafts. The outline included several grand schemes, such as a snow eagle that flies away, the arrival of Schelmerdine in a bi-plane, and setting the whole production 'in the fabric department of Marshall and Snelgrove'. Notes to John Cox accompanied the first draft:

As I was working on the synopsis, it began to seem a better and better idea to emphasise a certain quality as of country house charades, e.g. the servants becoming lords and ladies, and, especially, becoming the garden appealed to me a lot. (They can quite easily become an Elizabethan formal garden by standing around with pot plants, or privet bushes cut into antic forms over their heads, after all. They can't, obviously, become a Victorian shrubbery but they can convert a Victorian drawing room, with its plethora of indoor plants, into a shrubbery, perhaps.) Anyway, it seemed to me that a fluidity of decor – one scene running into another – is part of the dream-like quality of the whole; hence the use of gauzes, always a dream-like effect.

About the white eagle, snow eagle or whatever, that I've given Sasha to carry. This is out of a Russian fairy story; the Tsar asks the child to visit him 'neither without a present nor with a gift', and she brings a bird that flies away as she hands it to him. This seems to me the perfect image of a love-gift, and relates to the bird-like Shelmerdine's winged apparition during the wedding scene.

As Carter worked, she became more aware of practical problems of staging. It was agreed that the bi-plane could become a parachute, to take up less space behind the scenes. The last change that Carter made was the addition of a new prologue. Cox described her introduction of the character of the tutor as a significant step:

> By this time she had really begun to engage with Woolf's material, and was creating here a device specifically angled towards an operatic production. It was obvious that she was going to make the piece a great statement of Neo-Platonism, and she introduced a new major character (a 'co-star' as she called it).
> It lifted the opera away from the narrative episodes of the novel to something much more essential.

Partly for reasons of copyright costs, and partly because of Glyndebourne's current caution about new operas, the proposed production went no further than the second draft of the libretto, reprinted here.

Angela Carter supplied a list of the chief characters and their significance.

ORLANDO – is a being in time; his/her passage through time and the sexes is a movement towards the cessation of both time and the war of sexuality.

GLORIANA – mother, not necessarily a good mother.

SASHA – the winged bird that flies away; a variant of AMOR, the unachievable.

THE SERVANTS – are beings in place, like rocks or trees.

ARCHDUCHESS HARRIET – Mr/Ms Wrong; the eternal unbeloved, the recurring unrequited, the parodic shadow of Amor.

TUTOR/SHELMERDINE ETC. – AMOR in person.

SCREEN PLAYS

The Company of Wolves

Neil Jordan met Angela Carter in Dublin in 1982 and they subsequently discussed expanding the radio play of *The Company of Wolves* for the screen. Jordan recalls:

> What she had written – the adaptation of the story basically – was too short for a feature film. I suggested to her that we develop it into a Chinese box structure, using the dream of Rosaleen, and the thread of the granny's storytelling as the connecting points, thereby enabling us to integrate other stories and themes of Angela's own. This structure was inspired by a film – *The Sargasso Manuscript* [Wojciech Jerzy Has, 1964] – which we had both seen. Once we had agreed on the structure, the writing seemed to flow quite naturally from it, since it gave free rein to Angela's own taste for narrative subversions.

The screenplay grew from three short stories in *The Bloody Chamber* (1979): 'The Company of Wolves', 'Wolf-Alice' and 'The Werewolf'. During the early summer of 1983 Carter and Jordan mapped out an outline of proposed scenes, which she then wrote up. They reached a third draft by July 1983; and, Jordan adds:

> The visual design was an integral part of the script. It was written and imagined with a heightened sense of reality in mind. She was thrilled with the process, because she loved films, and had never really been involved in one. Subsequently, we tried to find other projects to work on together, but tragically things didn't turn out that way. At the time of her illness, we were discussing *Vampirella*, another of her radio plays that could have become a feature film.

The film was released by Palace Productions in 1984. The cast was as follows:

GRANNY	Angela Lansbury
FATHER	David Warner
OLD PRIEST	Graham Crowden
AMOROUS BOY'S FATHER	Brian Glover
YOUNG BRIDE	Kathryn Pogson
YOUNG GROOM	Stephen Rea
MOTHER	Tesse Silberg
HUNTSMAN	Micha Bergese
ROSALEEN	Sarah Patterson
ALICE	Georgina Slowe
AMOROUS BOY'S MOTHER	Susan Porrett
AMOROUS BOY	Shane Johnstone
WITCH WOMAN	Dawn Archibald
WEALTHY GROOM	Richard Morant
WOLF GIRL	Danielle Dax
DEVIL BOY	Vincent McClaren

DOWAGER	Ruby Buchanan
ANCIENT	Jimmy Gardner
EYE-PATCH	Roy Evans
LAME FIDDLER	Edwards Marksen
BLIND FIDDLER	Jimmy Brown

Producers: Chris Brown and Stephen Woolley
Director: Neil Jordan

The Magic Toyshop

The Magic Toyshop was commissioned by David Plowright for Granada Television in 1985, at the suggestion of director David Wheatley. The script adapts Carter's second novel, of the same name, but alters the ending to make the outcome of the fire more ambiguous. Among the films that influenced director and writer during their discussions, Wheatley cites *Valerie and Her Week of Wonders* (Jaromil Jires, 1970), a Gothic celebration of the passage through adolescence of a beautiful girl in a vaguely defined Transylvanian landscape, and *Tales of Hoffman* (Powell/Pressburger, 1951).

The Magic Toyshop was first broadcast on ITV on 5 November 1988. The cast was as follows:

UNCLE PHILIP	Tom Bell
AUNT MARGARET	Patricia Kerrigan
MELANIE	Caroline Milmoe
FINN	Kilian McKenna
FRANCIE	Lorcan Cranitch
MRS RUNDLE	Marlene Sidaway
JONATHON	Gareth Bushill
VICTORIA	Georgina Hulme
COPPELIA/NYMPH DANCER	Marguerite Porter
ARTIST DANCER	Lloyd Newson

Producer: Steve Morrison
Director: David Wheatley

Gun for the Devil

Carter was inspired to write a revenge tragedy set in the Wild West by Carl von Weber's opera, *Der Freischutz*, based on the German folk-tale of a forester ridiculed for poor marksmanship. To win a shooting match to decide the next head ranger and become eligible to court the girl he loves, the forester makes a pact with a wild huntsman for seven charmed bullets. Unknown to him, the huntsman, who is the Devil's alter ego, controls the last bullet. After being duped into firing the last shot, and believing he has killed his beloved, the hero confesses and is exiled, but is reprived when it emerges that it is a rival forester who is the huntsman's victim.

'Gun for the Devil' was originally written as a prose film treatment in the early 1980s (published in *American Ghosts and Old World Wonders*, 1993). The screenplay was commissioned by Brenda Reid at the BBC in collaboration with David Wheatley. The script was delivered in September 1987 but did not go into production and was written off in 1989.

The Christchurch Murder

In September 1987 Angela Carter was commissioned by Andrew Brown of Euston Films to write a screenplay based on a murder committed by two schoolgirls in Christchurch, New Zealand, in 1954.

Mrs Honora Mary Parker was killed by repeated blows to the head with a lisle stocking filled with a half brick. Her daughter, sixteen-year-old Pauline, and her friend, Juliet Hume, were charged with the murder. The two girls, daughters of a fishmonger and a prominent academic, had become friends two years before, and their relationship had become increasingly obsessive and driven by fantasy. They invented a make-believe world, keeping the imaginary company of Julius Caesar, Caruso and Orson Welles and renaming themselves Gina and Deborah. On hearing the news that Juliet was to be taken to South Africa by her mother, they pledged to each other that they would not be parted – Mrs Parker's refusal to allow Pauline to go away was the motive for her murder.

Euston Films failed to find a production company to make *The Christchurch Murder*, and the project was taken no further than a second draft of the script, delivered in August 1988. (A film based on the same subject was made in 1994 by Peter Jackson, as *Heavenly Creatures*.)

STAGE PLAY

Lulu

In 1987 Richard Eyre, Director of the National Theatre, approached Carter to write a play based on the two 'Lulu' plays of Frank Wedekind, *Earth Spirit* (1895) and *Pandora's Box* (1904).

Carter had long been fascinated by 'the role of the Life Force incarnate, Wedekind's earth spirit, the Dionysiacally unrepressed Lulu, who must die because she is free'. In an article for *New Society* in 1978 she discussed G. W. Pabst's vision of the role in his 1929 film:

> Pabst's screen version of the Lulu plays, *Pandora's Box*, remains one of the great expositions of the cultural myth of the *femme fatale*. It is a peculiarly pernicious, if flattering, myth which Pabst and his star Louise Brooks, conspired to both demonstrate irresistibly in action while, at the same time, offering evidence of its manifest absurdity . . .
>
> Brooks is the greatest of all the Surrealist love-goddesses, pitched higher in the pantheon, even, than Dietrich and Barbara Steele because she typifies the subversive violence inherent in beauty and a light heart. She is not at all obscure but positively a radiant and explicit object of

desire – living proof, preserved in the fragile eternity of the film stock, that the most mysterious of all is, as Octavio Paz said, the absolutely transparent. And, indeed, Lulu is transparent as sunshine; which is why her presence shows up all the spiritual muck in the corners. So she gets blamed for the muck, poor girl . . .

Lulu keeps repeating cheerfully that she has never been in love. This is the main thing that is wrong with her, according to Wedekind. No heart, see. A lovely flower that, alas, lacks perfume. Her loyalty to her old friends; her fidelity to her first seducer, the repulsive Schoen; her willingness to support her adoptive father and effete stepson by the prostitution she loathes – Wedekind records all this but cannot see it as any evidence of human feeling at all. She is the passive instrument of vice, he says. That's all.

The National Theatre commission, however, presented problems. Wedekind's plays had been subjected to much mutilation, largely by the author himself, who re-worked them throughout his life in the hope of satisfying the censor; although the National Theatre provided literal translations of the accepted German texts, a definitive German text, closer to Wedekind's intentions, was not available in 1987. There were also tensions between the demands of 'translation' and the desire to create a new work. In Richard Eyre's words:

Maybe it was a wrong marriage – if you take on somebody else's piece, you have to submerge your own personality in the original. I wanted Wedekind with the colour and graphic edge of Angela, which may have been an impossible combination.

In addition, there were differences of conception between Carter and the prospective director, Howard Davies. Although several of Davies's editorial suggestions were incorporated into later drafts in the summer of 1988, the project was eventually dropped.

Angela Carter

BURNING YOUR BOATS

Collected Short Stories

'A writer cultured in every sense of the word, whose syntax is ever artful, whose vocabulary is zestfully arcane, whose erudition manifests itself in her work in a shimmering play of parody and illusion. She was one of the century's best writers and her stories are among her finest works'

Lucy Hughes-Hallett,
Sunday Times

'*This* is the voice the young generation are flocking to read and study, and these marvellous collected stories wonderfully explain why no pigeon-hole could ever contain her creator. When you read all the stories collected together, a sense of joy erupts that such writing can exist'

Carmen Callil, *Daily Telegraph*

'A fine, fierce, incandescent talent'
Tom Adair,
Scotland on Sunday

VINTAGE

Also available in Vintage

Angela Carter

WISE CHILDREN

'A mistress-piece of sustained and weirdly wonderful Gothic that's both intensely amusing and also provocatively serious. This is a big and superlatively imagined novel'
Observer

'A glorious piece of work, a set-piece studded with set-pieces. The narrative has a splendid ripe momentum and each descriptive touch contributes a pang of vividness. By doing possible things impossibly well, the book achieves a major enchantment'
Times Literary Supplement

'*Nights at the Circus* is a glorious enchantment. But an enchantment which is rooted in an earthy, rich and powerful language ... It is a spell-binding achievement'
Literary Review

'A remarkable book by any standards'
Guardian

VINTAGE

Also available in Vintage

Angela Carter

THE BLOODY CHAMBER

'*The Bloody Chamber*'s interweaving of retold fairy tales demonstrates Angela Carter's narrative gift at its most shocking and seductive'
Observer

'Angela Carter has extended the life and richness of the fable form itself partly through language that is pellucid and sensual, but chiefly through imagination of such Ariel reach that she can glide from ancient to modern, from darkness to luminosity, from depravity to comedy without any hint of strain and without losing the elusive power of the original tales'
The Times

'Magnificent set pieces of fastidious sensuality'
Ian McEwan

VINTAGE

Also available in Vintage

Angela Carter

AMERICAN GHOSTS AND OLD WONDERS

'Angela Carter's admirers, denied the prospect of any more of her fat, rich, celebratory novels, will seize on the plump and piquant raisins in the book with gratitude'
Times Literary Supplement

'Myths and movies, fairy tales and pantomime mingle in celebration of her buoyant life'
Mail on Sunday

'Carter's perspective on the American dream is ironic and wry...the collection is worth buying for the Lizzie Borden story alone'
Michèle Roberts,
Sunday Express

VINTAGE

VINTAGE